CRAFT AND CONSCIOUSNESS

SECOND EDITION

COMMUNICATION AND SOCIAL ORDER
An Aldine de Gruyter Series of Texts and Monographs

Series Editor
David R. Maines, *Pennsylvania State University*

Advisory Editors
Bruce E. Gronbeck • Peter K. Manning • William K. Rawlins

CRAFT AND CONSCIOUSNESS
Occupational Technique
and the Development
of World Images

SECOND EDITION

Joseph Bensman and Robert Lilienfeld

ALDINE DE GRUYTER
New York

About the Authors

The late **Joseph Bensman** (1922-1986) was Distinguished Professor of Sociology at City College and at the Graduate Center, City University of New York. Dr. Bensman contributed regularly to major sociological journals, and was author and coauthor of numerous books, among them *Dollars and Sense; Small Town in a Mass Society; The New American Society;* and *Reflections on Community Studies.* With Robert Lilienfeld, he also wrote *Between Public and Private: Lost Boundaries of the Self.*

Robert Lilienfeld is Associate Professor of Sociology at City College of New York, and has also taught at New York University and the New School for Social Research. In addition to numerous journal articles and critical reviews, Dr. Lilienfeld is author of *The Rise of Systems Theory (Second Edition);* coauthor, with Joseph Bensman, of *Between Public and Private* and of the present book; coauthor of *Mass, Class and Bureaucracy;* and coeditor of *Interdiscipline.*

ALDINE DE GRUYTER
A Division of Walter de Gruyter, Inc.
200 Saw Mill River Road
Hawthorne, New York 10532

The paper used in this publication meets the minimum requirements of American National Standard for Information Sciences—Permanence of Paper for Printed Library Materials, ANSI Z39.48-1984. ⊚

Library of Congress Cataloging-in-Publication Data
Bensman, Joseph.
    Craft and consciousness : occupational technique and the
development of world images / Joseph Bensman and Robert Lilienfeld.
    —2nd ed.
        p. cm. — (Communication and social order)
    Includes bibliographical references and index.
    ISBN 0-202-30384-5. — ISBN 0-202-30363-2 (pbk.)
    1. Knowledge, Sociology of. 2. Attitude (Psychology)
I. Lilienfeld, Robert. II. Title. III. Series.
BD175.B39 1991
306.4'2—dc20   91-16326
                                                    CIP

Manufactured in the United States of America

10 9 8 7 6 5 4 3 2 1

To David and Hugo

Contents

Part III. Ideological and Political Consequences

Foreword

Arthur J. Vidich

In a secular, this-worldly civilization, our choice of profession determines our consciousness and provides us with meaningful 'gods.' *Craft and Consciousness* tells us that professional ideologies replace theodicies by providing us with meaningful world images.

Bensman and Lilienfeld's systematic analysis of the presuppositions lying beneath professional ideologies points to a multiplicity of incommensurate, contradictory, and frequently competing world images. Nevertheless, professional ideologies of the modern crafts not only provide us with our meanings in life, but shrink them into an occupational consciousness. Analyzing the occupational ideologies of musicians, composers, performing artists, journalists, politicians, bureaucrats, planners, historians, economists, psychologists, sociologists, lawyers, and doctors, the authors indicate how the several specialized and specific practices associated with each of these occupations define the way of life and the world images of the modern specialized professional. They maintain, furthermore, that those who so profess accept on faith the transcendent value of their occupational ideologies.

The power of Bensman and Lilenfeld's argument is best illustrated in their chapters on "The Religious Attitude," "The Attitude of the Intellectual," "Philosophical Attitudes," and "Craft and Meaning in Literature." Taking the religious attitude as the paradigmatic case, the authors argue that "religion as a form of thought is the prototype of all thought forms." When institutionalized it attempts, like the forms of thought in literature or in philosophy, to define the central meaning of lived experience. But, they go on, "every intellectual field or form faces the same conflicts, paradoxes, and tension that religion does." Each form is committed to a set of values, "which if taken as an absolute, places itself at odds with other forms of knowledge and with its secular world." Thus when the religious practitioner attempts to rationalize a system of religious thought, the resulting theology must confront a secular world that inevitably contradicts it.

Max Weber had also noted this problem when he stated: "The [more rationally closed] the development tends towards the conception of a transcendental unitary God who is universal, the more there arises the problem of how the extraordinary powers of such a God may be reconciled with the imperfection of the world that He has created . . . ." Bensman and Lilienfeld are following up ideas developed by Georg Simmel in his conception of the tragedy of culture, but in the process they extend Weber's point to include all other efforts to create closed systems of thought:

> In attempting to cope with the secular world, [religion] is forced to make compromises, but the nature of the compromises results in the incorporation of extrinsic values or elements into its original insight or vision. In gaining influence, power, prestige, and economic rewards, in becoming institutionalized, in coming to terms with society, it loses much of what gave it a unique claim for its value upon its society. This is the generic tragedy of all religion, but the tragedy is so generic that it is the tragedy of all other forms of knowledge. Thus, in escaping from this tragedy in religion to some other realm of value, one escapes only to another form of the same tragedy.

Seeking to escape this generic tragedy, another sociologist coming out of the German tradition of the discipline, Karl Mannheim, proclaimed a new role for the intellectual: that of being the bearer of autonomous forms of knowledge. Supposing that the freedom of the intellectual could guarantee his commitment to the discovery and dissemination of objective truth, Mannheim failed to note that, as professionals, intellectuals would be attuned to their own occupational and positional perspectives and interests. Bensman and Lilienfeld have generalized the inherent relativity of knowledge beyond the thesis presented by Mannheim; they argue that the development of every social position provides it a view of the truth, a view that is itself socially determined. This social fact about the sociology of knowledge is inherent and applies to all theories of knowledge, whether they be religious, literary, or philosophical. By the same token, the several occupational or craft-developed forms of knowledge are so many different ways of looking at a multiform world—a world that can allow, as we now understand, an infinite variety of perspectives.

New readers of this book will see that its authors are philosophically and sociologically well informed. They have drawn their perspective from the works of Kant, Descartes, Hume, Husserl, Schutz, and Hegel on the one side, and from Marx, Durkheim, Weber, Simmel, Freud, and Veblen on the other. However, basing their work in these predecessors, Bensman and Lilienfeld confront the problem of the relation between consciousness and existence empirically, by concretely examining forms of thought in relation to specific modes of experience.

The application of the sociological attitude to a variety of occupations reveals the multiple ethical and moral perspectives of the specialized professional crafts. Philosophers and ethicists who have in recent years begun to concern themselves with the moral and ethical problems and dilemmas of modern complex societies will find in this book an entirely new approach to the ethical and moral quandaries of our times.

A striking feature of their study derives from the authors' unusual ability to project themselves into the perspectives of others' professional and craft ideologies. It has been said that a truly sociological attitude exists only when the observer possesses the ability to see the world from the perspective of the other. Max Weber called this a mode of true sociology, *verstehen*, understanding the other from the other's point of view. It is only this capacity to trade places with the other that makes possible an understanding of the other's aims, purposes, motivations, and meanings. Those who recognize in Shakespeare's plays the drama of social reality will understand the special kind of sensitivity that is required to achieve this form of understanding. Members of the professions that are analyzed in this book will see that the authors have held a mirror up to their occupational reality. Sociologists will learn by the example of Bensman and Lilienfeld's craftsmanship what is meant by the sociological attitude.

Originally published by Wiley Interscience in 1973, *Craft and Consciousness* sold out quickly and was not reprinted. At that time, John Wiley and Sons, Interscience's corporate parent, disbanded the social science division of Interscience. As a result, *Craft and Consciousness* was never given the second printing that it deserved. Its limited availability restricted its distribution to the scholarly world and, consequently, its influence on the direction of social thought. In spite of this, it has gained an underground reputation among the cognoscenti as a classic study in the sociology of knowledge, and has left its mark on such fields of study as the sociology of occupations, phenomenology, hermeneutics, philosophy, and social theory.

The present volume contains a completely revised and expanded first chapter and additional chapters that did not appear in the 1973 publication. Before Professor Bensman's death in 1986, he and Professor Lilienfeld had completed two new chapters and had proposed a second edition. One, entitled "Legal Attitudes and Changes in the Law," is unique to the literature; it takes as its central focus the consequences of bureaucratization for judicial and legal practice. The authors' central concern is to query how justice can be maintained in a legal system that must somehow cope with a changing social order. The other, "Attitudes in Clinical and Scientific Medicine," examines how the medical profession has responded to the transformation of clinical-diagnostic medical practice into technocratic scientific medicine. For many years before he succumbed to an incurable disease, Professor Bensman had the opportunity to observe as well as to participate— as a patient—in the practice of scientific medicine in New York City. He notes that the new norms and principles of modern medicine involve choices made by networks of physicians rather than invocation of the ethical norms that once prevailed between physician and patient. Medical ethics has thereby taken a new turn, one that frequently involves recourse to legal adjudication of medical problems. These new chapters (12 and 13, respectively, of the present volume), conceived after careful reflection by the authors on their earlier work, have a thickness of texture and a comprehensiveness that make them models for any further analysis of the professions.

The authors do not treat the several crafts and professions they analyze as autonomous systems. As they put it, "If it were possible to see them all operating simultaneously together, we would have some notion of the 'totality' of human existence and society." However, this possibility they regard to be a methodological fiction because, in the face of a multiplicity of occupational world images, any conception of "society as an autonomous, self-enclosed system with clear-cut boundaries" is obtainable only by a form of verbal magic. Bensman and Lilienfeld reject as sorcery all claims made by social scientists who assert that the social order is system grounded on an underlying set of consensual social values.

Introduction to the Second Edition

The first edition of *Craft and Consciousness* received substantially successful acceptance, particularly in the use made of its ideas by others working in the field of the sociology of knowledge. But we, the authors, were aware of a number of its limitations. This may be because there are as many sets of attitudes as there are occupations and professions, and the attempt to restrict and categorize occupations and attitudes by such schemes as object-, symbol-, and people-oriented is far too gross. Thus a surgeon may be object-oriented (Chapter 13) as may a laborer (Chapter 18); and a poet and an accountant—while both dealing in symbols—may have little else in common.

Given the possible range of occupation and professional attitudes we were aware of some limitations in our selection of the crafts we studied. In other of our works, particularly "The Sociology and Phenomenology of the Performing Arts," in *Performers and Performances*, edited by Jack Kamerman and Roseanne Martorello (New York: Praeger, 1983) we have attempted to make finer phenomenological distinctions within and between the creative and performing arts than we did in *Craft and Consciousness*. But, even more importantly, we felt we lacked, in our first edition, studies of the great classical professions, medicine and the law. These, in the United States, were the first to organize as free, voluntary professional associations with, among other things, codes of ethics. Elsewhere they are among the oldest professions with long traditions and histories.

In including chapters on each of these two professions, we have raised questions related, we believe, to all craft attitudes and world images. These include the results of the attempt of a profession to "rationalize," self-consciously and rationally to control, the attitudes of its members in opposition to ever-present and continuous pressures upon a profession to meet the demands of external interests and ideologies of clients and other outsiders. Social change also results in profound technological, organizational, administrative, and financial changes, both internal and external to a profession, that alter its basic craft technologies and the social relations within it. How do these, we have asked, affect the very basic craft attitudes of occupations and professions?

Finally, in raising these questions we have raised the question whether occupational attitudes are relatively static ideas-in-themselves or ever-changing products of history, that is, the history of science, technology and macroscopic changes in the organization of society and its institutions.

We hope that our new chapters will at least point in the direction of raising useful questions.*

Joseph Bensman
Robert Lilienfeld

---

*The assistance of Dr. Marilyn Bensman in editing and revising the new chapters for publication in this edition is gratefully acknowledged by the publisher.

Introduction

This book attempts to develop an approach to the sociology of knowledge based on craft, or occupational technique. It is our contention that major "habits of mind," approaches to the world, or in phenomenological terms, attitudes towards everyday life, and specialized attitudes, are extensions of habits of thought that emerge and are developed in the practice of an occupation, profession, or craft. We emphasize craft since we focus upon the methods of work, techniques, methodologies, and the social arrangements which emerge in the practice of a profession as being decisive in the formation of world views.

The emphasis on craft as a generator of habits of mind is in contradistinction to an emphasis on class or a profession. These latter aspects of occupation, of course, do exist and contribute to world views and attitudes, but they have already been studied in great detail, perhaps to the point where the additional knowledge gained from such perspectives is minimal. In many of the following essays, we will, after exploring what we regard as the essential craft attitudes, describe the relationship of craft attitudes to occupational or "class" and positional perspectives. But we will distinguish between the three kinds of bases for knowledge.

We are concerned, basically, with the sociology of knowledge, substantially defined by Marx as relating the forms and content of knowledge to the position of the knower in the social, economic, and class structure of society, and thence back to the evolution and character of that economic structure. The Marxian approach is summarized by the statement: It is not the consciousness of men that determines their existence, but the existence of men that determines their consciousness. For Marx, in the statement above, existence meant initially class, and class interest as a determinant of ideologies, perspectives, and the forms and content of personality itself. These class determinants are reflections of situational placement as a product of the class structure, the forms of capital, technology, and property. Relationship to the market, wealth, income, and bargaining position with respect to the labor market are significant variables in the Marxist sociology of knowledge. The Marxist tradition in the sociology of knowledge has been amplified and developed by such Marxists as Lenin, Trotsky, and Plekhanov, and by such scholars as Mannheim and Lukács, among others.

Any person working in the field of the sociology of knowledge must acknowledge that the field would not be possible without the work of Marx. While others at various stages may have suggested social origins for the way reality has been perceived and described, after *The German Ideology* it became impossible to discuss the articulation and development of ideas, ideologies, and the growth of knowledge without reference to Marx. Thus we are forced to acknowledge his work. Moreover, the fundamental notion that much political and social theory is ideological, that such theories are screens behind which class interests and perspectives are concealed, is one that, once stated, is inescapable, and the notion that people in a given restricted social position will see the world from the standpoint of that position in terms not only of class position but also of saliencies, relevancies, and will fail to see other events, facts, and data because of the restrictiveness of their own position, is now almost a truism. It is often but not always true that the ruling ideas of an age reflect, as Marx put it, the ideas of the ruling classes.

Recognizing all of these contributions of Marx, we would depart substantially from a sociology of knowledge based exclusively or even primarily on Marx. Our criticisms of the Marxian point of view are to be found in Chapter 16, on social class. We can summarize them here briefly:

1. Class, no matter how defined, is rarely the basis of social perspective.
2. Occupation is usually as important or more important than class in the determinance of social perspective.
3. Occupational perspectives do not necessarily lead to class perspectives.
4. Occupational perspectives are based in part on the specific craft of the occupation, and occupations at similar class levels may have different techniques and methods. Moreover, the occupations at similar class levels may have different dynamics—rates of growth, expansion, and decline—which color the perspective of the craftsman.

There is an autonomy in the development of craft technique, attitudes towards materials and media, and the development of skill and virtuosity, which are indigenous to an occupation. They give it distinct and peculiar characteristics of its own. They create a sense of pride, loyalties, and attitudes of virtuosity and craftsmanship which isolate occupations from each other regardless of the similarities of their relationship to the market or to the ownership of capital. Marx was aware of these factors, especially in his description of feudal guild occupations, but he did not give them a general emphasis in his major theoretical focus [1].

These aspects of occupations are explored in the chapters that follow. It is important to note here that craft and occupational attitudes have autonomous and internal dynamics which are not deducible from the analysis of the external relationship of the occupation to the society at large. We hope to demonstrate that these internal dynamics produce world views that are exported to the society at large, and color not only the culture of that society but even its property relations (as the chapters on art and religion will show).

In focusing on craft, and consciousness induced by craft, we draw primarily on Veblen. While Veblen is best known for his motivational terminology based on instincts (the instinct of workmanship, the "predatory" instinct, etc.), he introduced the notion of "habit of mind" into the discussion of occupational perspectives. In characteristic manner, he bent Dewey's notion of habits of mind to fit his own perspective, and placed it into the context of occupational attitudes. Veblen spoke of the industrial habit of mind, and attempted to show how habituation to a given state of the industrial arts of industrial or economic institutions, produced a mentality that reflected such habituation. He could argue that every state of economic development produced occupations and professions that in turn produced a corresponding social character. In his *Theory of the Leisure Class*, Veblen showed that the same institutional developments produced a culture, secondary institutions, patterns of taste and styles, and types of knowledge that embodied these habits of mind. While we disagree with many of the specific formulations that Veblen attempted, his initial insight is a basis for much of this work.

Much of this book, too, is based on specific works of Karl Mannheim and Max Weber. Mannheim must be given full credit for the development of the sociology of knowledge as an explicit discipline. His work is based on the attempt to combine the ideas of Marx with those of Max Weber within the philosophic tradition which is in part based on Husserl and the phenomenological tradition. We are influenced by Mannheim in more ways perhaps than we can acknowledge. Mannheim's emphasis on the sociology of the intellectual and the effect of both the rate of production of intellectuals and the capacity of a society to absorb intellectuals or their output is highly relevant to our work. Even more important is the effect of the ability of specific institutions of the society to attach intellectuals to their specific occupational domain. Such differences affect, in both Mannheim's work and our own, the content of thought of specific groups of intellectuals.

The degree to which intellectuals become autonomous is important to us, as it was to Mannheim. Here we mean autonomous in the sense of the creation of separate and autonomous forms of knowledge, which do not reflect in a direct way any external social perspective, position, or class. At the same time we are not inclined to suggest, as did Mannheim, that the freedom of the intellectual is any guarantee of objectivity or truth. If objectivity or truth is to be established (or can be), it must be established on grounds other than those given by the social position of the propagators of a truth. We argue further that the development of any social position, whether it be that of free-floating intellectuals or not, creates occupational and craft perspectives, positional perspectives and interests, which warrant criticism of the truth from the perspective of the observer, even though that observer himself views the truth from a position which is itself socially determined. Mannheim has been criticized, rightly we think, for placing himself in an epistemological bind: that all those who would attempt to assess the objectivity or truth of a position are themselves socially and positionally determined, so that they lack the objectivity or the epistemological freedom to assess the truth or objectivity of a position from any other position than that of their own limitations. While Mannheim struggled with this bind, and failed to escape it, no one else seems to have succeeded in escaping it. But this trap in the sociology of knowledge is inherent in all theories of knowledge. The discovery of Descartes and Hume, that existing categories of thought govern subsequent forms of knowledge, has plagued all epistemologists. We offer no solution to this problem, except that the quest for knowledge is the successive uncovering of the errors of our predecessors, in the discovery of our similar errors by our descendants. Albert Salomon was perhaps correct in saying that there was no sociology of knowledge: there was only a sociology of error. But if this is true, then perhaps the development of knowledge is, in fact, the successive growth and replacement of old errors by newer ones, but that these errors constitute the framework of social existence at any given time or place. Perhaps all we can do is become conscious of the errors of the past as we move on.

In a larger sense, we are indebted to the work of Max Weber who, while he is not usually regarded as a specialist in the sociology of knowledge, we regard as the supreme master of the field. Weber most clearly developed the theory of the autonomous development of knowledge or, as he called it, intellectual rationalization. By this he meant the attempts of professional intellectuals, priests, scribes, and scholars to work out self-consistent, rational theories of explanation of the phenomena subject to their attention or professional interests, that were often independent of the external position of the professional. Thus theology, theory, law, philosophy, music, and art could have an autonomous growth that made them something more than mere reflections of external structures and interests. He demonstrated that such autonomously developed ideas could have consequences that modified or changed the external world. Yet in almost every specific instance he studied, Weber attempted to show how external factors influenced the production of knowledge, and how they modified the selection and implementation of knowledge. Thus Weber's statement, "Not ideas, but material and ideal interests, directly govern men's conduct. Yet very frequently the 'world images' that have been created by ideas have, like switchmen, determined the tracks along which action has been pushed by the dynamic of interest," constitutes the most powerful single statement governing this field. Again, it is not possible for us to state fully the extent to which we have used Weber's thought. Certainly our chapters on the philosophic attitude, the religious attitude, and on the intellectual and political attitudes specifically are based on his work. Our emphasis on the various modes of autonomy in the development of a field reflect his work as well as our focus upon the development of the consequences of elitehood in the chapters on the political attitude and the intellectual attitude.

In the chapter on the planning attitude, which is largely based on Weber's thought, we introduce a few minor objections, if only to escape from the sense of possession that haunts almost everyone who works in a Weberian tradition.

Edmund Husserl's concern for these questions is stated in somewhat different terms. In his philosophical language, the entire problem of consciousness and existence can be described under the heading of a struggle between two modes of thought. Objectivism takes the world for granted through experience, and seeks what in this world is unconditionally valid for every rational being; this is the objective truth. Objectivism sees the task of the scientist and the philosopher as that of carrying out the task of rational investigation in order to arrive at objective knowledge. Opposed to this is transcendentalism (a term used by Husserl in a special sense), which sees the meanings of the world and even the images of the world that men create and carry, as structures that are subjectively built up. The "objective" world of science is a structure at a higher level, built and based upon prescientific experiencing and thinking, or rather on their valid accomplishments. For Husserl, only a radical inquiry into the roots of subjectivity, and especially that subjectivity which is the basis of valid knowledge, can make objective truth understandable [2].

For Husserl, the split between science and the "life-world" originates in Galileo's mathematicization of nature, in his physics of mass and motion. With the triumph of this approach, virtually all the sciences and philosophy are drawn towards an abstract and technicizing mode of operation which made the connection of sciences and philosophy to the world of everyday life ever more tenuous. The subjectivist stream of philosophy, emerging with Descartes's *ego cogito*, and culminating in the dilemmas of Hume's epistemology, has never achieved a stable basis despite the efforts of Kant, Hegel, and later philosophers.

It was the goal of Husserl's philosophical labors to accomplish a rejoining of the transcendental-subjectivist roots of meanings to the objectivating procedures of modern science. Without this reunification, he saw the sciences as becoming ever more opaque, technicized, and "methodological" in character. Existentialist schools of thought (represented by such names as Heidegger, Merleau-Ponty, Levinas, Scheler, and others) though deplored by Husserl, claim his work as a major source for theirs. This split, which had culminated on one hand in the scientism which Husserl saw as dominating the sciences and humanities, and the irrationalist existential and subjective philosophies, which later Husserl saw as connected to the political irrational-isms of our time, had to be overcome by a return to the "life-world" as the foundation for scientific meanings and procedures. Phenomenology was seen as a means of clarifying the procedures of the sciences, and of laying bare their true relation to the world of everyday life.

It does not appear to us that Husserl accomplished the task he set himself, and it seems that many self-designated phenomenologists have redefined phenomenology as the clarification of pure meanings, an endeavor which while certainly part of Husserl's work was but a narrow segment of the field as Husserl saw it. There is no doubt, however, that this thought suggests some of the major themes and approaches in our work, and will prove fruitful in the future for all who work in his spirit.

Much of our formal method of analysis is thus based on our understanding and misunderstanding of the phenomenological method as presented by Husserl and particularly by Alfred Schutz. Historically our work began (in Chapter 1) with an attempt to extend the dimensions of the attitude of everyday life, and the scientific attitude, developed by Schultz from Hus-serl, to other forms of knowledge.

Chapter 1 represents our attempt to state formally and explicitly the basic definitions and concepts we use throughout the book. In the early chapters we attempt to apply and illustrate these concepts in their extension to such attitudes as that of the performing artist and the sportsman. As the work proceeds, we drop some of the formal vocabulary developed in Chapter 1, and assume that the methods used become part of the attitude of everyday life of the reader. But in doing so, we begin to add and treat other themes that go beyond the formal methods of phenomenology. These include such themes as the role of ideas in the development of a craft, the effects of the elite perspectives of an occupation, the degree of autonomy in the develop-ment of craft ideas, the borrowing of ideas among professions, and the effect of occupational success on the articulation of ideas. In addition, starting from our initial phenomenological perspectives, we deal with the effect of class and occupation position on the content of ideas, as well as the effect of the acceptance of occupational perspectives by a nonoccupational clientele. On the way, ideas are modified, accepted, or rejected. Finally, we deal with possible effects of craft-generated ideas on the structure of ideas, culture, and institutions in the society at large.

While our basic method is that of attempting to locate the origins of attitudes in the practice of a craft, we "discovered" quite early the phenome-non of the migration of ideas and attitudes to related fields. Sometimes such migration involved, from the standpoint of its original use, the development of the misapplication of attitudes, which serve as a screen for other attitudes which we thus hoped to reveal. Such "use" and "misuse" of attitudes led us quickly into a reconsideration of conventional problems in the sociology of knowledge, that is, problems of ideology. Once these problems were raised, we were able to view problems of political ideology—the ideologies of elites and of the conflicts of elites.

Our original perspective always forced us to keep central our focus on the effect of occupational craft on the production of ideologies. At the same time, we were able to raise the question of craft consciousness versus positional perspectives and class interests as well as the problems of ideologies that reflect the autonomous position of the craft, and those that reflect the relationship of a craft to both its sponsors and clients.

At some points we depart from the point of view of a purely phenomenological approach. Throughout this book we have been concerned with the problem of the kinds of bracketing and reduction which various occupations and crafts make in their approach to an infinite and multidimensional reality. Some phenomenologists would tend to say that the only permissible reduction is the reduction to the ideas themselves, that ideas are understandable only in their own terms, and that reduction to other orders of data is a destruction or denigration of the idea itself. In contrast, we would argue, as we do in Chapters 6, 9, and 18, that any reduction or bracketing is permissible provided that the analyst is aware of the fact that he is making a reduction, and that the analysis and findings that he makes as a result of his bracketing and reduction are a product of the methods that he uses, that the reality he discovers is only a partial reality and is made partial by the very fact that he has bracketed out all other realities, and has dealt with the resulting reality as a self-enclosed universe or province of meaning. If the analyst then proceeds to treat the resultant reality as a total universe, he creates, in Marx's term, a world of phantasmagoria and chimeras. We feel that this stricture applies equally to the phenomenological reduction as to the economic, psychological, epistemological, or any other reduction. We have attempted to indicate the range of reduction that it is possible to make. This is especially true of our chapter on the philosophic attitude.

In one additional way we have deviated from the phenomenological method. In concentrating on craft consciousness and craft attitudes, we have repeatedly been forced to recognize the role of the intellectual, the professional, and the artist in the creation of basic attitudes toward life. Wherever we have done so, we have discovered, as did Keynes, that much of what are regarded as the attitudes of everyday life are the shadows of attitudes that had been fully articulated by intellectuals and other professions who specialize in the articulation and dissemination of knowledge and ideas. Much of what is presented as the attitude of everyday life reflects the concentration of the phenomenologist on ideas or knowledge as they exist in the here and now, free from their historical sources and free from the institutions which convey these ideas to individuals in the here and now. Understood in purely phenomenological terms, such ideas can be viewed as they exist in the here and now. But to treat these ideas as if they were autonomous creations springing out of the personal interactions and experience of isolated individuals in their daily interaction is to create a world in which larger institutions do not exist, in which intellectuals and professionals do not exist, and in which there is no machinery for the dissemination of ideas nor for the selective introduction, diffusion, and control of ideas. Such a world patently does not exist except when viewed from the standpoint of a reduction that, once made, does not recognize its limits. We are aware, however, that this stricture applies much less to the work of Husserl than to many who have worked in his name. This error may be less the error of phenomenology per se, than it may be the grafting of phenomenology onto other traditions. These include the sociology of knowledge that derives from Durkheim.

Emile Durkheim and his students developed a sociology of knowledge based primarily on the study of primitive society, in which basic forms of knowledge are seen as reflecting the social organization and structure of the community, as a whole, with the fundamental categories of thought, the collective representations, all being determined by the collective life of the society. The function of knowledge was not only to represent the collective life of the society, but also to integrate the society, to create a collective consciousness, a social objectivity, within which society has an objectivity apart from the existence of its individual members. As society becomes more complex, due to its greater size, population density, and the division of labor, then the mechanical solidarity, the unity of the collective representations, is fragmented. This results in some cases in anomie, normlessness, and a reintegration of society on the basis of smaller groups, including occupational and professional groups. The contemporary world is conceived as being at most a degenerate form of the primitive world, in which all knowledge tends to be a relatively undifferentiated product of the overall unsegmented structure of a total group life. Durkheim emphasizes the parallelism between the forms of group structures and the resulting forms of knowledge without even attempting to analyze directly the institutions and mechanisms by which knowledge becomes articulated, disseminated, and diffused. At most he can point to "correspondences." Thus, notions of individual influences, class interests, and class mechanisms are absent from his analysis. But more importantly, the forms of correspondence which emerge in a primitive society in which personal relations directly reflect the overall culture of the group becomes the model for advanced societies; that is, he does not allow for the analysis of more complex institutional arrangements to show themselves in the articulation of specialized forms of knowledge. Even when Durkheim deals with the medieval guild, he treats the individual guild as if it were a total society, and the pluralities of guilds as creating separate worlds of knowledge. This would result in an absence of a total form of knowledge for the society in which the guild exists. But Durkheim does not treat the interaction, conflict, and specialization that takes place between the special guild forms of knowledge.

In a similar sense, phenomenology has been grafted onto symbolic inter-actionism, the philosophy of George Herbert Mead. From this perspective, all social norms result from the personal symbolic interaction of individuals who in their daily action and interaction create and re-create the world. The emphasis on personal interaction again precludes attention to the hierarchi-cal, organized, centralized institutions from which and through which knowledge is filtered. Finally, ethnomethodology, whose methodological prerequisites forbid the recording of all information other than what can be viewed by the direct observation of persons in interaction, makes for a world in which only direct interaction exists.

Linguistic and logical reductions, that is, the treatment of knowledge only in terms of its logical or linguistic structure, by the very nature of their concentrations, their bracketing and reduction, preclude all other worlds of knowledge. To the extent that they do so, they make it impossible for us to recognize the existence of other worlds, which, as either naive laymen, or as well-informed citizens in the sense meant by Alfred Schutz, we would take for granted. This critique of what we regard as the misuse of these and other forms of reductions, is developed in Chapter 6 and continues to our conclusion.

For having read and commented helpfully upon various portions of this manuscript, we wish to thank Arthur L. Anderson, Leigh B. Kelley, John Lukacs, Edward Quinn, Bernard Rosenberg, Murray H. Sherman, Em-manuel Tobier, and Arthur J. Vidich.

Several chapters of this book have appeared previously in slightly varied forms, as follows:

Chapter 1 appeared as "A Phenomenological Model of the Artistic and Critical Attitudes," *Philosophy and Phenomenological Research*, Vol. XXVIII, No. 3 (1968), pp. 353–367.

Chapter 3 appeared as "A Phenomenological Model of the Attitude of the Performing Artist," *The Journal of Aesthetic Education*, Vol. 4, No. 2 (April 1970), pp. 109–119.

Chapter 10 appeared as "Psychological Techniques and Role Relation-ships," *The Psychoanalytic Review*, Vol. 58, No. 4 (Winter 1971–1972), pp. 529–552.

Chapter 12* appeared as "Phenomenology of Journalism," *Diogenes*, No. 68 (Winter 1969), pp. 98–119, in slightly abridged form, and in Bernard Rosenberg and David Manning White (eds.), *Mass Culture Revisited* (New York, Van Nostrand, 1971), pp. 131–149, as "The Journalistic Attitude," also with minor revisions.

*At present Chapter 14 in the second edition.

We wish to thank the editors and publishers for permission to reprint these items here.* Our special thanks are due to Estelle Cooper for her careful typing of the manuscript, and for many helpful comments.

NOTES

* Chapter 12 of the second edition originally appeared, in a much-abridged form, in *State, Culture & Society*, Vol. 1, No. 2, (1985) pp. 58–84.

1. See, for example, *Capital*, Book 1, page 420 of the Modern Library Edition, in the description of medieval guilds.

2. See his *The Crisis of European Sciences and Transcendental Phenomenology*, translated by David Carr (Evanston, Ill., Northwestern University Press, 1970), pp. xxvi and 48.

CRAFT AND CONSCIOUSNESS

SECOND EDITION

PART I

PHENOMENOLOGICAL ORIENTATION

Chapter 1

The Artistic and Critical Attitude

The emergence of phenomenological philosophy—the path from Kant and Hegel to Edmund Husserl and Alfred Schutz—was a complex one, and required the development of methods and ideas that would enable it to become a working tool of the philosopher and sociologist. A more complete discussion of this development can be found in Appendix A. We would like to briefly discuss some of the more salient ideas of Schutz as a background to our own approach to the analysis of the various crafts, beginning with this chapter.

Schutz tried to define and describe the attitudes that govern ordinary social interaction and the constitutive elements that underlie them as if they contained systems of meaning. He described these as attitudes toward everyday life.

The task of the sociologist interested in describing and analyzing social action, according to Schutz, is to discover these systems of meanings as if they were selfconsciously created and understood by the parties in question. One of the starting points and basic foci of Schutz's work is his distinction between the attitude of everyday life, which he also referred to as the "natural attitude" and the "scientific attitude." Schutz's discussions of the natural attitude imply that in ordinary everyday life situations men are neither self-conscious nor reflective, and directly enter into social relations with others in terms of their immediate personal goals and their intuitive apprehension of a situation. Time is experienced in the psychological sense; its intervals are unequal depending on the depth of feeling and the degree of excitement accompanying an event and the passage of time *(durée)*. The individual takes for granted and shares with others in his* environment the

---

*Editor's note: Here and elsewhere subsequently, the authors use "he" in a generic sense where colleagues more recently might have opted for "he or she" or a similar construction. The focus throughout is on occupational perspectives rather than those of gender.

3

social meanings that underlie his intuitions and actions, and no one need make explicit or even put into words the meanings they share. These "provinces of meaning" may be so deeply shared that the parties to an action are not even fully aware of the meaning they project or introject. The meanings are simply taken for granted.

The scientific attitude implies that the holder is conscious of each concept, method, and procedure used, and accompanies them with formal statements that describe the ones he used. These statements must be rendered in objective and reproducible terms, so that each scientist who observes a particular action can attribute the results to the procedures and methods used in observing and measuring. In addition, in the scientific attitude, time is measured in terms of objective standardized units, independent of the personal feelings and reactions that characterize the natural attitude. This means that objectivity is defined in part as the ability to detach oneself from experience as felt, with all of the emotional overtones such a phrase suggests.

More importantly, the scientific attitude rejects the notion of implicit rationality (or "situational closure"). Means are postulated and results are predicted within the framework of what is logically possible, so that alternatives are open to rational analysis.

The distinction between the scientific attitude and the attitude of everyday life is basic to Schutz's work, yet it suggests a number of possibilities that go beyond his model. One such model we have constructed, which we call the *planning attitude*, is based on a combination of Schutz's polar types. Our model indicates that the boundaries he constructs may be more permeable or fluid than those in his dichotomy.*

In a large-scale bureaucratic society the planner "rationalizes" the process of decision making (as in Schutz's scientific attitude) by following a number of procedures specific to his field of expertise. A military planner, for instance, constructs a series of alternative plans of action based on all possible contingencies, and then weighs them in terms of the allocation of available resources. In this respect, he exhibits a scientific attitude, but as he moves from the planning to the action phase, his attitudes and motives may prove to be more analogous to a natural attitude. He may choose a line of action simply because of personal preference or style, or because he believes it more situationally relevant.

The planner in his capacity as actor deals only with situations over which he has the possibility of exerting control. (In a bureaucratic society planner and actor may be two different people.) After the action sequence is completed and he attempts to construct new plans, he may try to assess, after the fact, the relationship between the plan and the action. In doing so, he once

*See Appendix, Figures 1 and 2.

again adopts the scientific attitude after the fact. He becomes a researcher or evaluator.

As the process of planning becomes more central to bureaucratic organizations, the scientific research and development phases are built into the action phase; the scientific attitude is then allocated to a separate department that will not threaten to interfere with operations.*

THE ARTISTIC AND CRITICAL ATTITUDES

The ideas implicit in Schutz's natural and scientific attitudes have led us to construct other phenomenological models, to begin with, a model of the artistic and critical attitudes.

The attitude of everyday life, or the natural attitude, takes the world as a given (in Schutz's terms, as "social reality"), and the actor attempts to impose his motivation upon the world by a direct confrontation with it. He does not analyze except as related to his immediate motives and direct experience of it.

The *artistic attitude* attempts to create—or rather, the artist working in the artistic attitude attempts to create—an image of a world in such a way that it can be experienced directly, intuitively, emotionally, and naively. The work of art is thus a representation of a total and complete world, a province of meaning complete in itself, which the viewer can respond to in terms of an attitude of everyday life [1]. Thus, the naive response of the audience is a subspecies of the attitude of everyday life. The work of art allows the individual to diminish, suspend, or eradicate the sense of objective time by losing himself, or involving himself, in that world. He can, through the work of art, suspend the image of himself as observer of himself, and thus also achieve a form of unity with himself through the work. Thus a great painting, a performance of music, a play or film can make so powerful an impact on the viewer or listener that its meaning may cause the observer to suspend, at least momentarily, meanings that previously were part of his natural attitude.

Moreover, if the work of art is compelling, it looms up in its pervasiveness so that the viewer (or listener or reader) can suspend any notion of other realities or provinces of meaning while he confronts the work of art. This is sometimes called the "suspension of disbelief" or the "magic of the theater" [2]. This is an application in the world of art of Schutz's term, the *epoché* of the natural attitude [3].

The *attitude of the art consumer* is not the *artistic attitude*. It is, as we have indicated, a special kind of attitude of everyday life when confronted

*The implications are worked out in detail in the appendix to this first chapter.

with a powerful art object. What is characteristic of the artistic attitude is the attempt to create such a world as the result of a rational, conscious, methodologically inevitable systematic effort, by the application of highly developed and self-conscious procedures. This does not preclude the fact that the artist may in addition portray or include improvisatory, unconscious, and other self-projecting material in his art. In fact, it can be and has been argued that all great art always includes such material [4]. But that which makes it art is the presence of style, of artificial models that have been self-consciously taught and learned and adopted as conventions by a group of artists.

Art is not experience, but it may consist of the rearrangement and the selective heightening of elements that are possible in experience in order to create new forms and varieties of experience. The word "art" implies artificiality or artfulness, all of which suggests that the artificer is self-conscious in the use of his tools, methods, and procedures, to construct a world that looks as if it were artless [5]. The artlessness of art consists of the fact that the art product can be experienced without recourse to knowledge of methodology, techniques, or procedures on the part of the art consumer. Thus, a major ingredient in art is to be at the same time highly conscious of one's technique while concealing from the audience the fact that technique is used. The element of contrivance as merged with spontaneity is one of the elements by which a great performer or work of art is judged. If the artificiality of art is its predominant characteristic, then the work is usually judged as dry, dead, or academic.

Consciousness of technique parallels a central ingredient in the scientific attitude, but concealment of technique is antithetical to the scientific attitude and comes closer to resembling in its effects the natural attitude. Thus, until at least the latter part of the nineteenth century, with the exception of a few artistic epochs, a criterion of good art was the fact that the bones, the methodology, the technique, did not show. Clumsiness, awkwardness, lack of inspiration, and ordinariness were evidenced by the artist's allowing the machinery of art to show itself through the "natural" world portrayed in the work of art.

Some artistic epochs, it is true, have exhibited an emphasis on the effects produced by self-conscious stylistic experiments resulting from purely deliberate manipulations of materials; these tendencies, called "manneristic" or "mannerism" by art historians [6], are for the most part exceptional or transitory in character [7].

As a result of the artistic attitude, any work of art has two faces: (1) a presentation to the world to be comprehended in direct, immediate, natural terms; and (2) a complex, involved, self-conscious, systematically derived methodology, which is usually hidden in the work of art.

The first face corresponds in its manifest content to a "natural" world, and allows itself to be treated as a natural world in the same way that the scientist, using the scientific attitude, treats the natural world.

THE CRITICAL ATTITUDE

If an art-created world is treated by a critic as if it were the natural world, such that those elements in that world which give it its form, its content, its structure, and the functional relationship of its parts are dissected, we see the action of the critical attitude.

It is different, however, from the scientific attitude in that the natural world of science has no author, or at least no author who is directly accessible to the observer.

If the natural world were treated as having an author whose intentions and purposes are to be divined by the investigator, then the mode of investigation, we would postulate, would be critical, in the sense in which we use that term. Thus, the age-old conflict between science and theology appears as a difference between a scientific attitude and a critical one.

In any event, the natural world of art, the art object, has an author, a composer, a painter, who deliberately concealed his techniques in creating an artistic world in his art object. What the critic does is to tell the audience what the artist did to achieve his effects; he may even go beyond this in telling the consumer what the artist was unaware of doing when he attempted deliberately to conceal the means of creation of his art world.

In this sense, it is easy to see why there is a tension at the deepest level between the artist as creator and the critic as explicator. For the artist, concealment of technique is essential to his art, both for achieving the spontaneity and naturalness in the work of art and, correspondingly, for the direct and immediate response in the art consumer, as if he were responding to a "natural" world. In unmasking or exposing the techniques, the critic invites the audience to approach the art work from an attitude of "scientific" detachment, which makes the viewer a critic and which destroys the effect of the art product as being a natural world in itself. It upsets the suspension of disbelief and destroys the involvement of the audience by introducing the detachment of a pseudoscientific attitude into the act of experiencing the world as embodied in an art object.

Thus, the critic assists in the disenchantment of the art world in the same way as intellectuals and scientists have, by the process of analysis, helped to disenchant the natural world.

Of course, there are other, simpler, more obvious sources of tensions between the creator and the critic. But these are functional rather than phenomenological. The critic, especially if committed to some earlier or contending aesthetic school, can, of course, destroy or impede the success of an artist or a work of art by negative reviews. He can delay acceptance of a valuable work either by indifference, hostility, or obtuseness. When this happens the artist or performer responds in terms of a natural attitude rather than of an artistic attitude, but this response is evoked by the content of criticism and not by the generic nature of criticism itself.

The issue raised by many artists is that criticism falsifies relations between artist and audience. Criticism can replace creativity as the final product of the artistic enterprise. The *critical attitude* can, alternatively, be called the *academic attitude*, for quite frequently, in attempting to explain the process of creativity, the academician describes the techniques and processes of artistic production as if knowledge of the artistic techniques in and of themselves constituted a solution to the problem of creativity. It is perhaps necessary for an academician to do so, since technique is the most objective and discernible part of the process of artistic creation. Somewhere beneath these objective procedures lie the hidden sources of creativity, ideas, images, feelings, which guide and direct the techniques. The academician, if he lacks these qualities, can only reveal them through his critical work, for in art as in science the work itself is a higher form of communication than is the ex post facto explanation. Much of the apparatus of scholarship that takes the work of art as a point of departure for a wide variety of forms of reductionism—psychological, sociological, historical, and textual—constitutes a world that is autonomous vis-à-vis the world of art. At times, these industries appear to have more structure and foundation than art itself. Yet one cannot dismiss them. Their relevance to the world of art is determined not by their autonomous nature but by the extent to which they contribute to heightening the common-sense appreciation of art.

The critic must necessarily employ words to do his work, and he must employ them in discursive and logical terms. All forms of art, except that of the essay, deal with images available either to the other senses or to the imagination, as does poetry. In using words in a prosaic, quasi-logical framework, the critic attempts to translate the imagery of art into prose. If he could succeed, he would be destroying that which is unique to art, the images themselves. The artist, to the extent that he feels his art medium is unique, must feel that the act of explanation is a form of destruction [8]. In some cases, the artist or layman, habituated to the imagery of art itself, can read criticism in its prose forms and translate this criticism into the imagery that is imperfectly subsumed by the prose. If and when this reverse transformation of prose is successfully accomplished, the prose description need not be an act of destruction. It may, in fact, depending on the value of the analysis, be of great use to the artist, who expresses himself through the imagery of his art. But for prose to be useful in this way, the level of communication subsumed by the prose is one of highly subtle allusions to images that are distantly evoked by that prose. If this style of prose becomes highly developed in its allusive imagery, then critical writing claims an aesthetic value of its own, while being nominally directed toward the works of art of others. The journalistic piece that frankly and openly uses the techniques of poetry and fiction has been called the *feuilleton;* art criticism is increasingly written in this manner.

The attitude of the art consumer may or may not be affected by the critical attitude. A consumer may take for granted the existence of a highly developed artistic or critical attitude, and may simply be concerned with the world of art that presents immediate pleasure, the confirmation of existing tastes, ideas, and attitudes of everyday life, without in any way examining or questioning the work being enjoyed. Artists have sometimes deplored this attitude as that of the "philistine" who only enjoys works of art that are entirely familiar [9], that make no demands. Or, under the influence of the critical attitude, the consumer can look to the work of art to provide confirmation of current categories and standards of criticism that he has absorbed from media other than the work of art itself. In this sense, the consumer attitude, infected by the critical attitude, becomes a form of snobbery, of evidence of being "in," of being *au courant* or "trendy," and has little to do with the work of art itself. Perception of the work of art is clouded by critical images of it, whether favorable or unfavorable.

Yet neither of these two subspecies of consumers' attitudes can tell us why some works of art seem to have a currency or a salience that goes far beyond the critical fashions that may originally have been used to validate them, and goes far beyond the particular contents of the attitudes of everyday life of a given era. Thus works of art may endure while the contents of attitudes of everyday life seem to change substantially over time. One can only conjecture that particular works of art, by the depth of their perception, continuously call into question any temporary attitude of everyday life. They force the consumer to reassess and reevaluate his attitude of everyday life, and a major work of art that endures has a universality that allows it to question virtually all temporary forms of such attitudes. But because it does so, the work of art causes the consumer not to accept that work simply as a "taken-for-granted" form of knowledge that can be absorbed without reflection and thought: the work of art is forced to become an object of analysis; or rather, it forces the viewer or listener to treat it as an object of his analysis. Repeated experience may force him to attempt to understand the means by which the work of art achieves its effects, and the knowledge so gained may cause a deeper understanding of the work itself, of the medium of which it is an exemplification, and of the consumer himself. When this happens, the consumer becomes an active rather than a passive consumer. But such a transformation is not necessarily a product of a program, an intellectual desire to master the form in terms of critical categories. Rather, any major work of art produces its own criticisms in terms of the heightened awareness that it produces in the consumer—both of the work and of himself. And this is what great art always does.

The critic necessarily must transvalue and distort what he would reveal. Since discursive language is the medium of the critic or the academician, he must necessarily fail in doing what he would hope to achieve by the act of criticism. He can, of course, make criticism an end in itself, independent of or only nominally linked to the work of art he criticizes. This is necessarily so, since prose in some form is the stock-in-trade of the critic. And as a teacher of would-be artists and scientists, he must necessarily deal with those tools and media which he has at his disposal.

In earlier periods, before the rationalization of education, the teacher taught by example, and precisely that which was communicated was communicated not by words, but by a kind of osmosis of empathy and by demonstration.

With the rationalization of educational methods, the critical attitude is used to inspire the artistic attitude, or to direct or lead it. As a result, the methodological, technical, and procedural bases of the art form begin to overwhelm the art product as a means of the presentation of the work of art as a holistic world.

Under this aegis, the work of art begins to transcend itself, and becomes an exercise in criticism; thus, modern painting increasingly becomes an exercise in how to do modern painting, and modern music an exercise in how to compose. More than one novel has been written describing the struggle of the novelist to write the novel. The work of art now becomes important because it exemplifies and embodies the critical or academic attitude rather than the artistic or scientific attitude, and this too would have to be considered as an emergent type of phenomenological model. This has usually been called "academic" art (by musicians, *Kapellmeistermusik*). The manner is not too different from the one in which the critic operates with respect to science.

All of the above does not imply that criticism has no positive functions, though these functions are, properly speaking, consequences rather than phenomenological aspects of criticism.

First of all, the critic at his best can serve as press agent for new techniques, styles, and forms of art [10]. In doing so he may provide the terms by which a previously unrecognized style may be apprehended. Since it is the *terms* only that he provides, he does not provide for the possibility of direct communication of the art work itself; but rather in legitimizing new styles, he makes art objects in these new styles accessible to the act of experiencing. If he succeeds, and provides more than a new rhetoric for talking about art, his criticism is of value in enlarging the sensibility of the audience.

Second, the critic, within the framework of an established style or medium, provides an act of judgment that compares the art work as technique with the conventional canons of the style or medium. To the extent that such judgment is necessary, the critic serves this function of maintaining standards.

Third, the critic may actually succeed in enlightening the artist as to what he is really doing; in codifying the rules of art it is possible that artists may perfect techniques which they have intuitively or haphazardly stumbled into. Their work may also serve as manuals for the instruction of neophyte artists. If the artist can respond to his inner voices as well as to these manuals, he may be helped. It is only when criticism transcends art that it places itself in tension with it.

From his standpoint as an agent for the communication of art, the critic has a triple role to perform, each with respect to a different audience:

1. For the professional, the critic maintains standards, by alerting him to sloppy performance, underpreparation, and failure to maintain good taste. He prevents the artist from falling below the best technical standards.

2. For the mass audience, the critic provides the judgments and the terminology that enable that audience to know whether they have enjoyed a work of art, and the symbols with which to express enjoyment.

3. For the sophisticated lay audience, the elite among art consumers, the critic can serve as "prospector," discovering new works and styles of art, and rediscovering old works or styles of value that have been neglected. He reminds the audience of those works which can be appreciated and enjoyed if given the opportunity for sufficient exposure; at this level, he elevates the taste of the audience.

For the critic who functions primarily as a journalist, and who is required to provide a given number of columns for each edition, these functions remain even if only on the level of official rhetoric for the critical profession. These critics are often forced to tailor their criticism to meet the needs of their readers and are unable to meet the immanent requirements of criticism. Thus, in the long run, critics and academicians often do not live up to the standards they apply to others.

APPENDIX: THE PHENOMENOLOGICAL APPROACH

One of the major approaches to philosophy, on which we have already touched is called *phenomenology.* The phenomenological approach had its origins primarily in problems associated with Kantian philosophy. Kant's distinction between the *phenomenon* (the object as it appears in experience) and the *noumenon* (the object as it is in itself), and his view that we can never know the noumenon but only its phenomenal appearances, led to the notion that phenomenal appearances cannot lead to knowledge. In fact, early usages of the word **"phenomenology"** referred to the study of errors and illusions [11].

Hegel, in his *Phenomenology of Mind*, carried philosophy closer to the phenomenological approach of today by attempting to show the conditions under which phenomena are not illusory but revealing. Edmund Husserl, basing his work on that of Franz Brentano and Bernhard Bolzano, took the decisive steps toward a phenomenological approach through his analyses of those states of consciousness in which phenomena do not deceive but reveal. But whether they do the one or the other, they deserve study, according to this approach [12].

The opposite of the phenomenological approach is *reductivism*, that is, the analysis of the object of consciousness in terms of something other than the object itself. Thus the behaviorist, to use a modern example, reduces the qualities of mental productions, ideas in their inner relationship, to the flow of electricity along the nervous system through the ganglia to the brain and from the brain back through the nervous system to the effector muscles. In this process of description, the quality of the ideas disappears—or rather, is reduced to electrical impulses. In the same way, Freud's work can be criticized as reductivist in that the manifest content of an individual's ideas is reduced to diffuse hidden biological impulses and motives and emotions that have greater significance than the ideas themselves. Another form of reductionism is economic, in which economic categories, structures, and systems "explain" the behavior of individuals without recourse to their ideas or purposes, or their ideas are assumed to be masks for economic interests and motives. Because this reductive character is imputed, it is assumed that the imputed motives are primary and that the ideas individuals express can be disregarded without investigation.

The emergence of phenomenological philosophy was a complex development requiring methods and ideas that would enable phenomenology to become a working tool of the philosopher. . . . Such was the task Edmund Husserl would undertake [13].

In the United States, Alfred Schutz attempted to introduce phenomenology into sociology; in doing so, Schutz tried as we have already noted to describe attitudes toward everyday life, that is, to treat the attitudes that govern social interaction as if they were systems of meaning, and to define their constitutive elements as they underlay social action.

Thus, one of the starting points and basic foci of Schutz's work is the attitude of everyday life, or the "natural attitude" [14], as opposed to the "scientific attitude" [15].

THE "NATURAL" AND "SCIENTIFIC" ATTITUDES

In describing and analyzing the attitude of everyday life, Schutz developed a model for understanding the course of social action in terms of motives, which he expressed in phenomenological terms [16]. These motives are based upon shared understandings and meanings between the actors in question, though they may not be explicitly self-conscious of the meanings, concepts, and understandings they share. The understandings are implicit, not intellectualized, and not the objects of consciousness of the parties. Yet they frame and determine the actions that spring from them. The task of the phenomenologist is to discover the meanings and to present them as if they were self-consciously created and understood, and thence to ascertain their relationship to the action of the parties in question. The emphasis, however, is on the phenomenological definition of the meanings themselves.

The attitude of everyday life has two basic ingredients: (1) an attitude toward time [17]; and (2) an attitude involving rationality of action.

The attitude toward time is based on Bergson's distinction between psychological and objective time (Schutz uses the term "cosmic time"), a view similar to that of Husserl [18]. The attitude of everyday life implies psychological time, with unequal intervals based on the depth of feeling and the degree of excitement accompanying the experience of the passage of time (*durée*). Thus, in the attitude of everyday life the individual does not calculate time in objectively measured units, a process that implies objective distance between the observer and the person experiencing it [19]. The psychological concept of time implies minimal self-awareness and minimal distance between oneself as observer and as observed.

The common-sense attitude to rationality of action suggests that the actor takes into account only those alternatives which are immediately relevant to his action in his own immediate situation and over which he may have some control. Thus, he does not plot explicit, logically possible alternatives, which while logical are irrelevant to him and to the possibility of his acting upon them; rather, the alternatives, means and ends, are "taken for granted," assumed as part of the normal setting of the action. When this occurs there is no need for the individual to be conscious of his choice of means to any explicitly stated end. Rather his action is based upon the lack of necessity for self-conscious choice. It is taken for granted. In Schutz's words,

> "rational action" on the common-sense level is always action within an unquestioned and undetermined frame of constructs of typicalities of the setting, the motives, the means and ends, the courses of action and personalities involved and taken for granted. They are, however, not merely taken for granted by the

actor but also supposed as being taken for granted by the fellow man. From this frame of constructs, forming their undetermined horizon, merely particular sets of elements stand out which are clearly and distinctly determinable [20].

As a result, his common-sense actions are situationally egocentric in the same sense that psychological time is temporally egocentric, and neither is subject to rational, explicit self-consicious calculation and planning.

Implicit in the concept of the natural attitude is the counter concept of the scientific attitude. The latter is opposite to the natural attitude in two major dimensions. [21].

Harold Garfinkel in a paper entitled "The Rational Properties of Scientific and Common Sense Attitudes." has, like Schutz described scientific theorizing and the scientific attitude in phenomenological terms and contrasted it with the common sense or natural attitude. He states that if one contrasts the two attitudes in polar opposite terms, one is likely to overlook the fact that the basic concept, the natural attitude, has two "dimensions", one of time and the other the explicit rational calculation of alternatives. Given this dual character of the attitude, a logical "scientific" consideration of its opposite should include the opposite of each dimension. Thus, deviation from the natural attitude could entail deviation from each dimension as well as deviation from both. One can envisage three forms of deviation from the natural attitude, or four basic types of attitudes. Of the four possible cross combinations, Schutz mentions only two, as in the matrix below [22].

In the scientific attitude, time is measured in the objective sense of the term with standardized units, independently of a feeling of involvement which increases or decreases the experience of passing time. In a sense, this means that objectivity is defined in part as the ability to detach oneself from experience as felt and all of the emotional overtones suggested by the phrase [23].

More importantly, the scientific attitude rejects the notion of implicit rationality (what might be called "situational closure"). All logical alternatives are considered independently of the pressures of subjective time; that

Action   Time

	Objective	Subjective
Rationally calculated	Scientific attitude	
Common-sense rationality		Attitude of everyday life

Figure 1. Schutz's dichotomy of attitudes.

is, the sequence of time used up in assessing these alternatives is not considered relevant and is ignored. Within the framework of the logically possible alternatives, alternative means are postulated and alternative results are predicted. In this sense, alternatives are held to be open to rational analysis. Estimates of relative efficiency are then calculated, a decision is made, and the relative efficiency of the decision as against all alternatives is measured by subsequent research or evaluation. The cost of objective time is ignored, for under the natural attitude the time spent in making such assessments might, if thought out, be greater than any gain in efficiency caused by the assessment [24].

In addition, the scientific attitude implies consciousness of each concept used, each method and procedure used, and a statement of concepts, methods, and procedures, in objective and reproducible terms which allows the scientist as observer of his own actions as well as other observers to attribute the results to procedures and methods of observing and measuring [25].

The distinction between the scientific attitude and the attitude of everyday life is basic to Schutz's work, and suggests a vast number of possibilities in the development of phenomenological models that might be useful in work beyond that immediately contemplated by Schutz.

One distinction that we can tentatively suggest, already touched on in this chapter, would be a model called the *planning attitude*, which is based on a combination of the scientific and natural attitudes [26]. The discussion of the natural attitude implies an un-self-conscious, nonreflective man who directly and immediately enters into social relations with others in terms of his immediate personal goals and his direct and intuitive apprehension of a situation. He takes for granted and shares the social meanings that underlie his intuitions and actions; and neither party to the action or social relationship need make explicit or even put into words the explicit meanings they share. These "provinces of meaning" may be so deeply shared that neither party need be consciously aware of either the meaning he projects or those he introjects. The meanings are simply taken for granted.

In a large-scale bureaucratic society, the planner "rationalizes" the process of decision making by following, in his plan, all of the procedures specified in the planning attitude. A military planner may construct a series of alternative plans to deal with a vast number of contingencies, which are viewed as possible, and then attempt to allocate resources in terms of the probabilities and priorities implied in each alternative plan. In this respect, he is scientific. As he moves from the planning phase to the action phase, the action begins to involve attitudes and motives that are analogous to the natural attitude. Certain alternatives are discarded for reasons of economy of thought and action, and because they are either not situationally relevant or low in salience.

The planner in his capacity as actor (though planner and actor may be different persons) deals only with situations over which he has the possibility of exerting control. After the action sequence is completed and when the planner attempts to construct new plans, he may attempt to assess, after the fact, the relationship between the plan and the action [27]. In doing so, he again adopts the scientific attitude after the fact. He becomes a researcher or evaluator.

As the process of planning becomes more central to bureaucratic organizations, the scientific research and development phase is built into the action phase so that the scientific attitude is usually allocated to a separate department that does not interfere with operations.

In the same way, cell 2, in which time is viewed as objective but in which alternatives are not considered, suggests ritual and ceremony as means of organizing activity, especially in highly stylized or expressive ways. Alternatives are not considered and the control of the rhythm of time itself is a major function of the ceremony in inducing into the time perspective of the participants that objective rhythm of the ceremony or ritual. If we now complete the matrix implicit in the cross-analyses (intersecting the dimension of rationality with the dimension of objectivity-subjectivity in the attitude toward time), we would find the following matrix [28]:

If, as we have argued earlier in this chapter, the world of art is an "artificial" construction of aesthetic worlds that correspond in previously described ways to the world of nature, then there should exist a correspondence between each subtype of phenomenological approach for the world of art as for the world of nature. We would postulate the following correspondence of subtypes:

Action   Time

	Objective	Subjective
Rationally calculated	1. Scientific attitude	3. Planning attitude
Common-sense rationality	2. Ritualistic and ceremonial action	4. Attitude of everyday life

Figure 2. Fourfold schema of attitudes toward the natural world.

The Natural World

Action	Time	
	Objective	Subjective
Rationally calculated	1. Scientific attitude	3. Planning attitude
Common-sense rationality	2. Ritualistic and ceremonial action	4. Attitude of everyday life

The World of Art

Action	Time	
	Objective	Subjective
Rationally calculated	1. Criticism	3. Pedagogic art
Common-sense rationality	2. Ceremonial art	4. Creative art

Figure 3. Comparative fourfold schemata of natural world and world of art.

1. *The artistic attitude* presents an image of a total world; it is, as we have indicated, different from the natural attitude, though parallel to it, because the "natural" object is artfully created [29].
2. *The critical attitude* corresponds to the scientific attitude because it analyzes the artistic world in a manner similar to the way that the scientific attitude examines the "natural" world.
3. *The pedagogic attitude* attempts to specify the methods of construction of an art world. It contains elements of the critical and the artistic attitudes, as does the planning attitude.
4. *Ceremonial or ritualistic art* has all the elements of art, except that it is usually highly stylized in forms that limit the choices of the artist in selecting his technique, and is used to create effects that are external to the art experience itself, such that the art work may or may not be considered as having intrinsic interest for its own sake.

In much of modern science, academic criticism takes the form of constructing matrices and paradigms out of successful scientific work in which the critic suggests that if one followed the logical procedures (often unknown to the creator) implicit in one's work, one could discover the secret of creativity [30]. Usually such work results only in criticism and a scholarly commentary on work that has already been done. Going beyond the work of the creator implies new discoveries rather than logical commentary on old discoveries [31].

In the same way, a test of authenticity in art might well be that it creates what appears to be a natural world regardless of its methodological complexity, rather than being a commentary on itself in methodological terms.

NOTES

1.   A more detailed analysis would suggest that the viewer's experience of the art work takes place within a merger of the natural attitude and scientific attitude defined as play, i.e., nonpurposive action, as stated in Huizinga's *Homo Ludens*.

2.   These commonplace phrases are originally derived from English and German Romantic aesthetics.

3.   Schutz I., "On Multiple Realities," p. 229: "Phenomenology has taught us the concept of the phenomenological *epoché*, the suspension of our belief in the reality of the world as a device to overcome the natural attitude by radicalizing the Cartesian method of philosophical doubt. The suggestion may be ventured that man within the natural attitude also uses a special *epoché*, of course quite another one than the phenomenologist. He does not suspend belief in the outer world and its objects, but on the contrary, he suspends doubt in its existence. What he puts in brackets appears to him. We propose to call this *epoché* an *epoché of the natural attitude*."

4.   Friedrich W. J. von Schelling, *Concerning the Relation of the Plastic Arts to Nature* (1807), translated by Michael Bullock, in Herbert Read (Ed.), *The True Voice of Feeling—Studies in English Romantic Poetry* (New York, Pantheon, 1953), p. 331: "It has long been perceived that not everything in art is the outcome of consciousness, that an unconscious force must be linked to conscious activity and that it is the perfect unanimity and interpenetration of the two which produces the highest art. Works which lack this seal of unconscious science are recognizable by the palpable absence of a life which is autonomous and independent of their creator, while, on the contrary, where it is in operation, art simultaneously imparts to the work, with the greatest lucidity of the intelligence, that unfathomable reality by virtue of which it resembles a work of nature."

5.   E. M. Forster, "Art for Art's Sake," in *Two Cheers for Democracy* (New York, Harcourt Brace, 1951), p. 89: "*Macbeth* is furthermore a world of its own, created by Shakespeare and existing in virtue of its own poetry. It is in this aspect *Macbeth* for *Macbeth*'s sake, and that is what I intend by the phrase 'art for art's sake.' A work of art—whatever else it may be—is a self-contained entity, with a life of its own imposed on it by its creator. It has internal order. It may have external form. That is how we recognize it." See also Aron Gurwitsch, *The Field of Consciousness* (Pittsburg, Duquesne U. Press, 1964), pp. 389–390: "When a plurality of imagined

events [sic] concatenated, the several 'quasi-times' in which these events respectively occur are conceived of as phases of one quasi-time with reference to which the multiple imagined events are unified into one encompassing world of imagination. By its proper sense, no imagined event or sequence of imagined events requires insertion into a wider context. This unification depends entirely upon the discretion and fancy of the imagining subject. The imagining subject has complete freedom to unify as well as to abstain from unifying the products of the imagination, each one with its own quasi-time and, therefore, all disconnected from one another. Whereas each world of imagination must be kept free from contradictions, no question concerning consistency or inconsistency between happenings in different worlds of imagination may legitimately be raised. There are then as many independent and autonomous orders of existence as there are separate worlds of imagination. This is exemplified by the multiplicity of novels, plays and epic poems."

6.   Wylie Sypher, *Rococo to Cubism in Art and Literature* (New York, Vintage, 1953), p. 156: "Mannerism rephrases itself . . . after the loss of a style. . . . It is an aspect of pastiche and virtuosity." Also, p. 158: "Renaissance mannerists had a consuming interest in aesthetic theory, sometimes painting compositions only to see how far an accepted canon could be altered. Mannerist beauty is very sophisticated, a kind of dandyism in painting, resorting to what is unnatural, strained, over-cultivated. . . . Such beauty is synthetic—abstract, eclectic, painstakingly designed. . . . Mannerism is a result of different attempts to stylize, and is one symptom of the loss of a style, a revolt against a prevailing style, or a reformulating of style. It is prone to technical ingenuities."

7.   Detailed discussions of the attitude of the composer, the performing artist, and of craft and meaning in literature are presented in later chapters. In addition, virtually every chapter will deal with the relationship between technological self-consciousness and "meaning" in the various fields to be discussed in those chapters.

8.   Robert Lilienfeld, *An Introduction to Music* (New York, Macmillan, 1962), pp. 1–2: "Not that books on music have nothing to say—they often contain many observations that are excellent, or at least correct. Rather it is that such observations as books have to make, true as they may be, simply do not help the listener. A book may discuss music in a variety of terms: historical, emotional, aesthetic, or philosophical; or it may seek to explain music in social, biographical, or psychological terms. These are all translations of music into something else, and whatever merit a translation may possess, it does not help the reader penetrate into the original language." Also p. 124: "Everything he needs to know is in the sound itself, and no reference to anything else will help."

9.   The word "philistine"—already in common use to mean an "outsider," someone "not one of us"—came also to mean someone unimaginative or narrow in his artistic preferences, early in the Romantic era. The composer Robert Schumann, both in his critical journalism and in his compositions (his *Davidsbundlertänze*, piano pieces for the brotherhood of "Davids" at war with the philistines who accept only the familiar in art) helped give the term its currency.

10.   The critic as journalist is treated separately and in detail in chapter 14.

11.   Richard Schmitt, "Phenomenology," in Paul Edwards (Ed.), *The Encyclopedia of Philosophy*, Vol. 6 (New York, Free Press, 1967), pp. 135–151, especially p. 135.

12.   Hans-Georg Gadamer, in "The Phenomenological Movement" (1963), summarizes the conditions under which the phenomenological approach emerged and developed, in the collection of briefer essays titled *Philosophical Hermeneutics*, translated and edited by David E. Linge (Berkeley, University of California Press, 1976), pp. 130–181. Julian Marias, *History of Philosophy*, translated by Stanley

Appelbaum and Clarence C. Strowbridge (New York, Dover Publications, 1967, based on the 22nd Spanish edition, 1966), "Husserl's Phenomenology," pp. 403–417.

13.   Jose Ortega y Gasset, "Sensation, Construction, and Intuition" (1913), in *Phenomenology and Art,* translated by Philip W. Silver (New York, Norton, 1975), pp. 79–94. See also Herbert Spiegelberg, *History of the Phenomenological Movement* (The Hague, Nijhoff, 1960). The literature here is very extensive.

14.   Alfred Schutz, *Collected Papers, Vol. I, The Problem of Social Reality* (The Hague, Martinus Nijhoff, 1964) (referred to hereafter as Schutz I), "On Multiple Realities," p. 208: "The natural attitude of daily life and its pragmatic motive. We begin with an analysis of the world of daily life which . . . shall mean the intersubjective world which existed long before our birth, experienced and interpreted by others, our predecessors, as an organized world. . . . All interpretations of this world are based upon a stock of previous experiences of it, our own experiences and those handed down to us by our parents and teachers, which in the form of 'knowledge at hand' function as a scheme of reference." Schutz at times uses the phrase "common-sense thinking," as well as the "natural attitude" and the "attitude of everyday life," to express the same basic ideas. See, for example, Schutz I, "Common-Sense and Scientific Interpretation," pp. 7–10, and also "On Multiple Realities," pp. 208 and 229. In focusing on the "attitude of everyday life" as a descriptive phrase, we are following Garfinkel, simply because the phrase is most descriptive of the phenomenon embraced by the concept. See Harold Garfinkel, *The Rational Properties of Scientific and Common Sense Activities,* pp. 9, 10, and passim. The paper by Harold Garfinkel, "The Rational Properties of Scientific and Common Sense Activities" was later published in his book on ethnomethodology: Harold Garfinkel, *Studies in Ethnomethodology,* (Englewood Cliffs, N.J., Prentice Hall, 1967). See also, Harold Garfinkel, "Aspects of the Problem of Common Sense Knowledge of Social Structures" in *Transactions of the 4th World Congress of Sociology,* Vol. 4, 1959, pp 51–65. And his "Notes on the Sociological Attitude" (unpublished) p. 2 and *passim.* (Garfinkel here uses the phrase "attitude of daily life.") Unpublished papers, available on request from author. See also Peter L. Berger and Thomas Luckmann, *The Social Construction of Reality* (Garden City, Doubleday, 1966), pp. 40–43.

15.   Schutz I, "On Multiple Realities," pp. 248–249: "The theoretical thinker is interested in problems and solutions valid in their own right for everyone, at any place, and at any time. . . . The 'leap' into the province of theoretical thought involves the resolution of the individual to suspend his subjective point of view. And this fact alone shows that not the undivided self but only a partial self, a taker of a role, a 'Me,' namely the theoretician, 'acts' within the province of scientific thought. This partial self lacks all 'essentially actual' experiences and all experiences connected with his own body, its movements and its limits."

16.   Schutz I, p. 249: "We may now sum up some of the features of the *epoché* [a Greek word adopted by Edmund Husserl to mean a reduction or bracketing of phenomenological contents] peculiar to the scientific attitude. In this *epoché* there is 'bracketed' (suspended): (1) the subjectivity of the thinker as a man among fellow men, including his bodily existence as a psychophysical human being within the world; (2) the fundamental anxiety and the system of pragmatic relevance originating therein. But within this modified sphere the life-world of all of us continues to subsist as reality, that is, as the reality of theoretical contemplation, although not as one of practical interest. With the shift of the system of relevances from the practical to the theoretical field, all terms referring to action and performance within the world of working, such as 'plan,' 'motive,' 'projects,' change their meaning and receive 'quotation marks.' " See also Garfinkel, *The Rational Properties of Scientific and Common Sense Activities,* p. 11: "In . . . scientific theorizing quite a different role of

interpretive procedure is used. It provides that interpretation be conducted while holding a position of 'official neutrality' toward the belief that the objects of the world are as they appear. . . . [T]he activities of scientific theorizing are governed by the strange ideal of doubt that is in principle unlimited and that specifically does not recognize the normative social structures as constraining conditions."

17. Schutz I, "Choosing Among Projects of Action," p. 85: "Bergson, who has emphasized more than any other philosopher the importance of the two time dimensions—inner *durée* and spatialized time—for the structure of our conscious life, investigated . . . the problem of choice under this aspect. He handles it in connection with his criticism of the deterministic and indeterministic doctrines. Both determinists and indeterminists, so his argument runs, base their conclusions upon an associationistic psychology. They substitute for the inner *durée* with its continuous succession and the interconnected stream of consciousness the spatialized time in which there is juxtaposition of seemingly isolated experiences."

18. Bergson, *Time and Free Will*, Chapter II, p. 100: "Pure duration is the form which the succession of our conscious states assumes when our ego lets itself *live*. When it refrains from separating its present state from its former states . . . it . . . forms both the past and present states into an organic whole." And pp. 107–108: "When I follow with my eyes on the dial of a clock the movement of the hand which corresponds to the oscillations of the pendulum, I do not measure duration *(durée* . . . I merely count simultaneities, which is very different . . . withdraw . . . the pendulum and its oscillations; there will no longer be anything but the hetero-geneous duration of the ego, without external relation to one another, without relation to number." Also Schutz I, "On Multiple Realities," p. 215: "What occurs in the outer world . . . can be registered by appropriate devices and measured by our chronometers. It is the spatialized, homogeneous time which is the universal form of objective or cosmic time." Edmund Husserl, *Ideas—General Introduction to Pure Phenomenology* (New York, Collier Books, 1962), pp. 215–216: "Through the phe-nomenological reduction consciousness has forfeited not only its apperceptive 'at-tachment' (in truth only an image) to material reality and its relations in space, merely secondary though these may be, but also its setting in cosmical time. The same time, which belongs essentially to experience as such with the modes in which its intrinsic content is presented—and derived from these the modally determined now, before and after, simultaneity, succession, and so forth—is not to be measured by any state of the sun, by any clock, by any physical means, and generally cannot be measured at all. Cosmical time stands to phenomenological time in a relation somewhat analogous to that in which the 'extensity' *(spread)* that belongs to the immanent *essence* of a concrete sensory content . . . stands to objective spatial 'extension,' to that, namely, of the appearing physical object, manifesting itself in visual 'perspectives' through the medium of the sensory data in terms of which it appears."

19. Schutz I, "Concept and Theory Formation in the Social Sciences," p. 63.

20. Schutz I, "Common-Sense and Scientific Interpretation of Human Action," p. 33.

21. Harold Garfinkel has based a central part of his work on the difference between the scientific attitude and the attitude of everyday life (see the works cited above). Much of this essay is based on his work.

22. The missing cells will be treated in subsequent sections.

23. Schutz I, "Common-Sense and Scientific Interpretation of Human Action," p. 36: "This attitude . . . is that of a mere disinterested observer of the social world. He is not involved in the observed situation, which is to him not of practical but merely of cognitive interest. It is not the theater of his activities but merely the

object of his contemplation. He does not act within it, vitally interested in the outcomes of his actions . . . but he looks at it with the same detached equanimity with which the natural scientist looks at the occurrences in his laboratory.

24.   For this reason, many persons holding the natural attitude reject the scientific attitude as academic. The time wasted in making decisions is greater than the gain to be derived from assessing the efficiency of a host of alternatives.

25.   Schutz I, "Common-Sense and Scientific Interpretation of Human Action," p. 39: "His stock of knowledge at hand is the corpus of his science, and he has to take it for granted—which means in this context, as scientically ascertained—unless he makes explicit why he cannot do so. To this corpus of science belong also the rules of procedure which have stood the test, namely, the methods of his science, including the methods of forming constructs in a scientifically sound way. This stock of knowledge is of quite another structure than that which man in everyday life has at hand." See also "Concept of Theory Formation in the Social Sciences," p. 63.

26.   Joseph Bensman, in an unpublished paper, *The Use of Models of Formal Organization in Business*, discusses the planning attitude and its relevance to bureaucratic and planning structures.

27.   This planning attitude can be located in cell 3.

28.   This method of analysis we are using, substructuring, has been suggested and developed by Lazarsfeld and Barton, especially in "Some Functions of Qualitative Analysis in Social Research," *Frankfurter, Beiträge zur Sociologie* Vol. I (1955), pp. 321–361.

29.   See Joseph Bensman and Israel Gerver, "Art and the Mass Society," *Social Problems*, Vol. VI (Summer 1958), pp. 4–10.

30.   The matrices shown above may well be examples of this.

31.   When the academician-critic treats scientific theories and ideas from the standpoint of the critical attitude, that is, analyzes their properties, dimensions, structure, and thematic development, he converts the scientific theory into a work of art, and analyzes its aesthetics. The scientific theory becomes artistic theory because it is treated as such. Science in thus viewed primarily in terms of its logical coherence with initial assumptions, instead of in terms of its predictive ability or its ability to explain previously unsolved "problematics" of the external world.

Chapter 2

The Professional Attitude of the Composer

The composer, like other artists, seeks to create within a medium a world that is at times so rich and varied that it is possible for the listener to suspend all other worlds, and to enclose himself within it.

But music offers difficulties that the other arts do not. The poet, the novelist, the dramatist, the painter can all offer as elementary materials concrete images of persons, scenes, landscapes, flowers, and so on; that is to say, they can represent things concretely knowable to persons in the natural world. But musical tones represent nothing outside themselves, and music itself, besides, offers certain peculiarities that remain puzzling for theorists. The problem for the composer, then, is to create a world of experiences within the acoustical and tonal region, which region does not offer the representational concreteness available in words, painting and drawing, or in dramatic action.

This task for the composer emerges late in history. Music in its earliest forms always appears linked to other forms, as a dimension added to dance, poetry, drama, ritual, ceremony. In its earliest forms, then, the words, ceremonies, drama, choreography, all supply the concreteness, the imagery, and the "meaning," which the music serves to intensify and to heighten. But the late emergence of music as an abstract and autonomous art form now confronts us with its difference from all other art forms, a difference which occurs at various levels. The fact that music works on the selection and ordering of sounds is of course its unique characteristic, to be discussed in detail below. But within the ordering of sounds, music operates with special emphasis on time; not only the time of its rhythm and tempo, but also the fact that the act of listening can only take place with a continuous flow of attention directed by the composition or the score, as performed. Thus a painting can be viewed instantaneously in its entirety; or the viewer has the option of arresting his attention to now one aspect of the canvas by suspending his interest in all other aspects. In literature, the reader can control, direct, redirect the sequence of time in the act of reading, by stopping, skipping, or going back. He can pause over a sentence, and spend as much time as he needs for analyzing a word, phrase, sentence, or chapter. In a live performance, the music listener must surrender his control of time in order to understand the work as it is performed. Of course the professional or semiprofessional musical analyst can study the score as if it were literature, and thus analyze it. When he does this, he is surrendering the natural attitude of the listener. Or, with reproduction devices, he can skip, play back, stop, but in doing so he gives up listening to a musical entity, and therefore surrenders his perception of the overall idea of the music. To recapture the overall feeling and the flow of the music, the professional analyst must suspend his critical analysis of parts, and of the music as a whole, and listen as an amateur. In this sense of depending on the controlled flow of time, music has much in common with plays and movies, in which the succession of events is the major ingredient for understanding the work in its entirety. In this sense, there is a "dramatic" quality in the performing arts—music, drama, in recited poetry, dance, and, to a lesser extent, in the cinema, which are different from all other fields. In the novel, an extra feat of virtuosity is achieved when the work of art produces a flow of action which challenges the reader to put down the novel, that is, to even suspend the literary form of the novel itself. But this is not essential to the novel. The "dramatic" quality in music, the creation, release, and maintenance of dramatic tension, is thus an additional possible quality in music. All of this, however, is accomplished despite the fact that there is no direct representational quality in music. A play and a dance convey direct mimetic qualities; painting can be representational; literature has significant representation which can evoke the immediate appearance of the ordinary world of experience.

Poetry, in suggesting moods, feelings, and tones beyond the denotations of the words used, can move in the direction of nonrepresentational symbolism, as can any art form which attempts to transcend the merely representational. And, as the other art forms have evolved through time, a major form of virtuosity has been that of transcending the pictorial, the representational, the mimetic, or the denotative. But in all other artistic media, this kind of transcendence is a "leap," an escape from the essential mimetic or representational form, and all other art forms imitate music in this respect. Historically, of course, this problem did not present itself as the problem for music. Music in primitive and folk cultures, as we have noted, always had a representative character, not because music was representative per se, but because it was always interwoven with other activities; dancing, drama, ritual and work, warfare, death and marital rites, and religious and political ceremonies. Music presumably adjusted its emotive "tone" to that of the event, but the question now emerges: are there musical tones or combinations thereof that *sui generis* have emotional or other content that go beyond the conventional meanings attributed to music by virtue of past associations? As music gradually emerged more and more as an autonomous art, this question emerged with it.

Many early writers assumed naively that music had clear representational and emotive meanings [1]. The test of whether this is true or not would be accomplished if listeners could appreciate the emotional or symbolic significance of music when such listeners were drawn from cultures other than those in which the music originates. The burden of much research suggests that music does not have specific cross-cultural representational powers. Additional research suggests that on a first performance of expressive music, even relatively sophisticated audiences are not able to agree on the intended mood of the music, even when the intention of the composer was explicit [2]. Yet, as naive listeners, we must conclude that within the framework of conventional designations of musical expressiveness, musical performance can evoke powerful responses of moods that cause audiences to lose their sense of the ordinariness of experience.

But regardless of the lack of generic representativeness, composers have striven mightily to create works and theories of work that give to sounds, tones, sequences, and motives a representational power. At its simplest levels, this involves musical representation of sounds in nature—the cuckoo, the nightingale, the hunting horn, representations of out-of-tune tavern bands, peace suggested by quiet music, war by drums and trumpets, etc. At more complex levels, theorists and composers have attempted to suggest that certain scales and keys have emotional affinities. A popular misunderstanding is that minor keys suggest moods of resignation, plaintiveness, defeat, and tragedy, and major keys express direct, healthy, extroverted, joyous, even patriotic activity.

Yet within a culture, music may have profound symbolic meanings. Notions of grief, joy, bucolic simplicity, triumph are conveyed by sonority and tempo, and can be instantly recognized as such by an audience [3]. But the degree to which this is so depends on the existence of a musical tradition in which the association of tone, tempo, and rhythm, with word, phrase, affect and imagery is already established. Even within a culture, however, this parallel between sound and "meaning" cannot be taken as given, for in any period of artistic creation, musicians or composers, in creating new sounds, violate the accepted meanings, and become "misunderstood." The establishment of new meaning then requires new patterns of familiarity, habituation, and interpretation. At the same time, established forms of music at one time seemed to have self-evident patterns of meaning, or seem to have lost their meaning, or are not taken as meaningful in a self-evident manner. That is, they are not part of the natural attitudes of the consumer. In periods of revival, the reestablishment of meaning requires at times a willingness to explore self-consciously the meanings of previous styles of music, and familiarize oneself with such music in manners that require more than a natural attitude. Such revivals often require self-conscious "movements," pressure-group tactics, organizational activity, all of which cannot be taken for granted at the moment of inception of the "revival." In the same sense, the effects which at times became taken for granted were the products of earlier theorizing, indoctrination, education, and special pleading. Only when such movements were successful could the meaning of music within a culture become the "natural" meaning of music.

Many composers, especially in opera, recognize at least intuitively that the expressive quality of a theme or motif is conventional, and they simply use established conventions as part of the program for the work. Using these expressive definitions, the composer operates as if they were true, and within such a framework he is capable of writing highly expressive music. This is especially true for Wagner, Liszt, and such post-Wagnerians as Debussy, who operated on the notion that musical structure is to be totally subordinated to a mood or image.

Of course it would be a vast oversimplification to say that the meanings in music are either the product of the projection of natural attitudes into music, or the reflection of musical theorizing into performance and listening. Certainly external social institutions and organizations have profound effects on the character of music. A vast literature has demonstrated these external effects, and we can only suggest some of them here. The requirement of military organizations to provide a uniform rhythm of the march, morale, stately dignity, a triumphant tone, uniformity and discipline, has everywhere produced special kinds of music, though not everywhere is military music the same. Work may at times employ music to emphasize the integration of work crews, the dulling of pain, the celebration of unity, the overcoming of boredom. Religion will underline and accentuate the dominant religious themes of ceremony and rites, whether these emerge "naturally" over time, or whether the result of conscious planning to evoke specific attitudes and loyalties, and to establish uniformity within a sect or church and diversity from other religious organizations and their music. Religious themes are thus "objectified" in music; but various religions emphasize a wide variety of emotional themes [4]. Music may under these emotional themes result in an ever wider variety of treatments.

Music will often express ethnic and national traditions. In folk music such indigenousness may be the product of musical evolution over long periods of time based on the relative isolation of an ethnic group or tribe from other groups, but even here the amount of borrowing of folk music from one group to another serves to limit the amount of genuine indigenous music. The most one can say is that there are families of indigenous music based more on region than on ethnicity. However, with the development of nationalism or of ethnic self-consciousness, ethnic music becomes programmatic, and develops its themes and character as parts of intellectual movements which use music as a means, often, to nonmusical goals. In addition, with the development of musical self-consciousness, folk music becomes an almost inexhaustible reservoir of themes, motifs, sounds, rhythms, and even of musical instruments, which may be used in highly self-conscious non–folk musical schemes. And, if one wants to complicate the picture, one can further add that with the export of self-conscious, professionalized music into as yet "primitive" worlds, indigenous folk music borrows from sophisticated art music, and incorporates themes into its more "primitive" conceptions. A substantial part of popular music bases itself on the vulgarization of art music, which in turn may be sophisticated transformations of earlier folk music.

Certainly social class is a basic external factor in the development of music. Some types of music were based on the possession of relatively expensive instruments and training accessible only to the more prosperous classes. Other types of music could be universal in their accessibility. The needs to differentiate between types of music created a class character thus based on the possession of relatively inaccessible musical means. The necessities of class ritual and ceremony created musical forms and styles, as music derived from court dancing and court performance. Other types of music derived from the accessibility of music to places of performance. Thus, the ballroom, the salon, the grand opera, all confined some types of music to the upper classes. Conversely, such forms of music as street music or opera buffa could be based on less grandiose means.

Certainly patterns of social organization contributed to selectivity in the forms of music. The development of urbanism and civic government allowed for the development of community music—complete with guilds and municipally financed orchestras. Correspondingly, the aristocracy could afford to employ bards, troubadours, court orchestras, chamber groups, chapel choirs, ballet and opera companies. The churches could employ, depending on their place in the church hierarchy, massive choirs, organists, other instrumental accompanists. Moreover, all these groups could create music schools, and employ professional music directors, composers, *Kapellmeister*, and virtuoso performers, though the roles were not always or often separated.

The development of architecture was of course external to the development of musical styles and forms, but could clearly influence them. The development of churches with choirs separated by the nave allowed for the development of complicated multichoral part music, reaching a high point in the development of late renaissance and baroque sonorities.

Further developments in architecture led to the possibility of the giant symphonic orchestra, grand opera, and the concert as a new form of musical life, though all of these were accompanied by the rise of the middle class, who by numbers and affluence could, through the development of the subscription concert, financially support the music afforded by the new architecture. Beyond this, the aspirations of the middle class to be "cultured" reflected mobility strivings which could be expressed not only in music but in all cultural forms.

But equally important was the development of science and technology, as it was reflected in the development of musical instruments. Such technological changes made possible the standardization of instruments, and with it the possibility of precise performance, a possibility which could be realized only with the development of printing on a large scale.

The development of the piano with improved action, the tempered scale, and the cast-iron frame not only resulted in the enhancement of sonorities but helped to result in the simplification of the thematic or melodic presentation of music. In doing so, it made music more accessible to the middle classes, since the simplification made fewer demands on the listener. The technological changes, moreover, resulted in a reduction in the original cost and upkeep of keyboard instruments, and made previous types of keyboard instruments accessible in new forms to larger audiences. In a similar manner, the simplification of music, together with developments in architecture, and the subscription concert, resulted in the development of virtuosity in performance and composition, and the cult of the musical personality. The development of technology in music has continued unabated, though in the twentieth century its development has taken many forms. The recording and broadcasting of music has resulted in the enlargement of musical audiences, the accessibility of all kinds of music to all kinds of audiences, the vulgarization of vast bodies of musical performances, the greater use of incidental music, the employment of music of even the highest orders for essentially nonmusical uses, the replacement of live musicians by recorded music at weddings, dances, and other social occasions, and frequently the banalization of music. At other levels electronic music has permitted experimentation with sounds, rhythms, timbres, and combinations of the above, so that experimentation not only based on external technology but on the techniques of music itself seems replete.

In part, such development may be a reaction to the overblown, excessively simple virtuosic music of some currents of composition of the late nineteenth century; in part it may have been the result of the sense of the exhaustion of triadic harmony by the chromaticism of Wagner and his successors.

Western music in its history reveals a quality of disjunction between the natural world of naive folk, programmatic, and expressive music, and the highly formalized, abstract, intellectual, and methodological character of its art music. Music as a self-conscious, stylized art has forms, methods, meanings, and an autonomy which must be understood in its own terms. It also reveals that there is much more to music than its subservience to the external world as embodied in religion, warfare, work, social class, architecture, science and technology. Music is amenable to mathematical analysis. The division of strings into segments, with each segment producing a different interval, octave, fifth, etc., and a series of divisions producing a scale, all permit the intellectual analyst to perform rational exercises with these intervals, and to attempt to find perfect sequences of intervals, a perfection that, however, has eluded all musical rationalists of the last 2500 years [5]. Plato and Pythagoras, as mathematicians and philosophers, looked to the mathematical order of music as a key to the discernment of the order that lies in the secret of the universe. At the moment, we are not concerned with the secrets of the universe, but once the attempt has begun to rationally order the world of music, the rationalization has resulted in the conception of music as a series of alternative closed systems, each having definite order, definite rules, and musical taboos, which began to frame in highly rational terms what was permissible and impermissible in the composition of music. Once musicians began to accept these frameworks, music could no longer be naive, matter of fact, un-self-conscious, simply a "natural" given world, at least for the composer.

Within any era, however, in which the rules appeared to be stabilized for some length of time, the listener could regard the music to which he was accustomed as natural, given and self-evident, merely on the basis of familiarity. The composer could never completely make this assumption because he had to avoid the "mistakes" that were defined as such within the framework of the conventionally rationalized music. Of course, rationalized music has primarily been confined to those who are exposed to formal musical training and conventions. The primitive, the folk, is always present or reemerges among those who are outside the culture of rational music, as in perhaps the case of the Blues, though much of what is regarded as "primitive," or folk music represents the conventional music of earlier eras, as distilled by the musical nonelect, and simplified in their terms, and then accepted as given, natural, and self-evident. Conversely, much of serious, formal music rests on themes and ideas that are drawn from folk music, but which is then treated in terms of musical formalization and rationalization of whatever musical system the composer is working in at the time of composition.

This may be done in several distinct ways: a musical virtuoso may select the most banal popular themes and demonstrate, through musical treatment, his ability to transform the banal into the brilliant. Secondly, this may be done as a musical joke; thirdly, it may be done as a public relations or

journalistic device to demonstrate that serious musicians can produce serious, general music out of popular trash. Others, such as Bartók, were
genuinely interested in musicological research and the preservation of musical heritages, and "incidentally" used such materials as means of demonstrating the possibilities of musical systems that were not acceptable by conventional musical high culture. In this sense, the use of popular themes had a
creative function for the evolution of systematic musical theory.

Perhaps the simplest case of the use of popular music in the development
of formal musical theories and styles is in the establishment of musical forms
in the late Renaissance and Baroque periods. Such musical forms as the
sarabande, the musette, the gigue, the pavane were folk and popular forms,
especially dance and literary or poetic forms, which, when they evolved,
through serious stylization became no longer danceable or singable. But
through this very process of stylization, they became standard forms through
which serious music would have to express itself.

The rationalization of musical forms, theories, scales, and keys, and means
of thematic treatment, can be defined as aesthetic in the sense that they
constitute a set of self-selected limits, rules, and taboos for the composer,
and constitute a challenge to him to be able to develop a musical idea so that
it has variety, dramatic tension, and closure, while still staying within the
framework of fairly rigidly prescribed rules. High points in such aesthetic
rationalization include Bach's handling of the fugue, Haydn's and Mozart's
treatment of the rondo form, and Beethoven's mastery of theme-and-
variation techniques. Taking a very limited and highly defined medium,
Bach, through a series of brilliant exercises, demonstrated all the possibilities of treatment of musical ideas within the framework of that medium.
Having done so, there was little more that one could do with that genre.
Bach's work could not be surmounted, and the fugue qua fugue was virtually
abandoned. As a result, however, the fugue and fugal elements were imported into or helped to create other forms—the sonata, symphony, quartet, etc.
There are very few other cases which compress the nature of aesthetic
rationalization into so short a time period. Over longer periods of time, a
similar sequence appears to have happened with all musical genres, methodologies, schemes, etc.

The very limited nature of the musical scheme constitutes its challenge
within the framework of rationalized music, and serves as an impulse to the
professional, either to exhaust the form, or to demonstrate its perfection in
terms of a musical idea, or theme, which is independent of the form. But the
very existence of rigid forms, to some musical creators, constitutes a set of
limits to their musical ideas; for these musical creators, the problem is not
one of using up the resources of the style, but of bursting through the
boundaries of the "style." Thus, Beethoven's famous remark to his teacher
Albrechtsberger (about his breaking the rules) that the composition is right

simply because he dared to write it that way; but in doing so, Beethoven succeeded in imposing his musical standards upon other composers and upon musical audiences and in fact helped to develop a new musical schema. It is not just the fact that he "broke the rules" that is important. What is important is the fact that in breaking them he rewrote them and suggested new possibilities for musical development. But Beethoven's uniqueness in this respect is overestimated; Mozart, Haydn, and many others also violated conventions for expressive reasons [6].

Such departures, however, produce conflicts in musical theory, even more than they do in musical practice. Musical theorists, as critics, quite often serve as guardians of the conventional wisdom of musical methodologies. The practicing musician, in breaking the rules, is thus viewed as guilty of a kind of heresy and is often treated as a barbarian, and such treatment is likely to persist until the rules are broken often enough to constitute a tradition in and of itself, and then the violation is incorporated into the rules, and celebrated by a later generation of musical theoreticians [7]. In the same sense, when the musical methods are accepted as the conventional wisdom by audiences, the violation of the rules becomes a kind of barbarism, at least at first, or at early performances. Thus, Beethoven, in presenting each of his major symphonies, was regarded as a barbarian, but within a short period of time one symphony was regarded as acceptable because a later one was regarded as even more barbarous. Many works have travelled the path from scandal to orthodoxy in a relatively short period of time. Illustrations of this process could be multiplied almost infinitely.

There are historical periods when self-consciousness in the rationalization of musical systems becomes heightened, so that the development of these systems becomes an end in itself, a game in which the composer seems to say "This is what we can do." In a short run, such aesthetic development invites the listener to suspend judgment because the development of genuine musical ideas may come after the rationalization of musical systems. In the long run such rationalizations may produce nothing but their own transcendence. A generation or even longer may pass before one can say that the direction taken was a dead end or, at most, raw material for other rationalizations.

At the same time, innovating music sometimes achieves its success precisely because it breathes fresh air into a musical atmosphere which has become stagnant by the continuous circulation of musical banalities. The virtue of such music consists, at times, only in its momentary freshness. Once it is repeated, it is found that it contributes to an almost instantaneous stagnation. When this happens, a musical era will stagnate under the press of "innovation." Slight variations in the form and style will be used to demonstrate the self-conscious inventiveness of the composer. The individual works will be composed in order to demonstrate a novelty of sound, theme color, or sonorous treatment, that novelty being unable to go beyond the work in question. Thus, novelty consists of the discovery of striking fragments, the exploitation of tricks, of sensationalism, of a self-consciousness on the part of both composer and audience without having any intrinsic relationship to a flow of musical development in a work as a whole. Periods where such musical tendencies abound are frequently recognized after the fact as periods of stagnation and decadence. This practice is reminiscent of "mannerism" in painting.

The pure systemic play—play with rhythms, chromaticism, meters—produces a sense of artificiality, of mannerism, in the music, which may be so prominent that the music, even with repetition and familiarity, does not achieve a matter-of-fact status. This does not imply that there exists some absolute, true, or ultimate music, from which "artificial" music deviates. It does mean that a test of all music is that it can reach the stage of being "taken for granted" or accepted as a vocabulary for the expression of musical taste and feeling. Some music may always seem too highly intellectual, and therefore nonmusical, and other music may appear to have no other "substance" than the evocation of temporary "charm," "amusement," or "shock value"; that is, it appears incapable of development, expansion, or permanence.

THE COMPOSER AS CRAFTSMAN

A musical idea, in its narrowest sense, is a "theme" or a "motif" that is recognizable as a unique entity, and that has a character of concreteness. The ability to generate such uniquely concrete ideas is comparatively rare, and remains something of a mysterious process. It is usually understood as a lyric or melodic element; some composers seem to have an abundance of melodic inventiveness, but this by itself does not necessarily result in the capacity to sustain interest. The absence of drama, tension, or more important, the absence of development, all contribute to a sense of shallowness or incompleteness despite thematic inventiveness. These additional qualities—"drama," tension, transition—are equally subjective and intangible, though clearly recognizable after the fact. They too, by themselves, can only produce short-term interest. The capacity for the development of musical themes is a product of training in technique, but by themselves the formal attributes of musical training can produce highly skilled but relatively empty music. Such music may be perfect by the standards of contemporary music theory, and will be admired precisely because of its perfection, but like musical themes or melodies that are undeveloped, it lacks the capacity for sustaining interest. It is the combination of musical themes or shapes plus their development that in our definition will constitute a musical idea [8].

Musical ideas, themes, and melodies can emerge without reference to prevailing systems of music. However, some themes or melodies—dramatic tensions—would be barred by the rules of a given system of musical rationalization. To state it differently, musical ideas are not cumulative but systems of musical rationalization are, or claim to be. More important than the musical theme or idea is the musical paradigm, the fundamental framework within which music is expressed. This may be music composed in terms of a scale, mode, harmonic system, or tone row, or in terms of aleatoric procedures. As indicated, a particular work may be created within any of these "forms," and the reliance on a particular "form" may at times produce only sterile evidence of the mastery of the techniques of composition. Yet if one looks at the dynamics of music, it is the movement from "form" to "form" that constitutes the history of the development of western music, and, we would suspect, if we understood them better, the history of other kinds of music [9].

These rationalities of musical "forms" or styles include not only kinds of tonalities but also selective preferences or conventions with respect to the use of rhythms, timbres, textures, cadential patterns, accompaniments, or improvisations. The rationalization of music then includes the attempt to work out the full range and implications of the limited possibilities inherent in the rules or conventions of a form. And the exhausting, apparently, of the limits of a form (that is, if the composer believes that all he can do has been done before), to the extent that he wishes to be autonomous and original, forces the composer to change the formal rules. In some periods, such developments involve relatively slight changes, which are not programmatic in their intent, or if seen as "innovations," are not expressed in programmatic terms. Thus, the harmonic practices of such composers as Brahms, Dvorák, and Grieg include some chordal uses that are new but that remain within the framework of "romantic" chordal harmony. At other times, the accumulation of changes results in such a change in the initial paradigm that the musical theorist will either programmatically announce the change, or will programmatically call for such a change. Thus, the end of Renaissance style is implicit in Zarlino's formulation of triadic ideas, and in the programmatic "second practice" of the new composers of the seventeenth century. In some cases the change of program is expressed in music so radically different from the ongoing music of his time that the music itself is a declaration of the adoption of a new paradigm (as with Debussy, Wagner, Stravinsky, Schoenberg).

These programmatic changes, whether they are expressed only in the shape of music itself, or are presented with the statement of nonmusical literary or polemical statements, may if successful be turning points in the development of music. In part, such changes are intimately connected with changes in the external social institutions of music. Thus, the development of Classical and Romantic music is related to the various forms in which the rise of the middle class expressed itself, as in earlier times the development of church architecture affected polyphonic styles.

The battles over music are always expressed in musical terms, and musical development is incapable of presenting itself except in the capacity of musical theorists, not only as proponents and opponents to defend and attack new and old forms of music, but to create the music which they defend. Moreover, given any external set of circumstances, there is no one form of composition which embodies the external circumstances on a one-to-one basis. Thus, even among the opponents of the "old music" at any time and place, there are various forms of "new" music embodying the music of the future, and these forms of new music are often as much opposed to each other as they are opposed to the old music. And since all new music ultimately becomes old music, the old music has unity only from the standpoint of radical departures that emerge over time. In its own time the "old" music is not as unified as subsequent generations often see it [10].

Beyond this, the development of aesthetic programs implies the possibility of composers becoming conscious of their craft and separating themselves from the external demands placed upon them. The history of composition shows the musician as composer continuously straining to write music which is autonomous despite the demands placed upon him by audiences, patrons, sponsoring groups, and critics. Such struggles were not celebrated until the beginning of the Romantic era, though the evidence of such struggles goes back as far as documentation exists, and is embodied in musical innovation where other forms of documentation do not exist. In this respect music is no different from medieval religious carving and sculpture, where anonymous artisans insisted on leaving a personal mark upon their work by the use of covert initials and codes [11], but the opportunity and the ideology for personal self-consciousness and expression did not fully emerge until the nineteenth century; in part this was a product of the emergence of the composer qua composer, and the separation, to a large extent, of the role of composer from that of performer, *Kapellmeister*, etc. [12]. In part this separation occurred simultaneously with the separation of performer and musical director as such. Even when the great virtuosi of the nineteenth century excelled in several of these roles, they achieved recognition in their separate roles, sometimes serially.

Certainly the separation of the role of composer was made possible by the development of the printing of music and the enactment of copyright laws. In part the rise of the mass musical audience made it possible for various musical roles to be supported independently of a particular patron or organization. By the twentieth century, the support of the musician, especially the composer, by the university, and to some extent by foundations, allowed the composer to become almost totally independent of audiences. All of these developments assisted the composer qua composer to become conscious of the independence of his musical media from the requirements of particular patrons and audiences. It enabled him to become conscious of himself as composer, and provided him with a new audience, other composers who were similarly preoccupied with the musical paradigm itself, and not the particular musical work in its conventional meaning as known to musical audiences. Thus, by the last quarter of the nineteenth century, music as composition began to take on an objectivity in itself, became subject to musical criticism by composers as critics of musical systems or paradigms. In part, this criticism was itself a reaction to the vulgarization of music as embraced by nineteenth-century romantics who specialized in the evocation of overblown effects for their audiences. But the consciousness of music as an object of musical analysis by composers hastened the rate of musical experimentation. Established forms were no longer regarded as given or sacred, the forms were less accepted as points for small departures within a continuous and cumulative exhaustion of work within a paradigm, but the paradigms themselves became the object of analysis [13].

As a result, the rate of innovation began to accelerate and innovation began to take on a self-conscious experimental character in which composers simultaneously attempted to test the effects of the substitution of new forms for all aspects of traditional forms. In part, some experiments consisted of extending and changing the conventional sounds of music; others consisted of ignoring the sound of music in order to explore the possibilities of mathematical or rhythmical changes and combinations. In almost all cases the effect of such music on the audience was ignored, and audiences who for whatever their reasons were attuned to music, supported their interest by listening to older more traditional music, which at least had the advantage of familiarity [14]. Some musicians and critics would add that such older music had the further advantage of being based on a coherent tonal system. In any event the cleavage between composer and audience grew wider and wider, and because of this cleavage, the possibility of a continuous familiarization of the audience with musical innovations was made more difficult [15]. Thus while much new music ultimately became popular, the delay often took as long as fifty years, and even when such new music became established, it often became so only as a result of a delayed programmatic revolution imposed upon audiences by the desire of conductors, impresarios, and musical pressure groups to become up to date, or "in." Ultimately, much new music grown old has become familiar, often in time to celebrate the death of its composer. At the same time, new music makes itself familiar as incidental music in films, and the ballet, more than on the concert stage, and when it does make itself familiar in the latter sense, all too often it does so as a cultistic activity of self-conscious musical intellectuals, who achieve prestige by the exoticism of their taste. At no time since the eighteenth century has music been so far removed from its audience. But if this is true, it is true because musical self-consciousness, paradigmatic criticism (style analysis), and self-criticism have been major results of the technical revolutions of our time.

NOTES

1.   Eduard Hanslick, *The Beautiful in Music*, translated by Gustav Cohen (New York, Liberal Arts Press, 1957) (originally published 1854), pp. 86 ff.

2.   See Leonard B. Meyer, *Emotion and Meaning in Music* (Chicago, University of Chicago Press, 1956), pp. 258–260. See also Susanne K. Langer, *Philosophy in a New Key: A Study in the Symbolism of Reason, Rite, and Art* (New York, Mentor Books, 1951), pp. 181 ff.: "The results of such experiments add very little to the well-known fact that most people connect feeling with music, and . . . believe they *have* the feelings while they are under the influence of the music."

3.   Hugo Riemann, *Catechism of Musical Aesthetics*, translated by the Rev. H. Bewerunge (London, Augener & Co., no date), pp. 66 ff., on music as an expressive and pictorial art.

4.   See Chapter 5 for a more detailed treatment of these themes.

5.   Max Weber, *The Rational and Social Foundations of Music*, translated by Don Martindale, Johannes Riedel, and Gertrude Neuwirth (Carbondale, Southern Illinois University Press, 1958), especially Chap. 4, "Scale Rationalization in Terms of Fifths and Fourths: Foundations of Modern Tonality." See also Warren Dwight Allen, *Philosophies of Music History: A Study of General Histories of Music 1600—1960* (New York, Dover, 1962), pp. 190 ff.

6.   It is important to distinguish the various kinds of musical creativity. A "traditionalist" may accept established forms and rules as the basis of his art but perfect his music within the framework of those rules and forms, so that the perfection achieved is a creative act. Others like Haydn or Beethoven may change rules or forms so much that much of their work represents original and genuine creativity. Such creative work need not represent the highest quality in a field. Figures like Stamitz and Clementi were composers of great value in altering and defining the art of composition in their field though their work has been superseded by composers who were less "creative" in these terms.

7.   On this point, compare the scheme suggested by Thomas S. Kuhn in *The Structure of Scientific Revolutions*, 2nd ed. (Chicago, University of Chicago Press, 1970). The musical framework (the "rules" of style generated within a particular temporal and social locale) can be conceived in Kuhn's terms as a paradigm, when it is a result of self-conscious theorizing, rules, limits, and conventions, and when the framework is conceived of as delimiting the future development of specific musical works. In the sense that these frameworks are explicit, self-conscious, and the result of theorizing before even more than after the fact, the process of construction and alteration of these frameworks can be called the rationalization of music.

8.   Roger Sessions, *The Musical Experience of Composer, Performer, Listener* (New York, Atheneum, 1966), pp. 43–44: "What, then, is a musical idea? The term has acquired a somewhat stereotyped meaning, and curiously enough not because of our precise usage but because of an unduly vague and loose one. . . . I would say that a musical idea is simply that fragment of music which forms the composer's point of departure, either for a whole composition or for an episode or even a single aspect of

a composition . . . a 'musical idea' . . . can be virtually anything which strikes a composer's imagination. It may, certainly, be a motif . . . on the other hand, I could cite many examples where the most essential musical ideas consist not in motifs at all, but in chords, sonorities, in rhythmic figures, or even in single notes of a particularly striking context."

9.   Leonard B. Meyer, *Music, the Arts, and Ideas: Patterns and Predictions in Twentieth-Century Culture* (Chicago, University of Chicago Press, 1967); see the essay, "History, Stasis, and Change," especially pp. 98 ff.: "In what ways may we expect the arts to change in the coming years? I should like to suggest . . . that the coming epoch . . . will be a period of stylistic stasis, a period characterized not by the linear, cumulative development of a single fundamental style, but by the coexistence of a multiplicity of quite different styles in a fluctuating and dynamic steadystate." Change, then, will be not the rule but the exception. See also pp. 100–102: "in the arts, mutational change takes place when some aspect of the material, formal, syntactic, or other preconditions of a style were altered. . . . It should be emphasized that a series of developmental or of trended changes, no matter how extensive and prolonged, will not in themselves produce a mutational change . . . change and variety are not incompatible with stasis. For stasis . . . is not an absence of novelty and change . . . but rather the absence of ordered sequential change." See also Chap. 7, "Varieties of Style Change."

10.   Manfred Bukofzer, *Music in the Baroque Era* (New York, Norton, 1947), p. 1: "When Monteverdi in his fifth book of madrigals (1605) asserted that he did not follow the precepts of the old school, but was guided by what he called the *seconda prattica,* he spoke with the self-assertion of an artist fully conscious of a fundamental change in the conception of music. Monteverdi was retorting in his statement to an abusive attack by Artusi, in which this conservative critic and theorist found fault with Monteverdi's treatment of dissonance. By opposing the second practice to the first, and by implying that the standards of the old school could not be applied to the new, Monteverdi challenged the whole basis of the argument. Thus the eternal controversy between artist and critic about the standards of art criticism flamed up in the violent manner that is indicative of all periods of transition."

11.   See Otto von Simson, *The Gothic Cathedral,* 2nd ed. (New York, Harper Torchbooks, 1962).

12.   Robert Lilienfeld, *An Introduction to Music* (New York, Macmillan, 1962), p. 74: "His [the composer's] role, then, as an isolated literary figure, is somewhat unfortunate. Music seems to have been greatly influenced by the example of Beethoven, who was forced by his deafness to give up musical performing and to try to live by his composing. It seems best for the composer to remain as close as possible to practical music making. All the masters of the past have been at least competent performers."

13.   See, for example, *Contemporary Music Newsletter,* published jointly by the Group for Contemporary Music at Columbia University, The Departments of Music at the University of Maryland, New York University, and Princeton University. The *Newsletter* ceased publication in the early 1980s.

14.   Henry Pleasants, *The Agony of Modern Music* (New York, Simon & Schuster, 1955), p. 26: "It rarely occurs to the contemporary composer that the blame for his estrangement from the serious music audience might lie with himself." Mr. Pleasants' writings document the changing relations between composers and audiences.

15.   See also Theodor Adorno, *Einleitung in die Musiksoziologie—Zwölf theoretische Vorlesungen* (Frankfurt am Main, Suhrkamp, 1962), the eleventh essay, "Moderne," especially p. 198.

Chapter 3

The Attitude of the Performing Artist

Basing our work on phenomenological theory and method, we have, in the previous chapters, attempted to review and develop new approaches to phenomenological attitudes. These phenomenological attitudes are related to the process of articulating new images of the world and of acting within the framework of existing images of the world. Thus we reviewed Alfred Schutz's distinction between the scientific attitude and the attitude of everyday life, and, based upon Schutz's work, the planning attitude, the ritual or ceremonial attitude, the artistic, critical and academic attitudes, and the attitudes of consumer and producer.

Major attention was given to the artistic and scientific attitudes as primary means by which world images were constructed, and to the critical attitude, by which these constructions were dissected. The artistic attitude is one of creating a totally complete and self-enclosed portrait of a world, a province of meaning, which, while being the product of conscious methodological technical disciplines, presents itself so directly to the art consumer that it induces the consumer to suspend his awareness of all other worlds. He is, for the moment, contained in the symbolic world of art.

We have used the "attitude of the composer" to demonstrate the emergence of artistic autonomy and creativity within a field of the arts. But we have also attempted to show how the emergence of autonomy is related to and constrained by the "external" developments in the field in question.

In this analysis, the successful work of art directly and immediately creates its own world, which links the technical skill of the creator with the nontechnical experience of the spectator. Viewing a painting or sculpture or reading a novel is a direct experience in which, apart from the technical problem of getting the work into the hands of the audience, no intervening parties are involved.

The performing arts, sometimes called the "re-creative" arts, are different. Their apprehension and understanding by the art consumer involves the intervention of third parties. The composer, the dramatist, and the dance choreographer (unless also occupying performers' roles) are all separated from their audiences not only by the art work itself but also by technically trained artistic professionals who present the work in the form that allows the audience to suspend its awareness of the ordinary world while focusing on the world presented in the work of art. A dance, a play, or a musical composition is not immediately in the presence of the audience in the way that a painting or sculpture is; it must be performed in order to be made present. Thus, the act of creation for the performing arts involves a separation of the technical skill implied in the word *art* from the nontechnical realization of the work as involved in the act of artistic apprehension. Thus, in a performing art, the script, the score, or the choreographic notation may be totally unintelligible to all but a trained performer, and it is the latter who translates the technically unintelligible score into accessible arrangements of sounds, symbols, words, and actions. This of course is more true for music and the dance and less so for poetry or the drama, which can be experienced both as written literature and as performed art. At the same time, a fully trained and experienced musician can read a score, and in his imagination, "hear" the music without the presence of the performer, though the adequacy of this as a substitute for a real performance, especially with complex scores, is open to some question [1].

These partial exceptions aside, both the creative artist and his audience are dependent upon performers for the realization of the work of art. The performer thus serves the role of mediator and communicator. At the same time, the interpreter, if he is a professional, is likely to be highly skilled in his own right in aspects of performance, which may exceed the performing skills of the creator. He has his own vested interest in the act of performance, which, depending on personality and the state of aesthetic theory at a given time, may cause him wittingly or unwittingly to add elements to the performance which are beyond the "score" itself [2]. This constitutes a major problem in aesthetic theory which will be treated in detail later on.

The fact that the work of art comes to life only in the performance introduces other new dimensions into the essential quality of these arts.

PERFORMANCE AS AN ART FORM

In the creative arts, the painting or sculpture is presented to the audience as a finished, final product in one moment of time, in which all of the time spent in the creation of the work of art is encapsuled and assumed by the work itself. The artist can edit, revise, rework, and redo the work of art any number of times before the final work is presented. In certain types of painting, however, such as watercolors and egg tempera, the quality of the medium limits reworking, and therefore requires the painter to complete a finished product on the first try. The performing arts, which are to be enjoyed in their performance or execution, have this specific quality of finality at the moment of performance. The artist in performance cannot rework, rewrite, or re-edit, for, in doing so, he would destroy the elements of directness, spontaneity, and rhythmic completeness of the work as a whole.

As a result, he must give a totally finished performance in the act of performing. This applies both to judging the work of art as such, and to judging the performer as performer. At the point of performance, there is little or no room for mistakes, or for the kinds of mistakes that would mar the performance. The creative artist, as opposed to the performing artist, can make as many mistakes as he wants, as long as those mistakes do not enter into the final version, and this quality of the finality in performance is the distinctive element of the performing arts.

The element of finality, both in completeness of execution and in the induction of the audience into the reality of the world created by the work of art, causes the performing artist to prepare both his performance and his life as a performer, so that his total being is involved in the finality of the performance. This means that since he cannot permit himself the mistakes permissible to the creative artist, or the luxury of reworking during the performance, he must concentrate on preparing for the performance in a way that far exceeds that of the creative artist. Practice, rehearsal, discipline, anticipation of the performance all govern the total structure of his way of life. He must totally subordinate his physical and psychological being to the absolute finalities of the performance. This may require rehearsal, at least until he is in absolute control of all of the physical skills required, of from four to five, or even twelve to fourteen hours per day.

The requirements of performance tend to demand control of the total physical resources of the performer; the dancer will work years to master mental control over almost every muscle in the body, so that the body responds instantaneously to the requirements of the performance at the moment the control is needed. Similarly, the musician—pianist, violinist, etc.—will have rehearsed for years many hours per day to have absolute control over each muscle, over his sense of touch and of coordination, over the type of tone production, etc. The actor will perform the same kinds of exercises for control over vocal chords, chest, facial muscles, and body, as does the singer. The actor, in addition, who in the ancient theater and in popular entertainment often had to be skilled in acrobatics, song, and dance, must also be in physical condition to perform strenuous or heroic roles. Some of these, involving the simulation of dueling or other forms of combat, require purely physical skills approaching those of the dancer [3].

All of these forms of discipline are developed not merely in preparation for a specific performance, but even more with a view to developing the total physical resources of the performer, so that he may respond with full control to the requirements of the performance, as embodied in the score.

But in addition to the emphasis on the purely physical strengths and skills necessary, the pedagogical and professional traditions of the performing arts emphasize the mental elements necessary for the control of performance. The mental labors involved in mastering a composition, a role, or a dance are considered as significant as the physical drills. One does not repeat a movement in order to get it right; rather, repetition serves to make unconscious what at first had to be done consciously. "Everyone fixes his attention on cultivating the physical factor above all . . . but exercise is only a part of the physical training. It serves to *automize precise movements previously acquired*" [4]. The purpose of repetition and rehearsal is the relinquishment of conscious control. "That which in the beginning gives rise to reflection, is later on executed unconsciously or instinctively; then, to the extent to which technique becomes ever more automatic, the work of consciousness is always more diminished" [5].

This does not mean that the performance must be over-rehearsed, overly mechanical, unspontaneous, and dead. For the requirement that the performing artist create a world that evokes immediate response requires that, while the performer must have absolute control over both himself and the score at the moment of performance, his reading must be alive, fresh, spontaneous, and must contain elements of a self that has these qualities. Beyond this, the techniques of notation of a script, score, or choreography are such that it is impossible for any creative artist to specify with absolute exactitude the interpretation or reading to the point where the performer can exclude himself from the performance [6].

The element of rehearsal and preparation, or repetition until movements acquired at first with conscious effort become unconscious, has more than one purpose. First, it serves to give the performer as total a control over his resources as possible, and to eliminate the problem of technique from the requirements of the performance. Second, it serves as a bulwark against stage fright, a phenomenon from which the most experienced and accomplished professionals are known to suffer.

> . . . at the basis of nervous sensitivity in performance lies a general nervous irritability. It is not a sure mark of artistic temperament, but is nevertheless found among all real artists, as each artistic personality reveals itself by hypersensitivity. To put this sensitivity to good use by sure knowledge, instead of letting it degenerate into an impediment to play, is the fundamental idea. [7]

Third, the ability to relinquish conscious control over movements that have been acquired by rehearsal and repetition serves to free the performer to make those minute adjustments that add the qualities of spontaneity and freshness to the performance, and to orient himself more immediately and responsively to other performers in an ensemble. The dancer, in performing, must condition his response to the choreographic plan, the tempo of the music, the space across the stage to be covered, the probable appearance in the immediate future of a partner at a given place on the stage at a given time, doing all of this with movements that are fluid, lyrical, and in harmony with the overall mood of the music and of the dance itself; but at each moment the movements must be spontaneous, unforced, and must appear to be unplanned. The appearance of deliberation, of mechanical thought, of lack of spontaneity, of counting, or of metronomic precision all destroy the effect to be achieved when all of these complex elements are reduced to the level of spontaneous execution.

In the same way, in the performance of music, the exact execution of the notes can be, at one level, mechanical, unspontaneous, dead, forced, and "academic" in effect. The same score, played as accurately by an inspired artist, may have a quality of poetic or lyric immediacy that transcends the mere reproduction of the notes. It is this quality of immediacy and spontaneity within the framework of the score which is recognized as the greatness of performing art.

THE PERFORMER AND THE CREATOR

In the sense that a great performance always goes beyond what can be specified in the score, performance is a form of creativity. But another possibility also arises, that of great technical performance which involves little creativity, as, for example, in the salon pieces of nineteenth-century music, the concert etudes of Liszt, etc. Thus, there are works, the virtuoso pieces, which are difficult and make a point of advertising their difficulties in contrast to works which may be difficult but do not appear so, as their principal focus is upon their content. Thus, the sheer accumulation of technical virtuosity may at times appear to be an end in itself, in which the performer selects works to be performed primarily as vehicles of his virtuosity. Thus the showpieces of nineteenth-century music. Similarly, in the last quarter of the nineteenth century, up to the time of Diaghilev, virtuosity became the prime feature of the dance, and "ideas," poetry, imagery, and all other aspects suffered. One can almost declare an inverse relationship between virtuosity in performing and the presence of true art, when creative artists adopt or are forced to adopt the criteria of the virtuoso in the process of creating works rather than simply creating as their fantasy and skills direct. Similar preferences can be noted in the theater of the nineteenth century and the early twentieth, in which star performers often preferred melodramas serving for vehicles for their personalities to plays of better artistic caliber, though less spectacular.

When such tendencies develop, the technique of performance becomes the performance itself. This phenomenon is most likely to occur at precisely those periods when the institutional developments have arisen in which the machinery for instilling performance skills is perfected to the point where concern for performance skills transcends the concerns for the work being performed.

Thus, in all eras where the performing arts are stressed, the special technical qualities of the performance are emphasized at the expense of the score, the script, or the choreography. There are three types of performance-centered art. One emphasizes the quality of the technical skills of the performance itself, with the score devalued or reduced to an opportunity for the performer to show his wares, as described above.

A second type, which reflects the development of the critical rather than the artistic spirit, occurs when a *Kapellmeister*-turned-musicologist uses the score as a device for writing critical exegeses on the score itself. As a result, the performance is used as a device for presenting a lecture about a critical theory concerning the score or script. Aspects of the artist's intentions are outlined, underlined, heightened, or made clear. The music in itself has apparently not made this clear. The performance will thus have the quality of a lecture, a dissertation, or an exercise.

The performance thus achieves a quality of self-consciousness, of methodological and critical clarity, which destroys the spontaneous and naive encompassing of the spectator by the work of art. As a result, the audience never loses its consciousness that the performance is a performance, and that the work of art is a work of art. The ability of the work of art under such conditions to cause the audience to suspend its awareness of all other worlds, and to enter into the work or world presented, is nullified. If the audience consists of other performers, such devices are legitimate for methodological instruction, but the performance is not "artistic" in the generic sense of the term.

The third type occurs at times when the methodology of a work of art is complicated and difficult, and when half-educated audiences tend to appreciate the overcoming of difficult technical problems as a feat in and of itself. Then, the audience is not prepared to listen to the work but rather to watch the performance. In this sense, the aesthetic of performing transcends the aesthetic of the art work. Virtuosity becomes a form of athleticism.

The artist, who is more conscious of audience reaction to the score, the choreography, or the art form itself, will cater to the attraction of the audience for virtuosity as an autonomous trait.

To be sure, a composer, choreographer, or creative artist may be aware of the audience's respect for virtuosity per se, and may create works whose meaning consists only in the opportunity they provide for the virtuoso performer. This is especially true if the creator has totally mastered all of the methodologies included in his art as a craft, and few of those involved in the art as a means of constructing autonomous worlds of meanings. In such cases, virtuosity per se becomes the only meaningful image of the world.

A final nexus between performance and the work of art can be seen in the performer's sharing with the creator of the methodology of creation. To be a performer requires, at least to a minimal degree, a knowledge of the problems involved in artistic creativity. And the performer all too often thinks of himself as a second-class citizen because he is merely the performer. In resenting his second-class citizenship, he often will attempt to engage, in his performance, in the act of self-conscious creativity. In the drama, this takes the form of the attempt by the actor to rewrite his lines, to make them more "natural," "expressive," or meaningful. In music, the performer will alter tempos, introduce excessive *rubato* effects, produce innovations in dynamics and sonority, and will even at times rewrite the actual score. In some eras, and in some types of performing arts, the artistic conventions allowed performers these latitudes, as for example in the Baroque era of Western music, where the figured bass (the continuo) allowed the keyboard player some latitude for his performance. In such periods, it was assumed that the conventions of performance were sufficiently standardized, and that exact specifications were not only unnecessary, but that the element of improvisation introduced by ornaments, cadenzas, and by a figured bass actually enhanced the performance. At other times, it was assumed that the composer or playwright or dancing-master himself would direct or rehearse the performance, so that the quality of the performance would be subject to unwritten controls. But within the development of Western music, changes in styles of composing and performing occurred so rapidly, and the time elapsed has been so great, that by the nineteenth century the attempt was made to limit the freedom of the performer, and all parts were written out as explicitly as possible.

In some genres, however, the element of improvisation was considered desirable and welcome, within limits. Thus, for centuries, the popular musical theater assumed that the performing comedians would twist or improvise around the lines of the script, and introduce an element of topical (often ephemeral) satire on local personalities, or on the political events of the day.

According to the artistic era and the particular genre of the performing art, the element of improvisation may be welcomed, or it may be limited as much as possible.

By the middle of the nineteenth century, the great musical virtuoso performers began to feel imprisoned by the restrictions developed by the creators; in the assertion of autonomy by the performer, virtuosos began to alter aspects of a work, even to rewrite the work itself. In the field of conducting, Wagner and his disciples began to assert the importance of the conductor's personality over that of the score. In doing so, Wagner, basing himself on Liszt as performer and theoretician, began a tradition which has continued well into the twentieth century. Recently, under the influence primarily of the emergence of musicological research and such conductors as Toscanini and others, the opposite tendency, that of the reassertion of the rights of the composer and of the integrity of the score, was made, which tended (with numerous exceptions) to deemphasize romantic virtuosity. But this emphasis on the score went hand in hand with the development of a critical and academic spirit, in which research on the original qualities of performance often gave it the character of archeological, museum reconstructions.

Recent developments in the performing arts have suggested increasing control over the actions of the performer. New forms of dance notation have been developed, which make more and more of the actions hitherto left to the dancer subject to external control. Similarly, actors are more and more controlled by stage directors. The use of the Moog synthesizer and music programmed for computers, tend to eliminate the performing element completely. But contemporary with these developments have been the rise of aleatory music, in which performers are given extremely wide latitude, and the development of improvisatory or "free" theater, in which actors improvise within very broad limits. These latter developments appear to be attempts to reintroduce spontaneity and the performer as a concrete individual into the arts. The two are now divorced: the premeditated work of art, and the immediacy and spontaneity of performance. The permanency of this separation is uncertain.

When the musical values of the score are deemphasized in favor of the academic values of musicological or historical research, the spontaneity, the freshness, the liveliness, the immediacy of the performance as a means of suspending all other realities but the music itself is lost in the academic intellectualism of fidelity to the score as a methodological or intellectual exercise, rather than as a work of art waiting to be realized by its performance.

The dilemmas presented here are those to be faced by every performer and conductor. His specialization and professionalization as a performer, as an interpreter, and often as a quasi-historical scholar, all pose divergent and, all too frequently, conflicting role demands upon him, including those demands which cause him to dramatize himself as a unique individual apart from the character or work he is playing.

The performer, in the course of his career, will respond at different levels to each of the various demands. In the early part of his career, when the problems of acquiring technical mastery are central for him, he is likely to emphasize the mechanical aspects of his craft, and will (if given the choice) perform works that permit him to demonstrate the acquisition and perfection of technique. If his artistic growth becomes arrested at this point, he may go on to be a virtuoso in his field, but he may never become an artist. If the influence of the academy is too great, either because of idiosyncrasies in his training or if in the process of his career he becomes primarily a teacher or theoretician of performance, he is likely to emphasize the intellectual aspects of the work, and regard the performance of the work as the realization not of the composition but of the *theory* of composition or of performance. If this occurs he is likely to become a "performer's performer," having considerable esteem among other performers, while remaining little known by the general public.

If the performer is able to retain and then to transcend theory and technique, he reaches the point of becoming an artist. But this requires continuous growth and continuous preoccupation with performance as a means to the realization of the work of art. The audience carries a double awareness of the performer in that the members of the audience know that the performer is a living contemporary, while at the same time he is serving in an assigned role for the realization of a character or a work of art. The artist, by submerging his own personality into that of the part played, allows the audience to suspend its awareness of the performer in his actual identity, and to experience him as the person whose part he is playing, and thereby to enter the world of the work of art. The virtuoso, the star conductor, the "prima donna," and the "ham" actor, on the other hand, reinforce the audience's awareness of the performer, and obscure or obliterate the presence of the world which the work of art was intended to evoke.

The emphasis on virtuosity and on the technical perfection of performance has led to such recent practices as taping and splicing together portions of different performances. Such practices may simulate qualities of perfection which were not present in the actual performance, and which may transcend the limits of the human body. Thus, the development of techniques of reproduction has altered the medium of performance, but the limits of the human body constitute the norm, and the standard of intelligibility. With the development of recording tape it is possible to make performances (or rather records of performances) more perfect technically by substituting corrections for misplayed passages, wrong notes, etc. This has the effect of maximizing the technical perfection of the performance, but it devalues precisely that element of spontaneity and freedom in performance which bring the work to life. Thus, if one artificially perfects a series of imperfections which are caused by the limitations of the human body, by increasing the speed or means or volume of performance, one violates the sense of what is humanly possible, and as a consequence, even the appreciation of the virtuosity in a complete live performance becomes devoid of meaning.

But the performing artist who succeeds in submerging his personality in his quest for a spontaneous and living realization of the work of art is likely to create, in his performance, on the basis of both technical mastery and his understanding of the score, a world of art which realizes that world as projected by the creator. He is likely to actualize it not only for himself, but also for the audience. If he does, he achieves a unity between the composer as represented by the score, himself as represented by the performance, and the audience as participator in the work of art [8].

NOTES

1.   See Donald Francis Tovey's useful discussion in his essay, "Training the Musical Imagination," in *The Main Stream of Music and Other Essays* (New York, Meridian Books, 1959), pp. 375 ff.

2.   The term "score" will be used in this essay as a shorthand device, meaning either a dramatic script, a musical score, or a choreographic plan. Viewed phenomenologically, a score is the overall plan for a complex series of actions which are to be realized, usually by actors other than those who write or compose the plan. Such plans are usually so complete that the course of action specified by the plan and the outcome therefrom are included in detail in the plan. Some scores, as we indicate, allow intentionally and systematically for improvisation within an overall detailed plan, while all scores, except those written for computers and electronic synthesizers, must allow for and require some "interpretation" by the performer.

3.   "Actor, Actress, Acting," in Phyllis Hartnoll, (Ed.), *Oxford Companion to the Theatre*, 2nd ed. (Oxford, Oxford University Press, 1962), p. 10. In Greece, the tragic actor was static—a voice and a presence; in Rome he was lively, and, in the last resort, an acrobat. The *commedia dell'arte* demanded above all a quick wit and a nimble body; French tragedy . . . a fine presence and a sonorous voice; Restoration comedy . . . a polished brilliance and a gentlemanly insolence . . . the true actor still needs to be a little of everything—singer, dancer, mimic, acrobat, tragedian, comedian—and to have at his command a good physique, a retentive memory, an alert brain, a clear, resonant voice with good articulation and controlled breathing."

4.   Willy Bardas, *On the Psychology of Piano Technique* (Paris, Greenberg, 1931), pp. iii–iv.

5.   *Ibid.*, pp. 18–19. See also C. Whitaker Wilson, "Concentration and Pianoforte Technique," *Music and Letters*, Vol. 9, No. 2 (1928), pp. 145–51: "If, instead of 'technique,' Von Bülow had called the first essential in pianoforte playing concentration, the second concentration, and the third concentration . . . he might indeed have defined perfection in pianism." It should be noted that although the performing arts are the principal locus of the need for absolute finality of performance, this need is also found in other spheres, including surgery, sports, courtroom behavior, diplomacy, and acrobatics. The same qualities of rehearsal, muscular control, and controlled total spontaneity are required, because of the serious consequences of mistakes.

6.   The history of notation could at least in part be read as an attempt to make notation ever more explicit, and to narrow as much as possible the area of discretion, ornamentation, and improvisation left to the performer.

7. Bardas, *op. cit.*, pp. 6–7.

8. Julius Bab, "Theatre," *Encyclopedia of the Social Sciences* (New York, Macmillan, 1934), Vol. 14, p. 598: "Actor, dramatist, and public—they and they alone have remained the crucial elements in the theatrical process. Furthermore, a genuine theater comes into existence only when these elements are closely integrated; when actor and dramatist serve merely to articulate the sympathies and aspirations of the people as they undergo the hypnotic experience of identification across the footlights. Every theater, in the true sense of the word, is a unity, at the core of which is the living community finding some vital part of itself reflected in the creations of dramatist and actor."

Chapter 4

Games and Sports

In previous chapters, we have attempted to describe some aspects of: the performing arts as related to the creative arts. A central characteristic of the performing arts was indicated in the finality of performance.

In a live performance, the performing artist, in giving life or realization to a score, script, or choreographic plan, must produce a final, instantaneous, and temporal image of the world as embodied in the score without error, with full mastery of highly developed technical means of performance, and with sufficient warmth, spontaneity, and freshness to induce an audience to suspend its awareness of all other worlds but the world framed by the score and re-created by the performance.

A performance is not fully realized unless it achieves a quality of technical impeccability, together with spontaneity. Finality means that nothing interferes with the full realization of the values implicit in the score [1]. Reworking, revising, going back, hesitancy, "practicing," errors, and a lack of full performing proficiency all interfere with the realization of the score in performance.

To achieve this quality of finality, the performing artist must do his editing, reworking, thought, planning, and skill development in advance of the performance, by unrelenting and continuing practice and rehearsal. But having done so, if the performance is only evidence of continuous practice and rehearsal, he has not realized the goal of the performance. In addition to mastery, there is the element of freshness, spontaneity, and the subjective qualities of interpretation, spirit, mood, vitality, which go beyond mere technical mastery. The ultimate objective of rehearsal, practice, and technical mastery is to reduce the interval between thought and execution to zero. This allows for the development of spontaneity, precisely because the technical difficulties in the work have been overcome. Alternatively, the reduction of the gap between thought and action to zero means that the process of thought has been reduced to muscular activity. After complete mastery of the material through practice, rehearsal, and conquest of difficult actions, the individual thinks with his fingers, muscles, throat, arms and legs, depending upon the performing art. This does not mean that he is an automaton, but that he expresses his spontaneous evocation of the score by his physical being.

SPORTS AS A PERFORMING ART

It is in exactly this sense that sports and athletics are similar to the performing arts. In almost all sports, the level of technique required is high. And at the moment of "play," the individual commits himself, for that moment, to final and irreversible activity. It is final in the sense that once started, the activity is irreversible. To achieve this instantaneous quality of thought, decision-making, and action, the individual must rehearse and practice for years and years. He must, in the sessions before the actual play, break down the elements of the game into all the movements required of him at the moment of play, and for each element he must rehearse and practice so that at the proper moment his decision is automatic, instantaneous, and final.

But having done so, he must, in his practice, take larger and larger units of the game into account, so that he can move from one elemental situation to another automatically, instantaneously, and finally. This is precisely the same thing that a ballerina must do in the course of her training. She must master a plethora of extremely difficult physical movements to the point where each one appears to be easy, instantaneous, and spontaneous. Having done so, she must learn how to link them together in a series of smooth, lyrical, flowing *enchaînements*. In the same way, the instrumentalist will spend vast amounts of time mastering individual phrases, bars, lines, movements, only as a prelude to mastering the score as a unity or as a living whole.

As in the performing arts, the player rehearses, practices, and perfects his skill in each of the individual movements and aspects of the sport relevant to his position in the game. He strives to achieve full mastery over his body and to have instantaneous control of his action, so that the time between thought and execution is reduced to zero. Moreover, with respect to series of movements, he reduces the thought required between individual movements to habits, that is, to nonreflective actions. In team sports, the basic patterns of action between players are rehearsed over and over again, so that execution is virtually automatic, or, if thought is required, so that the mechanics of execution do not interfere with the thought. But unlike the performing arts, there is no "score"; that is, the flow and sequence of events is a function of the game situation in which the competitive players continuously attempt to disrupt the predetermined game plans of their opponents. Thus improvisation, revision of game plans, some calculated forms of spontaneity, are always a factor in the game. Related to this is the notion of poise or presence of mind, the consciousness of being "in good form," the basis of which is the confident mastery of individual movements, chains of movements, and cooperative patterns.

SPONTANEITY WITHIN THE "RULES OF THE GAME"

All games and sports involve the overcoming of obstacles. These include overcoming the opposition of a competitor or a team of competitors; overcoming the odds, as in aleatoric games of chance; overcoming nature, as in mountain climbing, hunting, and fishing; overcoming the limits of the self; in terms of endurance, speed, difficulty. Even mimesis (the imitation of persons and mythical beings by costumes, masks, pantomime), and ritualistic games, involve transcending the self by submission to an external style, persona, or rhythm. In all cases, the individual transcends and transports the self according to agreed-upon styles, rules, and conventions. In these respects also, games and sports are similar to the arts, whose styles, rules, and conventions constitute obstacles which must be overcome in performance.

One purpose of the rules, like the purpose of the obstacles, is that of creating genuine doubt about the outcome of the event. Obstacles that are too easy trivialize the event, while obstacles that are hopelessly difficult make the event meaningless. Hence the purpose of handicaps, such as extra weights carried by horses with consistent winning records, or the odds of pawn, rook, or knight that a champion chess player will give to a lesser rival. Although rules have the same function in both the performing arts and in sports and games, that of creating obstacles to overcome, there is a sense in which sports are more difficult than the performing arts. The performing arts operate within the framework of a score, a predetermined plan of action whose outcome is prescribed. The plan is thus a structure of actions expected of the performer, and known in advance by him. The score is provided by the composer, dramatist, or choreographer to outline a particular artistic image of the world within the framework of a set of stylistic rules and conventions which constitute the medium of the art form.

In sports, with the possible exceptions of wrestling, some boxing matches, and those competitive events in which a combatant or team is hopelessly overmatched, there is no "score" that determines in advance the drama and flow of events in the game. Of course, there is often a "game plan" or overall strategy that is designed to capitalize on the strength of one's team or self, to minimize one's weaknesses and limit the strengths of the opposition or capitalize on its weaknesses. But such "plans" cannot prescribe the detailed course of action of the game, nor is the hoped-for outcome of the game ever prescribed in detail by the plan. In the game, the actions are necessarily open, whereas in the arts—except for those situations which allow for improvisation—options are closed by the very existence of the score. Instead of a predetermined score as in the performing arts, the framework of the drama that ensues is contained only in the rules of the game and in the unit actions which combine to constitute skill in performance.

Unlike the performing arts, the "score" evolves spontaneously in the process of playing the game. In this sense, sports are analogous to the free improvisation which was frequently characteristic of instrumental performance at the turn of the nineteenth century and earlier [2].

Because there is no score, the structure of the game is determined almost exclusively by the nature of the rules themselves, which become the basis for athletic and competitive improvisation within the framework of the rules. Piaget has attempted to find an analogy between the "rules of the game" and a naturalistically based social contract which rests upon the fact that over the life cycle of the youth, the youth begins to learn that if there is going to be a game, the individual must discipline himself toward accepting the rules, so that he cannot enjoy the fruits or benefits of the game without the rules. If one is to spend one's time fighting about the rules, there cannot be a game [3]. According to Piaget, the major process of socialization consists in the internalization of the rules of the game, and the moral judgment of the child develops by stages when the child begins to realize that there cannot be a game if the players are unwilling to accept the rules. For Piaget, the acceptance of the rules of the game implies that the rules already exist, and that the child's major function is to adjust to the game by internalizing its rules. He does not have to evolve them. We argue that the analogy between the game and society is doubtful, simply because Piaget's game takes place within the framework of an established order of society which is always maintained in part by force. In games, if the individual does not like the rules, he can withdraw, play some other game, or play no game at all. It is precisely because the game does not constitute the whole of life that the individual has the options of accepting or rejecting the rules. When society is the game itself, then debate about the rules may constitute attacks and defense of the whole structure of society, a society which is ultimately dependent on force and which frequently makes actual use of force. The "game" of society is based historically upon accepting or rejecting the rules, but when rules are rejected the structure of society is threatened, a price that individuals and groups appear willing to accept when the rules are intolerable. Society is not just a game in Piaget's sense. The problem for the study of society is not just one of determining how individuals internalize the rules, but of discovering the conditions under which individuals and groups accept, reject, and change the fundamental rules. Thus, while Piaget may have produced an analogy between games and society which is not too enlightening, he has produced an excellent description of the phenomenology of games and sports.

SOCIETY SEEN AS A GAME

Jan Huizinga, in both *The Waning of the Middle Ages* and in *Homo Ludens*, uses the analogy of the game as a means of interpreting society [4]. He sees in the rich, complex, ceremonial life of the late Middle Ages an attempt of the aristocracy to provide a pageant of life in which the pageantry is both a mock performance of a game and a device by which individuals dramatize themselves in adjusting to rules that are external to themselves, even though they are aware of themselves as players in a game. One plays the game of courtly love according to highly stylized rules, or the game of chivalric knighthood in which the rules of chivalry are viewed as artificial conventions, sufficiently artificial in their nature such that the game is played with tongue in cheek.

In the same sense, the religious penitent may look over his shoulder to see if anyone is watching. In this sense, regarding life as a game can be understood as the achievement of a relatively high degree of self-consciousness regarding conventions which in simpler times may have been immediately meaningful in and of themselves. Such conventions, in a period of decline in faith, take the form of mannerisms in which this ceremonial activity becomes self-conscious and achieves the artificiality of a game.

Huizinga demonstrates with extraordinary detail how serious, nonplay activities are converted into play as these activities lose their original meaning, function, or intent. The collapse in meaning results in their quasi-parody, though with the seriousness that intense play may assume. Huizinga makes the point that even in play the player may take a serious and apparently all-encompassing attitude toward his play, and at the same time recognize that the activity is a playful one that is not ordinary. The actor is able thus to move out of the attitude of play into the ordinary activity of nonplay life or action. The shift in attitude and perspective constitutes a recognition that no matter how serious play may be, it is still play.

In *Homo Ludens*, Huizinga takes an entirely different stance. While he emphasizes even more the distinction between play and "ordinary life," he argues that play is intrinsic to all culture, that it precedes culture (in the animal kingdom), and that it pervades every aspect of culture. He also argues that the deemphasis of play in modern society conceals the dominance of play in archaic societies. But in emphasizing the pervasiveness of play in all aspects of society, he ignores nonplay forms. As a result, his distinction of play as being outside the boundaries of the ordinary is not maintained in the application of this concept, because he does not consider nonplay or the ordinary in any case beyond that of making the definition.

Our analysis focuses on society as a game and as a nongame, on the ordinary, and on aspects of society which are not subject to the rules of a game. It enables us to examine the relationship between play and nonplay.

Roger Caillois [5] attempts to generalize beyond Huizinga, to develop a typology of games that includes four types of play: *alea* (games based on chance and luck—dice, cards), *agon* (games of struggle against an opponent—boxing, wrestling, football), *mimesis* (charades, mimes, masquerades), and vertigo (forms of play involving dizziness, fear, and visceral excitation—roller coasters, whirling rides, feats on the trapeze). He also attempts to demonstrate, as did Huizinga, that play is an essential aspect of man's condition. Like Huizinga, he indicates at times that play is a necessary response to the "seriousness" of life and is therefore reactive. At other times he suggests, by reference to the animal kingdom, that play is basic to man's biological nature, and is not reactive. The two positions are not resolved. Both Huizinga and Caillois see the play element in culture as a stylizing and sublimating influence, transforming fights and combats into more sporting forms, and trial by combat into more rational procedures, under the influence of rules. Caillois, like Huizinga, states that societies have game-like values in their nongame institutions (courtrooms, for example), but he does not explicitly suggest the order of causation between game and nongame. He does, however, present as a theory of society the dominance of agon and alea forms of society over forms of vertigo and mimicry. By implication, society is a game.

Harold Finestone uses the Huizinga model to understand the Negro hipster, narcotics addict, and jazz fan, who creates the world of the "cat" or hipster as a game—in many ways a parody of middle-class life—in which manners of dress, speech, the use of "chicks" as hustlers, and styles of boasting constitute an artificial world. This world, in its cultural density, is inaccessible to anybody but the hipster. Its very cultural density creates the clues which provide for mutual recognition and for the exclusion of outsiders. The element of the game is present in the fact that this is removed from the ordinary world of work in which the hipster can "make it" by conventional means. Thus, the game becomes a means by which the hipster avoids the problem of not being able to deal with the dominant society in the dominant society's terms. His game is an ironic substitution of middle-class symbols and methods with a parody of middle-class symbols and methods [6].

The "cat" creates this culture, or game, in self-conscious "play," simply because he cannot take the game of ordinary life seriously. This he cannot do because ordinary life is inaccessible to him, devaluates him, and rules him "out of bounds," making his participation in terms of the normal game all but impossible. Like Huizinga's aristocrats, and to some extent like Frazier's black bourgeois, play is an alternative to accepting ordinary life as serious and as directly meaningful.

In the same way, E. Franklin Frazier describes the world of the black bourgeoisie as a game in which the black bourgeois emulate what they originally perceive to be the special ritual of the plantation-owning slave owners [7]; Horace Cayton and St. Clair Drake conceive of the overinvolvement of the middle-class Negro in social activities as a ritualistic parody [8].

Thorstein Veblen takes a different view [9]. He describes economic life as a game in which the business classes, in their normal business activities, are playing a zero-sum game in which the object of the game is the acquisition of differential advantages rather than the creation of utility. Thus all the *normal* activities of a business civilization represent trophies of victory in the game, in which conspicuous consumption, idleness, waste, and manners are proofs of victory in the game of life. Veblen's theory is based on the notion of a predatory instinct which becomes sublimated by means of conspicuous consumption, idleness, abstention from serious productive work. The predatory instinct, however, enters, interferes with, and controls serious productive work, giving that work much the quality of play, but infecting it with a military exploitative character, in which the rules of the game are imposed upon the players by force and by controls of the system—or the game. Since the guiding spirit is the predatory animus, the rules of the game are continuously being destroyed and re-created by the predators, who are not limited by the rules of the game, though they may be limited by the force that other predators can impose on them, and at times by the constraints imposed by changes in the media on which it acts, technology, peaceful production, and the state of the industrial arts.

Ruth Benedict emphasizes that most of the social ritual in primitive society has the quality of a game, or contest, in which, like Veblen's businessmen, social ritual is either agonistic or a means of expressing deference and dominance to the victors [10]. The patterns of behavior are reflections and embodiments of these struggles. Once institutionalized, the struggles become games in the sense of performances. The individual is required to learn in detail a host of behavioral patterns which express preexisting societal game plans. Not all societies play the same game. Some games are directly competitive, as among the Kwakiutl; others tend to verge in the direction of the performing arts, as among the Zuni, and among the Japanese of classical traditions. Other games exist with relatively few rules, and the struggle is to violate the rules or to determine the rules.

The central game plan for a society, Ruth Benedict finds, is embodied in the central values of a culture. It proliferates throughout its institutions, and emerges in the unique history of the society [11].

In a peculiar, noneconomic sense, Erving Goffman in all of his work treats the process of social interaction as a dramaturgic game in which the actor attempts, by managing the presentation of himself, to devalue and deflate his gaming partners, and to prevent them from devaluing him. In this sense every social transaction is a zero-sum game, in which the actor comes out ahead or behind in terms of these elements of psychological victory, defeat, or exploitation. Thus, all of Goffman's analyses stay within the framework of these types of gamesmanship by presenting oneself for these purposes. Each individual arranges the appearance of his personality in terms of a frontstage and a backstage as devices in the game. He sets up the scenery for the play in terms of scientific terminology and technology, and collaborates with others in presenting a spontaneously arranged scene that will implement these gamesmanship motives of the actors. Thus, in the asylum studied by Goffman, the doctors, nurses, and ward boys are so concerned with their performances with respect to each other and the patients that the health of the patient is one of the lesser considerations.

At the same time, the patient discovers that if he is to defend himself against the onslaught of the others' gamesmanship against him, then he must learn to play the game. Some of his behavior is designed purely to frustrate the gamesmanship of his superiors, and thus to defend himself from their games. Other aspects of his behavior are that of action in terms of the expected roles of the institution, in order to achieve the institution's imposed image of sanity which the patient himself believes to be insane, in order to escape the clutches of the gamesmanship of the others. Thus, sanity consists of obeying insane rules. In this sense, all of life, for Goffman, is a series of performances in which the fundamental processes are learning and mastering the rules in order to carry off successful performances and so to win the game [12].

In emphasizing the theme and motives of the game in providing dramatic self-enhancement and self-defense, Goffman disregards all other motives and aspects of behavior. Thus, the restaurant becomes a device by which self-presentations and defenses are made, but the cooking and serving of food is simply regarded as given, and the fact that one might earn a living from such activities, or that one might enjoy the cooking and eating of food, or that there is a need to do both are for his purposes irrelevant.

The structure of any organization, even of the total institution, has no purpose or function other than that of providing the scene or setting for the game that Goffman describes. Ideas, ideologies, or theories have no other meaning except that of advancing individuals, groups, or professions in the game of society.

Social or role distance, for Goffman consists primarily of the consciousness of the actor of his act. The actor is self-conscious in the moments when he is attempting the skill to act the game, and at the moment he has acquired the skill, so that he is able to demonstrate to others that he has transcended the mastery of the role. The individual then defines himself as a master actor in the dramatic sense of the term, and thus achieves his identity through alienation.

GAMES WITHIN SOCIETY

In contrast to Veblen, Goffman, and even Huizinga, who in various ways take the game as a kind of evidence of alienation, Malinowski (like Caillois), as the exponent of an important anthropological position, emphasizes the element of playfulness and ritual as part of the basic psychology and philosophy of the primitive [13]. For Malinowski, the primitive man is an individualist who makes very complicated dualistic and parallel rules for himself in organizing his society, the rules resembling in many ways the rules of a game. But the primitive man is not an unself-conscious individual unaware of the fact that the rules are conventions. He acts out the elaborate social ritual which constitutes the framework of his society, but in his self-consciousness and individuality he satirizes, bargains, and parodies the rules, and he emphasizes his triumph as an individual against his partner in the exchange, while upholding the rules of the game. Stephen Potter and Eric Berne are simply popularizing these traditions, which are serious attempts to reconstruct those images of society in terms of society as a game or games used as a device by which individuals escape from the overseriousness of society [14].

But all such attempts to reconstruct society as a game or the game as a defense against society, must rest on the knowledge or theory of the game as a social form.

THE IMPORTANCE OF RULES

Sports are a special type of game involving bodily and athletic activity, and in most cases zero-sum outcomes. But at their core is the structure of rules as a matrix within which the game is played; the rules serve to define narrowly the limits of all actions within the game, and are sufficiently interlocking and finite so that the whole of the game can be played within the framework specified by the rules. Within this framework however, there are legally standardized options which allow for choice, and which thus allow the actor to exercise strategy or tactics, acts of judgment and skill, in order to win.

If there are no options, then the game becomes a ritual or a ceremony. If there are few options, the game provides little opportunity for the exercise of skill or imagination. If the game provides a vast number of options beyond the capacity of the players to exercise, then the lack of rigor made possible by the overabundance of options makes the game a series of random choices in which there is no challenge or skill to determine the outcome [15] (a game of chess, for example, between children or unskilled adults). In short, the game through its rules involves the arbitrary restriction on permissible kinds of actions. The restriction constitutes a set of obstacles which take skill and imagination, so that the victory involves not only overcoming the opponent but overcoming him in a series of actions that involve challenge to one's own capacities. If there are too many choices, the player can grow in skill as a result of practice, or the game can shrink in its demands on the player, but the game does not operate at the level of taxing the participant. This is why a game between unevenly matched participants is "no contest." It either overtaxes or undertaxes the player, and may become only an exhibition. The game has this aesthetic quality which makes it different from raw life in that the participants agree, in advance, to discipline themselves to the rules in order to have the game. In short, the limitations implied by the rules are *by explicit definition* inherent in the very nature of the game. But insistence upon the rules consists of a set of self-limitations which contradict the requirement of victory in a zero-sum game. In amateur sports, in the traditional sense of the word, where the sportsman is conceived of as an upper-class gentleman, the act of being the sportsman involves an aesthetic in which compliance to the rule is regarded as being more important than victory. Thus, in those sports—tennis, golf, sailing—which are popular with the upper class, the emphasis on sportsmanship is dominant.

INTERNAL NORMS

In tennis, one is supposed to call one's own fouls before the linesman does, and if the linesman makes a mistake in judgment, the favored player makes a deliberate error. In golf, the conventions require that all golfers report their own scores. It is assumed that all golfers are gentlemen in both the sporting and upper-class definitions of the term. The major form of social control is humor. When golf becomes professionalized, and victory produces material rewards, then the assumption that all sportsmen are gentlemen comes into jeopardy, and external controls become necessary.

In sailing, while in general the same respect for the dominance of the rules is part of the conventions of the sport, the aesthetics of victory permit the leader to maneuver in such a way as to rob the follower of the wind. But this is defined as acceptable within the framework of the rules.

In other, more professionalized sports which tend to involve face-to-face opposition by individuals and teams, and which are defined as "lower class," though this designation should probably be middle class, the balance between respect for rules and desire for victory is different. In these kinds of sports—basketball, football, hockey—with basketball the supreme example, the individual attempts to estimate what the consequences are of violating the rules in terms of the foul that one will assume if one is caught. The probability of the opposition profiting from the foul is estimated; this is compared with the consequences of not fouling the opposition in terms of their scoring opportunities and the consequences of their getting the ball after the foul shot. All of these alternatives are calculated in terms of the game situation (who is ahead), the existing foul situation, and the length of time remaining in the game. Fouling is then undertaken or not undertaken as a result of these calculations, and purely on pragmatic grounds. Thus, breaking the rules occurs within the framework of the rules, similar to the analysis of Malinowski, and the rules are not respected per se. Of course, such violations occur at levels which permit the game to go on. Other violations, like assaulting the opposition, a fan, or a referee, involve stiffer penalties, fines, banishment, and rest on the structure of an external organization with means of sanctions that are outside of the game itself.

EXTERNAL RULES AND AUTHORITY

These kinds of violations cannot be corrected within the rules of the game because, in a sense, playing the game requires a prior agreement to abide by the rules or else there is no game. To save the game, the players need recourse to a higher authority outside the game that provides sanctions.

But even where external authority is used as a means of enforcing the possibilities of the game, in those games which permit institutional deviations from the rules, the special definition of the game involves the use of the rules which limits and defines the structure of activities, so that special difficulties are invented for the participants in order that they may exercise their skills in restricted fields. It is in this sense that the game is different from nongame situations, in which the rules are conceived of as external constraints which one must accept because of their compulsion rather than as a convention which permits the game. Or, the rules may be so internalized that the norms or rules are not perceived as conventions.

In crisis situations, during which the violation of the internal rules results in the possibility of the disruption of the game, recourse is almost always made to external authority. Thus, in boxing, state boxing commissions are set up to control the fraud and corruption in the sport; in baseball, magnates appoint and create "czars" and commissioners who rule over the game and at times have the authority to punish or suspend and force out of the game not only the players but the magnates themselves; racing commissions have the power to ban jockeys, trainers, and owners. In some instances, a commissioner or czar can become a despot in Hobbes' sense, in others he may be overthrown or severely limited by the most powerful barons of the game. But ultimately conflicts or extreme conflicts are resolved by the intervention of the police and the state, and the game becomes subject to external political regulation.

If society is conceived of as a game, then sports proper can be conceived of as a set of games subject to larger external games. The attempt to make society into a game can only be completed if societal values and institutions are redefined so that they fit the requirements of game theory.

Those aspects of norms that are supported by external sanctions must be treated as conventions and the "external" character must be devalued. Thus, power and differential access to sanctions are deemphasized, for the rules of the game are usually interpreted in a conventional sense to mean that equal justice is available to all participants, and that equal sanctions are applied to all violators. In order to fit society into a game theory, it is necessary to make these assumptions about society. Much political and social theory emphasizes the conventions, the consensus, the rules that are agreed upon in the making of society, and devalues the force, power, coercion, and conflict out of which society emerges and which is always an ultimate resource in the maintenance of the game called society.

To fit the behavior of the individual into a game theory of institutions, the individual should be treated as if all norms are conventions, and as if he is conscious of the norms as rules in order that he may play the game in a self-conscious way.

In fitting society to game theory, much social theory emphasizes the voluntaristic nature of society, both the agreement of individuals concerning the rules, their awareness of the rules, and their willingness to accept the rules. The various forms by which individuals abstain or are excluded from the game are necessarily minimized. Thus, ignorance, apathy, resentment, and rebellion are devalued in order to make game theory work.

Thus, values are emptied of all other content except what is required to play the game. And the "game" of life has no meaning other than that of a game.

SPORTSMANSHIP AND THE EVASION OF RULES

If we treat not society as a game, but rather sports as a game within society, and the rules as a matrix which includes penalties for violation of the rules of the game, then we can specify further some of the variations within gamesmanship as related to sportsmanship.

impose upon the professional athlete standards of sportsmanship based on sanctions which are outside the rules of the game. Conspicuous violators of major rules, attackers of umpires, and users of obscene gestures can be fined, suspended, or barred. But what is important here is that the form of the sanctions, and the source of sanctions are outside the rules of the game. They rest, not on the voluntary acceptance by the athletes of the rules, but upon the fact that owners and managers have sanctions, both legal and economic, that are exterior to the game. They can be imposed upon the players for purposes that are exterior to the game. Sports thus becomes societalized, that is, they do not depend upon a voluntary social contract of the players, but on the use of sanctions that are external to the sport. In this sense sports were seen as resembling the operation of society, where the rules of the game are mediated and directed in terms of economic, political, ideological, ethnic, and other status interests. These interests allow the game to exist at one level in terms of an intrinsic set of rules, and at another level allow the rules to be the by-product of the collision of interests among the interested parties for purposes of maintaining the game.

Society can become a game when individuals act out highly stylized and formalized roles in a self-conscious manner only for the sake of enjoying their own and others' performances and not for other external results, and when all other nongame values or motives appear to be incapable of realization or devoid of meaning. Thus, the treatment of society as a game is an ironic adjustment to the futility of a social order or class, and of the values of a culture.

PLAY AND CONSTRAINT

Even in the most serious institutions, especially when individuals are constrained to act according to norms which are independent of their personal purposes, at those times when they are not subject to sanctions, forms of play involve the parody of the ordinary. Thus, burlesquing, irony, satire, and humor are acts of withdrawal from the ordinary which involve being playful. The suspension of the ordinary does not involve a different physical setting or a different time or an independent, formalized set of rules. It does involve a notion of bracketing the ordinary while one parodies, burlesques, or satirizes it. In this sense, the glint in the eye, the tone of voice, the appearance of excessive seriousness, and the exaggeration of gesture all suggest playfulness. Playfulness can surround all ordinary activities without suspending those activities except in a psychological sense. In this way, it may be as pervasive as the more serious play of less sophisticated, less disenchanted societies.

Given the change in the forms of play, there may be more play in modern societies than in primitive societies.

The fact that this form of playfulness exists in the midst of serious, ordinary, nonplayful activities does not deny the fact that when serious external consequences of the action are involved, the actors suspend their satire.

Periods of stylized playfulness, according to Huizinga, emerge at the waning of an age, and in societies in which the possibility of individual achievement of deeper values is perceived as not realizable. In this sense society becomes a game only when there are no motives, interests, or values that have deep enough meaning to cause the parties to the game to transcend the sport-like qualities of gamesmanship. Or, conversely, it becomes a game when the worship of "society" or "community" in their abstract form becomes the only meaningful religion available [17].

NOTES

1. "Score" is used here to mean the "plan" of the original creative work, as embodied in symbolic form, that is, a dramatic script, a choreographic plan, or a musical score.

2. The rules of figured bass permitted keyboard performers to improvise details within a generally determined framework of harmony. Similarly, operatic singers could improvise cadenzas and ornaments at certain places in operatic arias, as could soloists in concertos. The rules of voice-leading and of harmonic succession provided the overall framework within which they operated. Similar procedures were evident in the *commedia dell'arte,* in which comedians could improvise within the framework of certain stock situations and stereotyped characters.

3. Jean Piaget et al., *The Moral Judgment of the Child,* translated by Marjorie Gabain (New York, Free Press, 1965); see Part I, "The Rules of the Game," *et passim.* The views of George Herbert Mead on the function of play and games in socializing the individual are perhaps too well known to cite. But Mead does not extend the model to cover society as a whole. The social process as a whole enters the individual's thinking via play and game but is not itself seen as a game. See *Mind, Self, and Society* (Chicago, University of Chicago Press, 1962), pp. 152ff., reprinted in Anselm Strauss (Ed.), *The Social Psychology of George Herbert Mead* (Chicago, U. of Chicago Press, 1956).

4. Jan Huizinga, *The Waning of the Middle Ages* (Garden City, N.Y., Doubleday, 1954), and *Homo Ludens—A Study of the Play-Element in Culture* (Boston, Beacon Press, 1961).

5. Roger Caillois, *Man, Play, and Games,* translated by Meyer Barash (New York, Free Press, 1961).

6. Harold Finestone, "Cats, Kicks, and Color," in *Social Problems,* Vol. V, No. 1 (1957), pp. 3–13, reprinted in Maurice Stein, Arthur J. Vidich, and David Manning White (Eds.), *Identity and Anxiety* (New York, Free Press, 1960), pp. 435–448.

7. E. Franklin Frazier, *Black Bourgeoisie* (New York, Free Press, 1957) especially Chap. IX, "'Society': Status without Substance."

8.   St. Clair Drake and Horace R. Cayton, *Black Metropolis: A Study of Negro Life in a Northern City*, rev. ed. (New York, Harper & Row, 1962), Vol. II, Chap. 19 "Style of Living—Upper Class," and Chap. 22 "The Middle-Class Way of Life."

9.   Thorstein Veblen, *The Theory of the Leisure Class* (New York, Macmillan, 1899, and many reprints including New York, New American Library, 1953, Chapters 3, 4, 7, 11, *et passim*).

10.   Ruth F. Benedict, *Patterns of Culture* (Boston, Houghton-Mifflin, 1961), and *The Chrysanthemum and the Sword; Patterns of Japanese Culture* (Boston, Houghton-Mifflin, 1961) (originally published 1946).

11.   The central game plan is involved in "the pattern of culture," an overall system of central values as distinct from "patterns of culture," discrete configurations of behavior which, according to Benedict, embody the central pattern.

12.   Erving Goffman, *Asylums—Essays on the Social Situation of Mental Patients and Other Inmates* (Garden City, N.Y., Doubleday, 1961); *The Presentation of Self in Everyday Life* (Garden City, N.Y., Doubleday, 1959); *Behavior in Public Places* (New York, Free Press, 1963).

13.   Bronislaw Malinowski, *Argonauts of the Western Pacific* (New York, Dutton, 1961) (originally 1922); also, "Myth in Primitive Psychology," *Magic, Science and Religion* (New York, Free Press, 1948).

14.   Stephen Potter, *Gamesmanship* (New York, Holt, Rinehart & Winston, 1951); Eric Berne, *Games People Play, The Psychology of Human Relationships* (New York, Grove Press, 1964).

15.   Norbert Elias and Eric Dunning, "Dynamics of Group Sports with Special Reference to Football," in *The British Journal of Sociology*, Vol. XVII, No. 4 (December 1966), p. 398: "The group dynamics which rules help to maintain . . . determine whether rules persist or change. The development of football regulations shows very strikingly how changes of rules can depend on the overall development of that which they rule. . . . Thus, in football the tension level may flag, not simply because of the distinguishing characteristics of individual playing groups or of their individual members, but because of set characteristics of the configurations which they form with one another. In 1925, for example, the 'offside' rule in soccer was changed . . . the older rule, skillfully exploited, had led to a stage where stalemates had become increasingly frequent . . . the balance had moved too far in favor of defence." Also, p. 395: "The whole development of most sport-games . . . centered to a very large extent on the solution of this problem: how was it possible to maintain within the set game-pattern a high level of group tension and the group dynamics resulting from it, while at the same time keeping recurrent physical injury to the players at the lowest possible level. The question was, and still is, in other words, how to 'steer the ship,' as it were, between the Scylla of disorderliness and the Charybdis of boredom."

16.   See Caillois, "The Corruption of Games" *op. cit.*, Chap. IV, pp. 44–46: "What used to be a pleasure becomes an obsession. What was an escape becomes an obligation, . . . a source of anxiety. The principle of play has become corrupted. It is now necessary to take precautions against cheats and professional players, a unique product of the contagion of reality. . . . The corruption of *agon* begins at the point where no referee or decision is recognized."

17.   See Huizinga, *The Waning of the Middle Ages*. For an important description of forms of "playfulness" under tyranny, see Czeslaw Milosz, *The Captive Mind*, translated by Jane Zielonko (New York, Random House, 1951), especially Chap. 3, "Ketman."

PART II

THE SPECIALIZATION OF CRAFT ATTITUDES

Chapter 5

The Religious Attitude and Corresponding Religious Institutions

EMOTIONAL AND INTELLECTUAL BASES
FOR RELIGIOUS ATTITUDES

In a sense, much of what is described as the religious attitude and religious institution is not an intellectual attitude, but a profound quality of emotion [1]. The sense of awe and wonder, the sense of the infinity of existence, and of man's incapacity to grasp in intellectual terms this infinity, defines, for some phenomenologists, the religious attitude [2].

Other emotions stressed by religions—pietism, ecstasy, quietism, religious frenzy, orgiastic states—are also, in this sense of the term "emotion," religious attitudes.

Religion is an attitude toward the ultimate, the absolute, the infinite, expressed or personified in a god or gods, or in a state of being that is free from the limitations of everyday life. In that sense, religious values express an ultimate state of escape from the limits of time, place, and the ordinariness of existence. This is true even though religions prescribe forms of enduring and acting in everyday life in order to achieve, at some other time or place, an escape from the vicissitudes of everyday life.

We are primarily concerned here with the self-conscious attempt to define religious attitudes in systematic, logical terms. We are more concerned with problems of theodicy and theology than with the way these are felt. It may well be that religious emotionality precedes religious theorizing, both in historical terms and in ontogenetic terms (Freud's "oceanic attitude," for example). But once religion becomes formalized and professionalized, religious emotions are both defined in explicit terms and are induced systematically by religious training, ritual, religious art, rewards, and punishments.

71

Correct religious emotionality is rewarded by access to religious values and punished by denial of grace, salvation, or of the rights to participate in the communion or community of the religious [3].

The inducement of religious emotions at some occasions and places is the primary end of the ceremony or ritual. At other times, they are the emotional supports to religiously prescribed actions, which in turn are defined by religiously defined theories. One can thus construct a formal paradigm of the relationship between religious theory, religiously defined action, the means of religious indoctrination, and the means of inducing religious emotions. These can be presented in the following matrix of religious attitudes, a matrix not unlike the paradigm of artistic and critical attitudes.

Religiously defined action: The end-product of all religious activity, the incorporation of religious attitudes and actions into the everyday life of the religiously qualified. If successfully induced, the religious definition of the action is so incorporated into the everyday behavior of the actor that religious activity is not problematic to the actor. It requires no sense of estrangement from the "nonreligious" actions of the actor because religion defines not only the religious but also the nonreligious. Needless to say, for reasons to be elaborated later, this state as a "pure state" is rarely achieved.

Theology and theodicy: These are the systematic, self-conscious attempts to define, in logically self-consistent ways, the theoretical basis for the religious attitude. Attempts at such definitions are professionalized; theology and theodicy are conceptually difficult and abstract, and usually inaccessible to laymen who are the objects of and respondents to such attempts. The success of religion is measured not by the number of individuals who understand religious theory, but by the number who respond to it and incorporate it into their everyday action [4].

Religious indoctrination: This includes the means and devices by which theology is translated into terms, maxims, mottoes, and ideas which make it accessible to incorporation into everyday life. This includes preaching, homiletics, teaching, exemplary behavior, and religiously defined performances which concretize, personify, dramatize the abstractions which are necessary to religious theory and theology.

Religious Attitudes—Orientation

	To Outside World	Internal
Action	Religiously defined action	Religious indoctrination
Theory	Religious ceremony or ritual	Theory and theodicy

Religious ceremony and ritual: These are the kinetic and autokinetic processes by which desired emotional attitudes are induced in a population which otherwise may be defined as inaccessible to religious messages. Thus, religious ceremonies and rituals evoke the feeling of awe, wonder, or ecstasy, of orgiastic freedom, humility, piety, or control, depending on the attitude which has been previously defined as theologically desirable. At times, emotional states, which are attitudes already characteristic of a population, are selected and stressed by a religious body in order to link feeling tones to explicit theologies.

In the Counter-Reformation, ritual and ceremonial elements, art, music, aesthetic and architectural developments, and educational innovations were channeled by an organizational and rational bureaucracy to direct religious emotions, attitudes, and character into forms of behavior and loyalty that were rationally—that is, theologically—defined.

However, the paradigm shown above does not necessarily re-create in any linear way the history of particular religions. It may well be that in the original primitive religions, attitudes of wonder and awe were the supreme social values of religions, and that these preceded theology and theodicy.

But theology and theodicy, once they make their appearance, provide logical and theoretical rationality for attitudes and behavior, which at other times could have been realized without theological and theodistic explanation. But once religious rationality enters the picture, whole new sets of processes intervene. The introduction of theoretical rationality into religion, then, as we shall see, subjects religious theory and behavior to criteria of rational criticism and consistency. Once this happens, the "self-evident" nature of religion weakens and religious theory and behavior becomes subject to entire new processes and dynamics of intellectual rationalization [5].

At any given moment, however, religious theory becomes the basis of religious planning. Theology becomes incorporated into the framework for religious indoctrination and for the design (often rational) of religious ceremony and ritual. If effective, both of the intervening devices can successfully implant attitudes, emotions, and values that concretize and embody the theology in such a way that the religious actor need not be aware of the theoretical grounds for his action. The theology is then imbedded in his character structure.

Thus there is a tension between the unconscious acceptance of a religious attitude of everyday life and the theological or theoretical system that creates that attitude. The breakthrough of religious self-consciousness among those whose attitude was an attitude of everyday life may be destructive to that attitude of everyday life. In this sense it may be necessary to segregate the deeply religious, in a theological or critical sense, from the practitioners of everyday religion.

THEOLOGIC AND THEODISTIC DEFINITIONS
OF RELIGIOUS ATTITUDES

We would argue that to the extent that the theology and theodicy are based on a professionalization of religion, they come relatively late in religious evolution. Moreover, as theology and theodicy become highly professionalized, abstract, and inaccessible, the impulses toward the expression of religious emotion may be found outside the formal structure of theologically defined religions. Thus, folk religions, storefront religions, evangelical and ecstatic religious cults may exist within the framework of religions which do not stress these emotional expressions within their formal theoretical structure. In fact, the tension between theology, theodicy, and the expression of personal emotionality is a fundamental problem in almost all religious bureaucracies. Spontaneous, religious emotionality may be difficult to control and may violate religious intellectuality and rationality [6]. Religious organization requires at times a form of religious genius in containing these two diverse and contradictory elements within the same religion, a genius which was most conspicuously revealed in the Catholic Counter-Reformation.

Our paradigm, thus, is, at a simple level, a specific application of the tensions between the attitude of everyday life, and the scientific, artistic, and critical attitudes, as presented in Chapter 1. But it is our contention that religion, representing the first systematic form of knowledge, contains within it the basic tensions and contradictions that occur in all other forms of knowledge.

The paradigm, however, states only the formal relationship between theological attitudes and everyday religious attitudes; it says nothing about the content of such attitudes. It is of course an obvious point that religions have a variety of religious contents, and produce different attitudes of everyday life. The specific themes and contents of various religions are the product of historically unique institutional and intellectual developments. But the starting point of all religious development is in the attitude toward the infinite, the absolute, to God or the gods.

But from such unique starting points a variety of alternatives has developed historically. Weber has attempted to explain these starting points in terms of the differential experience of good and bad fortune, experiences which raise questions as to why good or bad fortune happens, especially to the private individual [7].

The quest for the answer to these theodistic questions causes communal religion, religion oriented exclusively toward communal goals; to be transformed into religions which attempt to explain the life-fate of the individual. Out of the attempt to answer this question arose a professional priesthood who began to specialize in the problems of theodicy via the means of theology. The breakdown of the basic questions of the incidence of good and bad fortune into more specific questions resulted in the classic and universal problems of not only all religion but all knowledge. These questions are: What is the relationship of man to the universe (and this includes the attempt to define the universe)? What is the relationship of men to each other (and how should men act toward each other)? What is the relationship of man to himself? These are not only the questions of theology and theodicy, they become the underlying questions of philosophy, and the increasingly specific questions which underlie all rational science. In this sense the questions that are evoked by the fundamental problems of theodicy, once raised, have never left us, and all intellectual life whether consciously based on religion or not is the attempt to answer these questions on different grounds, as successive answers appear to be inadequate in removing the original questions.

It is not our purpose here to trace out the specific theodistic answers evolved by the various world religions. These involve the notions of community, of responsibility for man's transgressions, redemption via rebirth, the myth of the savior, submission to an omnipotent and omniscient God, the promise of grace, and the sanctity of acceptance by the community of the elect. The specific ontological and metaphysical assumptions of the great world religions of course vary. While each set of assumptions is subject to a process of intellectual rationalization, and, as we shall see, various forms of institutionalization, the particular manner of rationalization works or operates within the framework of the basic selection of assumptions that are historically made for a religion. The religious intellectual, innovator, or theologian, even when creating the most radical changes in the religions to which he addresses himself, is likely to operate within the framework of intellectual and institutional limits which are part of his received world.

RELIGIOUS RATIONALIZATION

The development of such religious theory is the product of religious intellectuals and priestly bureaucrats who created theologies that defined in systematic terms the sacred and the profane. But simply by defining the sacred, the profane as an object of consciousness must come into existence in order to provide a counterimage to the sacred.

It is possible to speculate, and many thinkers have speculated, that at some point in time, the whole world of primitive men was suffused with awe and wonder. God was nature, and all action was the propitiation of or identification with the gods. In this sense, the religious attitude was not separated from nonreligious attitudes to everyday life. All action, and all nature, was sacred. The "profane" did not exist. When religious developments, and especially rational religious development defined what was *peculiarly* sacred, *peculiarly* appropriate to God or a god, then what was inappropriate was defined as the profane [8].

Much of the world was disenchanted, stripped of its magic, the religious was confined to one particular sphere, which because of its confinement, could be intensified. Beyond this, the existence of the profane, the non-sacred, and the ungodly make it possible for men to be alienated both from God, nature, and from other men. Thus, it could be argued, that the source of alienation resides in rational professional religion. A basic form of alienation is thus experienced originally in religion, and as we shall see, repeats itself in all other forms of intellectualized knowledge, even when these forms have as their central purpose an attempt to escape from the alienation caused by previous attempts to escape from alienation.

Once the profane is defined, the world is divided between the sacred and the secular, the exalted and the ordinary. The unity of the total wonder and awe of a primitive world is rent by the dualistic division of the world. In this sense, religion invents the nonreligious, the ordinary, and introduces an alienation between the religious and nonreligious worlds. This dualism, however, may well reflect a division between the world as controllable by men and a world that is controlled by forces that are not understood or are not easily brought under control except, hopefully, by religious magic. The development of professional priesthoods results in religious specialization, in the art or act of theorizing [9]. The religious intellectual becomes a specialist in (1) reading, writing, and literature, and (2) criticizing, evaluating, philologizing, and in logical analysis, and (3) makes a financial and economic claim upon the community and upon individuals within the community, by promising them redemption, salvation, and religious assurance. It is, for the moment, the first two points that we are interested in.

Simply because of his intellectual specialization, the priestly intellectual develops his intellectual talents as a set of autonomous traits, autonomous from the religious message per se. He is thus able to evaluate, criticize, "research," analyze, and find flaws in received religious traditions. In doing so the religious intellectual develops the quality of intellectual rationality, which in its specialization is separate and opposed to religious emotionality.

He is thus able to destroy, through increasingly refined levels of analysis, received religions that appear to be irrational, emotional, or which could result in logical contradictions, and to substitute for them newer formulations which for the moment are more capable of resisting his critical and analytical abilities. Thus, a process of theological evolution begins to take place. It results in higher and higher levels of criticism, and it destroys the higher levels of complexity of religious theory which is the product of past attempts to answer past criticism [10].

The theological changes that are induced by past religious criticism result in a continuously more intellectually elaborated theology that is highly rational in form, and made increasingly subtle and complex in answer to rational and scholarly criticism. At some points, we shall see that such rational elaboration results in the growth of new forms of religious "irrationality" as rationalized intellectual religion appears to be incapable of answering more "primitive" questions placed upon it by those whose religion is not intellectualized.

In this process of religious evolution, religion has continuously destroyed and remade itself. But in the modern world the destruction of religious theory has resulted less and less in the replacement by newer forms of religion capable of inducing a religious attitude of everyday life. Why this is so requires some explanation.

At the simplest level, theology and theodicy are not, for their intended audiences, simply exercises in criticism, analysis, research, and evaluation. They spring from the attempts of religiously alienated men to explain their existence. The basic questions of theodicy must be answered in ways that conform to the questions raised by their immediate experience in a continuously evolving historical present. If and when theology becomes so abstract, so removed from the ordinary capacity of men to find correspondences between religious theory and the events of their everyday life, religion loses its relevance and is rejected not necessarily on programmatic bases but on grounds of being inapplicable or incomprehensible.

When theological developments present a religious world that finds immediate correspondence with the existential world of its congregation, then theology becomes immediately relevant, it becomes an immediate factor in the lives of people who live in a historically experiential world. Thus, the Reformation, while being based on relatively abstract theological premises, was transformable into terms that could correspond to the experiences of the individual whose experience was modified by evolving institutional and historical processes [11].

RELIGION AS A CREATOR OF NONRELIGIOUS RATIONALITY

The continuous rationalization of religious theory by religious intellectuals leads at times to the rejection of religion by intellectuals similar in interest to those who were originally its exponents and guardians. If religion is the primary form of systematic knowledge, then the failure of religion to answer the questions it itself raised resulted in the emergence of new ways of posing the basic questions, and new theories in response.

Thus, religion gave birth to philosophy, and philosophy, for similar reasons (as we shall see in the next chapter), gave birth to the natural sciences, and these in turn gave birth to the social and psychological sciences [12]. And yet, in their generic form, all of these newer forms of knowledge attempt to deal with the same problems: the nature of the universe (the physical sciences), the relations of men to each other (the social sciences), and the relationship of men to themselves (psychology and the humanities).

While each of these disciplines come into existence in the attempt to answer the same basic questions as does religion, the choice that they make constitutes an alternative strategy in locating the areas in which answers are to be found. Each area—as a modern university catalogue would suggest—becomes an autonomous area with autonomous methods, concepts, theories, and habits of thought. Each discipline develops its own aims and goals, based on the development of its emerging internal autonomy. And each area tends to raise its own aims and goals as supreme values for its quest. As a result, a proliferation of separate values begins to occur. Thus, knowledge, beauty, art, science, social organization, and forms of community become the ultimate values for their respective practitioners. To the extent that these values are ultimate values, they have the characteristics of religion, since religion originally is defined as a stance toward absolute, ultimate, and infinite values. Thus, by the very development of the continuous rationalization of original religious values, religion breeds alternative values which can be and in fact are treated as religions. Thus, religion not only suffers from the internal tensions and conflicts introduced by its self-rationalization, but also creates a world of autonomous children who become competitors for the original values inherent in "purely" religious activities. Conversely, the alternative forms of knowledge have, in their formal sense, the same essential characteristics as religion; they take a stance toward one or another value which they regard as absolute, they attempt to explicate the theory, methods, and concepts of their fields to make the world consistent in terms of these methods, theories, and concepts, and so far as we know, are no more successful than religion in accomplishing the original purposes of religion. This "lack of success" can be inferred by the continuous rejection and substitution of theory in the respective fields.

Thus, it is possible to argue that the world is not becoming less religious or more secular, but rather that the worlds of religion are becoming more pluralistic in content and form. The problem facing us today is that we face the competition between an overabundance of ultimate values which in their loyalties and potential demands are each as absolute (and are functional substitutes for religion) as religion [13].

Each of the major fields of knowledge deriving from aspects of religious thought itself, once it becomes autonomous from religion, begins to develop in a manner similar to the way religious thought originally developed. The new form of thought develops its own specialized assumptions, concepts, rhetoric, terminology, method, and, of course, set of values. Each ultimately becomes professionalized, and the work of practitioners and theorists in each world of thought becomes subject to the critical analysis of men who, as we have already indicated, become expert in criticism. Each then becomes subject to a system of autonomous intellectual development, which causes the system of thought to develop in substance, in complexity, and in methodological and conceptual difficulty. And as each field of knowledge begins to develop an internal complexity in both its theoretical and organizational aspects, each field begins to subdivide, subspecialize, and to develop separate worlds of ultimate values [14]. But as this occurs, the value-pool that constitutes the total realm of values in a society at large is so great and yet so splintered that the total world so defined becomes inaccessible to any individual in it. Each, by virtue of its professionalized and academic critical stance, becomes difficult to understand by laymen who were originally committed to the values implicit in that form of knowledge. As a result, the theoretical, methodological, and conceptual complexity alienates all but the professionals in the field. Journalistic popularizers (see Chapter 14) become necessary, and increasingly, the integration of knowledge is left in the hands of charlatans. In addition, those who seek, in new forms of thought, answers to the essential problems of the senselessness of the universe are forced to seek even newer formulations which readdress themselves to the original questions. Thus, each of the new forms of thought becomes subject to the same kinds of dynamics that the original form of thought, religion, was subject to. It appears that this process is endless. The evidence for such an appearance is the fact that new forms and figures of knowledge continuously re-emerge despite the fact that older forms have attempted to deal with essentially the same questions.

PROBLEMS IN THE INSTITUTIONALIZATION
OF RELIGIOUS IDEAS

Up to now we have treated religious ideas, theologies, and theodicies as if they were determined solely on intrinsic, autonomous grounds. It is important to recognize the autonomy of intellectual phenomena. But to say that religion or any other intellectual system develops solely on the basis of intrinsic, autonomous processes would falsify history as much as does vulgar Marxism. The external basis for religious rationalization is the need for laymen to experience the world as meaningful. The criteria of meaning, however, are independent of religious theory per se; that is, "sense" is judged from the standpoint of everyday matter-of-fact "natural" experiences of men in their immediate historical, cultural, and social existence. Thus, the intellectual attitudes of men are, in part, determined by the entire evolution of their world with all its problems, contradictions, uncertainties, and sense-lessness as that mold operates upon them. Men use religion and other forms of social and philosophical theory, including the arts, as means by which the fragmentations, the contradictions, and the disorders of experience are to be unified. If a religious or other theory fails to unify this experience, men will look for other theories which do so. They thus accept or reject theory on the basis of these relatively simple external and pragmatic grounds.

In addition, men in their particular historic, social, economic, and political positions will view religious theories from the standpoint of the ways their thoughts and interests have been determined by their external position. They will make demands upon religion to justify themselves as they exist in a time, place, occupation, or social position, and they will demand that reli-gious thought be modified, reinterpreted, and emphasized from the stand-point of these external positions. Moreover, given the fact that different groups within the society possess different degrees of economic, political, and social power they have different means of exerting pressure upon organized religions. Thus, religious leaders, especially as religion becomes professionalized, develop an administrative, personnel, and cost-structure of its own, which requires for its existence that it come to terms with those who make demands upon it and who contributed to its maintenance. Profession-alized religion must respond to these salient external demands of the world despite its own autonomous development. Moreover, since the economic and social processes of a society continuously unfold, the typical life experi-ence of an underlying religious population and the balance of powers be-tween these groups continuously changes. This means that if religion does not change its content or message somewhat in phase with external develop-ment, interest, and demand, it risks the danger of becoming intellectually obsolete or of losing its clientele. If it changes purely in response to its own internal logic, it also risks the danger of becoming obsolete. Moreover, in a complex society—and we would argue that almost all societies are com-plex—as the balance of power within society changes, and new leadership emerges, it risks alienating some segments of a population simply by virtue of the fact that it is especially meaningful to other segments of the population [15].

Some religious theory, such as medieval corporate theory, attempts to develop a notion of the unity of society and thus to heal the rifts that occur within society. It may attempt to unify societies which in themselves are not unified. At times, this appears to be successful. But the emergence of new rifts, new conflicts, has tended to destroy even this attempt at religious unification [16].

At an even simpler level, religious bodies develop vested interests which necessarily determine aspects of their intellectual position. As they become institutionalized, the nature of the means of their institutionalization frequently provides them with vested interests which are of the same nature as those of secular bodies. Thus, ownership of land by a religious body will at times sanctify ownership of land in general, and cause it to reject other forms of capital.

The source of income for a church may be derived from one class, occupation, or group within a community, and the alienation of such a group would deprive a religious body of its economic, political, or social support. As a more extreme case, the patterns of recruitment of religious officials may be such that either the major part or the most influential part of the religious bureaucracy is drawn from one social or economic stratum which imposes its own common-sense attitudes and vested interests on the church and upon the ideas that emanate from the church. Where the church draws its officialdom from different strata, or when different officials drawn from the same stratum are differentially alienated from that stratum, then the conflicts that exist in the secular society are reenacted within the confines of the church. The conflict, that is, between "religion" and society is reenacted within the confines of the church.

One final major type of relationship between religion and society remains, within our present context, to be discussed. This occurs when the church, on religious grounds, develops a secular message. Typical examples occur in Confucianism, Brahmanism, in classical Egyptian civilization, to some extent in early Calvinism, and in Jesuit Catholicism. In these cases religious leaders developed an ideology, or a myth, of their indispensability to the management of secular affairs. Religious leaders became political leaders or advisors to political leaders. Their success at religious leadership is measured by the extent to which they convinced secular leaders of their indispensability, and by their success in the management of secular affairs. As a result, the boundaries between sacred and secular, while existing to justify religious intervention, collapsed in practice, and the secular interests were imported directly into religious definitions of experience. The acceptance and rejection of religion by the underlying population in such situations is measured directly by success in the exercise and justification of claims to power.

THE INSTITUTIONALIZATION OF RELIGIONS AS A PROTOTYPE FOR SECULAR RATIONALITY

We have argued that religion as a form of thought is the prototype of all thought forms. We would continue the analogy by arguing that the institutionalization of any thought form creates the same dilemma for all thought forms.

In the same sense, literature and philosophy are attempts to define the meaning of experience. They develop autonomous aesthetic and technical criteria for their respective forms. But the value of the literary or philosophic message to laymen is based upon the extent to which the medium clarifies or expresses the meanings of experience. Literary leaders will respond, quite frequently, to the audiences that select themselves as the objects of their messages. These leaders will attempt to write, define, stylize, their work for their particular audiences. The audience then determines the content of the literature. This is sometimes called "hack writing," but is so named only when it is done self-consciously and poorly. When the writers are recruited from the same classes as the audience, the message and form is frequently judged to be a product of the unity of a society, though we have argued that no society, except a mythical primitive one, is ever unified. At other times, writers, philosophers, and all other professional exponents of the forms of intellectual knowledge, become co-opted into the external establishments of a society. As such, both the form and content of the field of knowledge serve the higher purposes of the rulers of the state, and the elites within a society become the functional equivalents of high priests, but not the high priests of their autonomous system of thought. In societies in which the external establishments are less directly politicized, the determination of form and content is executed by managers, impresarios, business firms, foundations, and other agencies of the external society. Lastly, leaders of the profession-alized purveyors of knowledge attempt to organize themselves in order both to determine the form and content of their field, and to improve the conditions of professionals in their field, to improve or propagate the values and methods of their fields for lay audiences. This includes at times the securing of government support, funds, legislation, and monopolistic juris-dictions from their government. In no case that we know of have these intellectual leaders succeeded in achieving the power and predominance that religious leaders have secured in selected times and places in the past. This may be due to the fact that all other forms of knowledge have emerged in more pluralistic worlds than existed at the times of religious paramountcy or dominance. Thus, all other forms of knowledge have had to compete with much more fully developed forms of knowledge, and all such power strivings have tended to limit each other. Another possibility may be that the value-sweep of religion is so wide and deep that only as an intellectual form does it provide the basis for a unified image of the world.

Regardless of these qualifications, it would seem to us that in their stance towards the external world, every intellectual field or form faces the same conflicts, paradoxes, and tension that religion does. Each commences with a commitment to a set of values, which if taken as absolute, places itself at odds with all other forms of knowledge and with its secular world. In attempting to cope with the secular world, it is forced to make compromises, but the nature of those compromises results in the incorporation of extrinsic values or elements into its original insight or vision. In gaining influence, power, prestige, economic rewards, in becoming institutionalized, in coming to terms with its society, it loses much of what gave it a unique claim for its value upon its society. This is the generic tragedy of all religion, but the tragedy is so generic that it is the tragedy of all other forms of knowledge. Thus, in escaping from this tragedy in religion to some other realm of value, one escapes only to another form of the same tragedy [17].

We would think that this tragedy is inescapable. It is part of the condition of man. Solutions may exist, but these are the solutions of the individual man who follows his own vision. They are not solutions for the field or a form of knowledge itself.

NOTES

1. This chapter is an attempt to combine what we regard as the essential thrust of Weber's sociology of religion as related to the intellectual rationalization and disenchantment of the world, with later philosophic attempts to deal with the phenomenology of religion. The extent to which Weber is not adequately acknowledged in footnotes merely reflects our overall incorporation of his point of view.

2. See Rudolf Otto, *The Idea of the Holy: An Inquiry into the Non-Rational Factor in the Idea of the Divine and Its Relation to the Rational,* translated by John W. Harvey, especially Chap. II–V (New York, Oxford University Press, 1958) (first published 1923); Emile Durkheim, *The Elementary Forms of the Religious Life,* translated by Joseph Ward Swain (New York, Free Press, 1951), pp. 37ff.; Herbert Fingarette, "The Ego and Mystic Selflessness," in *Psychoanalysis and Psychoanalytic Review,* Vol. XLV, No. 1 (1958), pp. 5–41, reprinted in Stein, Vidich, and White (Eds.), *Identity and Anxiety* (New York, Free Press, 1960), pp. 552–583; see also Gershom G. Scholem, *Major Trends in Jewish Mysticism* (New York, Schocken Books, 1961) (originally published 1941); Paul Radin, *The World of Primitive Man* (New York, Henry Schuman, 1953), Chap. IV; and Robert Redfield, *The Primitive World and Its Transformations* (Ithaca, N.Y., Cornell University Press, 1953), pp. 116ff.

3. Henri Bergson, *The Two Sources of Morality and Religion,* translated by Audra and Brereton, (Garden City, Doubleday, 1954) Originally published in 1935, especially pp. 240ff., on the impulse to explain the world; see also Joachim Wach, *The Comparative Study of Religions,* edited with an introduction by Joseph M. Kitagawa (New York, Columbia University Press, 1961), Chap. 2; and Mircea Eliade, *The Sacred and the Profane: The Nature of Religion* (New York, Harcourt, Brace, 1959), pp. 8–13 and 65ff.

4. See Robert A. Nisbet, *The Sociological Tradition* (New York, Basic Books, 1966), Chap. 6, especially pp. 233ff. Nisbet cites Durkheim, Tocqueville, and Burke on the need of persons for precreated values to enable them to act in a multitude of situations which could never be dealt with by purely rationalistic methods.

5. See Peter L. Berger, *The Sacred Canopy: Elements of a Sociological Theory of Religion,* Chap. 3 (Garden City, N.Y.. Doubleday, 1969).

6. Ernst Troeltsch, *The Social Teaching of the Christian Churches*, Vol. I, translated by Olive Wyon (New York, Harper, 1960) (original German publication 1911, English translation 1931), pp. 331ff., indicates the institutional forms corresponding to this conflict.

7. Hans H. Gerth and C. Wright Mills, *From Max Weber* (New York, Oxford, 1961) (originally published 1946), from the essay, "The Social Psychology of the World Religions," p. 275: "The metaphysical conception of God and of the world, which the ineradicable demand for a theodicy called forth, could produce only a few systems of ideas on the whole—as we shall see, only three. These three gave rationally satisfactory answers to the questioning for the basis of the incongruity between destiny and merit: the Indian doctrine of Kharma, Zoroastrian dualism, and the predestination decree of the *deus abscondidus*. These solutions are rationally closed; in pure form, they are found only as exceptions. . . . The rational need for a theodicy of suffering and of dying has had extremely strong effects. As a matter of fact, this need has molded important traits of such religions as Hinduism, Zoroastrianism, and Judaism, and, to a certain extent, Paulinian and later Christianity."

8. See Mircea Eliade, *op. cit.*; Max Weber, "Religious Rejections of the World," in Gerth and Mills, *op. cit.*; and Owen Barfield, *Saving the Appearances: A Study in Idolatry* (New York, Harcourt, Brace & World, 1965) (originally published 1947).

9. Max Weber's entire body of work on the sociology of religion is central to this discussion, including not only the essays cited above, but also his studies of China, India, and ancient Judaism.

10. Histories of theology give ample illustration of the elaboration of doctrines. See J. F. Bethune-Baker, *An Introduction to the Early History of Christian Doctrine to the time of the Council of Chalcedon* (London, Methuen, 1903); H. R. Mackintosh, *Types of Modern Theology—Schleiermacher to Barth* (London, Nisbet & Co., 1937); Reinhold Seeberg, *Text-Book of the History of Doctrines*, 2 Vols., translated by Charles E. Hay (Grand Rapids, Mich., Baker Book House, 1956); and Adolf Harnack, *History of Dogma* (New York, Dover Books, 1961).

11. Erich Fromm, *Escape From Freedom* (New York, Holt, Rinehart, 1941) (Avon, 1965), Chap. 3; see also Karl Jaspers, "The Axial Age of History," in *Commentary*, Vol. VI (1948), pp. 430–435, reprinted in Stein, Vidich, White, *Identity and Anxiety*, pp. 597–605. Jaspers' philosophy as represented in such works as *Reason and Existenz—Five Lectures*, translated by William Earle (New York, Noonday, 1955), attempts to deal with meaninglessness by establishing limits beyond which reason should not attempt to reach by risk of foundering, and Michael Novak, *Belief and Unbelief* (New York, New American Library, 1965).

12. On the birth of cultural institutions out of religion, see Georg Simmel, *Sociology of Religion*, translated by Curt Rosenthal (New York, Philosophical Library, 1959), pp. 4–5: "Out of the visible and the conceptual, which we also experience in the realm of reality, the religious world arises in new tensions, new extensions, and new syntheses. The concepts of soul and existence, of destiny and guilt, of happiness and sacrifice, even the hair on our head and of the sparrow on the roof, are its concern also—but augmented by standards of value and shades of feeling, arranged in different dimensions and assigned a quite different focus and perspective. Thus the very same material seems to produce the empirical, the philosophical or the artistic order. The religious life creates the world over again; it interprets the whole of existence in a peculiar key. . . . Only if religion is accepted as the totality of the world-picture, co-ordinated with other theoretical and practical totalities, will it and other systems of life achieve a harmonious state of inner interdependence." Simmel's entire essay is essential to this discussion. See also F. M. Cornford, *From*

Religion to Philosophy: A Study in the Origins of Western Speculation (New York, Harper Torchbooks, 1957) (originally published 1912), and Arnold Hauser, *The Social History of Art*, translated by Stanley Godman (New York, Random House, 1951).

13. See Weber's "Religious Rejections of the World and Their Motivations" in Gerth and Mills, *op. cit.;* also, Karl Mannheim's *Ideology and Utopia*, translated by Louis Wirth and Edward Shils (New York, Harcourt Brace, 1965), Chaps. IV and V.

14. Thomas Luckmann, *The Invisible Religion: The Problem of Religion in Modern Society* (New York, Macmillan, 1967), Chap. VII. The author suggests the emergence of new spheres and values that assume sacred status.

15. See Peter L. Berger, *The Sacred Canopy: Elements of a Sociological Theory of Religion*, Chap. 7; and Peter L. Berger, *The Noise of Solemn Assemblies*, Chap. 9 (Garden City, N.Y., Doubleday, 1961).

16. Ralph Henry Bowen, *German Theories of the Corporative State, with Special Reference to the Period 1870–1918* (New York, Whittlesey House, 1947).

17. Perhaps the most common form of substitute for religion is politics. See Richard Crossman (Ed.), *The God That Failed* (New York, Bantam Books, 1965) (originally published 1950); also Eric Voegelin, *The New Science of Politics* (Chicago, University of Chicago Press, 1952), Chaps. V and VI, on gnosticism as a civil theology. Similar sanctifications of the arts and science are almost as common. The entire work of Jacques Ellul is significant here, e.g., his *The Technological Society* (N.Y., Knopf, 1964), *The Political Illusion* (N.Y., Knopf, 1967, etc.).

Chapter 6

Philosophical Attitudes

Initially, philosophy took as its object a world of explanations which previously had been generated by myth, by religion, by magic, and by "superstition." The myth, magic, and religion were contained in legends and symbols which were not abstract, general, or subject to logical analysis. Philosophy is based on the discovery of the concept, a general, abstract, and explicit statement of the idea it wished to use as a means of description and analysis of the world. The use of the concept made possible and facilitated the use of logic, the attempt to assess whether a statement based on an abstract general concept inevitably flowed from the relationship specified by the concepts used. Thus it became possible to criticize statements in terms of either their adequacy of fit to the concept or the logical relationship of concepts to each other. Discovery of the concept had two consequences. The first was a demystifying one; myth, magic, religion, became subject to conceptual criticism, that is, the world of experience, of events, became accessible first to speculation and later to description which, based upon the concept, had to be subject to relatively careful observation, though not necessarily scientific observation. Thus, the development of philosophy led eventually to an interest in the empirical world, and the description of that empirical world demystified it by subjecting it to careful and precise observation. Thus the early philosophers were more than creators of concepts; in applying concepts to the world they began a process of description and analysis which made the world accessible to logical and critical analysis, but which in the initial process resulted in an increased awareness of the varieties of experience in the operation of the world. Natural philosophy thus became the precursor of science [1].

Secondly, the discovery of logic resulted in a further partial demystification of the world because it introduced the category of reason as the ultimate criterion for the explanation and understanding of the world. At one level it resulted in the elevation of logic as a method that was superior to all other methods of inquiry; at another level, since reason was to be the basis for efficient causation and logical order, the object of its investigation, it looked for logical order as the basis for the operation of the universe and the world of experience; it postulated as possible the existence of logical orders in nature and the discovery of those orders as the object of its effort. But beyond this, it looked for first and ultimate reasons as a means of explanation for the operation of the world.

This involved two distinct operations which necessarily tend, in the long run, to destroy all logical, closed systems. The discovery of new facts or new facets of experience which were philosophically and logically precluded by established philosophic systems forced the philosophical system-builders to revise continuously their theories in order to incorporate experiences previously excluded. But beyond this, as the empirical world continuously opens itself up to disclose new worlds of fact, observation, experience, and measurement (which have become incorporated in new fields that have spun off from philosophy), the task of mastering these new worlds has become so specialized, so methodologically and technically complex, that a lifetime can be spent within one narrow area of these newer worlds, without recourse to the general philosophic systems that purport to encompass all the specialized worlds of knowledge of science [2].

The philosopher as integrator or systematizer cannot have the specialized knowledge, concepts, techniques, methodologies, and procedures of each of the new fields in order to systematize them into larger general systems. The philosophic enterprise gave birth to new sciences, new disciplines, new specialities, which developed their autonomy from philosophy. In their development, they were often antagonistic to or defiant of the attempt of philosophy to embrace its offspring. Thus philosophy, if not queen of the sciences, is mother of the sciences, a mother incapable of controlling the destiny of her offspring.

As each of the specialized disciplines developed and grew in substantive technological, methodological, and conceptual density, philosophy has had to abandon that discipline, leaving it to the new specialists. The field of a special discipline separated itself from the reach and boundaries of philosophy. And since this has happened in almost all areas of human knowledge, the substantive worlds to which philosophy had formerly addressed itself have removed themselves from philosophy. The quandary of modern philosophy is that it has no substance, no external world, to address itself to. Philosophers have increasingly resolved the problem of lack of substance by emphasizing other aspects of philosophy than that of being the grand summarizer, integrator, and systematizer of all knowledge. Philosophy has been shifting in focus and concern to other grounds. These most prominently are the following issues:

1. The logic of inquiry and the analysis of meanings;
2. How we know, i.e., epistemology;
3. The linguistic structures used to describe the world, in terms of the study of grammar as logic, and of the signification of the terms used;
4. The fundamental structures of reality that exist below the level of empirical knowledge.

With respect to the logic of inquiry and the analysis of meanings, philosophers are likely to describe and prescribe general rules for the methods of thought among scientists as well as for themselves and for laymen. But scientists, engaged in their own specialized researches according to procedures that have been developed within their respective fields, are likely to be unaware of the rules by which philosophers say they think. So far, it has not appeared to inhibit them, though at times when they leave their detailed specific inquiries to reflect upon the "meaning" of their work, they are likely to use the philosophy of science constructed by philosophers, not scientists, as a general defense and ideology for their work. They are also capable of constructing their own philosophies of science or theologies for such justificatory processes. The value of their detailed work, however, is usually determined by its contribution to the solution of specific scientific problems, and not by its philosophical or ideological significance.

Philosophy to some extent has attempted to maintain, if not its intellectual preeminence, at least its professional jurisdictions, by developing subspecialties in the areas which emerged with the replacement of philosophy by new fields of primary work. The emergence of each new field has tended to deprive philosophy of a function as primary investigator of the phenomena of the new field. When this happens, a new kind of philosophy emerges, which takes as its subject matter the primary work of the field that originally replaced philosophy. Thus, we now have the philosophy of religion instead of theology, the philosophy of science, political philosophy, social philosophy, the new philosophies of the arts, of history, of mathematics, and so on [3].

This has had several consequences. First, philosophy in each subfield tends to become so specialized that the subfield begins to lose its identity with philosophy as a whole. Second, within each such field philosophy becomes a form of criticism and employs the critical attitude with respect to primary work being done by substantive specialists in what is now the primary field. Third, the use of philosophy as a device for educating laymen in the mysteries of the substantive fields results in the conversion, in some instances, of the philosophical attitude to the journalistic attitude [4] (see Chapter 14). Depending on the way this is done, as indicated in Chapter 1, this is not necessarily bad [5]. Finally, the development of extreme specialization in any primary field inevitably throws into question issues and philosophies which appear to have been resolved in previous philosophical work. Thus, the development of science at almost every stage has raised questions concerning the meaning of life as defined by philosophers and theologians, and has forced philosophers to reconsider their previous work, if only to defend their past work and to repair the damage done to philosophic systems by past scientific or other discoveries. Philosophers have been forced to become specialists in specific fields to deal with the effects of these fields upon their work. But beyond this the development of each field raises new issues for philosophy and produces an external dynamic for the development of philosophy. This expansion, via criticism and destruction, is not dissimilar from the effect that philosophy and the sciences have had upon religious theorizing.

Advanced systematic logic can, as we have indicated, be used as a technique of criticism to provide a commentary on scientific work, to criticize scientific work, and to specify rules by which such work in the future is to be done. At this level, the commentary and criticism concerning programmatic logic for science would, if followed, replace the specific logic involved in the detailed work itself; but while argument, debate, and discussion about the nature of science and the scientific enterprise continues unabated, scientists, unaware of these higher levels of debate, continue to make scientific discoveries and solutions, despite deficient logic, unsystematic procedures, "intuitive," or unrigorous mathematical procedures, and deficiencies, and even ignorance of the "rules" by which they are said to operate.

THE LOGICAL REDUCTION

To state it differently, the formal logic of a proposition can be treated independently of its content as a substantive statement. Thus, the specific substantive content of the statement loses its particular relevance in the reduction performed by treating the statement in terms of its formal logical properties. Thus, a series of substantive statements can be treated as a series of logical propositions without reference to the fact that they may address themselves descriptively or synthetically to "statements about the world," about experiences, or about events in the world. Logical defects can be noted, or implications that are more general than those presumed in the substantive statement can be derived; but all of this can be done without reference to the empirical significance of the statements. In this sense, the empirical world loses its relevance, or may be precluded from analysis or study. At best, such analysis is a form of criticism. At its worst, logic becomes the object of its own analysis, and the world described therein has no meaning or relevance other than for the playing of logical games. Thus there is a fundamental tension between philosophy as a science of logical reductions and philosophy as a means of interpreting experience and the world.

The perfected development of logical criticism, when carried to extremes, can then destroy any substantive approach, replacing the world referred to by endless discussion of what it would require to reach and discuss, at logical levels, the world referred to, if it were ever to be reached [6].

If a scientific study is of sufficient importance to come to the attention of the logical positivist, he will, after the fact, discover that the methods used correspond to his philosophy.

In this sense, philosophy narrowly conceived as logical analysis becomes a special type of the critical attitude to explain after the event and in other terminology that which was fruitful and clear in its own terms before the fact and up to the fact.

THE LINGUISTIC REDUCTION

The semantic or linguistic reduction is based on the fact, that the world that presents itself to an observer, a scientist or an analyst must always be described in terms of some set of symbols or language adequate either to communicate to other observers—scientists and interpreters—and at the same time adequate as a mode of communication.

But the structure of language is in itself a phenomenon that has meaning and form in its own terms, apart from that which it manifestly communicates. Its structure affects what is communicated about the world in the signification of language. At one level, the awareness of the centrality of language to the way assertions about the world, the specification of conditions for these assertions, and the description of events that can be made following from such assertions all become subject to the constraints imposed by language itself. This awareness leads one to be self-conscious about the use of language and about intentional and unintentional bias inherent in the use of language. It also forces one to become specific and accurate about the use of terms in such assertions, and forces one to define terms so that there is a direct relationship between the definitions used to describe experience, and the experiences to be described. Thus, in extreme form, it forces one to operationalize one's concepts. At another level, statements about the world can be analyzed in terms of the grammar and structure of the statements themselves, and unintended meanings, conventional meanings, and meanings that reflect a natural attitude (those that are taken for granted), and are therefore not specified.

Thus, the object of such semantic and linguistic reductions is to clarify the statements used to describe the experience. But since such clarification is based upon reductions that are independent of the substantive content of the statements, it is relatively easy to drop from consideration what in fact the statements assert, and content oneself with linguistic or semantic problems. It is on such grounds relatively easy to find linguistic and semantic deficiencies in any statement. But the discovery of such deficiencies does not constitute a correction of the deficiencies in the statement. Such a correction would imply new and more precise assertions about experience and about events in the external world. But since linguistic analysis is by now a field which is extremely complicated, developed, and specialized, focus on that field virtually precludes the making of substantive statements, and linguistic reduction methodologically precludes such statements, the result of the use of these reductions precludes discussion of the worlds of experience. When this happens, language ceases to describe experience: the use of language *becomes* the experience itself; and language has no other meaning than its own formal properties, its own internal logic and structure. In this sense, linguistic analysis becomes a form of specialized criticism, and again, in the extreme, has no other object than itself [7]. It precludes contact with the world, with science as philosophically more naive people know it, and with the world as it is directly experienced.

THE EPISTEMOLOGICAL REDUCTION

The problem of how one knows is an even more important problem to philosophy than the problem of how one reasons or what one knows. A central philosophic problem has always been to explore the essential nature of reality as unaffected by any attempt by the observer, analyst, philosopher, or scientist to describe it. But almost from the beginning of the philosophic enterprise, long before the announcement of Heisenberg's "uncertainty principle," philosophers were fully aware that the attempt of the individual to know the world altered the world that was to be known, that the observer of the world was himself determined by the world that he attempted to know, and that the concepts that he used to know the world were themselves particularistic concepts which were products of the unique location of the individuals who in a given time and place were attempting to observe the world [8].

If the logical and linguistic reductions are among the major methods and approaches of philosophy, then the epistemological reduction is even more basic. On the basis of vulgar, direct, and intuitive experience, men make assertions about the external world, and attempt to validate their assertions by observing events and experiences presumed as conditions for their assertions.

Depending upon the level of sophistication in making assertions this process may be a relatively simple trial-and-error process, or may be very complicated, specified, and limited. But one can always ask the questions: How do we know? How do we know what we think we know? How do we know the categories with which we think we know? What is the origin of these categories? Are the origins of these categories themselves determined by the very processes which allow us to judge or evaluate the experience? In short, is our knowledge of experience subject to the experience itself in such a way that we cannot judge or evaluate it? The raising of this question at some levels has forced men to specify what their assertions are, what the conditions are under which they can judge whether the assertions are true or not, and what is a satisfying set of observations which will enable them to meet the requirements of judging the adequacy of an assertion. At another level, the quest for a grounding of knowledge that is totally independent of the experience of men has led them to push further and further back into the analysis of the sources of knowledge so that the object of the quest for knowledge is precluded. In this sense, epistemology can become, as in the instance of logical or linguistic reductions, a special kind of philosophic reduction, a mode of criticism, which abstracts itself from the phenomenon originally in question, and becomes the object of its own method. It thus removes itself from the experiential world originally under consideration, and precludes that world from its operation. Again, this is a tension between philosophy as a mode of analyzing and explaining experience, and philosophy (or science) as an object of its own epistemological method.

The same focus on methods of inquiry operates within science. Since the world could not be known except in terms of the attempt of men to describe it, then the extent to which the world can be said to exist is only ascertainable in the methods by which men attempt to describe it. This means that both the scientific and philosophic enterprise give increasing emphasis to the precise observation and recording of the methods used in describing the world. And the precise description of the methods can be viewed as constituting the world which presents itself through the methods. Thus, the logic and methods of science are not just the logic and methods of science, but are science itself, and, more than that, the world itself. In this sense, epistemology and methodological analysis replace ontology, essence, and metaphysics.

In following this strategy, some observers are inclined to think that the image of a scientist describing a scientist describing a scientist, an infinity of mirrors, becomes the only reality which is philosophically defensible, replacing what the vulgar layman calls the world. And while our summary may seem harsh, it is a necessary conclusion after following each step in the logical grounds [9].

On intuitive grounds, most men not specializing in philosophy or in methodological criticism are not trained to follow its conclusions regardless of where they lead. They are likely to reject the conclusions of our logical chain on intuitive grounds, although they reject them on what they regard as empirical bases. They accept, perhaps only as an assumption, the fact that they exist, even though on philosophic grounds the statement may be unprovable, doubtful, or meaningless. They accept as axiomatic not only their own existence but the fact that the world exists. And having done so, the problem of knowledge becomes infinitely more simple [10]. It is possible for them to proceed from such questions to others based on an initial question, "What do we know?" rather than the question, "How do we know?" The difference between these two questions constitutes the difference between a sterile criticism which brackets out of existence all knowledge and the external world, and all attempts to describe and analyze the appearances of the external world. Following the epistemological question always leads back to the study of the known in terms of the processes of knowledge of the observer, the investigator, and away from the world allegedly known. The description of the objective world results in a radical subjectivity which precludes knowledge.

The debate that ensues is always a debate on how one knows, and the question of what is known is ruled out of the debate. If the latter question is posed, then the focus of the discussion is confined to the external world, and the argument is expressed in terms of theories describing, perhaps synthetically, the external world, and not things about the nature of the investigator or about investigation in the abstract. Where individuals disagree as to the nature of the external world, such disagreements can be resolved about what additional "facts" or observations of the external world would resolve the disagreements, so that resolution of the conflict could always be expressed in terms of visible or hypothetical appearances within the external world.

THE METAPHYSICAL REDUCTION

The fragmentation of the world into a series of limited, discrete, temporary, and temporal observations which have no unifying order has been a difficult notion to accept. Why this difficulty exists is itself a difficult problem. Certainly if the world were thought to have fundamental structures, essences, and universals which operate below and are more basic than the world of mere appearances, then it might be possible to posit ultimate values and universal codes for action; it might be possible to reconcile the contradictions between any set of observations about a particular segment of the world with other observations. Decisionmaking would become easier, and men would have an easier time of reconciling their extremely difficult but immediate goals with the necessities placed upon them by a world which otherwise appears to be senseless and disorderly. As John Dewey has argued, the quest for certainty has led men to seek a metaphysical unification of the world, whether in fact such unification can be achieved within their own experiences or not [11]. In one sense, then, this philosophic approach is in harmony with fundamental theological approaches that in themselves attempt to construct theories of universal world order. But it has been pointed out in thousands of ways that the world does not yield itself easily to theories of order. In a perverse way, the operation of the world and of past experience produces new experiences and new knowledge that continuously violate the experiences and theories we have gathered from our past experience and probing.

In a philosophically more important way there are fundamental problems in the quest for universal order and essences. The problem is as follows. The universals, essences, ultimate orders, or structures exist at levels below the level of experience. Events, experience, and observation always present themselves to the observer or experience in terms of discrete, limited, temporal facts and impressions of everyday life. To achieve a "description" of the ultimate, the universal, or the essential, a process of reduction must be performed in order to strip the appearances of this temporal, accidental, or "merely natural" appearance. This process may be called the metaphysical reduction. The problem that remains is how is this reduction to be made? Are there invariant rules by means of which one can reach the level of the fundamental from that of the merely apparent? If we pose the question of these rules, the rules become subject to the same criticism that can and have been made of the logical reduction, the linguistic reduction, and the epistemological reduction. We could therefore argue that since the methods of achieving a knowledge of ultimate forms and structures of nature and experience are subject to the very limitations and criticisms made of mere appearances, then until these other problems are solved, the problem of solving this basic problem is itself unsolved.

To state the point differently, if several philosophers, all geared toward constructing and describing essential forms differ as to the nature of these forms, then the problem becomes on what grounds does one discriminate in making a choice? Since the ultimate forms posited by different investigators are themselves different, then they cannot be the basis by which one judges the difference. The differences could be reconciled possibly only in terms of the appearances which the postulated fundamental structures explained, predicted, or ordered. If that is the case, then the fundamental structure is merely a hypothesis, a model, or a predictive statement which is validated

by the occurrence and the nonoccurrence of events in the world. If that is
the case, then such a structure can be viewed as universal or valid only to the
extent that it predicts, explains, or orders discrete and limited facts of the
world. But again, if that is the case, the structure is not fundamental,
essential, or universal. If the decision as to the essential nature of the
essential is made on the basis of method, then the extent to which there is
agreement about what is essential is based on the extent to which there
is agreement both on method and on the application of method. If that is the
case, then the definition of the essential is based on the consensual, and
the essential can be abrogated by any disagreement among definers of the
essential. The extreme of this latter position is that the world is not knowable, since every attempt to know the world in its essential terms is based
upon the attempts of individuals using concepts which are the products of
their limited, finite, subjective notions of the world. Thus it is possible to
prove that the world does not exist, that it is only an illusion manufactured
by subjective men who cannot prove that they exist. If the world could not
be known directly and immediately because of the limitations of those who
would know the world, then the extent to which the world was knowable
could only be defined, not as it existed in any essential form, but only to the
extent that the methods used to define the world became, by their use, the
only available definitions of the world [12].

If, however, the debate should focus on the issue of the nature of the
methods themselves, turned back into issues of logical analysis or linguistic
analysis or epistemology, then there are no external references by which the
issue can be resolved, and the radical subjectivity of criticism as science
takes over.

The response to the posing of the question of what we know, rather than
how we know, results in some limitations. We are forced to accept the
strictures implicit in our own approach. If we say the fundamental question
is what we know, then we are forced to confine our knowledge to knowable
appearances, and to the use of hypothetical models which may enable us to
predict knowable appearances. As a result, we will, within the framework of
our own assumptions, be unable to say anything about fundamental forms of
knowledge, absolutes, or essences, which lie below the level of knowable
appearances, and hypothetical models from which we can derive knowable
appearances. As such, the world we know is likely to be a series of limited
and discrete scientific observations which have no overall synthetic, unified,
general order.

Given these considerations, the problem of a unified general and essential
order of the world is, so far as we can know it, ruled out by science. To the
extent that we as individuals feel the necessity for a unified general order
that is closed, synthetic, in the sense of a philosophic system, we, even in a
scientific age, make acts of faith, attachments to value systems, and to

secular or sacred theological systems, which provide an order that science is unable to give.

In much of our analysis, we have suggested that the onrush of science, of specialized knowledge and discipline, have shrunk the areas within which philosophy in the distant past has operated. The more recent attempts to give substance to philosophy by converting it into a philosophy of science, logic, epistemology, linguistic analysis, and logical positivism, have led philosophy into a sterile academic criticism.

Thus it has appeared that we have suggested that there is no place for philosophy in the modern world. At the same time we have suggested that science does not provide the answers that philosophy once attempted in synthetically supplying images of the world that unify man's experiences. It would seem to us that now, more than at any time in the history of the world, there is a need for these unifying images.

PHILOSOPHY AS PRESENTING IMAGES OF THE UNITY OF EXPERIENCE

In a sense, literature, poetry, and drama attempt to provide these images. There is no reason that philosophy, being more generalizing and systematic, could not attempt to meet this gap. The kind of intellectual production imagined would be the attempt to describe the larger wholes which science cannot. Such wholes would not be "scientific"; they would be speculative, imaginative, and hypothetical. To the extent that they were successful, they might provide frameworks to meaning and guides to action which no other disciplines could provide because of their specialization. In a world of specialists, there is a need for the nonspecialist, provided that the non-specialist does not become an arid specialist in the methodology of non-specialization, or a generalizing dilettante.

Social philosophy, philosophies of history, the philosophers of grand systems, and speculative philosophers—Hegel, Kant, Schelling, Croce, Ortega y Gasset—all attempt, on the basis of what might be technically inadequate grounds, to construct and reconstruct images of a world that is otherwise fragmented; this fragmentation is in part a product of a fragmentation and reductionism within philosophy itself. It is further fragmented, as we have indicated, by the very specialization and technical complexity of science per se, and it is perhaps even more seriously fragmented by the historical development of the world in which all systems of thought, ideologies, religions, and philosophy itself, are rent by emerging social, political, and economic trends and movements. Despite all attempts since the emergence of theology and philosophy to impose intellectual order on the world, the world refuses to be orderly. But since we can postulate that in some terms men demand an orderly world, a major task for philosophy is to address itself to the existing problems and forms of disorder, and to attempt to construct, frankly and avowedly, speculative systems which appear to provide a form of order that is otherwise lacking [13].

With the recognition that all systems of the past which attempted to postulate ultimate order, and to transcend the merely historical have failed, perhaps the speculative systems of the future could be more limited, time-bound, and therefore more historical and more aware of the possibility of becoming transcended. Since in fact this is what has happened to the philosophic systems of the past, more modest speculative systems of the future can in fact be no more limited than the modesty which was ultimately forced upon the speculative philosophies of the past. But for a time, each philosophy may help to provide part of the order that seems to be necessary for the existence of society and of men in society. In this sense philosophy is a form of myth-making, poetry, or art, in which the images of the world created by the philosophic enterprise become part of the world that philosophy attempts to analyze. Philosophy, on these grounds, cannot be "scientific" or merely technical. It addresses itself to and creates values within which the scientific and technical are always forced to operate [14].

NOTES

1.   F. M. Cornford, *From Religion to Philosophy: A Study in the Origins of Western Speculation* (New York, Harper, 1957) (originally published 1912); Wilhelm Windelband, *A History of Philosophy*, translated by James H. Tufts (New York, Harper, 1958) (originally published 1893), pp. 1–22; Alexandre Koyré, *From the Closed World to the Infinite Universe* (Baltimore, Johns Hopkins University Press, 1957); Arthur 0. Lovejoy, *The Great Chain of Being: A Study of the History of an Idea* (New York, Harper, 1960) (originally published 1936).

2.   Thus virtually every philosophical subject is to be found in Plato: cosmology, logic, aesthetics, logic, political theory, etc. In Aristotle their separation into formal genres is more evident. Logic later becomes the province of the mathematician, cosmology of the astronomer, aesthetics of the art historian, ethics and morals of the theologian; little remains for the philosopher but critical analysis.

3.   Examples are legion. See Stephen Barker, *Philosophy of Mathematics* (Englewood Cliffs, N. J., Prentice-Hall, 1964); in the same series are philosophies of art, language, history, religion, education, natural science, etc. Also, see Arthur Danto and Sidney Morgenbesser (Eds.), *Philosophy of Science* (Cleveland, World Publishing Company, 1960); Hans Meyerhoff (Ed.), *The Philosophy of History in Our Time: An Anthology* (Garden City, N.Y. Doubleday, 1959).

4.   One of the major forms that this has taken has been in the development of a phenomenology of the field in question. The phenomenologist attempts to express in phenomenological terms the logic, meaning, structure of ideas, and implications of

the field in question. These essays in part may be an illustration. In addition, every major school of philosophy attempts to absorb into its "system" the subject matter of the new field; thus while there may be a philosophy of art, such a philosophy is subdivided into a phenomenology of art, the Hegelian dialectics of art, pragmatics of art, platonic theories of art, positivist and "linguistic" theories of art, "communications" theories of art, etc. Thus, while philosophy attempts to clarify the substantive fields, the lack of consensus as to what philosophy is may, to the cultivated layman, result in a compounding of confusion. Yet this may be inevitable, given both the wide range of fields to which philosophy addresses itself, and the range of division by school or approach within philosophy. In this sense, the overproduction of "culture," as Weber has indicated, may become a source of intellectual alienation.

5.   The nontechnical writings of Werner Heisenberg and Banesh Hoffman are of both scientific and philosophical importance. But the efforts of some scientists— psychologists and biologists among them—to construct world views on the bases of their findings or of their methodologies have often proven to be philosophically amateurish forms of scientism, often repeating the errors of past scientific philosophies. See Werner Heisenberg, *Physics and Philosophy: The Revolution in Modern Science*, with a useful introduction by F. S. C. Northrop (New York, Harper, 1958); Banesh Hoffman, *The Strange Story of the Quantum* (New York, Dover, 1959) (originally published 1947).

6.   Erich Heller, "Wittgenstein and Nietzsche," in *The Artist's Journey Into the Interior and Other Essays* (New York, Random House, 1968), pp. 210ff.; Frederick Copleston, S.J., *A History of Philosophy*, Vol. 8, Part II (Garden City, N.Y., Doubleday, 1967), Chaps. 18–21; see also J. N. Findlay's review of Edmund Husserl's *Erfahrung and Urteil*, in *Mind*, Vol. LIX, No. 237 (April 1950), pp. 262–268.

7.   In addition to Heller, Copleston, Findlay, above, see the remarkable essay by Owen Barfield, *Speaker's Meaning* (Middletown, Conn., Wesleyan University Press, 1967), and *Worlds Apart: A Dialogue of the 1960's* (Middletown, Conn., Wesleyan University Press, 1963), pp. 101–106.

8.   Edmund Husserl, *The Crisis of European Sciences and Transcendental Phenomenology*, translated with an introduction by David Carr (Evanston, Ill., Northwestern University Press, 1970), pp. 84 ff., the sections on Locke, Berkeley, and Hume.

9.   George Santayana, *Scepticism and Animal Faith* (New York, Dover, 1955) (originally published 1923).

10.   Edmund Husserl, *Formal and Transcendental Logic*, translated by Dorion Cairns (The Hague, Martinus Nijhoff, 1969), p. 5.

11.   John Dewey, *The Quest for Certainty* (New York, Putnam, 1960) (originally published 1929).

12.   See P. S. Strawson, *Individuals: An Essay in Descriptive Metaphysics* (London, Methuen, 1959), for an attempt in metaphysics.

13.   Stephen C. Pepper, *World Hypotheses: A Study in Evidence* (Berkeley, University of California Press, 1950), attempts to typify such systems in terms of root-metaphors. Like Strawson, his work is objectivist in character.

14.   Wilhelm Dilthey, *Pattern and Meaning in History*, edited with an introduction by H. P. Hickman (London, Allen & Unwin, 1961); José Ortega y Gasset, *What Is Philosophy?* translated by Mildred Adams (New York, Norton, 1960), Chap. 11; also his *The Origin of Philosophy*, translated by Toby Talbot (New York, Norton, 1967), Chap. 10.

Chapter 7

The Historian

It is our contention that the attitude of the historian in approaching his work is that of the artist. By this we mean that the historian constructs a particular image of a past world which is so arranged that the image has order, unity, clarity, and completeness. In short, it is aesthetically satisfying. At the same time, the writing of history is subject to greater constraints than art is in that, once completed, it must "make sense" of the facts known at the time of the writing. But like art, it is not arbitrary.

But beyond this, the order and unity of history is simply not the invariant order and unity of the events observed; that is, it is not an objective quality of nature. Rather the unity is given by the skill, the methodological competence, the ideas, and the artistry of the historian [1].

Any historical era reported on is subject to an unlimited range of interpretations. Thus, if one considers the post-Civil War period in America, it could be seen as an era of great industrial giants transforming a nation through the process of industrialization, modernization, and technological and industrial change. Or, it could be seen as an era in which robber barons, immoral captains of industry, and financial pirates plunder and exploit a nation's resources for their own profit. The social benefits gained by industrialization, urbanization, and modernization may be viewed as inevitable consequences of the development of the economic system and of the availability of natural resources, with the robber barons being seen only as unwitting agents of "the system." One could maintain that the social benefits referred to may be less than they might have been were it not for the deflection and misuse of natural resources practiced by these captains of industry [2]. The changes of this era may be viewed as the objectification and realization of ideas, the ideas of the Protestant Ethic or of the frontier mentality, which in their realization produced the changes in question [3]. With all of their moral dereliction, the captains of industry can be viewed as necessary agents for economic growth. Their morality or lack of it can be

101

evaluated as not unusual or out of phase with the temper of the times, but alternatively they and their total being can also be assessed as representative individuals appropriate both to their time and to the necessities of America in its time.

All these interpretations can be and have been made of the period, all derived from the same reservoir of "facts." Each image in some way corresponds to one or another interpretation of the same period. Thus, one interpretation of a period may be generated as a reaction to other ideas of that period, each idea with its own perspective on verifiable facts or selection of new facts, which justifies its existence and negates earlier facts and interpretations [4]. Thus the dynamics of historiography may to some extent be independent of the dynamics of history itself. In the sense that there are options and choices in the selection of the imagery with which one refers to a period, history is an art and not a science [5].

Before we can fully assess history as an application of the artistic attitude, it might be advantageous to exlore the intentionality implicit in historical work, in order to derive some of the perspectives which govern its operations.

One of the impulses to historiography is the attempt to establish a sense of the identity of a people or a group with its past. Thus, the writing of history may serve to establish a sense of legitimacy for a new group, a new nation, an ethnic group, a class, institution, or a new social movement. Where a newly ascendent, newly self-conscious or newly dominant group reaches that stage in its development when it can make a claim for social recognition, the very newness of the group constitutes a source of disesteem. It is, in a symbolic sense, illegitimate. It confronts older groups whose legitimacy is established by a direct institutional or legal history, and whose length of tenure or of institutionalization constitutes a claim for treating the new group as an upstart. Because the new group must defend itself against these claims of illegitimacy, it must discover, in its past, "precursors," "forerunners," and "embryonic ideas" which the new group realizes and personifies. Thus, its new ascendancy will be seen as only the fulfillment of a "historic mission." In this sense, the history so written will be optimistic, pointing from the continuity between the old embryonic ideas and the emerging and changing present to a future where the historic mission of the group will be fully realized. Thus, "black history" can only be understood in terms of the emergence of black nationalism and the civil-rights movement. In such movements, there is the necessity to discover a viable past in order to justify claims made in the present and to find hopes for a claim upon the future. The absence of such a history can be interpreted as the failure of historians to recognize the importance of the group in the past, and as evidence of the bias and lack of sensitivity of the historians of the past. The attempt to fill the gaps of the past is an attempt to suggest the importance of a population in the past. In addition, it is an attempt to document the injustices of the past as they operate up to the present. It is an attempt, in its selective emphasis, to create viable self-images and patterns of identity for a group in the present. It constructs, hopefully, models of one's group, ideals, loyalties, and images of one's enemies. It substantiates a political program. The extent to which there is lack of consensus over the ideals to be striven for, the strategies of action or contemplated action, and immediate tactics to be used, all suggest different bases for the history to be projected, and the craft of history as well as its content will be a source of contention. Some historians will be attacked or discredited because they perpetuate the sins of the past. Others will be charged with incompetence because they, in their desire to create an "instant history" from whole cloth, do not know the craft of historiography. Others will be viewed as "sellouts" or as irresponsible because they misrepresent events in the past in order to make short-term capital out of their strategies for the present.

All these charges and countercharges occur within the framework of contemporary black history. All such charges and countercharges emerge in the construction of any new history or any major attempt to revise the traditions that dominate the history of a group, a nation, or a people [6]. Every social and political movement thus produces its own history, and its own particular approach to history. This by itself cannot be considered an "evil," for corresponding to any impulse to historiography, there may exist a world of facts, events, which become evoked by the very consciousness that makes history relevant at a given time or place. Whatever "evil" there is emerges when the historian's craftsmanship is submerged by ideological or propagandist needs.

Thus it can be argued that the potentiality for history is infinite, and the construction of a particular history is, from the standpoint of history, arbitrary. Such arbitrariness may disappear if in the process of its construction, the history reveals a world that one can say, with some degree of certainty, did exist, and had a definite form and content.

In such treatments, the imagery of the historical past cannot be understood except as derived from the needs of the present. Thus, the historian, whether professional or amateur, attempts—perhaps only subliminally or intuitively—to assess and portray the present. But the manifest media of his portrayal of the present are expressed in terms of research, description, and analysis of the past. The arrangement of the sequence of events works itself out so that the past, whatever it may have been, "inevitably" produces the present, and if we are dealing with an ascendant group, it will "inevitably" produce the future as projected.

A similar process of historical reconstruction may be presented by older groups who, having arrived, must justify their existence in the face of newer groups who are making historical claims for legitimacy and identity. Historical research, in this instance, is now concerned with which is the "more real." Newer claims are devalued, and older claims are pushed into an ever more distant past, so that the date of origin of a class, a function, an institution, or an idea, constitute authenticity in the present. In its more vulgar sense, the art of heraldry, and the search for genealogy constitute basic pre-professional sources of historiography. And, as an institution, the local historical society institutionalizes a form of amateurism in history which, despite its origins, quite frequently preserves authentic sources, documents, publics, and interest for the benefit of more detached historiography. All of the above analysis may, in its emphasis on the sources of interest in history, oversimplify and vulgarize the process by which historical interest is determined.

In any time of crisis, of ambiguity, of challenge and threat to one's historic position, where institutional, economic, or political change threatens one's established notions of identity and of the ability of a group to take its existence for granted—that is, to have a natural attitude about itself—the historian as artist, using the techniques and methodologies, the awareness of time and of the possibilities of rational action, evaluates the past in terms of the critical decisions from which the present emerges, creates an image of the present which, if aesthetically satisfying, can provide closure to an ambiguous and threatening present. In this sense, history may be likened, like art, to a form of therapy. While using "scientific" techniques, it makes possible the return to a natural attitude of historical un-self-consciousness in eras when the decomposition of accepted realities has made a sense of alienation and estrangement from one's past a source of anxiety [7].

Perhaps a relatively simple illustration of this phenomenon can be seen in the treatment of the recent past, a past that frequently embraces the early youth of the historian or celebrates the childhood tales told to the historian and/or his audience by his parents and the adults he knew as a youth. Thus there is the attempt to recover the sense of innocence, romance, a time when life was infinitely simpler, when the complexities and troubles of the present were absent. When current problems, conflicts, and threatening groups were absent, and the problems that seemed threatening in the past are either resolved or replaced by other problems. Thus, the history of the Thirties, the Twenties, the Great Depression, America's entry into World War I, the romance of the late frontier, were celebrated in the recent past as in earlier times the Grand Army of the Republic, the frontier, and the old Confederacy had also been celebrated. The history of the past is always emergent, new histories must inevitably replace old histories. Whether or not such histories become attempts to institutionalize nostalgia, to create golden ages, and to escape the problems of the present, is a subject always for current conflict and debate among historians and their audiences. But again the reconstruction of history is an inevitable process of the operation of history. The forms such history may take, however, will reflect not only these external circumstances, but also what historians will do, both in their historiographic work and in their debates over the meanings of history and the meaning of their craft.

In still another sense, historical research and analysis can provide at its best the hope or the claim that the knowledge of history can provide a guide to the formulation of social policies which will enable a society to solve its present institutional problems and quandaries, and reach a stage where the anxieties, confusions, and malaise of the present will be solved by the application of scientific history to the solving of these problems [8].

To maintain this position, however, certain assumptions must be made with respect to the nature of those events which, when analyzed, constitute history. First of all, history must be viewed as repeatable, at least in some respects, and so subject to general laws which exist below the surface of mere events. These uniformities and generalities are considered discernible by the application of scientific historiographic methods [9]. Once the uniformities and generalizations are determined, their applications to a specific historical period can be assessed, and the appropriate policy derived. Such an ideology can, in a professional sense, become the occupational ideology of a historian, for if the claims made are true, then the historian must necessarily play an important role in the formulation of social policy, and is entitled to the rewards of his technological utility, and the social wisdom derived therefrom. But in a more serious sense, in periods in which faith in science and reason are pronounced, as in the period of the Enlightenment, or with respect to Marxism as allegedly scientific history, the faith that the historian as scientist can understand the laws of history leads enlightened, serious, and dedicated men to study the past, the decline of empires, and the growth in the past of models for the present, with a seriousness and an intensity which under other circumstances would be difficult to imagine. Thus, the *philosophes* of the Enlightenment and the rationalists of England and France studied in detail the decline of the Roman Republic and the later decline of the Roman Empire in order to draw lessons for constructing the new republics and for developing policies for these republics, and to develop justifications for destroying corrupt and degenerate monarchies. In the same sense, the Marxists studied the French Revolution, the revolutions of 1830, 1848, and later, the Commune, in order to draw lessons for revolution and the reconstruction of society. The optimistic belief in a scientific history still remains part of the faith in history, and much of this faith is part of the intellectual armory of the historian.

The sense in which the claim for scientific history is only a claim or an act of faith depends upon whether its assumptions can be validated; that is, the sense in which history is repeatable, subject to uniformities, generalizations, and law. While the claim is still being made in this age of disenchantment, there is a tendency to think of history and social life as not being subject to laws which transcend the phenomena of history itself. In other words, the very course of events alters the basic framework of subsequent events in such a way that the cumulative operation of history always introduces changes in the basic situation of history. While the past precedes the present, the past introduces a unique imprint on the present so that each historical situation is new. It is not derivable from general laws but only from the study of a unique past. If this is true, the study of history is at most a recording of man's existence on an infinite path into an unknown future. Such historical pessimism, in addition to its own meaning, denies the validity of history as either a claim to prophecy or to the guidance and formulation of social policy.

Whether or not there are laws of history that can be formulated in direct scientific form, and from which one can easily deduce policy, one can perhaps derive from the study of history a sense of the constraints which history places on the social planning of a given present. If history proves anything, it proves that the historical present carries with it into the future its problems and difficulties. But history also proves that history continuously emerges, that it is impossible to stay the flow of history, that no era, regime, or order remains fixed at a given point. History cannot be used as an image to deny all change, though those inclined to deny all change, or especially the changes they are opposed to, will use history as an essential ingredient in their ideology.

While history permits, we would think, neither position, it would suggest the limits and difficulties to be found in any absolute position. It denies the easy optimism suggested by those who could cut themselves off from the past in programmatic revolutions that are based on an *epoché* of history, or on the reification of history. What it suggests is that history is the cumulative progression of small changes which are in part the result of individual actions and in part the consequence of the blind effect of thousands of unrelated actions in the present. Thus, if history suggests anything, it might suggest a modification of delusions of grandeur, but not an attitude of total resignation. But it also suggests that the invocation of history as a legitimating device is a practice that must be done with some recognition of the difficulties that historians encounter when they attempt to describe even a simple event or set of events.

Another approach, exemplified by Lévi-Strauss' work on structural anthropology, is that of seeing the society at any given point in time as partial and fragmentary expression of a structural whole. The task of the cultural historian, anthropologist, or art historian is to reconstruct that historical world, cultural theme, or artistic manifestation, as if it were fully realized in its logical and conceptual unity, wholeness and realization. Having done so, one can organize and relate the partial and fragmentary aspects revealed in society, nature, and culture to their ultimate realization. Such a procedure would give unity to the fragmentary and contradictory nature of events. In historiography such an approach would result in the creation of analytical models of historical epochs in their essential and underlying characteristics. The development of such a model, if thought of as scientific, would result in analytical predictions within the framework of the abstract analytical model. Such predictions would be predictions of the order of events as they appear in a hierarchical sense. At a "nonscientific" level, such models would present the order of underlying themes in history to which it is possible to reduce the order of events in nature or in history.

The danger of such an approach is that it is imagistic. One can select from the whole world of knowledge, from sociology, psychology, anthropology, aesthetics, poetry, philosophy, and theology, an image that may be highly relevant in its own field, and tend to document the image by the use of the documents, events, and data of history. Since such data are infinite, they can document any image: the notion of a self-enclosed structure, status anxiety, consensual society, conflict society, the world as embodiment of one poetic theme, of art, of the attempt of men to comprehend themselves, etc. Thus any image or theme can be imported into history, and history will document all themes. What is more, the judicious selection of data can make any image seem all-encompassing, unifying, and integrating. As new images in related fields emerge, or as old images are refurbished, the data of history are salient and available. One can become creative and inventive simply by the application of new images and themes from other fields to the field of history. It is difficult to describe in principle the weaknesses of such an approach. In part one can discover whether such an approach is merely imagistic by assessing whether the historian simply grafts onto historical material a set of images because in doing do he does not work through the ideas contained (or suggested) in the image. He merely superimposes those ideas on the materials. The failure to grasp the theme, or if one wishes, the externality of the image, is evidenced by the fact that the image is often exhausted by the third chapter. Moreover, such imagery tends to lead the historian to neglect the detailed description of specific events, because such events are likely to conflict with or operate at cross purposes with the image being documented [10].

The pursuit of an image is likely to lead the historian to stress all elements that document the image, and neglect those elements which contradict it. The view of a society that emerges is one of greater unity, order, and integrity than could be derived from alternative models. It is at this point that imagistic theories can be tested, for the criterion of the adequacy of an image is its ability to absorb and exhaust relevant data which can be drawn from opposed or dissimilar models. The process then of a pluralistic presentation of many images by different historians tends to invalidate the exclusive use of any one image. Needless to say, some images may be more useful than others, and usefulness is based on the ability of an image to order and absorb greater amounts of material than others. Conversely, some imagistic histories require little refutation because they collapse under their own inability to order, absorb, or "give sense" to the materials they seek to order. In some cases such histories have the value of providing novelty or cleverness for short periods of time. These periods of novelty will often correspond to the period of currency of a particular image in the nonhistorical field from which the image emerges, and because of time lags necessary for the production even of novelties, may persist beyond the currency of the image [11].

Regardless of these impulses to historiography, the definition of the historical attitude can be derived not from its intentionality but rather from the very methods and procedures and habits of mind of the historian in the process of doing historical work. Historiography, as a serious and committed professional activity, develops in its practitioners characteristic attitudes toward work which in a deeper sense than its ideological impulses or intentional bases characterizes the work and attitude of the historian. The three hallmarks of the historical attitude are to be found in the attitudes towards the past, towards documentation, and to events.

THE ATTITUDE TOWARD THE PAST

The historian, especially as he begins to specialize in a country, an age, a century, or even a decade, begins to develop a sense as well as a knowledge of the milieu, the culture, the personalities, the institutions, laws, and events of the period he specializes in. All of these, the culture of the period, develop a detail, a richness, density, texture, sharpness, and imagery which make the period come alive for him. And as he immerses himself in the ambience of the period, it develops a reality, a vividness, and an immediacy that may be even more immediate than the present. He may know the personalities of that era through an accumulation of biographic detail, letters, documents, biographies, as well as he knows his personal acquaintances.

The historian prides himself on dealing with changes in the titles and names of historic personages, of being able both to coordinate exactly the appropriate name with the age and stage in the career of the personage, and to designate the wrong name for the age of the personage as both a methodological and sociological *faux pas*. Since the historian's time and energy are limited, his preoccupation with the culture of an age can frequently become an exclusive and all-demanding activity. As the richness and detail of imagery surrounding one's knowledge has all the immanence of the present, it is possible for the dedicated historian, by neglect of the actual present, to have an impoverished, barren, and stereotyped notion of the actual present [12]. There is some charm in discovering the specialist in twelfth-century Provence whose knowledge of the era is so great and so immediate, so "present" to him, that he is comfortable only within the framework of that century and that area, and who has the additional charm of total innocence in dealing with the present, whenever the present intrudes itself into his awareness. The present may be a source of surprise and wonder for him. In some instances, the quest for a past era in its total, encompassing nature, can be understood as an escape from the vulgarity, the materialism, the stress, and the anxiety, of the present. And past eras can be selected because they are allegedly more poetic, more virtuous, more heroic, more romantic than the immediate existence. This, however, is a problem for history only when the quest for these alleged virtues of the past forces the historian to neglect the unseemly aspects of the past. Such problems can be dealt with at the level of historiography, in which, as we have pointed out, the dialectics of historiography result in the continuous attempt to correct previous distortions of the past, perhaps by the introduction of new distortions [13].

At its best, however, the historian's attitude toward the past can result in his ability to communicate the past in its own terms. In this sense, historiography results in emphasizing the discontinuities of history, by allowing other historical periods to communicate themselves directly in their own terms [14].

The historical work thus serves as a communication between past and present in the same sense that the art object serves as a communication between the world of the artist and the world of the audience, and the historian, in making such communication possible, serves as a performing artist, either realizing or improving upon the "score" provided by the documents of history. The historian, to be sure, because of this tendency to become immersed in the past, may lose the present in his pursuit of the past, and so become unable to communicate to the present.

Historiography, then, as a communications art, requires a double-double consciousness, for both the past and the present; the ideal historian must know the symbolic level at which communication is possible. But in mediating between periods, he must place distance between himself and each period, so that he can translate the imagery of each period into the other without becoming a creature of that imagery. If he does, the imagery of either the past or the present becomes opaque. If he does not, he is more than a historian, he becomes an artist.

THE HISTORIAN'S ATTITUDE TOWARDS DOCUMENTS
AND DOCUMENTATION

A major claim for historiography as a science, or at least as a profession, rests on the attitude of the historian towards documents and documentation. For the historian, as a professionally trained and dedicated methodologist, the concern with accuracy in documentation represents his unique methodological characteristic and advantage. The historian, in dealing with the past, has some advantage over the social scientist who deals with the present, because he is dealing with a universe that is hypothetically closed. It is closed in the sense that the events of history have already occurred, and the task is only that of description. It is open, however, in the sense that both the documents and the perspectives from which events can be described can never be closed. New documents, new "artifacts" (in the archaeological sense of the word) are always possible. New methods of interpreting old data continuously emerge. Scientific discoveries, such as carbon dating, enable the historian of the earliest periods to reassess works of history. As historians themselves become the object of historiography, the methods by which documents are interpreted become subject to criticism, revision, and reinterpretation, so that the final answers of one period become the provisional or even the refuted answers of another. The use of totally new techniques, such as aerial photography or archaeological investigation in the study of relatively recent history, enables the reinterpretation of events beyond those based on purely written documentation. The degree of technical specialization in historiography, in philology, in the analysis and collation of sources, reaches such a point of technical specialization that concern for accuracy, detail, and evidence is primary. Awareness of the possibilities of overenthusiastic acceptance of evidence and documentation, followed by rejection of the interpretation as based on error, lack of judgment, gullibility, or self-deception, is sufficiently present so that most historians, as a matter of course, develop habits of skepticism, of critical ability, and a hardnosed respect for both the difficulties of conclusively establishing a point, and respect for facts if and when such facts emerge above and beyond the shadows produced by an intensely critical attitude. In this respect, then, historians are "professionals." They are unlikely to be taken in by easy generalization, shallow speculation, or poetic license. If history is a science, its claim to science can best be made on the rigor of its method and on the criticism and evaluation of facts. But the word "science" is an ambiguous term. Another term used to describe an academic field is "discipline," and in the sense that historians respond to the problem of documentation, verification, and evaluation, their work can more exactly be described as a discipline.

The idea of discipline in habits of work can be and is related to fields which are not sciences.

THE ATTITUDE TOWARD EVENTS

The description of past events within a framework that is meaningful within the past, by means of documentation that requires rigor and discipline, represents the unique contribution of historiography as a disciplined profession.

Some historians will devote their lives to universal or world history, in which the time period or territorial subdivision that serve as the universe for historiography is so broad that the act of writing and of research becomes one of synthesis. This is not to say that such work is not of value, for, in making broad comparisons between vast eras and areas, some generalizations may emerge that are not possible from a more narrowly focused approach. At the same time, other historians will use as their universe a single day, such that vast and complex portraits of events will be focused in terms of the events that occur on that day. Other historians will use a single event, the disputed election of 1876, or the Kennedy campaign of 1960, or "The Guns of August"; others will focus on a decade, a century, or perhaps a "year of decision," or an era between two events, the events themselves being regarded as transitional points during which trends in history take different direction. Since history is continuous even in its discontinuities, the bounding of any event or period by a label, a category, or a historical or artistic convention, is in some sense arbitrary, a product of the historian rather than of history itself [15]. Each philosophical, religious, and methodological innovation in history calls to the attention of the historian a new world of "facts" which become salient and available to historical research, by virtue of their relevance to the new ideas. Thus every reinterpretation or idea in history expands the world of data available to the historian. Since we are aware of no principle which *sui generis* limits the number of ideas that can be applied to an event, a period, or a place, there is no limit to the data that are potentially available. There are, of course, limits placed on interpretation by the fact that since history deals with data and documentation which has usually been collected for some restricted purposes, and which have been discarded, sometimes permanently, for other purposes, the data that may document any particular idea may not be accessible or available.

Conversely, with the development of historical craftsmanship, and the treasuring of data qua data, the discovery of the availability of documents, a collection of records, a series of diaries, or commercial records, may evoke new ideas, theories, or reinterpretations of existing ideas, simply because the documents exist as an object for historiographic craftsmanship.

One means by which the problems caused by the lack of "natural" units for historiographic work, and the infinity of perspectives are handled is the increase in specialization as the total range of materials that history can deal with expands; a specialized division of academic or professionalized historiography emerges. Thus, the professional historian can specialize in narrower and narrower periods of time, which in turn becomes, within a particular framework of academic and technical specialization, the total relevant universe of a branch of history. In addition, the cutting points of historiography can be specialized by subject matter, as, for example, intellectual history, art history, legal, political, musical history, the history of science and technology, all serving to allow the historian to narrow his focus to a very limited spectrum of data within the infinity of events that make up the totality of general history. Thus, the senselessness of an infinity of historical data can be obscured by specialization. Beyond this, the "cutting points" of the data of history—the definition of eras—the density of documentation, the levels of data which one considers appropriate for analysis—biographical, demographic, economic, military, historical, artistic, legal, social, biological or medical, linguistic, and so on—are all available as potential dimensions of treatment. Given the concern for accuracy of documentation, along with the multidimensionality of possible cutting points for the study of history, it is easy to ascertain that the study of history for a single event or even a single year, let alone an age can be endless. The injunction of the historian to treat each event as it actually occurred could make of historiography the infinite accumulation of facts, such that the totality of facts would be indigestible and incomprehensible. Under such conditions, historiography would be incapable of making sense of history. The lack of order would be a product of the infinite dimensions of orders with which history can be treated. Scientific historians of the nineteenth century such as Ranke attempted to exhaust history; they succeeded only in exhausting themselves and their readers.

For all of the above reasons, history as a discipline or as a science does not produce an inevitable set of units within which the historiographic enterprise can be conducted. Beyond this, historiographic methods by themselves produce no limits by which the inundation of the world in total documentation and description can be overcome. The problem of historiography then becomes that of developing a set of units within which to conduct historical work. Historians have managed to solve the problem without too much difficulty, though in doing so they have opened themselves to criticism on grounds of violation of the principles of historiographical purity. The solution that in fact becomes the operative principle of historiography within which the narrower and more accurate methods are used is that of the use of *ideas* in history [16]. The ideas, however, are ideas which are not immanent in the process of historical research, but are ideas which may emerge from philosophical speculation, literature, poetry, or commitment to values, ideologies, or to religions of a sacred or secular variety, which once posed become the cutting points for the entry into the process of research, and which serve as limits to the data which are relevant to the questions evoked by the ideas directing the process of historiography [17]. To the extent that these external ideas operate from outside history or historiography itself, then, for the historian they must be regarded as givens or as a priori. The historian, in selecting one set of givens or another, makes his decision on grounds which, from the standpoint of the materials themselves, are "arbitrary." They are subject to the same criticism of a dependence on either the "absolute" or on the a priori that has been made of all philosophic thought since Descartes or Hume. The leap to philosophy may be a rejection of history as the mere accumulation of detail, but the leap to philosophy places the historian in the same bind that the philosopher has found himself since Descartes. But even when the historian does make this philosophic leap, we repeat, he subjects himself to the constraints of facts, in order to justify that leap. Once such ideas serve as cutting points, as definers of units and limits of methodological work, the historian can proceed in a professional and technical manner, in terms of his preoccupation with the spirit of the age, accuracy of documentation, and completeness of coverage of the relevant data. However, since the historian operates within the framework of a restrictive organizing idea ("restrictive" is not here used in a pejorative sense), he does not deal with the totality of events, perspectives, data or units, that are possible [18]. The sense of restriction occurs at the onset of the statement of the historical problem, but once having made his restrictive convention, he strives for total accuracy and completeness, which are as much his habit of mind as they are his conscious methodology. The historian, in attempting to achieve completeness within the framework of a finite set of ideas or problems, can of course exhaust all the potentialities of the statement of a problem, but he does not exhaust history. When the possibilities inherent in any world view are exhausted by the technical work subsumed under its operation, history as an autonomous activity or rather the sense of craftsmanship of the historian will force him to alter his statement of the problem, his organizing principle, so that other aspects of the infinity of history become available to him. In the same sense, the fact that the organizing principles within which disciplined historical work takes place are themselves originated by ideas and values outside the sphere of technical history, and are, from that point of view, arbitrary, permits several historians to work on the one historical era, problem, or event from their own individual perspectives. Historiography then becomes a battleground among historians over philosophic, intellectual and ideological perspectives which are themselves not intrinsic to historical method. The battlegrounds are less a question of the accuracy of various statements of historical fact, since most historians are technically capable, but of the relevance or salience of different sets of historical facts. The relevance and salience are not functions of historiography per se, but of the philosophic perspectives which are outside the framework of technical historiography.

HISTORY AS CRAFT, IDEOLOGY, OR PHILOSOPHY

From much of what we have stated, it appears that at the heart of historiography are some fundamental dilemmas. The constant search for accuracy in recording and describing events creates the possibility of assembling an almost infinite amount of materials of such complexity and volume as to overwhelm all but the professional specialist. The specialist can escape this threat only by narrowing and subdividing his field of specialization to where he covers only slivers of time or of events. But since his goal remains that of purely technical competence and specialization, his reasons for selecting a particular sliver of time, a particular event, or structural specialty are increasingly on an ad hoc basis. As a consequence of all this, history loses any meaning in the sheer accumulation of data and in the arbitrary fragmentation of specialization. This leads to the problem of recovering the sense of the unity of history, a problem which can be solved at several levels.

One of the most obvious methods is that of allowing the reassembly of historical unity to be left to the journalist, or the popularizer. The latter, in order to achieve the dramatic values that are possible in any recording of human activities, will personify, dramatize, and stress the spectacular and the unexpected, and so seek to violate the expectancies of everyday life. In this latter respect, he will take the norms of prevalent public opinion or historiographic assumptions and attempt to invert them in order to introduce the idea of novelty, excitement, and "news" in the writing of history [19].

Another solution is that of the textbook writer, who, as a conventional historian, will attempt simply to "boil down" and compress the almost infinite work of the historiographic researchers; if he stays within the framework of the technical virtuosity of the professional, he will introduce no ideas into the writing of history, he simply compresses, orders, and balances the universe of monographs. Such history usually has the professional virtue of being competent, dull, and empty. If there are distortions, they are the distortions that come from a lack of ideas rather than from their presence.

In attempting to deal self-consciously with the problem of the overabundance of facts and the infinite expansion of history because of this overabundance, historians have attempted at a level that is far more serious than textbook writing, quite self-consciously to write in terms of larger units of time and place. Thus, world history, or histories of civilization, or what used to be called universal history, have come into vogue. Such history, whether serious or journalistic, makes history more meaningful, but to the extent that it does so, relies more and more on the primary research done by others and on organizing principles, usually philosophic, that are increasingly removed from the primary investigation which must be considered as basic to the craft of historiography. In doing so, it necessarily becomes more and more philosophical and less and less "historical."

To escape from this horn of the dilemma, still another solution may be attempted, that of exploring history from the vantage point of a specific idea, theme, principle, philosophical position, or set of values. In fact, the prehistory of historiography involved the application of historical methods, theological, philosophic, humanistic, and nationalistic ideas, among others, to the specific research and writing of history. Technical historiography, then, operated within a framework of philosophic and value assumptions that were outside the methodology and technique of history itself. Thus, to overcome the vastness of historical materials, and the problems of over-specialization, the quest for ideas could become a search aimed at compensating for the deficiencies of pure craftsmanship. Philosophies, thematic inquiries, heuristic theories, all became the basis for new histories, each new history being new for a while. But each new history became the basis for intense research and accumulation of data which, in its accumulation, lost its capacity to stimulate and provoke.

THE HISTORICAL REDUCTION

The attempt to substitute for causal, structural, ideological, or other forms of analysis, a description of historical sequencing, can be called the historical reduction. This means that the sequence of events in almost infinite detail, treated strictly chronologically, becomes a substitute for all other forms of thought and analysis. Since, as we and many others have argued, there is no beginning or end to such sequencing, the process is infinite. When a beginning and an end are assumed, the process is arbitrary. At the same time, the events, as well as the documents which are considered in the sequencing process, are selected out of an infinite pool of events, documents, and other data, the criteria for selection are not given by the process of sequencing itself. The process of selection is given by the sense of a problem, Weber's "value-relevance," that is, theoretical considerations that are outside of the sequencing itself but which determine it, or by ideological considerations, or by the unconscious acceptance of taken-for-granted theories of the investigator. In other words, the attitude of everyday life of his occupation at a given time.

In addition to this, the succession of ideas, themes, and philosophies in history has resulted in a new industry, the history and criticism of history and of historical thought, of which this essay is, possibly, an example. Moreover, as new histories developed, they began to attract proponents, opponents, publicists and counterpublicists. Thus, the fragmentation of historical theories became a subfield within history [20]. Furthermore, historical concepts are introduced at uneven rates, and have uneven durations, while older concepts retain or regain currency. New specialties emerge while old ones continue. Thus, history speaks with thousands of voices, so that while no voice is wholly lost, none is fully heard. In this sense, history is no different from all other fields of intellectual or artistic creation.

As historical criticism continues, a major discovery is made, that all history contains and embodies value assumptions, biases, and beliefs. Even the purely professional technician of history who attempts to avoid value judgments takes the given world as the only possible world. The specialist, by the very act of specializing, has made a judgment of the relative value of the importance of his choice. The fact that he is unaware of the basis of his choice, and that it may be due to the accidents of his professional training, or to his estimations of professional opportunities, does not mean that he is not making value judgments. Perhaps value judgments that are not consciously made are the most biased, as the judgment-maker is unable to control his bias.

But if we learn that value judgments are implicit in the process of historical research and writing, we may tend to devalue the history of the past, and increasingly to write new histories which are increasingly value-oriented, ideologically committed, and aimed at producing specific societal changes in order to produce specific ideological or value-oriented goals. When this is explicitly done, the great temptation is that of consciously neglecting some facts while stressing others. Another temptation is that of stressing ideological purity as a major criterion in evaluating history and historians, and if this occurs, then history as a craft disintegrates, to be replaced by the warring camps of sloppy, propagandizing ideologues.

The dilemmas and contradictions indicated above are inherent in the framework of historical work, as they are inherent in all intellectual, artistic, and cultural work. There is, we think, no easy solution. Each historian facing his work must face and resolve these problems anew, both in terms of the development of his field at a given time, and in terms of his personal values and goals. The great danger, to repeat, is that of ignoring the problems, or of seeking a false or facile resolution of the problems, and in some act of righteousness or of "total" commitment, proceeding as if the problems do not exist. Intellectual honesty involves recognition of the difficulties and dilemmas within one's field, and intellectual honesty is the one element which cannot be sacrificed if there is to be a craft, as well as an art, of history.

NOTES

1. E. H. Carr, *What Is History* (New York, Random House, 1961), pp. 9, 24: "It used to be said that facts speak for themselves. This is, of course, untrue. The facts speak only when the historian calls on them: it is he who decides which facts to give the floor, and in what order, or context . . . the facts of history never to us 'pure'. . . . they are always refracted through the mind of the recorder." G. M. Trevelyan, "Clio Rediscovered," in Fritz Stern (Ed.), *The Varieties of History* (New York, World, 1956), pp. 230, 239: "Ought it not to be not merely the accumulation and interpretation of facts, but also the exposition of facts and opinions in their *full emotional and intellectual* value to a wide public by the difficult art of literature? . . . I use the word literature because I wish to lay greater stress than modern historians are willing to do, both on the difficulty and also on the importance of planning and writing a powerful narrative of historical events." These views approach that of the authors; others of course conceive of history differently, claiming scientific status for it. For another view, see John Lukacs, *Historical Consciousness or the Remembered Past* (New York, Harper & Row, 1968), pp. 5–6: "I believe that the most important developments in our civilization during the last three or four centuries include not only the applications of the scientific method but also the growth of a historical consciousness; and that while we may have exaggerated the importance of the former we have not yet understood sufficiently the implications of the latter . . . history, for us, has become a form of thought. . . . We can describe and, consequently, understand a person, a nation, any kind of human society, virtually any kind of human endeavor, not only through their material or spiritual, their physical or psychic characteristics but through their history. . . . There is no field of human action that may not be approached, studied, described, and understood through its history."

2. These interpretations are to be found among such historians as Frederick Jackson Turner, Charles A. Beard, Carl Becker, and Vernon Parrington. See David W. Noble, *Historians Against History* (Minneapolis, University of Minnesota Press, 1965). Examples of a similar nature, demonstrating a multiplicity of interpretations of other historical events, are discussed in Herbert Butterfield, *Man on His Past* (Boston, Beacon, 1960), pp. 173ff.

3. Noble, *op. cit.*, pp. 80, 170.

4. J. H. Hexter, in *Reappraisals in History* (New York, Harper & Row, 1961), presents a survey of such multiple views.

5. Jan Huizinga, "Historical Conceptualization," in Stern, *op. cit.*, pp. 290ff., also approaches this view in slightly different language.

6. See J. Anderson, "Styron and His Black Critics," in *Dissent* (March–April 1959), pp. 157–166; also John Henrik Clarks (Ed.), *William Styron's Nat Turner: Ten Black Writers Respond* (Boston, Beacon, 1968); also Henry Pachter, "Teaching Negro History," *Dissent* (March–April 1959), pp. 151–156.

7. J. H. Plumb, *The Death of the Past* (Boston, Houghton Mifflin 1970), pp. 76–77.

8.   E. H. Carr, *op. cit.*, pp. 87ff.
9.   See discussions by Maurice Mandelbaum, *The Problem of Historical Knowl-edge* (New York, Harper & Row, 1967), Chaps. 7, 8; also Friedrich Meinecke, "Values and Causation in History," in Fritz Stern (Ed.), *op. cit.*, pp. 267ff. Also valuable is L. R. Perry, "The Covering Law Theory of Historical Explanation," in W. H. Burston and D. Thompson (Eds.), *Studies in the Nature and Teaching of History* (London, Rouledge and Kegan Paul, 1967), pp. 27ff. Especially valuable is John Lukacs, *Historical Consciousness, Or the Remembered Past* (New York, Harper & Row, 1968), Chap. IV. "Thinking about Causes, or the Structure of Events."
10.   See Robert Stover, *The Nature of Historical Thinking* (Chapel Hill, University of North Carolina Press, 1967), pp. 59ff.
11.   Some examples are violence as a central theme in history; the central value approach; structural-functionalism; urban history; melting pot history; black frontier history; cold war "revisionism," etc.
12.   This of course is a risk undergone by scholars in fields other than history.
13.   Cf. Hexter, *op. cit.*, Chap. 6, "Storm over the Gentry."
14.   Cf. Jan Huizinga, "The Task of Cultural History," in *Men and Ideas* (New York, World, 1959), p. 54: "One does not realize the historical sensation as a re-experiencing, but as an understanding of music, or rather of the world by means of music. Re-experiencing as a method of cognition assumes a more or less continuous perception constantly accompanying the labor of reading and thinking. In reality this sensation, vision, contact, *Ahnung*, is limited to moments of special intellectual clarity, moments of a sudden penetration of the spirit.
"This historical sensation is apparently so essential that it is felt again and again as the true moment of historical cognition. . . . The most modest historical research, that of the genealogist and the students of heraldry, that of the local dilettante, can be exalted and ennobled by this intellectual preoccupation. Their work has its own full-fledged goal if the scholar or the reader experiences that sensation from it."
15.   *Ibid.*, p. 67: "The division of history into periods, however, indispensable it may be, is of secondary importance, always vague and imprecise, and always to some extent arbitrary. Colorless names derived from external and chance breaks in history are the most preferable designations for periods."
16.   J. H. Plumb, "The Historian's Dilemma," in J. H. Plumb (Ed.), *Crisis in the Humanities* (Baltimore, Penguin, 1964), pp. 34ff: "All are equally guilty of wilfully rejecting the one certain judgment of value that can be made about history, and that is the *idea of progress.* If this great human truth were once more to be accepted, the reasons for it, and the consequences of it, consistently and imaginatively explored and taught, history would not only be an infinitely richer education, but also play a much more effective part in the culture of western society."
17.   J. H. Plumb, *The Death of the Past* (Boston, Houghton Mifflin, 1970), pp. 138ff.
18.   Max Weber, " 'Objectivity' in Social Science," in *The Methodology of the Social Sciences*, translated and edited by Edward A. Shils and Henry A. Finch (New York, Free Press, 1949), p. 82: ". . . the naive self-deception of the specialist who is unaware that it is due to the evaluative ideas with which he unconsciously approaches his subject-matter, that he has selected from an absolute infinity a tiny portion with the study of which he *concerns* himself."
19.   See Chap. 14.
20.   Butterfield, *op. cit.*, p. 161: ". . . there is a model specimen of the anomaly in the *Cambridge Modern History* where the subject of the origins of the Seven Years

War was divided between four authors, evidently not on speaking terms with one another, and even at variance in respect of the greatest of the controversies in the 1890's—the Russian section of the narrative standing entirely on its own. What you have in such cases are two separate stories impaled and transfixed, and a trained historian could not marry the Russian story with the European one because what are omitted are just the things which provide the dovetailing and the joints between them."

Chapter 8

The Economist

Economics has been called the dismal science [1], primarily because in the nineteenth century, economics was used to justify the lowest possible wages, the employment of children and women, starvation, and so on. The iron law of wages held that the impersonal, remorseless operation of the free market forced wages, through free competition, down to a level barely adequate to avoid starvation [2]. It was "dismal" in another sense, in that the liberal economists of the nineteenth century argued that such was the best of all possible economic worlds, and that governments should do nothing to alleviate these conditions. Economics could also be called "dismal," though other adjectives have been applied, because it reduced all other phenomena to prices, wages, costs, and material elements. It stressed cold, rational, impersonal calculation at the expense of the warm, human, emotional, poetic, cultural, and artistic faculties of men. And even when it dealt with such phenomena, it reduced them to elements that could be understood in terms of economic factors. In a sense, economists have accepted this criticism insofar as they have claimed that economics is a science. If economics is a science, then the dominance of objective, calculable, rational, impersonal factors are the virtues of economic calculus.

IDEOLOGICAL BASES FOR ECONOMICS

As we go back into the history of economics, it becomes increasingly clear that at each stage in the development of economic science, the policies that sprang from the operation of economists were moral in character, ideological, committed to one or another party in political and economic struggles, and that those moralities, ideologies, and values were part of the initial assumptions on which their economic calculus was based. Thus, Adam

Smith's *The Wealth of Nations* was a political document aimed at the liberation of the bourgeoisie from mercantilism, the power of the crown, and the favoritism of the court and the nation. The technical demonstration of the ideology was the attempt to prove that, on purely economic grounds, a laissez-faire system would be more productive of the wealth of nations than the structural inefficiencies that were part and parcel of mercantilism. In the first half of the nineteenth century, when economic liberalism had been implemented as a social policy, the same types of economic calculus by such men as Ricardo and Nassau Senior were used to justify policies that were to lead to the most intensive exploitation of workers yet experienced [3]. For the justification, necessity, especially scientific necessity, was invoked. The economic system had properties that were intrinsic to it, and the full operation of the system justified, on systematic grounds, this exploitation of labor. It was science—natural economic law—which made legitimate what seemed inhuman in previous cultures and generations. It is again from the hindsight of history, though at the time there were opponents to this version of natural law, that the conditions under which the new economic policy was to operate did not actually exist, and, what is more, had never existed, and it was therefore "unnatural." Thus, it was presumed that businessmen were rational, and calculated rationally, that hedonism, the avoidance of pain and the maximization of pleasure, was the primary motivating force in society, that the market was to be so free that no single producer was large enough to affect the market, that totally free competition could and would exist, and that the substitution of factors of production was instantaneously available in response to profit opportunities between various industries and segments of industries. It is obvious that none of these conditions existed before the adoption of laissez-faire as either a philosophy or a policy, and moreover that they did not exist after the policy was adopted, or existed only in partial form. At most, then, it can be said that the presuppositions of economic liberalism were an abstraction, and the science of economics, as it emerged in England, was based on treating an abstraction or ideal as if it were a reality, deriving policies from that abstraction and applying them to an historical reality to which it did not in fact apply, or applied imperfectly. The effect, however, was to give the doctrine an objectivity, and legitimacy that it could not gain if it were presented as an ideology [4]. In the same sense, in France, the Physiocrats, speaking for a different class, and for different social policies had earlier created the beginnings of an economics which was based on entirely different grounds. Here, the conception was that land was the basis of all wealth and the monopolization and the misuse of land by a restricted class resulted in the impoverishment of a nation, that freedom and rights of accession to land would be an instrument for the maximization of the wealth of nations, that it would also result in the decline of the feudal class. Its replacement by a land-owning middle class of smallholders and farmers was simply a by-product of the character of the scientific analysis [5].

The attraction of science, of course, has appeal in and of itself. The appeal has been to the rational, educated intellectual, at a time when the physical sciences were beginning to have glamor, drama, and the promise of freeing the world from ignorance, superstition, poverty, and social and political abuses. Science, to the ideologists of an ascendant liberal middle class, provided an optimistic view of the future, in which all of the diseases of the past—of feudalism, and the dark ages—could be eradicated. In this sense, the idea of the intellectual philosopher-king, now a positive scientist, who could remove himself from the "bad" history of the past and create, in the sphere of economics, an economic order which would run solely by scientific principles, became a major basis for economic thinking [6]. August Comte, borrowing from Saint-Simon, used the same ideas to justify planning by sociologists (see Chapter 9). The methodology of science, as applied to economics, would become the dominant institution of the society, and of course all other institutions would have to give way. Thus, it would appear that not only the institutions, but the values of all other groups in the society would have to change and be replaced by the new values of science in the service of the nation. The nation, as the unit within which planning would take place, would necessarily be elevated, and those of the separate estates would have to be subordinated, a subordination which had not yet appeared in the eighteenth century. For Saint-Simon, the means by which this was to occur was not clearly specified, except that the superiority of science and the visibility of that superiority would, through persuasion and demonstration, provide the basis for the policies [7].

The appeal of science was not confined to ideologists of the bourgeoisie or of the intellectual classes, but was extended to ideologists speaking in the name of the "proletariat." Thus, Marx defended his version of Utopia on the basis of science. He too discovered a natural law that materialism transcended the extant ideas of history. He would as a scientist apply that new natural law over the resistance of all those who were dominant despite the operation of natural law. To be sure, he argued, the direction of the operation of the system would bring forth the conditions which would dramatize the violation of "natural law." The contradictions in the system, the concentration of capital, the impoverishment of the masses, the increasing misery and the generation of new masses by that system would bring forth the doom of the system. But natural law could not be counted on, in part because the populaces subject to natural law could not understand it. They were brainwashed and given to false consciousness, and thus the system could exist despite its own "unnaturalness," unless Marx, the scientist, the philosopher-king, showed the victims not only how the system worked, but organized, propagandized, and agitated against the system [8].

And yet Marx in his own writings demonstrated at other levels the moral, the ideological, and the philosophic—the existence of values which are independent of and which precede the scientific basis of his mode of analysis. These values and ideologies are, in their own terms, highly admirable. They include the emphasis on man as a total, integrated, bundle of capacities who ought to develop an even, balanced maximization of his potentialities. He objected to the exploitation of man by man, the separation of men from each other. He advocated the sharing between men of warm emotional communitarian values, so that while each man could be complete, richly endowed and independent, yet he could enjoy all of the graces of an unalienated social existence. It is not that we argue with these values, but only that those values were the preconditions of his economic science. And Marx, because he was an outsider, a spokesman for outsiders, an ideologist and propagandist of revolution, had to make his ideological presuppositions clearer than the laissez-faire economists he opposed but from whom he drew substantial parts of his technological, scientific apparatus.

Marx, then, can be understood both as a scientist and as a prophet [9]. Marxism represents one critique among many others of the liberal economics, and each critique was based as much on the value assumptions and preconceptions, ultimate goals, and images of the past, present, and desired realities as much as it was based on differences in the technical and "scientific" analysis. Thus, liberal economists and economics have had to face both the moral criticism of both revolutionary and reactionary ideologies, and the criticism that its assumptions have no relation to historical realities. This latter criticism has been one of the major rationalizing forces within the mainstream of academic economics. It is true, however, that even at the present, some economists such as Milton Friedman and Frank Knight attempt to maintain the initial assumptions of classical liberalism, especially the notion of the perfect market as a basis of their thought [10]. In order to maintain the reality of their assumptions, it is necessary to advocate changes in the institutional frameworks of economic institutions so that their assumptions can become operative. Others simply have ignored the historical reality.

The history of nineteenth-century economic thought going well into the twentieth century is a triumph in the development of the technical and methodological refinement and perfection of methods of analysis which were virtually outmoded at the beginning of that process of analysis. Alfred Marshall's thought is the perfect example of a highly sophisticated, highly developed system of thought that despite its development, has little relationship to any reality except that of the tradition in which it was developed [11].

Other economists, working within the framework of the classical tradition, or basing their work upon that tradition, attempted to modify the tradition to bring it into line with emerging realities or the emerging consciousness of the discrepancy between the tradition and existing realities. Thus, thinkers like Chamberlin, with his economics of imperfect competition, Keynes and his disciples, who emphasized macroeconomics and the concept of the total income flow within an economic system, modified and to some extent changed the assumptions of classical economics so that at times the older basis of the new work was virtually unrecognizable [12]. Yet in all of these innovations, the moral and ideological foundations of the new as well as the old economics are transparent. Thus, within the framework of Keynesian economics, it is possible to be a left-wing Keynesian, committed to economic planning, social welfare and reform, or a right-wing Keynesian, whose policy of stimulating productivity within an economic system tends to emphasize monetary and fiscal manipulation rather than economic planning, and economic advantages that accrue to totally different groups [13]. The methodological contribution of Keynes thus permits a wide variety of ideological and political positions. Conversely, those with a wide variety of political and economic positions can find in Keynes a means of justifying and implementing their own positions, and thus the methodology is not decisive in the determination of social policy. What appears to be decisive is the selection of particular economists and schools of thought by noneconomic policy-makers in order to justify and extend political and ideological policies based on noneconomic grounds.

METHODOLOGICAL BASES FOR ECONOMIC SCIENCE

Quesnay, Turgot and Quetelet developed the basis for vast fields of descriptive statistics, of economic surveys, of methods of economic measurement, which are as yet unexhausted. The development of economic censuses, of government reporting, measures of income flow, of bank credit operations, housing construction starts, inventory flows, utilization of labor, carloadings, employment and unemployment statistics, and the construction of complex economic indicators has reached vast proportions, so that today knowledge of what statistics are available in a given field represents one of the great assets of a professional economist. Knowledge of the means of processing such statistics becomes a highly technical skill which takes years to acquire, subject to continuous refinement as new techniques become available. Thus, the preparation of data for the computer, the development of mathematical and statistical procedures in terms of the computer becomes a science in itself, and being able to interpret the results of computer printouts is no mean skill. Linear programming, operations research, Monte Carlo methods, statistical analysis, Boolean algebra, and forms of matrix construction as related to statistical operations become the basis of subspecializations. Beyond this, it requires considerable skill to assess the means by which data is initially measured in order to estimate the error, duplication, and "artifactuality" of the statistics so derived. It requires, for instance, considerable knowledge to know when an estimate is an estimate, especially when the form of the estimate has the "factuality" or concreteness of a number [14].

MATHEMATICAL ANALYSIS IN ECONOMICS

Statistical economics can be subdivided into two basic types. The first type, pure empiricism, rests on the assumption that the techniques and procedures yield valuable information. Such information is of use to government agencies, local and regional planners, banks, business firms, trade unions, and other public and private institutions. Because such data collection and analysis lacks a theory, and appears to be purely descriptive, it takes on the character of being "value-free." However, since such methods are justified by their usefulness, and the demand for the measures so derived comes from the decision-makers of the institutions, the values which both evoke the measure and which determine their use are the values of the decision-makers. Thus, in economics as in all sciences, technically neutral work is not value-free work. The economist's commitment to values is a commitment to values other than those of the scientist [15]. For instance, one could construct a series of measurements which would indicate how slowly a worker can work and still look like he is working. One could do this with the same objectivity and precision as one would use to define maximal effort; but so far as we know such measurements have not been called for, even by trade unions. They have not been called for because the measurements are not based on the value assumptions that usually govern decision-making in economics. The scientist in developing measures thus accepts the values of others as a condition for being able to do the technical work he desires to do. This can be stated as: the decision to accept or reject a value-commitment is based upon the decision as to whom one will work for.

The second major type of statistical economics involves the use of explicit higher-power models. A model is a generalized abstract and formal statement of the economic or social system within which the presumed measurements are supposed to apply. It is a synthetic statement of a hypothetical universe. The description of the conditions under which statistical procedures hold is not an empirical description of an institution or a firm or of an income-disposing or income-distributing system. Rather the generalized properties of such a system are abstracted, formalized, and treated as if they were a universe for further work. In some cases this synthetic description is presented in mathematical or statistical terms. There is no special need for the synthetic system to resemble any empirical reality, since the model can be assumed as a given. Once, however, the givenness is assumed, the statistical and logical procedures can be performed on the basis of consistency with initial assumptions. The only danger is that solutions to problems as derived from the model may be applied to realities which are based on different empirical assumptions. In one sense, this problem is always present since the empirical or historical realities are never logically closed. That is, each empirical or historical factor is connected in almost uncountable ways to other factors which in turn can effect the given specified factors. Thus the fate of much work done within the framework of statistical models is undone by the fact that "unanticipated factors" external to the model impinge upon the reality under consideration and alter the hypothetical relationship between the prediction and the outcome. Thus, while all statistical work and mathematical calculations can be done flawlessly, the model becomes inappropriate simply because emerging realities continuously upset the assumptions of the model. In this sense, "history" always intrudes upon the formal, logical "abstractions" from history, and willy-nilly makes all abstract models into "historical" models. They become "historical" when decisions and policies about the "real" world are made even when those decisions are derived from purely hypothetical models. This is to say, the continuously superseded models of the past record the attempt of positivistic theoreticians to escape from the particularities of given historical eras, and it is in this sense that scientific, model-based statistical inquiries are no different from the models used in pure mathematical or analytical economic theory. The assumptions of any given model reflect in the same way the needs of a time or of an age and the values implicit in the particular agents of a time and age and a social structure.

Some of the more sophisticated models reflecting these developments include cost-efficiency models and input-output analysis, reflecting the needs of government planners to anticipate the secondary costs and re-source-displacements caused by any particular budgetary or spending program. Operations research, linear programming, and some forms of econometric analysis are all models of this order. Such models go beyond a simple application of a particular technique, and beyond the mere collection of data and provision of information. They have the dignity of science, and of theory, even though to the theorist the theory is of a low order.

THEORETICAL ECONOMICS

Theoretical economics is the heart of economical analysis. It tends, as we have previously indicated, to posit the generalized assumptions of an "economic system," or in modern parlance, a "model," and to develop by logical analysis the implications of the specified assumptions and the rules of logic that are deemed appropriate to that system. As we have indicated, its chief distinction for economics is the assumption that all economic behavior can be summarized by prices, costs, or by monetary units. This does not mean that actual statistical work need be engaged in, but rather that the logic of mathematics rather than of statistics has increasingly become the basis of modern economic analysis. Originally, economics was based on pure but nonmathematical logic. Geometric formulations, as developed in the drawing of curves, such as geometric representations of marginal utility, or indifference curves, were used. Neither marginal utility nor indifference were measurable quantities, but were inferred from the shape of the curve, as economists increasingly relied on mathematics, especially calculus. It was assumed that businessmen were rational calculators, or that the system would work as predicted if businessmen were rational calculators, obeying the rules of the system as defined by economists. The results of such analysis frequently seemed to indicate that businessmen are not rational calculators or that they frequently refuse to obey the rules of the system as defined by economists. A current illustration is as follows. Economic theory teaches us that as minimum wages are increased, the rate of unemployment goes up, since with each increase in wage rates it is desirable for employers to lay off the least efficient workers and replace the time lost by extended overtime for more efficient workers. Each increase in wages may result in the enforced unemployment of the less skilled segments of the society, and greater affluence to those who remain in the working force. One could argue that since increases in minimum wages affect all industries equally, allowing for different mixes in the proportion of highly skilled and marginally skilled workers by firm and by industry, the effects of minimum wages would be to restore the previous competitive situation to all firms. Thus, the effect, in eras of full prosperity, might be inflationary, but it would not increase unemployment as predicted. More importantly, the effect of minimum wages on unemployment is an empirical question, resolvable by research. At present the research available suggests that the deductive theory described above need not be as predicted.

The development of the application of mathematics to economics has now gone far beyond calculus. Sophisticated systems of matrix algebra, simultaneous equations, complex mathematical models are employed, all within the framework of the assumptions of the particular model or system.

HISTORICAL AND INSTITUTIONAL ECONOMICS

Historical and institutional economics have all the problems that all other forms of historical and institutional analysis have. The problems are: What are the appropriate data available for analysis (records, etc.)? What are the leading ideas around which data is to be collected? And, what are the ideological and valuational biases that determine the selection of data, the selection of problems, and the interpretation of data? Given these problems, historical and institutional economists have, like all other economists and historical and institutional analysts, adopted a wide range of problems, values, ideologies, and solutions. They have been Marxists, laissez-faire theorists, and non-Marxist critics of laissez-faire. What is unique, however, is that the historical attitude, the high valuation placed on specific, concrete evidence which has governed their work has tended to force them to reject the idea of perfect analytical or theoretical systems. They tend to question the truth of the *assumptions* of analytical economists. In the quest for the unique, the empirical, the historical, they ask the question: How accurate is the description of the firm, the economy, or of the men who act in economic situations? They tend to find that the reality is much more blurred than the assumption of perfect competition, that men are not economically rational, that firms have problems of mechanical efficiency, of morale, and of leadership, which limit the operation of logically derived economic models. They also tend to find that sentiment, tradition, and customary practices of the trade become the framework within which economic decisions are made, and which govern and limit economic decisions. As a result, they tend to provide descriptive studies of the way economics, firms, and economic actors behave or operate. In doing so they provide us with virtually the only available picture of the actual operation of the historical and institutional economic systems under which we live and have lived. It is the work of such men who force theoretical economists to alter their assumptions because it reveals the lack of "reality" of such assumptions. Moreover, as they begin to describe the historical operation of business cycles, forms, and industrial structures, they increasingly provide the parameters within which the models for statistical analysis are created, the measurements necessary for quantitative description. Most of their work, however, is of a low order of generalization. It involves the digging, sorting, and sifting of documents, reports, contracts, and laws. It has little of the glamor of science, it is not abstract, general or "powerful." As a result, men with a bent for theoretical analysis at high levels of generalization are likely to look down their noses at these low-level diggers into history or institutions. As a further result, institutional and historical economics falls more and more into disrepute at a time when, simply because of its complexity, economic science becomes more and more removed from any other reality than that of its own creation. Despite the virtues of historical and institutional economics, it is relatively easy to see that most such economists are subject to values, biases, ideologies, and commitments which govern their own and other fields in general.

A methodology based on historical methods or institutional analysis does not remove men from the necessities of delimiting their problems on some grounds other than the techniques they use [16].

NOTES

1.   Term first used by Thomas Carlyle. See Joseph Schumpeter, *History of Economic Analysis* (New York, Oxford University Press, 1954), pp. 409–411.

2.   Schumpeter, *op. cit.*, especially Part III, Chap. 4, "Review of the Troops." For a popularized discussion see also Robert L. Heilbroner, *The Worldly Philosophers*, rev. ed. (New York, Simon & Schuster, 1961), Chap. IV, "The Gloomy World of Parson Malthus and David Ricardo."

3.   This does not imply that economists such as Smith, Ricardo, Senior, or Marshall were themselves heartless or exploitative. As with Marx, distinctions must be made between theories and the uses to which they are put. See in Karl Polanyi, Conrad M. Arensburg, and Henry Pearson (Eds.), "The Place of Economics in Societies," in *Trade and Market in Early Empires* (Glencoe, Ill., Free Press, 1957), reprinted in George Dalton (Ed.), *Primitive, Archaic, and Modern Economies— Essays of Karl Polanyi* (Garden City, N. Y., Doubleday, 1968), Chap. 6. See also Schumpeter, *op. cit.*, p. 486n, and Heilbroner, *op. cit.*, Chap. VII. For an important defense of economic liberalism, see Silvio Gesell, *The Natural Economic Order*, translated by Philip Pye (London, Peter Owen, 1958).

4.   In this sense Marx was correct when he argued that the particular qualities of a given age are given universality by the particular proponents of an ideology.

5.   Schumpeter, *op. cit.*, pp. 232 ff.

6.   See George Dalton, *op. cit.*, p. xliii, and Joan Robinson, *Economic Philosophy* Garden City, N. Y., Doubleday, 1964), pp. 85ff.

7.   Schumpeter, *op. cit.*, pp. 415ff. Also Frank Manuel, *The Prophets of Paris* (Cambridge, Mass., Harvard University Press, 1962), Chaps. III, IV, and VI (Harper Torchbooks reprint, 1965).

8.   See Chap. 18 for a more extended criticism of this point of view.

9.   Joseph Schumpeter, *Capitalism, Socialism, and Democracy*, 3rd ed. (New York, Harper, 1950) (Harper Torchbooks reprint, 1962), Part I, "The Marxian Doctrine." Also Polanyi's essay in Dalton, ed., *op. cit.*, Chap. 7, "The Economy as Instituted Process."

10.   Frank Knight, *The Economic Organization* (Chicago, University of Chicago Press, 1933) (Chicago reprint 1963), and *On the History and Method of Economics*, especially the essay "Free Society, Its Basic Nature and Problem," reprinted from the *Philosophical Review*, Vol. LVII, No. 1 (1948); Milton Friedman, *Capitalism and Freedom* (Chicago, University of Chicago Press, 1968), and *Essays in Positive Economics* (Chicago, University of Chicago Press, 1970).

11.   Schumpeter, *History of Economic Analysis*, Part IV, Chap. 7; also, Adolph Lowe, *On Economic Knowledge* (New York, Harper & Row, 1965), p. 44ff., and Heilbroner, *op cit.*, pp. 176–180.

12.   Edward H. Chamberlin, *The Theory of Monopolistic Competition: A Re-Orientation of the Theory of Value* (Cambridge, Mass., Harvard University Press, 1946) (originally published 1933); see also Schumpeter, *History of Economic Analysis*, Part V, Chaps. 1 and 2. Also Gunnar Myrdal, *The Political Element in the Development of Economic Theory*, translated by Paul Streeter (Cambridge, Mass., Harvard University Press, 1954) (Simon & Schuster reprint 1969).

13.   See Joseph Bensman and Arthur J. Vidich, *The New American Society* (Chicago, Quadrangle, 1971).

14.   Especially instructive is Oskar Morgenstern, *On the Accuracy of Economic Observations*, rev. ed. (Princeton, N. J., Princeton University Press, 1963).

15. See below, Chaps. 9, 16, and 17. See also Daniel Bell, *Work and Its Discontents* (New York, League for Industrial Democracy, 1970).

16. See the works of Karl Polanyi, Adolph Lowe, Gunnar Myrdal, Joan Robinson; see also Andrew Shonfield, *Modern Capitalism* (London and New York, Oxford University Press, 1965); W. Arthur Lewis, *Theory of Economic Growth* (London, George Allen Unwin, 1955); John Kenneth Galbraith, *The New Industrial State* (Boston, Houghton Mifflin, 1967); Emile Benoit, *Europe at Sixes and Sevens* (New York, Columbia University Press, 1961); Richard Caves, *American Industry: Structure, Conduct, Performance* (Englewood Cliffs, N. J., Prentice-Hall, 1967).

Chapter 9

The Sociological Perspective

We will attempt here to define the various strategies, dimensions, and issues which constitute the framework of contemporary sociology. We are concerned with the range of differences within the field, and with the attempt to discover whether there is a common core of meanings that underlies these differences. We are not initially concerned with stating in paradigmatic terms a set of dimensions which becomes the basis for our analysis. We posit the works of four major sociological thinkers who provide what we believe is the full range of sociological perspectives. In analyzing their overall approach to the field, we hope to develop a paradigm that includes the major dimensions of sociology.

The classical sociologists in question are: Comte, Simmel, Durkheim, and Weber. We recognize, of course, that each of these figures was not without intellectual ancestors; we recognize, in addition, that each sociologist, in his own time, was not unique with respect to the approaches that became identified with him. But we assert that the approaches suggested here become major dimensions of the traditions of sociology, though not all of the followers of the tradition are necessarily aware of their intellectual ancestry. In part the work of the intellectual ancestors of contemporary social science has been so thoroughly absorbed that their descendants can appeal either to more direct links in their lineage or to a more generalized spirit or tradition within their field.

AUGUSTE COMTE

Auguste Comte, the first man to use the term "sociology" [1] developed one of the basic perspectives for the field. While many of his ideas are rejected by contemporary sociologists, the framework of his thought suggests much of the range within which the development of sociology has occurred.

There are three leading ideas in Comte's work. One deals with the nature of sociology in relation to society, the second deals with the relationship of sociology to the other "sciences," the third deals with the uses of sociology as applied to society.

First, sociology was to be the introduction of positive science into the study of human affairs. The sociologist would discover the laws by which events in the world occurred, and would be able to predict the occurrence of events. Being able to predict the occurrence of events would allow the sociologist to control the operation of events. The sociologist would then be in a position to be the philosopher-king who could use his knowledge of the laws of society to introduce reason into the governing of men and societies.

In this respect, Comte followed in almost literal terms the ideas of Saint-Simon, who saw in the application of the methods of physical science to society the means by which society could escape from magic, superstition, ignorance, and incompetence.

Quite naturally, with such an ambitious program, sociology would be the queen of the sciences. It would organize, synthesize, and generalize from all of the other physical and social sciences, in order to develop the laws necessary to provide prediction and control under the guidance of "reason."

Such a program involved the use of the comparative method, in which sociologists would study all societies, classify and characterize major institutions and structures within society, and determine the interrelationship between social structures. In doing so, they would discover the general characteristics of social structures independent of their specific and historical specificity, and, having done so, would deduce the general laws governing social structures. The knowledge of these laws would permit the intellectual together with the businessman to manipulate social structures in such a way as to produce the outcome that was most beneficial for society [2]. Moreover, the sociologist could define the values and moral structures that, with science, would provide the framework for a rational society.

By now, much or most of Comte's work is regarded as hopelessly naive and primitive, but much of it has been modified by other sociologists in response to the discovery of its weaknesses, and it remains, in disguised form, in the work of other sociologists.

At its simplest level, most sociologists reject the notion that general laws exist that govern society in all its forms; they believe that man's experience is cumulative, and by living cumulatively through time, that is, in history, men modify their experiences, cultures, and societies, such that their societies become amenable only to historical description. Generalizations occur only within specified times or historical periods. There are no generalized laws. The "laws" that emerge are not constant but are modified by their own operation. As a result, the historian cannot predict from a generalized model, for the very basis of the prediction is itself subject to change [3].

Such predictions as can be made (apart from those that are based on the purely physiological and noncultural aspects of men) are subject to historical limits which are only discoverable in the failure of predictions, a failure that occurs after the prediction. Thus sociologists tend to devalue even "laws of history," laws that tend to posit necessary stages in the evolution of society.

The weakness of this aspect of Comte's position is not just a weakness of his argument. It derives from the realization of the failure of the optimistic positivist rationality that governed the era of the enlightenment [4], for if Comte's system would not work, then the unilinear aspect of progress would be halted by the failure of history or society to yield its secrets, or its laws, to rational men. The faith in science, in progress, and in the belief in the ability of men to eliminate both irrationality and suffering do not, however, die easily. The failure of science to discover the laws of nature in the world of social affairs, while it has created depths of existential despair, and worship of the irrational among those who were never inclined to science anyway, has only resulted in a shifting of the basis upon which science would be justified. In Comte's work, science is justified by its ability to discover the underlying structure of the social world. In modern social science, science is justified by its method. Thus, while it may be true that social science does not yield eternal truth, it does yield, within a given period, the information, the generalization, and the knowledge of the operation of the society suffi-cient to form rational social policy which will solve the problems of igno-rance, poverty, war, and domestic unhappiness.

Thus, the modern positivistic social scientist comes equipped not with truth but with *methods*, which—if he is allowed to practice—can assure his society or its relevant agencies better solutions to current problems than are currently available [5].

The second aspect of Comte's work deals with the idea of the philosopher-king, the positivistic intellectual. While the superstitious, irrational, unrea-sonable, and ignorant have in the past made social policy, now the objective, unbiased scientist and scientifically oriented businessman can formulate policy from outside these social encumbrances that in part are the source of the problem. Thus, it is assumed that the process of becoming a scientist rids the practitioner of his biases, prejudices, and values. In the hundred-odd years since Comte's work, we have discovered that regardless of the scien-tist's ability, there is no guarantee that the scientist frees himself from values that are independent of science. Most social thinkers tend to think of science as having instrumental value, that is, as a means by which values originating outside of science can be realized, but that science itself does not provide the values. The one exception to this generalization is that the capacity to do scientific work itself is dependent on the realization of one cluster of values; this cluster includes freedom of inquiry, freedom to define one's own prob-lems, to define, within the limits of other values, the means by which such inquiry is to proceed, and the right to communicate with other scientists concerning one's methods, hypotheses, and results. But if the logic of the need for freedom for science as science is consistent, then there is nothing in science per se that requires freedom for anyone else except the scientist, or even the scientist of one particular school of thought within a discipline.

If, apart from this, science is instrumental in the realization of other values, then science by itself does not provide the basis for the solution of problems; rather, it depends on a consensus about the priority of other values.

This is most clear when expressed in terms of the power of the scientist. For Comte, like Plato, assumed that the intellectual-scientist could arrive at a social position which would allow him to make independent studies, to formulate social policy based on science and the knowledge of universals, and to implement those policies with the world as his laboratory. This image of the scientist as philosopher-king rather than as technician has haunted the world since the beginning of science, whether the thinker is Saint-Simon, to whom Comte owes most of his ideas, Comte himself, Marx, or such later thinkers as Stuart Chase, Clyde Kluckhohn, B. F. Skinner, or Kenneth Clark. This image operates today in terms of the new behavioral sciences, policy sciences, system theories, and the ideologies of the major foundations, who would innovate and change from the standpoint of a social position which is presumably independent of the narrow class, economic, and political positions which define everyone else's thought.

Comte was innocent of many of these problems. He hoped that the validity of applied science as a means of governing would be self-evident; the kinds of controls of science, the concessions the sociologist would have to make in order to practice his science, were less apparent. Today with the development of vast agencies that use science, the problem of sponsorship, of direct or indirect control, and of self-manipulation and the manipulation by others have become much more apparent. But none of these has resulted in the rejection of science as a means of defining and controlling social policy, at least in major scientific quarters.

Strangely enough, the rulers of the social establishments of the world have not graciously stepped aside and allowed the scientist to "exorcise his demons." Instead, recognizing the technical and instrumental value of science, they have employed scientists to achieve whatever goals were appropriate to their respective social positions, with the scientist serving only as an advisor, as a consultant, a provider of information, and not as the maker of a scientifically determined social policy. The scientist, including the social scientist, had to discover that the operation of science, and the livelihood of scientists, is based on the possession of funds, and of authorization to practice one's trade. In order to practice, one must come to terms with those who have the authority and the funds.

This lack of freedom for institutionalized science with respect to the defining of problems, methods, and results, is less true in a free society than it is in totalitarian societies with respect to the development of policy based on such definitions. Thus, the major freedom of scientists has been that of selecting, whenever possible, those external agencies which the scientist chooses to serve. But this selection for the total technician can be based either on the freedom to exercise techniques within a favorable value climate or on the agreement between scientist and sponsor with respect to extrascientific values. In neither case is the operation of science freed from the bonds of nonscientific values.

This second aspect of the Comtean perspective operates on the assumption that the sociologist, on the basis of science, can independently produce the means for transforming the world and making it amenable to reason, and that it therefore provides the basis for an implicit and explicit activism which becomes the means for a revolutionary transformation making the world more subject to ideals which in fact are higher than and beyond those of instrumental science. The impulse to transcend science for what are in fact higher realms of being is one of the genuine impulses to sociology. But this impulse, while it justifies itself as science, comes closer in fact to the prophetic and revolutionary activism of sacred and secular religions.

This prophetic and revolutionary religiosity that is at the heart of so much sociology reveals and recreates itself in numerous forms. Such a prophetic mission for sociology can be involved in salvation through planning, reform, revolution, and a return to simpler and more pristine times and virtues. Yet all of these ideological and utopian promises can be justified within the values that are attributed to science and once asserted can be intensified by all the righteousness that possession of a scientific technique and mystique can give.

The third major aspect of Comte's work, the claim that sociology is the queen of the sciences and that it governs even intellectual, academic, and scientific disciplines, is apparently the most modest one, since this demand is not to understand or rule the world, but only a small section of it. Since the target for positivistic sociology is so specific and focused that it confronts an immediate reality, the goal, in theory, is more actionable.

But not only is the goal more actionable; the resistances to the goal are more specific, direct, and "reactionable." In the light of the immediacy of resistance, this aspect of positive sociology has been abandoned almost immediately, for now it is not dealing with the world, the laws of nature and society, or science, but with visible colleagues down the hall. One would suspect that sociologists secretly have been least willing to surrender this aspect of their claim, though it is pressed indirectly, for sociologists have invented a myriad of subfields that embrace the total experience of men. Thus, there are fields like the sociology of science, the sociology of art, of the family, of physical and mental health, of government, politics, religion. The failure, however, of these subdivisions to embrace the totality of the world is caused not by the aspirations of sociologists but by the subspecializations of sociology. The field has fractured and splintered into a host of separate fields, with separate techniques, rhetorics, methodologies and findings, which are incomprehensible to all but specialists in that field. To be sure, this process is not peculiar to sociology; in psychology, economics, and philosophy, the same processes of specialization and fractionization are seen to occur.

Thus, sociology has failed to become the queen of the sciences not only because of the resistances to it from the other sciences, but also because sociology has failed to develop a sovereign within its own realm [6].

GEORG SIMMEL

The approach taken by Georg Simmel is at the opposite pole from Comte. There is nothing in his work that suggests either the intellectual, academic, or social imperialism implicit or explicit in the Comtean tradition, despite the fact that Simmel, like Weber, in his personal knowledge and genius, was as well-equipped as any man to be an intellectual imperialist. Simmel, at least in his philosophy of social forms, attempted to locate that which is unique and separate about the "social." He attempted to abstract from the concrete, historical, and empirical data what was peculiarly the product of the form and processes of social interaction. This tended to remove or to abstract from the concrete data the economic, historical, and cultural materials, and to leave, apparently as a residue, only the form of action itself.

By and large, this approach resulted in some of the most brilliant psychological and philosophical generalizations ever made, but it told little about the concrete historical social events which were the raw materials of Simmel's work. Simmel, like most other sociologists, was concerned with discovering a naturalistic basis for the objectivity of the social. He rejected the notion that social categories were immediately transcendant either in religion or in laws or in nature. Nor were they simply taken as given or "reflections" of group activity. He attempted to ascertain the emergence of social forms and categories out of the behavior of individuals, and emphasized, as a neo-Kantian, that only the individual was real. But the interaction of pluralities of individuals produces social products, forms of thought and behavior that become independent of the thought or action of any one individual. This independence becomes a form of objectivity and constraint upon individuals which in part "tyrannizes" over individuals. Simmel was in part an individualist, attracted by the freedom and opportunity for the individual qua individual in large and loosely organized societies, but he was aware that freedom could easily overburden individuals and become a source of social and individual pathology.

His overall explicit methodological aim was to discover, in a world-historical examination of social institutions, what was purely social, devoid of the historical "accidents" and particularities of time and place. The result of this, to the extent to which Simmel has been directly and indirectly followed, has been to devalue the empirical, the concrete, and the richness of historical data, and to lead to a quest for generalized and abstract models of the processes of history and of social systems. In following this path, one is led to the notion of transhistorical social forms which become the equivalent of laws, as in Comte's quest for laws.

In this sense, Simmel's contribution to sociology is sometimes overlooked. It is clear that Leopold von Wiese and Wiese-Becker [7] followed directly in the footpaths laid out by Simmel. At a more significant level, the small-group work of Bales and his school [8] follows directly in the Simmelian tradition by emphasizing the formal processes by which groups are organized, integrated, and maintain themselves. The reduction to generalized nonhistorical processes is characteristic of his work. The substantive content of group tasks, the concrete values and motivations and the specific actions of the test group members are bracketed out of the study, with the focus placed only on the forms of interaction. In this sense "abstract scientific sociology" derives directly from Simmel.

The attempt to find generalized categories of meaning appropriate to a given social act, the meanings implicit in such phenomena as loving, empathy, degradation, alienation, and the absurd can also be derived from Simmel. They are so derived in the sense that the specific historical content of ideologies, ideas, myths, and motivations are bracketed out of the discussion, after such historical contexts are introduced by the use of comparative "empirical" or historical methods. It is thus deemed possible to develop a general catalogue or, possibly, vocabulary of generic emotions, phenomenological states, or motives. While it is true that such a lexicon could be the product of Simmel's work, one could base such an attempt on the works of Jaspers, Husserl, George Herbert Mead, Alfred Schutz, Durkheim, and even Max Weber. With respect to Mead and Weber, some stretching is required to use them for such purposes.

In the same sense, Talcott Parsons, in developing highly generalized abstract models of social systems, and even more abstract, "the" social system, at the expense of the specific historical and empirical material within which the presumed social system is located, follows the direction outlined by Simmel even though Parsons consciously derives the technique of systematic model-building from Pareto [9].

Sociology abounds by now with hundreds of conceptual schemes, each of which is totally formal, logical, and abstract. Each is independent in its design of the specific historical materials to which it might be applied. At best, each will, subsequent to the use of the model, use historical or empirical materials to illustrate the viability of utility of the model. History, then, is not explored, analyzed, or explained; the model is. In this sense, the empirical world is reduced to a priori categories. However, since at these later stages, empirical or historical materials are used, the so-called research is considered empirical. Howard Becker described the process trenchantly as pouring new wine into old bottles. It could also be called a highly sophisticated method of Procrustean philosophical analysis. In short, the conceptual model becomes the functional equivalent of the Platonic essence.

EMILE DURKHEIM

Another solution to the problem of making sociology scientific is provided by Emile Durkheim. The starting point is Durkheim's analysis of the problem of the social investigator who, by the arbitrary nature of his stance with respect to events imposes his point of view on the data under consideration. In short, the investigator is the product of the events which he attempts to analyze. Durkheim finds a solution to the problem of the definition of social reality in the nature of social reality itself. Social reality is not the arbitrary construction of the investigator who is free to define reality as he wishes; rather, social reality is constructed by the operation of the society itself. Social facts are as much constraints, not only to the society, but to the investigator, because they cannot be ignored. They are social because they involve the objectified activities and symbols of two or more individuals, and they are constraints because if they are ignored, there occurs a violation of the fundamental agreements by which the social facts are made. Social facts are the product of the group life of the total operation of a society, so that even symbolic data, myth, ritual, folklore, because they are social in nature, have this quality of "hard fact." To be objective, sociologists must ignore the purely subjective and psychological meaning of these facts. They discover their meaning in terms of their objective functions and consequences for the operation of the group. The evolution in the meaning of the social facts of the symbolic or collective representations are the results of fundamental but objective changes in the structure of group life. Thus, the change from a society based on mechanical solidarity to one based on organic solidarity is a change based on the division of labor. From a methodological point of view this means that one set of social facts is explainable in terms of other categories of social facts. No recourse to subjective meaning is necessary or desirable. Thus, such an apparently "subjective" datum as a suicide can be objectified in terms of the rates of suicide, but these can be explained by the conditions of social solidarity or its absence (anomie). It might be possible to infer that anomie is a "psychological" state (as interpreted in Merton's work), but for Durkheim it is an objective structural fact, measurable in totally objective terms [10].

If Durkheim's solution is a solution, then the arbitrariness involved in the selection of facts is ruled out. Society as a producer of social objectivity produces that objectivity which allows the sociologist to be free from the arbitrariness of his subjective or positional perspective. This would be true if the society presented itself to the analyst in relatively direct and unambiguous terms, and the analyst had no freedom from the objective constraints that society imposes upon him. But if this were the case, the analyst would be unable to perform his job because he would not have the freedom and the distance from society to take it as an object for his analysis. Instead, the analyst would become a mythmaker, a manufacturer of collective representations, unconscious of the social processes that determine his analysis. And of course some psychologically oriented sociologists and epistemologists claim, as did Marx, that social theorists are mythmakers who reflect the temporary historical conditions of their times in terms of their specialized relationships to those times. In short, the only "objective realities" are the myths of un-self-conscious men.

The difficulty with the Durkheimian position is that at least in a complex, large-scale society, and we have argued that all but the simplest primitive societies are complex, society presents itself in an infinity of facts. Society is multidimensional, and each possible dimension of analysis is capable of almost infinite extension. Therefore, society does not present itself in a direct, unambiguous, and constraining manner. Instead, the social analyst selects his facts in terms of some perspective which is independent of the facts, but having arrived at a perspective, he can order the facts that had been selected only because he uses a particular perspective. However, once the sociologist begins his investigation, he cannot legitimately ignore facts that violate his perspectives or preconceptions [11].

But if the perspective is independent of the facts, then elements other than scientific ones may well determine the criteria by which facts are allowed to present themselves to the analyst. Such elements may include the positional perspectives, values, psychology, and—horrors!—the unconscious, personal life of the investigator. We do not deny the objectivity of the facts, but we do suggest that the criteria by which this objectivity is defined are independent of society *as a totality* in defining it.

Durkheim's solution, however, has many advantages. It allows one to think of society as an integrated, self-sustaining, closed system. All elements in such a system are explainable in terms of other elements in the system, each set of social facts can be explained by other sets of social facts.

It is thus possible to set narrow limits to the data which one would consider relevant to analysis, and to escape the infinite regression of history, the infinite extension of an infinite number of multidimensional elements which focus upon single events or sets of facts. The Durkheimian method allows one to limit his area of work to manageable proportions, and to work at the level of the a priori interrelationship between abstracted structural elements which presumably are functionally related or interrelated to form a self-sustaining abstract social system. We must rush to indicate that the construction of structural-functional systems is not the work of Emile Durkheim, but that of followers who combined the abstractness of system-building à la Simmel with the notions of closed systems derived from Durkheim. Thus, Simmel is not to be blamed for all the philosophic exercises which he prefigured, nor is Durkheim to be blamed for the abstract structural-functionalism which later thinkers have attributed to him. Regardless of method, Simmel was preeminently empirical and historical, though he handled such data in terms of implicitly closed systems. It is only the combination of philosophic abstraction with the idea of closed social systems that permits the contemporary structural-functionalist to treat the historical world as if it were an analytical model invented by a logical or analytical sociologist.

MAX WEBER

The problems of the relationship of the social sciences to the natural sciences and the degree to which the social sciences were amenable to the methods of the natural sciences was a central problem for Max Weber [12]. He was concerned with the fact that the intentionality of man's activity, his motivation, made the study of social action fundamentally different from that of the study of brute and blind nature. He devoted a great part of his life to methodological issues, but at the same time he was continuously concerned with the solution of concrete, substantive problems of his day, not only as historiographical problems, but as problems of history.

He was concerned with the problems of the uniqueness of historical data, and the difficulties of developing generalizations about the historical process at a methodological level. At the philosophical level, he wrestled with the ghost of Karl Marx in trying to solve the problem of the determinacy and indeterminacy of history, to understand the extent to which rational men are free to make their own history or whether they are the slaves either of the dialectics of history or of historical, social, and economic institutions. Beyond this, he was concerned with the extent to which the independent social analyst was free to observe, interpret, and analyze the processes of history [13].

In response to the problem of motivation and meaning in social action, Weber argued that the subjective nature underlying social action was a brute fact of man's existence. If this were so, no methodological *caveat* could allow the sociologist to ignore anything that was relevant. The problem was not one of ignoring the subjective element in human action, but rather that of finding methods by which these subjective elements could be made accessible to analysis.

Weber argued that the *ideal* types, especially those relating to motivational complexes which are historically revealed but which are artificially sharpened for the purposes of analysis and prediction, could become the basis not only for the imputation of motives, but for the understanding of social actions based upon such motives when placed in relevant historical and empirical contexts.

In addition, analytical types of motivation could be constructed in order to determine the logical consequences of a given set of motives. The motivational analysis would be purely logical in the sense that the "economic man" provides a basis for analytical predictions within a system, but in itself is not empirical.

These methodological innovations, even when they involve the use of abstract concepts, categories, and "systems," however, are not used to develop deductive systems which are formal, abstract, and general in nature. They are used to resolve problems in historiography and economic history. Weber confronted two schools of thought. One dealt with the notion of developing a deductive abstract economic analysis derived from English and Austrian marginal-utility analysis. The other was the totally unique historiography of Schmoller, reflecting the tradition of Ranke. In that tradition, Weber argued that the process of historiographic research provided no basis for determining the relevance of a problem or of data. The method could only result in the sheer accumulation of ad hoc factual data. Weber argued that in fact the method was not followed; in order to escape from the infinity of perspectives, dimensions, and data, the researcher would have to adopt an implicit definition of his problem and an implicit set of norms from which the concrete data of any historical research deviated. Because the fundamental categories within which research was conducted were implicit assumptions, the researcher was intellectually unable to control his biases or to separate normative statements from factual statements.

The concept of the ideal type was designed as a means by which the analyst or researcher could make explicit the theoretical assumptions and frameworks which governed his work.

The ideal type was a general statement of theoretical assumptions that were relevant to the statement of an explicit problem in sociological, historical, or economic research. But having developed his ideal type purely as a pragmatic method for solving specific problems, the object of the use of the ideal type was to facilitate research on the specific and unique aspects of the structures or areas under research. While the ideal type appeared to be general, in fact it was not. In the first place, the type is not a statement of some underlying essential reality. It is a purely artificial device aimed at facilitating work, which could be abandoned, modified, or changed as the focus of interest of the researcher changed. Its validity was not determined in its essential correctness but only in its value when applied.

When the ideal type was used, its pragmatic character was determined by its application to unique, specific, empirical, and historical problems. In developing a generalized type, the researcher wanted to find out in what way the given historical phenomenon was different from that assumed in the generalized type. The problem of research as a totality is to find what is unique and specific about the empirical phenomenon. The generalized type is only a device by which this is done.

Talcott Parsons, in concentrating on the ideal type—"the system"—as a general model, the development of which is apparently the end-product of his research, reverses the order of reduction. He ends up constructing general systems and general models which are suprahistorical. To the extent that historical problems and materials are involved in this process, they serve as the raw material for model-building and as illustrations for general, abstract models. But to the extent that they do not serve as mere devices to illuminate the specific substantive character of events and structures, they become the equivalent of Platonic essences, and the opposite of the Weberian ideal type.

Weber's procedure then, is exactly the opposite of that suggested by Simmel, in which the specific data are abstracted in order to find the general matrix which covers a class of actions or social relations. In this sense, Simmel's work is primarily philosophical in nature while Weber's work is historical in nature. But the focus on historical data is designed to escape the trap of an endless study of infinitely extending events. Weber reaches for more general conclusions of an historical nature. This is done by a comparative method in which both the type and the historiographic research are produced with reference to two or more historical periods or *loci*, in which comparative research is aimed at proving how unique features of an historical situation produced different consequences in various societies.

Weber's *Sociology of Religion* is an attempt at such a comparative sociology, but even here the comparative sociology is aimed at the solution of a very specific problem: What are the social, ideological, legal, economic, and other conditions necessary and sufficient to produce or prevent the emergence of a rationalistic capitalist economy. The use of a comparative method allows for some level of generalization within the historical uniqueness of the data embraced by the study. But Weber's respect for the intransigency of historical data did not permit him to think of an abstracted formal comparative method, as exemplified in the works of Eisenstadt, Etzioni, Zelditch, or, in anthropology, in Goldschmidt or Murdock. It meant, for Weber, for each society studied, an intensive historiographic investigation of that society as a unique case, governed not only by the factors necessary to approach his general problem, but also by the uniqueness of the historical data of that society as it emerges in the process of investigation. Thus, Weber has little use for formal abstract paradigms which determine in advance the data to be covered. Because this is true, Weber found it difficult to study systematically a wide range of societies in any one study [14]. Each society had to be studied with a degree of intensity that precluded highly formal comparisons of dozens of civilizations. He devoted his lifetime to the study of relatively few societies, even though it is still a source of astonishment that any one man could have mastered as much material as Weber did.

Still, all of the above discussion does not allow us to explain the factors which determine the selection of problems, and the major part of Weber's methodological writings are related to the extent to which science does or does not govern the selection of problems. Weber's solution is to reject the notion that science or objectivity governs these processes of selection. The concept of value-relevance means that the problems selected are related to the implicit or explicit values, biases, conventions, or traditions of an investigator as an individual or as a member of a society which experiences the problems as relevant to its values. This is necessarily so because, theoretically, the number of problems that could be investigated is infinite. The act of focusing one's attention is itself a decision that some problem or some datum is more valuable to study than others, and when an individual does focus his attention, it is because his value-system is in some way affected by the possibilities of the data in question.

Weber does not mean that all social-scientific research is biased, arbitrary, or capricious. He merely means that the selection of problems has an individual or historical relevance to values. Once the problem is defined and stated, then the methods of research and the objectivity of the researcher are brought to bear on the resolution of the problem. At the level of the technical work itself, it is possible to debate the work and its findings in objective terms. This is precisely the point that Alvin Gouldner appears to have misunderstood in his essay "Anti-Minotaur" and in his more recent book [15]. Nothing in Weber suggests that social scientists can separate value from their work. On the contrary, all work in the social sciences is relevant only because of its connection to values. Furthermore, the notion that value-relevance means that a value-free science is impossible does not imply that "value-correctness" determines the correctness of the scientific work; there may exist "good" and "bad" Marxists, and the difference between "good" and "bad" is not a question of the "Marxist" but a question of the technical quality of the work. As long as we are willing to concede that there are differences in the technical quality of the work, then we can say that freedom from values is possible.

Regardless of what values animate the social scientist in the selection of a problem, the problem is resolved when it ceases to be a problem, that is, when the tension between value and fact which created the problem no longer continues to exist. In this case, the original problem will be superseded by new ones as new findings place themselves in tension with old or emerging values. It must be pointed out, however, that Weber does not point to any self-validating machinery that establishes the objectivity of the work itself. Whatever objectivity or value there is in the work is resolved in the discussion of the findings, of their relevance, of their subsequent utility to other workers, and of their value. Thus, issues are resolved not at the methodological level, but at the level of the accuracy of the substantive findings, and the extent to which the data resolves the original research problem posed.

The attention, then, is continuously focused, despite the vast amount of methodological writing in Weber's work, on the substantive work and not upon the methodology.

Weber himself took as his major problem the development of rationality in society [16]. He defined rationality both in terms of the intellectual articulation of systems of thought, and the use of rationality in systems of action and administration.

He contrasted the growth of rationality with the loss of the sense of unity in society and in the life of the individual in society. He saw a dialectic: as rationality emerged, the natural unity and emotional harmony of individual life was destroyed. Intellectual rationality resulted in the disenchantment of the world. Formal rationality resulted in the growth of rationality for large complex organizations, or bureaucracies, and in the decline of any form of substantive rationality for any individual in or subject to the bureaucracies. Within society itself, he saw the polarization of values, the professionalization, institutionalization, and bureaucratization of all value-complexes. The result was that all values were placed in competition with all other values because each value-dimension became the exclusive and competitive jurisdiction of competing institutions. As a result, individuals in a society were subjected to the presentation of competing, exclusive values, which they are forced to internalize and harmonize in order to maintain a unified psychic life.

This statement of the central problem of Weber's work makes it clear that Weber himself worked within the framework of systems of thought, as Benjamin Nelson has pointed out, of value-relevances of ideas close to Lutheran theology [17].

It would appear to us that the four sociologists described above provide the total range within which sociological thinking takes place. Within this range there are vast differences which might suggest that there is no one unified point of view. The differences suggested concern the following issues:

1. Whether sociology is a science, insofar as it is objective and valuefree.
2. Whether it involves subjective, phenomenological materials exclusively, or whether it deals only with objective, quantifiable social data and methods.
3. Whether its purposes are to improve, modify, or change society, or whether its objective is only to describe and analyze the operation of society.
4. Whether—if society is not accepted, or if change is desired—the change should take place in reaffirming aspects related to the past, or by emphasis on hope for a future state of affairs. Related to this is the attitude to be taken toward society or toward the "establishment"; whether the change is to take place within the framework of the present dimensions of society, or whether it is to be radical change.
5. Whether sociology is an historical, empirical, descriptive discipline, aimed at treating and analyzing the unique phenomena of history, or whether it is an abstract, generalizing science, the end-product being, if not laws, then at least analytical models which either reflect the generalized essential nature of social events, or generalized models underlying the uniqueness of empirical events.
6. Whether sociological data encompasses all that is not alien to mankind, or whether it deals with the uniquely social.
7. Whether it deals with the major phenomena that determine the structure and issues of society in macroscopic forms, or whether it focuses on the minute detail, the miniaturistic milieu within society, without focusing on macroscopic features.

As indicated above, taking only the four men in question, there is a vast variety of approaches to these issues, and men who agree with each other on one such issue do not necessarily agree on other issues.

But if it be true that men in agreement on some of these issues disagree on others, then there is no one sociological perspective. The vast variety of specialized approaches and perspectives within the field of sociology can be comprehended in terms of differences of the combinations in a matrix of these dimensions.

However, it seems to us that there is one area in which all of the men discussed above agree, with the possible exception of Georg Simmel. All of them emphasize the interrelatedness of social, economic, political, psychological, cultural, normative, and other by-products and attributes of human existence; all, in their work, tend to explore self-consciously and systematically, either some, or hopefully all, of the social interconnections between various aspects of human life. Simmel, the exception, does this in fact, though on methodological grounds, in his formal sociology he focuses on the primarily social, so that in fact he is not an exception.

Comte made the exploration of the interconnectedness of these phenomena the basis for his program, not only in determining the laws of human existence, but also in what appeared to be his conception of sociology as the queen of the sciences.

Durkheim, in his focus on the interrelationship between social facts, focuses on these interconnections in explicit methodological terms.

Weber does so in all of his substantive sociological work, though it is not a major tenet of his methodological work. Thus, his major methodological device is to explore systematically within each society the relationship between institutional orders; between religious and economic ideas, legal arrangements and economic arrangements, politics or the state, and economic institutions, and so on. In fact, a textual analysis of any particular essay will suggest a successive rotation of perspectives surrounding a given problem, so that by completion of the essay he has examined all the major institutional and societal areas which in their interconnectedness surround and frame the area in question. We emphasize that Weber did this in the manner of his characteristic work, rather than as a focus of his methodological program. In addition, he did it in terms of his vast scholarly grasp of a particular area in all of its multifaceted dimensions. He achieved an emphasis on the interconnectedness of social phenomena more by virtue of his erudition than by conscious design.

In this sense, Weber was able to follow Comte's dictum that sociology would be the queen of the sciences because the sociologist would integrate all relevant knowledge concerning the operation of the society or problem under study. But again, he was able to achieve this aspect of the sociological imagination on the basis of unique intellectual and personal qualifications. All sociologists in some way focus on the interconnectedness of social phenomena, and all aspire to the integration of the social sciences. The fact that they fail is due not only to their respect for academic boundaries, but also to the fact that they are unable to acquire the mastery which would make a claim for total knowledge of materials either possible or valid. But in the sense that they aspire to explore, systematically or not, the interconnectedness of social phenomena, sociologists have a subliminal acceptance of the Comtean aspiration. Functionalism, which operates programatically to make explicit the interconnectedness of social phenomena, is in the main line of the sociological tradition. From a Weberian perspective, the major criticism one could make of functionalism is that it substitutes its program, and the concepts and definition of the program, for the task itself. This has been made abundantly clear in Kingsley Davis' paper, "The Myth of Functional Analysis" [18].

While the dominant sociological attitude focuses on the interconnected-ness of events, not all sociologists agree on the events to be connected. The Weberian image, perhaps in response to Marx, focuses on such phenomena as social and economic class, bureaucracy, ideologies and ideas, political and economic structures, class interests and conflicts, as they affect each other and the whole of society. Other sociologists focus on the interconnectedness of the purely social, or on the functional relations within the small-scale or on the functional relations within small-scale or abstract social systems. The choices between the macroscopic and the microscopic, and between the abstract and the historical, have become a permanent division within sociology.

NOTES

1. First printed at the beginning of the fourth volume of his *Cours de Philosophie Positive,* published 1838. Cf. *International Encyclopedia of the Social Sciences,* Vol. 3, p. 202.

2. So far as we know, much of this program is implicit in the Platonic notion of the philosopher-king. In the modern world, it derives most closely from Saint-Simon. As we shall see, the ideal is present in much of sociology, especially among logical positivists.

3. There are many discussions of this problem. See, among others, Karl Jaspers, *The Origin and Goal of History* (New Haven, Conn., Yale University Press, 1953), pp. 258–261, and John Lukacs, *Historical Consciousness* (New York, Harper & Row, 1968), Chap. 1.

4. The development of this failure is traced in H. Stuart Hughes, *Consciousness and Society: the Reorientation of European Social Thought, 1890-1930* (New York, Random House, 1958), Chaps. 4 and 8.

5. See Paul F. Lazarsfeld, William H. Sewell, and Harold L. Wilensky (Eds.), *The Uses of Sociology* (New York, Basic Books, 1967), pp. xiff.

6. See Raymond Aron, *Main Currents in Sociological Thought,* Vol. I (Garden City, N. Y., Doubleday, 1968), pp. 73ff.

7. *Systematic Sociology—On the Basis of the Beziehungslehre and Gebilde-lehre of Leopold von Wiese,* adapted and amplified by Howard Becker (New York, Wiley, 1932).

8. See Robert F. Bales, *Interaction Process Analysis* (Cambridge, Mass., Addison-Wesley, 1950); A. Paul Hare, Edgar Borgatta, and Robert F. Bales (Eds.), *Small Groups: Studies in Social Interaction* (New York, Knopf, 1955).

9. Talcott Parsons, *The Structure of Social Action,* Vol. I (New York, Free Press, 1968), Chap. V.

10. Emile Durkheim, *Suicide: A Study in Sociology,* translated by George Simpson (New York, Free Press, 1951), Chap. 5.

11. See Raymond Aron, *Main Currents in Sociological Thought,* Vol. II (Garden City, N. Y., Doubleday, 1970), pp. 73ff.

12. See Max Weber, *The Methodology of the Social Sciences,* translated and edited by Edward A. Shils and Henry A. Finch (New York, Free Press, 1949);

Reinhard Bendix, *Max Weber: an Intellectual Portrait* (Garden City, N. Y., Double-day, 1960); Hans H. Gerth and C. Wright Mills, *From Max Weber: Essays in Sociology* (New York, Oxford University Press, 1958), pp. 55ff.; Raymond Aron, *German Sociology* (New York, Free Press, 1958), Chap. III.

13.   See Raymond Aron, *op. cit.,* p. 76.

14.   Of course, Weber, because of his astounding erudition, was able to illustrate any one point in an essay, by citing materials from a vast number of contemporary and historical societies. Yet, when it was necessary for him to do explicit comparative studies, the number of societies he studied was small.

15.   Alvin Gouldner: "Anti-Minotaur: The Myth of a Value-Free Sociology," in *Social Problems,* Vol. 9, No. 3 (Winter 1962); also reprinted in Maurice Stein and Arthur Vidich (Eds.), *Sociology on Trial* (Englewood Cliffs, N. J., Prentice-Hall, 1963); Alvin Gouldner, *The Coming Crisis of Western Sociology* (New York, Basic Books, 1970).

16.   See Bendix, *op. cit.,* pp. 68–69; the theme permeates Weber's studies in the sociology of religion; see also the introduction by Don Martindale and Johannes Riedel to Max Weber, *The Rational and Social Foundations of Music* (Carbondale, Southern Illinois University Press, 1958).

17.   Benjamin Nelson, "Review Article," *American Sociological Review,* Vol. XXX (August 1965), pp. 596ff.

18.   To the extent that this has been called functionalism, then all sociologists are functionalists, but such functionalism existed long before the term came into exis-tence, and exists among those who do not regard themselves as functionalists, and who reject the formal reification of a self-evident starting point. See Kingsley Davis, "The Myth of Functional Analysis," *American Sociological Review,* Vol. XXIV (De-cember 1959), pp. 757ff.

Chapter 10

The Psychologist

ASSOCIATIONAL PSYCHOLOGY AND BEHAVIORISM

Today we conceive of psychology or of its numerous branches as being one of a series of highly professional fields, boasting relatively advanced methodologies, techniques, vocabularies, and procedures. Some branches are highly experimental, others base themselves on advanced statistical procedures, but all branches including the clinical have devoted much attention to the development of explicit methodological models, and to the creation of specialized techniques, whether those techniques are of therapy, research, or reporting.

Though psychology is a relatively young field, dating perhaps from the work of Descartes, it is a field that contains many schools, divisions, and subdivisions. Each major school within psychology has subdivided and re-subdivided again and again, and each major school bases its subdivision on the development of specialized concepts, techniques, vocabularies and parentage, as well as on loyalty structures. As a result, it would be difficult to describe the logics of psychologies without exploring vast and perhaps uncounted variegations in psychological approaches [1]. Because of the development of so many subspecializations in psychology, it is difficult to conceive of psychology or psychologies as having generalized logics or attitudes of their own apart from or underlying each of the specialized professional and technological apparatuses.

In this chapter, we will discuss what we regard to be the major underlying logics of major schools of psychology, recognizing full well that each particular school will qualify and differentiate itself from even the major logic that most resembles it. Moreover, we recognize that the process of division and subdivision among psychological schools includes the combination and recombination of elements from other schools which in their pure form were originally antagonistic, and contained antithetical logics.

There are various schools of gestalt psychology, some of which derive their basic assumptions from behaviorist psychology, others from Freudian psychology. There are schools of behaviorist psychology which draw major ideas from Freudian psychology into behaviorist molds, to be verified by experimental and behaviorist methods. The reverse is also true. Some schools attempt to synthesize Freudian and behaviorist psychologies by using models of interpersonal behavior as a base, others by using symbolic interactionism as a base. We recognize all these complexities, but persist in attempting to discern the minimal, irreducible elements in psychological attitudes.

The professionalization of psychology and of schools of psychology frequently obscures the nonpsychological orientations that become the basis of the school. Much of the basic attitudes in psychology are revealed in their origins and in the attitudes of everyday life which are accepted as givens by their practitioners, and it is at this level that we shall commence.

The major impetus toward "scientific" psychology rests not on the scientific nature of that psychology but in the attempt to answer essentially philosophic questions by means that transcend philosophic methods.

One basic problem plaguing philosophy almost from its origins is the problem: How do we know? The difficulty in answering this question is that the knowledge which enables us to answer this question rests on knowledge which is already given in the attempt to answer the question. Thus, every attempt to explore the nature of human consciousness rests on knowledge taken as given and assumed as existing prior to the answers given in the attempt. Thus, the pursuit of the epistemological question always confounds itself on the fact that the information necessary to answer the question is given by the very terms used in answering the question. To avoid this givenness, one explores at another level the givenness implicit in the original question. But in doing so, one retreats to the other levels of givenness, and therefore the process must be repeated. The attempt is made to escape from a priori thought, but the judgment of what is a priori is itself an a priori judgment, and therefore the consciousness that validates other states of consciousness is subject to the same suspicion that the original state of consciousness was.

Psychology emerged in the attempt to pose the question as an empirical question. The problem became not how do we know, in the abstract, but how do *men* in fact learn, the assumption being that if we could answer the question as an empirical question, we could solve the problem as an epistemological problem.

The early attempts to answer this question were done in terms of associationalism. That is, men are *tabulae rasae*. Sensations and impressions impress themselves on their consciousness. Consciousness is a faculty, a potentiality, that reveals itself by the very fact that men respond to the stimuli that are impressed upon them from the outside world. This solution became, for a relatively long time, the basis of a procedure which recorded the correspondences between men and their experience or environment. It could be criticized because it implied the existence of a consciousness which anteceded the experience, and made men able to experience and reflect their experience and environment. At the same time, the notion of *tabula rasa* assumed that men were passive agents, merely reflecting the stimuli presented to them [2].

One of the problems that plagued all associational psychology is that men actively seek stimuli, and do not merely record stimuli, an insight which became the basis of the instinct psychology of McDougall, Freudian psychology, the symbolic interactionism of George Herbert Mead, and latter-day behaviorism, which incorporates the dynamic elements from Freudian psychology.

At other levels, it became possible to demonstrate that individuals exposed to the same experiential and environmental conditions do not record with equal intensity the experience or the environment presented to them. Associational psychology, at least in its sociological implications, produced great advances over the philosophic psychologies that preceded it. It demonstrated that men in particular times and places developed, at least at gross levels, characteristics, personalities, social particularities, or at least character masks, that corresponded roughly to the quality of their social experience. Thus, an associational psychology could produce concepts of occupational personalities, or personality types that are relevant to an age, a social environment, a cultural configuration, or any other particular social world. In this sense, we have not as yet fully absorbed or extracted the value implicit in associational psychology.

Karl Marx's famous dictum that it is not the consciousness of men which determines their existence, it is the existence of men that determines their consciousness [3], could well have been derived from associational psychology, as in fact it was. The derivations available from this dictum are exactly what one would derive from associational psychology, except that Marx drew character types (or personality types) whose historical and social particularities were derived from relationships to the means of production, from class position, and from economically determined partial exposures to the world of experience. Associationalists believed other kinds of exposure to experience affect personality or character. Marx, using his crude version of associational psychology, influenced the development of an entire school of social psychology based on sociological experience as the principle by which character formation is achieved. Some of those who used a Marxian social psychology were Ferdinand Tonnies, Georg Simmel, Max Weber (through Tonnies and Simmel)—but not necessarily exclusively—and Robert Park and Robert Redfield through Simmel. Through Redfield, a whole host of anthropologists and social psychologists used Marxian social psychology. The concept of personality so derived did not deal with personality as we now understand the term, but rather with social type, social character, or character mask. Associational psychology did not by itself suggest or describe the methods by which experiential impressions recorded themselves upon the consciousness of men, nor did it solve its original problem because it had to assume the existence of a consciousness, a faculty to respond to experience.

The scientific interest in psychology led to an interest in discovering specific physical and scientific processes which intervene between the experiential input and the behavioral output. This quest for a specific demonstrable mechanism led to the exploration of the physiological systems, the electrical and chemical bases by which external impressions are picked up by receptors, transmitted through the nervous system, recorded in ganglia, stored in the cortex, and reinvoked by secondary stimulation producing behavior by a reverse flow of electrical and chemical processes through the same nervous system to the effectors which produce the action.

Such a bald and incomplete summary can hardly do justice to the gigantic body of physiological, experimental, statistical research which has been going on in this field for the past one hundred years and which still continues [4]. Mechanisms of learning and behavior have been discovered, learning theories have evolved, and specific processes by which behavior is evoked have been described in detail. A vast literature of behaviorism has emerged in which experimental replication, testing, and confirmation have been developed. Behaviorism, with its theories of stimulus and response, and with the development of specific descriptions of the physiological, electric, and chemical processes that take place between stimuli and responses, has gone far in closing the gaps left open by associationist psychology. It left unanswered, however, many questions which evoked the original philosophic questions posed of associational psychology. The raw experiential stimuli which become the imput to action are experienced in their own terms as discrete items of sensation. The problem of how such discrete items of sensation are organized into broader modes of conception is a problem that behaviorist psychology has grappled with but not solved. The behaviorist mechanisms as currently presented go little beyond describing men as more than the great apes in construction, analysis of form, size, color, etc.

As naive individuals in our attitudes of everyday life, and not as scientific behavioralists, we take as given that man is capable of highly symbolic thought, poetry, myth, art, literature, feelings, and sensitivities which are much more complex than the unitary and discrete sensations that behaviorism at its best describes. We take as given that man not only responds to such complex phenomena, but creates them as well. As a result, the cultivated layman would ask that the behaviorist must explain what for him would be the ordinary aspects of his life and his symbolic experience.

Behaviorism has attempted to deal with the symbol as well as the sign, but its presentation of the symbol has been as a series of only slightly more complex signs. In defense of these inadequacies, it has been argued in effect, that science is long and life is short, and that behaviorism's youth has as yet not enabled it to grapple with more complex phenomena of basically the same order as its simpler accomplishments. A question that remains is: Are these more complex symbolic materials of the same order as the more simple significant materials? Another question is: How much time is enough? It could be said that psychology's youth is its oldest tradition. In the meantime, the problems unresolved by behaviorist psychology remain and must be dealt with simply because the phenomena that psychology seems to be unable to deal with are so much a part of our lives.

In other words, psychology tends to reduce the qualitative, symbolic, and meaningful aspects of experience to electrical impulses and chemical processes. While it would be difficult to argue with the idea that there is a chemical or electrical aspect to every human experience, the reduction of these meaningful or qualitative aspects of experience to electrical or chemical properties destroys and distorts the quality of the experience itself. Behaviorist psychology thus appears to be unequipped to deal with the basic phenomena of experience. As a result, it neglects those experiences. In attempting to solve the problem of consciousness, behaviorism banished consciousness as a concept. The concept of mind was taboo, at least until very recently, in behaviorist thought because behaviorists were unable to deal with consciousness or mind by the methods they selected as being scientific. Again, the fact that mind or consciousness exists is a fact that behaviorists cannot ignore in their daily experience in their enjoyment of music, poetry, drama, or literature, or in the very pattern of their own response to and participation in events and social relationships, the moment they leave the laboratory. (The fact that we all have taste buds does not explain the taboos on beef among Hindus, and the taboos on pork among Jews and Moslems, the enjoyment of bird nest soup and age-old eggs among Chinese, or, for that matter, the enjoyment of chocolate-covered ants or rattlesnake steaks among some avant-garde Americans.) If the behaviorists are right, then all human populations learn in approximately the same way; what they learn, however, is quite different, and what meanings they attach to what they learn, do not learn, and what others learn and do not learn may vary tremendously. Even if the description and analysis of behavior is correct within behaviorists' framework, that framework deals with a small part of human mental experience.

FREUDIAN PSYCHOLOGY

Freudian psychology, in principle, did not reject physiological, electrical, or chemical explanations of behavior, but chose to explore the mental life of the individual. It was content to have faith that there would be a physiological explanation of that mental life. It would not wait to do its proper task while other mechanisms were being discovered. This assumption appears to be correct since there is fairly good evidence that there is a physiological basis for the repressed unconscious and for the persistence of memory.

The use of hypnotism to reveal repressed memories, a similar use of drugs, and the use of mechanical probing all reveal that no thought or experience is wholly lost; thought and experience may be latent or repressed, but under therapy, or chemical or physical manipulation it can be brought to consciousness [5]. The "unconsciousness" of the id, its "obscurity" by definition remains inaccessible, for if the unconscious were readily available to consciousness, it would be no longer unconscious. However, an outsider, a therapist perhaps, can infer an unconscious motive or thought and can validate his inference by analyzing (retrospectively) the actions that are based on the unconscious. Moreover, he can validate his inference by discovering the existence of the imputed unconscious motive or thought as it becomes conscious.

Freudian psychology did not emerge from an attempt to solve philosophical or epistemological problems. It emerged from the clinical practice of medical doctors, and out of the medical and custodial practices developed in dealing with the insane. As a result, Freudian psychology has always had a pragmatic basis, despite the fact that Freud had strong theoretical interests and a desire to create a system. The clinical basis of Freud's practice of psychology caused him continuously to revise, modify, and expand his system. In his own life, it was never complete. Most subsequent practitioners emphasized technique as developed within the field, more than theory. Only since Freudian psychology became respectable, and fell into the hands of academicians, has there been a strong attempt to make it into a logically closed theoretical model.

As theory in the arts, the social sciences, literature, philosophy, popular psychology, and the mass media, Freudian and neo-Freudian theory has emerged as something quite distinct from its clinical practice: As clinical technique, its method is still relatively small scale, confined to middle- and upper-middle-class patients, the clients of a relatively small number of trained psychoanalysts and psychiatrists. But as a set of habits of mind, or as a set of theories that can be used to explain human experience at almost all levels, it has been the most revolutionary theory to emerge in modern society since the Reformation [6]. Only Marxism and Darwinism have had as much influence. It has resulted in fundamental changes in our image of man, human nature, sex, personality, and in the role of society in expressing and containing man's biological and human nature. It has altered our concepts of work and leisure, of public and private behavior, of the place of the individual in society, and it has helped alter the concept of what is rational and irrational. This is true whether one agrees or disagrees with Freud. It has altered our concept of knowledge, for it has taught us that much of what had been regarded as knowledge is in reality a screen, myth, "ideology," rationalization, or defense. It has taught us to look behind the manifest meanings of much social presentation and behavior, and it claims that much of our culture, institutions, and social organization are means of expressing motives and needs that are otherwise not expressed.

In the extreme, it has led us to devalue the ideas themselves, in a quest for a reality that is more real than the ideas expressed by individuals, for themselves or for their groups. In this latter sense, it contains all of the dangers that are inherent in Marxism and behaviorism. Nothing is as it appears. Everything has a level of meaning which the thinker is at best only partly aware of, and which presumably the auditor or observer can be more aware of. The most powerful critique of this aspect of psychoanalysis is offered by Karl Jaspers, in *Man in the Modern Age:*

> Psychoanalysis collects and interprets dreams, slips, and blunders, involuntary associations, that it may in this way plumb the depths of the unconscious whereby the conscious life is determined. Man is the puppet of his unconscious, and when the latter has had a clear light thrown into it, he will become master of himself. . . . But their doctrine is never unified, not even heuristically for a brief space, in order to advance from a clear statement of a problem into the realm of effective investigation. The psychoanalysts even plume themselves on being empiricists, that, year after year, while presenting an infinite quantity of material, they may go on reiterating what is fundamentally the same thing . . . so does psychoanalysis believe itself able to disclose this same spiritual life as the sublimation of repressed impulses; and what, by these lights is still spoken of as civilization or culture is constructed like an obsessional neurosis. . . . Not only must the Godhead be dethroned, but likewise every kind of philosophical faith. The most sublime and the meanest are dressed up in the same terminology that, tried and found wanting, they may be driven forth into Nothingness [7].

To be sure, this assumption of omniscience and omnipotence may be less true in the actual practice of clinical psychology than it is true of Freudian

theory, as a general mode of sensibility, but again the great revolutionary
ideas resulting from Freudian psychology are due to its acceptance and
practice by those who do not engage in actual clinical practice. To this
extent, Freudian psychology has resulted if not in the destruction then in the
weakening of the importance of ideas per se, and the unwillingness of
individuals to trust the ideas of others or themselves, or to trust the whole
process of discussion, debate, or reason. As a result, in the absence of a
higher rationality that Freudian psychology presumes will emerge as a result
of clinical practice, issues are more and more solved and resolved by pressure, will, and force.

As a clinical technique, Freudian psychology imposes its own brand of
social relations upon its practitioners and its clients. Classical Freudian
therapy involves a one-to-one relationship between patient and practitioner.
The patient enters therapy not lightly, but because he has experienced
anxiety, deep emotional or behavioral problems which he perceives as a
threat to himself or his functioning. The process of therapy results, presumably, in the patient unburdening himself of his illusions, delusions, intimate
thoughts, memories, recalls of past perversions, sources of guilt, trauma,
weaknesses, etc. Almost literally, he strips himself naked before the psychologist. The psychologist does not enter a relationship of equality with the
patient. He remains "clothed." In the recall of all that which indicates his
frailty and weakness, the patient must at times diminish himself, become
small. In comparison, in this relatively intense continuous relationship, the
therapist grows larger, if only because he remains the same while the patient
grows smaller. It is for this reason, perhaps, that transference takes place.
They psychologist acquires the strength, omnipotence, wisdom, and authority of a parent, and the patient takes on the role of a child. Therapeutically,
this may be effective, for it permits the patient to identify with a father and
perhaps to reconstitute an image of a father, though the therapeutic father is
not as communicative, "real," or as self-revealing as an actual father. Nevertheless, the transference permits identification and the possibility of the
reenactment and reliving of events that took place in the distant past.
Looking at this relationship from the standpoint of the psychoanalyst, the
analyst increases in size, as the patient diminishes in size. His authority,
omnipotence, wisdom, and strength increase as the patient, out of his own
response to his self-diminution, invests the analyst with these attributes.
And a busy analyst sees the reality of the external world primarily through
the eyes of his patients. In terms of his social and work environment, the
reality presented to him is a reality reported to him by neurotic patients, a
reality upon which he has little independent opportunity to check. His
professional peers provide him with additional reports of reality, which
derive from the same sources. As a result of these processes, the effect of the

flow and direction of self-definitions is to confirm him in a sense of his own authority, wisdom, power, and strength. Patients may hang on his words, depend on his advice, and treat him as if he were omnipotent. If the analyst has any tendencies toward megalomania or authoritarianism, the response of the patient to the analyst will strengthen them [8].

If the patient resists, rejects, or differs from the analyst's advice, prescription, or role definition, he is after all either neurotic or psychotic, or is in the process of transference, living out infantile struggles against a father or authority figure, or acting out his neurotic or psychotic tendencies. In any event, the analyst has it both ways. He is, or can become, immune, because of his own occupational and positional isolation from the need for a communication that is as responsive from him as it is to him. The patient is expected to communicate from his position of weakness, illness, or dependency, but the analyst communicates from his position of authority, omnipotence, concealment, and psychological and moral superiority. In all such cases, going far beyond the situation of psychoanalytical therapy, the injunction to the other to "communicate" is an injunction to communicate on "my" terms, such that "I" will judge whether "your" communication is adequate. But because "you" do not have the moral, mental, or psychological capacity to be my equal, my communication will start from fixed positions which are inaccessible to you.

In all of these situations, the call for "communication" is a screen for power [9].

We have indicated that the role of the analyst resembles the role of a father, and the role of the father, psychologists indicate, is often attributed to God, for God is authority, wisdom, and omnipotence. God is symbol of the all-powerful father. The analyst, by virtue of the nature of his practice, is placed in a role resembling that of an all-powerful father. If, as we have indicated, he identifies with that role, he can assume the right to play the role of God. This includes the right to interfere with, manipulate, punish, and reward psychologically, and become the life model for the patient. Whether the psychologist chooses to play this role or not depends on his own ability to resist the temptations that are inherently built into the very structure of the therapeutic role relationship.

We do not claim that all psychologists choose to play this role. In some cases their own needs for additional analysis may limit their tendencies toward megalomania. In other cases they may have very little tendency toward megalomania to begin with. Still others may gain insight into this process and struggle against it. We do claim that the nature of the role relationship in one-to-one psychoanalytic and psychiatric relationships tends to enhance the possibility of such a response if there is any latent megalomania present in the character of the analyst.

Patients, of course, can be in the process of transference and subsequent therapy, rebel against the father or their totemic god. If the rebellion occurs as an assertion of their independence, of their capacity to deal with their own problems, then the rebellion may be an indication of a return to health. If it is merely a reenactment of an earlier rebellion, then it may be only a stage in reliving their problems. The analyst, however, must permit the patient to rebel, to assert himself and become independent, despite the fact that at major stages in the course of the therapy, the cards are stacked against the patient. But if he enjoys his own omnipotence and acts to preserve the dependency of the patient, he commits perhaps the most serious crime possible, the denial of growth. And yet not to commit such crimes is to deprive oneself of the grandiosity and pleasures of omnipotence. Strangely enough, there is nothing to limit this possibility in psychoanalytic technique, except continual reanalysis of the analyst.

Analysts have not been unaware of these problems. This is true even of orthodox Freudian analysts who developed most extensively the one-to-one analytic session, with the patient in the supine, dependent position, and who emphasized that the analyst had to play the father role in order to achieve transference. Other analysts, neo-Freudian and anti-Freudian, have rejected the idea of transference, and perhaps the idea of the patient reliving his earlier life in the process of therapy, and thereby reliving the relationship to a father and authority figure.

They concentrate primarily on reality problems in the present, on behavioral problems, on the structure and network of interpersonal relations, rather than on the intrapsychic subjective response of the individuals. But in all of these cases the psychologist presents himself as an agent of reality, of judgment, and as a guide to mental health, to a patient whose presence indicates his psychological inferiority. The problems of authority, godhead, and fatherhood can be presented in either historical or functional terms. Freudian analysis favors a historical presentation of the problems of authority, and allows the patient to relive the godhead and omnipotence of the father, the struggle against authority, and hopefully, allows for the recreation of the men as images of God, but separate and removed therefrom [10]. Neo-Freudian and many forms of anti-Freudian behaviorist and existential therapies reject this historical recreation of authority problems. They deal in functional terms with the same problems viewed not in their historical sense, but in the way they act themselves out in the present. But the relationship of the psychologist to the patient is necessarily similar. The psychologist necessarily symbolizes health and strength, the patient, illness and weakness; the patient reveals himself, and the analyst operates from a concealed and therefore superior position.

GROUP THERAPY

In group therapy the overall model of the strong authoritarian father in a one-to-one relationship is concealed. Group therapy takes other patients as the primary reference group for the individual patient. The therapist remains in the background, directing the flow of the discussion, attention, and line of analysis. It may be difficult to establish the psychological origins of group therapy. It can be argued that in a world where the authority of the patriarch is no longer present, reliving the roles of father and son may not be relevant to patients. They cannot recreate what never existed.

Certainly group therapy either reduces cost per patient or alternatively, increases income per session, or both. In terms of the content of the sessions, it overcomes the isolation of the patient and the therapist from all but the psychological realities of the individual neurosis. The therapist is allowed to view the presentation of psychic material by an individual patient in terms of the response he provokes and receives from other patients, even though these other patients will not necessarily represent the normal non-treatment world of the patient. Yet he may be able to view the characteristic patterns of interpersonal relations of his group. He may be able to use the response of the others as a means of correcting the delusional behavior of the presenting patient.

At another level, the pattern of group response becomes a substitute for the approving or disapproving response of the therapist. In a sense, the substitution of the group judgment for the therapist's judgment may reflect, and be appropriate to, an age where fathers lack the strength to make their own judgments, and where peer groups, social collectivities, and other formal organizations become the primary agencies of social and psychological control and sanctions.

In short, the development of group therapy reflects the substitution of group controls for individual controls, and collective responsibility for individual conscience. If this is the parallel, it can, however, be pursued further. The therapist, while using peer-group controls as a major device for introducing "reality" into the psychic life of his patients, cannot do this haphazardly. If he were to do so, he would only be required to set up a series of group therapy sessions, and allow the group to conduct its own therapy on the basis of evolving group standards. Or, at the extreme, the situations which may well have brought the patient to the therapist were ones involving the operation of group structures and processes upon an individual.

It is quite obvious that the therapist controls, directs, and manipulates the group for therapeutic purposes. This is, at a minimum, necessary in order to create some kind of orderly group process. But additionally it is assumed that the therapist has some techniques, theories, abilities, talents, and training, which are of value to the group and to the specific individuals who make up that group. In order to make use of these abilities and talents, he must in some way impose them on the group. In using group therapy, he abandons the role of the strong authoritarian father whose authority emerges at manifest levels in the process of therapy, and the problems of which become the major problems worked out in the course of therapy.

In abandoning this "strategy," the patient develops a more "equalitarian," more "democratic" approach to therapy. In order, however, for the therapy situation to operate, and for the therapist to contribute to that operation, the therapist must in fact control the situation. But his control is subtle, indirect, manipulative, subliminal, "democratic," and suggestive. The therapist selects and uses the responses of others to demonstrate points which he wishes to make, but often does not directly initiate these points himself. He may, however, evoke from others the responses which he wishes to make. All of the elements of an authority situation are present, but the authority elements are concealed in democratic manipulation. The therapist, instead of acting the role of the strong father, acts out, possibly, the role of the older brother or a democratic father, a peer-group leader rather than a father.

But all of this implies that he does manipulate and control. He uses authority but he conceals the use of authority. His use of the big brother role depends on his ability to conceal the manipulative ethos.

He thus develops an approach of warmth, friendliness, ingenuousness, sincerity, spontaneity, openness, and support. His professional ideology is to provide warmth, supportiveness, ego enhancement, and the development of intensive group structures. In short, he desires to create a therapeutic climate or a group culture that supports him, the group process, and ultimately its members. Group morale and group loyalty become major supports to this process. At times such group characteristics may transcend the individual members, including the therapist, and their problems. The maintenance of the group and its process becomes a supreme value, and its members may become dependent upon it. This applies even to the therapist. The older psychologist, working on a transference theory, could expect his patient to develop hostility, to react against the father and the god, and if he had autonomy, could expect himself to be overthrown. The group therapist is likely to define himself as a "nice guy" and become dependent upon the group for this definition. Or, to state it more accurately, the phenomenological consequences of this type of group structure are to support the role of the good guy, to select good guys for the role, and to reward therapists able to maintain that role [11].

The role of the good guy, however, often conflicts with the role of the therapist. At times it becomes necessary to confront the patient or to evoke confrontations of patients by other patients. That is, he must point out what elements of a patient's behavior are delusional, defensive, neurotic, not based on reality. If he avoids or delays this confrontation in order to be a good guy, he postpones therapeutic resolution of the patient's problem.

Fortunately or unfortunately, there are limits to such procedures. Patients almost invariably recognize the manipulative direction of the group discussion. They respond to the therapist in his role as big brother; they become his sibling rivals; and as they learn and identify with his methods, they are likely to turn upon him. And in the innumerable combinations of alliances and alignments that make up the network of social relationships in group discussions, they are likely to unite in resistance and opposition to the therapist. At that time, it takes considerable skill to resolve the conflicts in role between being a good guy and being an authoritarian therapeutic manipulator. Perhaps only superiority at manipulation will result in a higher synthesis of the two contradictory elements in group therapy.

But at another level the problems of group therapy are manifold. Since the group functions best when group enthusiasm, morale, and cohesion are strong, and since effective therapy may create dependency on the group, then the problem of the termination of therapy becomes a great one. Theoretically, individual therapy ends when the patient feels strong enough to stand upon his own feet. Occasionally it ends at a point in negative transference when a patient is most vulnerable to his own hostility and aggressiveness. This is of course true where the therapy is voluntary. Group therapy can at times produce such a strong collective ego that the members of the group can function only as members of the group. When this is so, group therapy becomes interminable. Fortunately the collective overthrow of the authoritative brother provides at best a "natural" point of termination, whether or not the problems of the invididuals in the group are resolved. And of course group therapy can be terminated when it is replaced by individual therapy tolerable to individuals who would not otherwise accept it. And finally a natural termination point can occur with the development of mutual boredom or hostility.

Assuming that the group goes through stages other than those characterized by mutual antagonism, hostility, or boredom, such a termination is not inappropriate. But if and when the group as individuals or collectively decides that all they are doing is disturbing old garbage, that nothing further is coming out of the group, then perhaps it has accomplished all that it can. And the termination of group therapy is positively realized when its members (or a member) realize that they could be spending this time and money in more valuable ways than rehashing old issues.

If this stage is reached, it may well mean that the old problems are no longer salient. Group therapy, then, usually ends with a bad taste in the mouth for both members and for therapist, even when it is successful. To the therapist, however, the experience that it may have been successful may not be confirmed by the attitudes of members at the moment of termination. As a result, therapists need constant reassurance that their efforts have not been a failure. The patient may terminate therapy with a sense that it is a waste of time, but he can do so because he feels that he is now able to do other, more profitable things.

Beyond this, he may well discover that in an age of therapy, having participated in it is in itself a valuable social attribute. He may have priceless stories to tell, he can participate in post-therapeutic communities and be able to understand those arcane cultures when presented by others. In short, he is no longer "out of it."

This is by no means a negative aspect of therapy. It does become one when the participation in therapy, individual or group, is conceived of primarily as a device to achieve the prestige and benefits of participation in therapy or post-therapeutic communities. When this happens, participation in therapy becomes a charade which is guaranteed to have little chance of success. But the prestige of therapeutic culture is so high that the demand for it is relatively great, and there is no shortage of charlatans who are willing to meet these demands.

As a result, new forms of therapy, procedures, gimmicks, devices, and schools continually proliferate, and are a major source of invention or innovation in the field. It has been our experience that many new forms of group therapy appear to be designed to collapse the advantages of post-therapeutic narcissism into the course of therapy itself. Persons who think they have no problems enter groups with others who think they have no problems. The enjoyment of psychological exposure and of voyeurism provides a sense of pseudo-community and a sense of freedom from the restraints which are normally associated with everyday life. The sense of daring, danger, and thrill are all made legitimate by the camouflage that they are undergoing therapy and learning to become spontaneous. Such feelings are, in addition, legitimated by the opportunities to express a sense of liberated elitehood before those who have not had the privilege of being a group member. The value achieved is that of *épatant le bourgeois*, even if the bourgeois is themselves [12].

THE SOCIETAL SETTING OF THERAPY

We have indicated that, while Freudian, neo-Freudian, and some anti-Freudian forms of therapy have very strong theoretical bases and rationales for their respective methods, the social framework, the patterning of social roles within the therapeutic process helps to define the meaning of therapy itself. Individual therapy tends to maximize the visibility of authority relationships, which in turn may be viewed as father-son relationships, or as God-man relationships. Group therapy tends more to become a brotherhood or peer-group relationship, in which authority is masked but always present, and techniques of "democratic" equalitarian manipulation govern the course and process of therapy, even in their unintended consequences.

Beyond this, we have suggested, at least minimally, that the therapeutic relations become surrogates for different kinds of family relationships whose applicability in part is determined by the appropriateness of these kinds of family relationships to different stages in the development of society. Thus, Freudian analysis appears to be most effective in societies where authoritarian fathers still exist. Group therapy appears to become more appropriate in societies where peer groups replace parental authority. Of course, since changes in the nature of family authority occur at unequal rates over time, it may well be that, depending upon the individual's family background, different types of therapy may be appropriate to different individuals. Moreover, to the extent that different kinds of family constellations may produce different kinds of problems, different kinds of therapy may be appropriate for different symptomologies.

If this is the very structure of our argument as related to Freudian psychology, what can we say of behaviorism, in terms of its social origins and consequences? Regardless of the many manifest varieties of behavioristic psychology, the essential model remains its original model—that of the effect of stimulation, reward, and reinforcement on subsequent responses. The external environment, through a system of selective external stimuli, operates on the nervous, chemical, electrical processes of the physiological individual to produce responses which are coherent with the nature and organization (and disorganization) of these stimuli. As a theory it has the advantages and disadvantages indicated above. But theory never remains pure theory. It develops an affinity for users and usages. If the behavior of individuals is determined by the response to stimuli, then the "natural" questions that must follow are: Who provides the stimuli? Who provides the responses? Historically, these others may be rats, mice, or students. Occasionally, they are prison inmates, or persons employed at relatively low wages. In wartime situations they may be troops, prisoners of war, or residents of guardhouses. They may be internees.

Since the experimenter is the stimulator, and the function of the subject is to respond to the stimuli provided by the experimenter, it is easy to understand how it is possible for the experimenter to see himself as a mover and the others as the moved. Within the framework of the experiment, the experimenter has the power, the authority to initiate action; the others have the freedom to respond both in terms of the experimenter's stimuli, and in terms of their prior personal and social existence up until the moment of the experiment. But quite often these other characteristics are subject to "controls." Given the structure of the experiment, and the nature of the implicit authority relationships involved in the experiment, it is easy to see how the experimenter can conceive of himself as the omnipotent mover, the controller, the manipulator of others.

In this sense, the possibility of developing an authoritarian manipulative mentality, deriving from the nature of the work itself, is as strong within the framework of behavioral psychology as it is in clinical psychology. In fact, since the pattern of interaction between analyst and analysand is more continuous, more intense, and is reciprocal, the patient, with all of the limits implied in the patient role, is more able to defend himself, and to limit the megalomania of the therapist, than the subject is in relation to the experimenter. Moreover, the course and development of clinical psychology makes manifest the irrational elements in the patient, the therapeutic process, and possibly the analyst.

In experimental psychology, the experimenter responds within a framework of scientific rationality, precision, control, and logical deductiveness. The experimenter assumes, because of the very nature of the rational and scientific methods that he uses, that he is the agent of rationality and of science in the experiment. It is also equally possible for him to confuse the values of science and rationality that are implicit in his technique with all other values that he or the subjects of his experiment may have. He is therefore likely to construct from his technical methods, a world view that he believes is superior to the world view of all others, and thus to prescribe the values for all others, for the society as a whole, and for "less rational" and "less scientific" leaders of the society. In fact, it is possible for him to conceive of the society as a vast experiment, with himself as the experimenter [13]. The experiment does not provide a theoretical framework by which the patient can challenge the logic of the experiment. The findings of his behavior, however, may challenge the hypotheses which the experimenter may test. But there is nothing in the nature of the social relationship between experimenter and subject which could constitute a check upon the scientific, logical righteousness of the experimenter. Thus, the patient is seen as raw material, at times intransigent, but only as resistant to the logically oriented omnipotence of a rather distanced and removed authority figure.

Yet it is not the quality of the social relationships in behaviorist psychology that presents its greatest threat to men as men. It is rather the correspondence of the logic of the experiment to the logic of manipulation present in other authoritarian bureaucratic institutions in our society. The logic of behaviorism assumes that the experimenter has the freedom to initiate actions upon a compliant respondent. At most, the respondent may resist but never does the respondent initiate actions to which the experimenter responds. In this model the psychologist has freedom and authority, and the omnipotence of the psychologist is maximized.

In nonexperimental situations this represents at most an ideal, for outside the laboratory the psychologist does not have this omnipotence. At most he is a handmaiden to those who have the economic and political resources to apply what is essentially the model of behaviorist psychology. Thus, the advertising agency, the mass media, the large-scale organization, the army, the business firm, or the government department are each centralized. Relatively few individuals have the authority or resources to transmit stimuli to which masses either within or outside the organization are supposed to respond.

Research on the audience and research on the effects of previous experiments are designed to assure maximum effectiveness in the selection of stimuli, in the selection of media, and in the proper differentiation of stimuli and media appropriate to the intended audience. The psychologist may assist in the technical design of such experiments in the control of audience response, but by now the logic of control has reached a point where a whole host of occupations, sociology, market research, political science, business administration, industrial engineering, industrial psychology, and so on, apply basically the logic of science to human social relations. It is interesting that at this level the different preconceptions of behaviorist and Freudian psychology need not be opposed to one another; the Freudian, with his knowledge of unconscious motivations and irrational elements in behavior, provides models for more effective selection of stimuli, cues, images, and symbols, which become part of the content used by a mechanism based on the logic of experimental science.

In neither case, however, is the model or the symbol decisive, but rather where psychology is applied in these ways, it is the logic of power—power as used in large-scale centralized organizations—that is decisive. It would be unfair to blame behaviorist psychology for the uses that are made of it. Behaviorist psychology developed its logic independently of the logic of bureaucratic manipulation, but the similarity of the fundamental logic of psychology to the necessities of pacific domination of a population were such as to make it immediately useful. Such usefulness has not been overlooked. Bureaucrats of all kinds have seen the possibilities inherent in both behaviorist and Freudian psychology, and wherever they had the resources to do so, have applied them, and have applied them increasingly [14].

Seen from this point of view, the modern world is a multiplicity of experiments in which the subjects to those experiments are most often unaware of their role as subjects. If psychology and the related fields that use the psychological models as their methodology are to be blamed, it is for their willingness to serve. The one hopeful sign in all of this is the fact that the experiments in empirical control are not, from the standpoint of the laboratory, good experiments. That is, in a world in which all organizations attempt to experiment on the underlying populations, the subjects of those experiments are frequently subject to an uncountable number of simultaneous and often contradictory experiments.

In short, the stimuli in the experiments are contaminated. In a rat lab, this would be likely to drive the rat mad, and to some extent this may occur. Even here the sheer multidimensionality of experimentation may not have the effect of producing direct conflicts in conditioning. The multiplicity of stimuli may have the effect of cancelling the effects of any one set of stimuli. For separate populations differentially exposed to a set of stimuli, the effect of the experiment may result in a statistical tendency of the respondents to act in a given direction but as long as it is impossible to isolate the respondents from alternative conditioning, they do not respond in total to the stimuli, as rats in a maze.

Beyond this, the subjects are not rats. At times they respond not only to the stimulus itself but to the meaning of the stimulus, and resist not only the stimulus but also those whom they know to be the creators of the experiment. Thus, it appears difficult for any set of experiments to be too successful for too long a period of time. Russian and Czech populations have been subject to as intensive propaganda, brainwashing, and manipulated control as any population one can imagine. At the first opportunity of presenting evidence of some freedom in response, the subjects of these experiments have indicated that they never were brainwashed. The freedom to respond, the "thaw," indicates the development of counterexperimental attitudes that must have been in existence all the time in order to have been so well developed at the moment of the "thaw."

Such opportunities for freedom may result in orgies of freedom which go far beyond what is necessary for survival and may be as destructive in their immediate consequences as the initial brainwashing itself. But the exultation in freedom, self-determination, and autonomy is as basic to the development of the psyche as the possibility of experimental manipulation. In the same way, the attempts of an industrial society to condition its youth and its lower classes has resulted in a rebellion both against the process and against the agencies of such socialization, a rebellion which is often as irrational and as destructive as the pure exultation in freedom from control which momentarily emerged in more totalitarian societies.

The logic of control, however, seems to be an inevitable accompaniment to the institutional development of large-scale bureaucratic societies, whether they emerge from within the framework of more decentralized democratic societies, or from the attempts of more totalitarian societies to decrease the costs of domination. The use of this logic of domination then becomes independent of the specific methodologies which have become major instruments in this process. Once such methodologies are discovered, it is difficult to imagine their disappearance. Regardless of design, we may be forced to live in a world in which the logic of psychology is a major institution.

The problem is to discover the means by which this logic is not carried through to its ultimate conclusion. That conclusion is to convert men into rats. But we have indicated that this by itself does not work. The experimental situation is most effective when, at the institutional level, men have no choice but to respond to the experiment. They are isolated from all other stimuli, and are offered no opportunity to attack or destroy the experiment. In other words, experimental science never works unless the experimental scientist has, in addition to his science, the power to force the respondent in the direction indicated by the experiment. Thus, if conditioning is dependent on providing positive or negative rewards for acceptance of the indicated behavior and for reinforcement of that behavior, then the experiment becomes effective if all other alternative rewards offered to individuals outside the framework of experiment are eliminated. Thus, five dollars an hour paid to be an experimental subject is not likely to be a strong inducement to millionaires.

The logic of experimental science or psychology is most effective in totalitarian situations, or at least those in which traditional restraints and conventions can be evaded, as is often the case in laboratories, hospitals, mental institutions, and prisons. To prevent the conversion of men into laboratory rats requires that we be opposed to the totalitarianism which is always implicit in the experiment. At the academic or laboratory level, and to a lesser extent in the therapist's offices, the psychologist may be free to play his scientific games. When the same logic is applied to the normal, natural, empirical world, it becomes even more of a menace. The task of the humanist is to prevent conversion of the world into a laboratory.

NOTES

1. R. A. Harper, *Psychoanalysis and Psychotherapy: 36 Systems* (New York, Prentice-Hall, 1959); R. S. Woodworth, *Contemporary Schools of Psychology* (New York, Ronald, 1931).

2. F. S. Keller, *The Definition of Psychology* (New York, Appleton-Century-Crofts, 1937).

3. K. Marx, "A Contribution to the Critique of Political Economy, Preface," in L. Feuer (Ed.), *Marx & Engels: Basic Writings on Politics and Philosophy* (Garden City, N. Y., Doubleday, 1959), p. 145.

4. W. R. Hess, *The Biology of Mind* (Chicago, University of Chicago Press, 1962); R. C. Oldfield, "Experiment in Psychology—A Centenary and an Outlook," in J. Cohen (Ed.), *Readings in Psychology* (London, Allen & Unwin, 1964); K. H. Pribram and D. E. Broadbent, *Biology of Memory* (New York, Academic Press,

1970); 0. Zangwill, "Physiological and Experimental Psychology," in J. Cohen (Ed.), *Readings in Psychology* (London, Allen & Unwin, 1964).

5.   K. H. Pribram and D. E. Broadbent, *op. cit.*

6.   P. Rieff, *The Triumph of the Therapeutic* (New York, Harper & Row, 1966), Chaps. 4, 8.

7.   K. Jaspers, *Man in the Modern Age* (Garden City, N.Y. Doubleday, 1957), pp. 167–168.

8.   There have been several studies of the misuse of therapy. See H. L. Lennard and A. Bernstein, *The Anatomy of Psychotherapy: Systems of Communication and Expectation* (New York, Columbia University Press, 1960), pp. 121–122. A popularized description of this problem is M. Shepherd and M. Lee, *Games Analysts Play* (New York, Putnam, 1967). Shepherd and Lee offer the thesis that therapists' manipulations can vastly extend and impoverish the course of therapy.

9.   Since the 1930's, major sets of theories have been based on the needs for communication. These theories have emerged in managerial studies, in sociology, in the field of intergroup relations, anthropology, and political science, as well as in psychology and in behavioral science. In all of these fields, we would feel that those who call for communication assume that it is *others* who must communicate, either with them or with still others. The communications practitioner assumes that since he understands the theory and practice of communication, it is his function to stimulate the communication from others. He assumes that his communications are rational, scientific, objective, and necessary from the standpoint of the communication system while others use communication as a screen for less worthy purposes. In this sense, he develops the possibility of a megalomania that is not unlike that which is inherent in the social situation of analyst-patient.

10.   P. E. Slater, *Microcosm: Structural, Psychological, and Religious Evolution in Groups* (New York, Wiley, 1966), Chap. 2, "The Attack on the Leader."

11.   If, as in some schools of therapy, the group leader becomes an open, democratic, responsive, and unauthoritarian group leader, he surrenders whatever technical advantages that he might have as a psychologist. He might do so, however, if he has faith in his ability to direct the discussion and intergroup relations without recourse to his personal or technical authority. If he follows this latter path, it merely means that he hides his confidence in his ability to control a group on the basis of his knowledge, insight, and technical skill. He merely conceals a sense of superiority that is necessary for the practice of group therapy. All of this is only to say that there are contradictions and role conflicts at the very heart of group therapy.

12.   J. Howard, *Please Touch: A Guided Tour of the Human Potential Movement* (New York, McGraw-Hill, 1970). See also J. Mann, *Encounter: A Weekend with Intimate Strangers* (New York, Grossman, 1970).

13.   The popular writings of eminent psychologists and psychological journalists reveal at almost every stage in the history of psychology new and up-to-date versions of this application.

14.   R. A. Harper, *op. cit.* See also Charles Rycroft, editor: *Psychoanalysis Observed* (Baltimore, Penguin, 1960), and Perry London; *The Modes and Morals of Psychotherapy* (New York, Holt, Rinehart and Winston, 1964).

Chapter 11

Craft and Meaning in Literature

THE LITERARY REDUCTION

In our previous discussions of occupation and professional attitudes, one of the chief characteristics of each attitude has been its tendency to make a reduction away from the primary phenomenon itself to an aspect of the phenomenon which is relevant to the special occupational specialization, technique, or methodology of the field. Thus, the same phenomenon can be viewed as "psychological," "economic," "sociological," "historical," "ideational" (or intellectual). But given each reduction, the data reported, the terminology and models used are so different that it might be difficult to recognize that each field is reporting on the same events or phenomena. The literary attitude, with the exceptions to be noted below, operates at an entirely different level [1]. Classically, literature attempts to reconstitute the wholeness, the irreducibility of life, and to suggest the unity of the worlds that make up a life. This does not mean that it necessarily creates a unity where that unity does not exist; rather, that it may portray men in the process of attempting to live a unified life even when the forces in society appear to tear such a life apart. The central unit in such classic literature is the whole person. The portrayal of an individual, heroic, tragic, even insignificant, may be involved, but the central organizing principle is that experience be expressed through the life of an individual or a set of individuals. Thus, abstract social forces, historical processes, even fate and nemesis are experienced as personifications. The individual deals with these forces in personal terms, and attempts to solve problems by his own actions. Abstraction, formalization, impersonality, as techniques of portraying the world, are usually avoided. As a result, the world is depicted so that it can be comprehended in almost visual terms. *Events* are described as the products of men, not "social forms" [2]. Narrative, the detailed description of events, is still the primary basis of the literary attitude. The art of storytelling is central to the literary attitude, no matter how prosaic and matter-of-fact, undignified, and unpretentious it may be [3].

Of course, this approach is also a "reduction." It may be argued that the complex life in a complex society is so diffuse, so subject to abstract, impersonal forces that a "realistic" treatment involves the portrayal of these forces in their own terms. This is to say that the psychological, economic, political, and sociological reductions must be made in order to analyze the events themselves. The classical novelist would reply that each of these aspects of experience are presented in concrete visual-narrative forms.

This is to say that no matter how abstract and formal a social or spiritual force may be in classical literature, the force is embodied in concrete personal forms.

At another level, it can be argued that life constitutes an accumulation of an infinity of details, sensations, and experiences which thrust themselves upon an individual without apparent reason. Simply recording these sensations as they thrust themselves upon individuals would lead to an accumulation of unrelated ad hoc details that are as senseless as life itself. Some naturalistic novelists have attempted to do exactly this, in the name of accuracy, representation, and completeness of recording of a process by which lives are lived.

Novelists who attempt to record in excessive detail the way the world impinges upon them may not succeed in ordering their experience. Balzac, in the guise of the omniscient observer, accumulates vast amounts of detail. Robbe-Grillet, by contrast, is no omniscient observer. The reader apparently experiences the senselessness of events along with the protagonist, and the reader is forced to make his own relevant selection along with the protagonist, even though he may lack the selective mechanisms that determine the framework of relevances possessed by the protagonist.

Thus, classical authors, in giving a sense of order to lives and to events, that is, treating them as if there were a narrative and dramatic continuity of events and a unity within each of the personae, provide or imply a set of categories that go far beyond the recording of discrete, unrelated sensations. Thus, the process of giving narrative and dramatic order to personae and events constitutes a kind of classic literary reduction which some modern literateurs, as we shall see, have rejected. Others, focusing on the process by which sensation is experienced, will attempt to record the thresholds of experience where undifferentiated stimuli are presented to the protagonist or to the reader, and the immediate, undifferentiated response of the protagonist is presented, perhaps as an interior dialogue, and the reader is asked to reassemble, in visual, dramatic terms, the actors in the situation, the actions in that situation, and the response of the protagonist [4].

Thus, the job done by a classical novelist or storyteller is left to the reader, and if the reader fails, it is his own deficiency. In this sense, modern literateurs have abandoned the classic unities, the classic virtues and programs of literary work. [5] An understanding of this process is of interest. In part, it may be that the attempt to create work in a classic mode is based on the attempt to gain understanding of events, and understanding of the personalities that deal with events as an attempt at self-understanding by an author for an audience. The attempt to understand events and personalities is a product of the sense of being imprisoned by events. Clarification is a process by which the individual liberates himself from a sense of not understanding, or from misunderstanding the complexity and fragmentation of experience.

Literature, in this sense, is the attempt to reconstitute a fractured or incomplete world so that it is amenable to intellectual control and understanding. The unity portrayed is a unity striven for, not a unity achieved. Literature from Homer on has been a major process by which men have sought to come to terms with a dimly understood life, to put intellectual order in that life, to put intellectual insight into it, and to cope with new sources or new kinds of fragmentation, misapprehension, complexity, and confusion.

Other major aspects of literary craftsmanship are explored by critics such as Erich Auerbach, Wayne Booth, Northrop Frye, and Kenneth Burke. Classical authors do not "simply" narrate events, as though they created literary genres entirely free of prior influences. They worked within, and emerged from, old established forms of myth, ritual, and legend, which tightly circumscribed what they could describe and how they could describe it. Thus the portrayal of reality was often limited to relatively few modalities: a dignified tone where noble personages were portrayed, and low comedy where everyday life and ordinary persons were represented. This, for Auerbach, is "realism" as classical authors interpret it. But periodically, writers rebel against these rigid categories and struggle to portray not only "external" but psychological realities in forms and styles appropriate to their expressive instincts or theories. Thus, literary craftsmanship includes both a use of existing modalities of realistic narration and of rebellions against these modalities in search of extended accuracy in the portrayal of experience [6].

Northrop Frye develops a typology of literary genres corresponding to the status of the protagonists and their relationship to their environments. Where a protagonist is superior to other men, and superior to natural and social environments, a myth or legend is enacted. Where the protagonists are superior in rank to other men, but not to natural or social environments, then epic or high tragedy is the appropriate genre. Where the protagonist is superior in rank to men, and is in some respects above the limitations of nature, then the genre is termed *romance*, as in the legends of the Arthurian knights. Where the protagonists are "people like us," the genre is that of "low mimesis," low comedy or realism. Where the protagonists are portrayed as inferior persons (in a moral rather than a social sense), then the ironic mode portrays the antihero. Beyond this, the craftsmanship of the writer includes not only the development of appropriate tonalities, language, and incident, but the handling and reworking of a large vocabulary of myths, symbols, archetypes, and legends that are the residues, both for writers and their audiences, of literary, cultural, and religious traditions. Some genres require realistic, others more idealized modes of treatment; the conventions adopted are as much social as they are literary in character [7].

A writer may at times depart from these conventions for the sake of specific effects. Thus Sean O'Casey's *Juno and the Paycock* presents a mixture of low comedy with bitter tragedy in ways that violate the conventions of tone and mood of the traditional genres. In avant-garde literature, of course, such violations of norms have themselves become a norm. For Kenneth Burke, dramatic forms have become archetypes of human thought-forms. In his *A Grammar of Motives*, he describes the five dramatic terms: act, scene, agent, agency, and purpose—what was done, the background against which it was done, the person performing the act, the means used, and the motivation. In various literary and philosophical genres, these five terms may stand in varying relations to one another, and in turn generate ways of understanding the world. Thus, a philosophy of pantheist determinism places primary emphasis on the scene as primary agent; pragmatism, on agencies or instruments; a social psychologist may describe the transforming effect of the robes of office (the "scene") on the man assuming the office. Poetic, narrative, and dramatic modes reflect varying uses and relations between these five dramatic forms, and the craft of the poet or dramatist includes a conscious mastery of these forms and their internal relations [8].

Thus, the attempt to comprehend a complex world involves, as much for the literary artist as for the philosopher, the theologian, or the historian, the development of categories, methods, and genres corresponding to the needs both of artists and their audiences, to understand their world.

As new problems arise, and as new populations enter a scene, for which intellectual awareness and probing becomes possible, new literatures develop which have the quality of personification, concreteness, and unity in its basic form. Thus, even when the dominant literary forms are complex, methodological, technical, and virtuosic, old classic forms are recreated and reasserted at precisely those points where the need for intellectual comprehension and reconstruction of a total world is necessary. The Russian novelists of "the thaw" attempt to reassess the meanings of politically submerged experience, by use of the most oldfashioned forms and styles, attempting to recreate images of total societies and of total persons struggling to deal with the fragmentation of their experience.

LITERARY CRAFTSMANSHIP

Literature is more than an attempt to reconstruct worlds, more than a system that embodies personal philosophies, ontologies, or world images; it became, at a relatively early age, a professional activity. It developed methods and techniques of its own, and the preoccupation with technological development became a major goal of the craft of literature. First of all, literature is concerned with the use of words, and becomes subject to the dynamics of that concern. At times the art of writing a simple sentence appears to be almost the exclusive concern of the literary craftsman. At other times, the art of writing an elegant sentence, an ornate sentence, an "educated" sentence, or one replete with obscure, informed, and archaic literary allusions becomes the goal of writing a sentence. Poetry is a special and more intensive application of the concern with language, of course. It is less concerned with narrative action, and more concerned with the moods, feelings, and evocations that words, images, and allusions can present. Within this framework, the following discussions of the relationships of form to content, of craft to final product, are, we feel, applicable. One might argue that within the dynamics of a craft, most literary periods will select one of these stylized frameworks as a basic methodological principle, and explore the possibilities of writing within the framework of its assumptions, until mere repetition destroys the novelty and challenge, or the technical gratifications produced by the attempt. Boredom may set in, and new problems are posed for the stylist. Another assumption is postulated, either in continuation of the original or in direct opposition to it, which provides a basis for new aesthetic experimentation and innovation.

Poetry, in its concern with the meaning and evocative powers of even a single word, a symbol, or an image, and with the arrangements of sound, of mood and overtones produced by a relatively small number of words, does not need to produce an orderly or panoramic vision of a total life. It may produce an illumination of, an evocation of, or a resonance with, a small corner of life. It thus aspires to a deeper and not necessarily an extensive image of life. In concentrating on an image, it attempts to capture the essence of an experience, a feeling, a mood, or a tone; but it does not do this philosophically, that is, does not strive to be general, abstract, and prosaically explicit. Rather, to the extent that the mood portrayed is universal, it is private, subjective, and specific. It thus establishes a form of communication at levels deeper than can be put into ordinary language [9].

Poetry may be closer to music than to other forms of literature. In its concentration on the nuances of mood and feeling, created by the selection, sequence, order, and sound of words, it requires a harmony, balance, and precision in the selection and order of words that may not be necessary in prose. This kind of craftsmanship may be of a higher order than can be expected in other forms of literature. That is, it is possible for great novels to be weak in craftsmanship of this order, whereas poetry devoid of such craftsmanship is necessarily bad poetry. But the concentration on poetic craftsmanship, when it results in such a self-conscious specialization, will result in an experimental attitude towards sounds, word arrangements, meter, and beat, that quite often transcends the meanings and evocation of the imagery itself. It can produce a kind of experimentalism with respect to its technique that is not unlike the experimentalism in all other areas of methodological and stylistic concentration. The fact that poetry does have this unique specialization does not by any means preclude its use in other forms of literature.

The element of thematic conflict in literature is of course most likely to be present in the drama, and underscores the fact that the drama has separate meanings from literature. The drama not only emphasizes, in heightened form, the confrontation of opposing forces within an individual or within society, but it may be a means of performing ritualistic, ceremonial, cathectic, and symbolic functions for the audience or the society at large. Such functions derive from the fact that drama when publicly performed can evoke an immediate response and collaboration between the audience and the actors. The immediacy of the performance in its public setting provides an emotional setting to the drama that can be of a different order than the immediacy of response by a reader to the printed page or a viewer to painted canvas. The drama is more social in its character, and contains the possibility for an emotional contagion and catharsis that is unique to its form. With the development of the self-consciousness of the dramatic craft, it becomes an objective of the dramatist and the actor [10]. These elements become separate from literature. However, since much of literature, poetry, and folk "literature" developed in performance, whether by bards, troubadours, or troupes of performers, this dramatic and poetic element has remained as part of the fundamental impulse to all literature. It has become part of the literary tradition even when performance is no longer central to its media.

While drama evokes an immediate emotional response because it is social in its performance, yet all literature, good and bad, and regardless of form, creates images and moods, conceptions of personality, and characters which influence audiences far beyond the currency of the work itself. Du Maurier's *Trilby* became the model for millions of American career girls, just as Emma Peel of television's "The Avengers," had become a model in dress and manner for another generation of liberated women. For the ancient Greeks, the drama was a means of expressing the myth, the spirit, and the conflict in Greek society. Homer helped to fix conceptions of virtue and heroism at even earlier periods. Ideals of love have been offered by Sappho, Ovid, Laura, Heloise and Abelard, Don Juan, Dante, Petrarch, Carmen, Violetta, Werther, Jane Eyre, Lucky Jim, Tess, and Scarlet O'Hara. Literature has symbolized the national aspirations of a culture, a social class, the ideals and demands of youth, the travails of the seeker for autonomy and freedom, the heroism of the religious virtuoso, the struggles of man against nature, and has provided models and images of behavior that could be emulated by individuals who saw themselves in the situations portrayed in a poem, a play, or a novel.

Beyond this, poetry especially has given expression to and legitimacy for personal moods, styles, and emotional traits which at most might have been individual forms of expression. The cultural objectivity of literature, its accessibility to those who can read and to those who emulate those who can read, means that literature dignifies and makes acceptable moods, perceptions, and behavior which individuals might otherwise have felt were purely subjective, private aberrations. In identifying with such publicly accessible symbols, the reader can feel free to publicly express his private behavior, or even more, make himself over to fit a style that seems attractive when presented in literature.

Events in the classic formula are usually shown from the standpoint of a central protagonist, but variations in craft may result in shifting the protagonist, so that the same events are seen through the eyes of a number of persons, some of whom may not be identified by the author. The job is left to the reader who reconstructs the momentary protagonist by seeing him through the eyes of other protagonists who have been previously been presented. Narrators may turn out to be unreliable, and their narrations may be "corrected" by other, equally unreliable narrators. In such an approach, the unity of events is presented by inference since each protagonist sees only a partial segment of those events. The reader must reconstruct the sequence of events as if he were a participant in or a historian of the events, being presented only with fragments, and making his own reconstruction. The dominant theme of the novel may be to present the ambiguity, the lack of form, the lack of closure of events, and presumably judgment is left to the reader. However, all the materials on which such a judgment can be made are usually offered by the novelist. Finally, the unity of character need not be presented. Each person may present an image, his own partial image, of the other characters. But each person's image of the others is fragmentary, based not only on his limited experience with that other and on the filtering of that experience by his own misunderstanding of himself and his motives, as revealed by the misunderstanding of him by others.

The modern novel is often a highly intricate puzzle, ambiguous and obscure, and places the reader in the position of being willing to play a game of literary detection, first to find out what the novel is about, what actually happened in it, what its characters were like, and what the novel or play actually said. These ambiguities and absurdities seem to be the explicit intention of the novelist, and the dominant characteristic of the novel (or play) is that of a puzzle. Yet strangely enough, the same ambiguities of event or of character are present in almost every great novel or play based on the classic unities. Critics can engage for centuries on the meanings involved in the events or characters of Hamlet, Prince Hal, or Falstaff, or of the heroes of the Iliad. The methodological self-consciousness of the novelist as crafts-man leads him with much straining and affectation to produce what the best literary artists produce within a framework of classical simplicity.

LITERATURE AS SOCIAL PHILOSOPHY

We have indicated that the generic method of the novel is the dramatic narrative, storytelling through the verbal reconstruction of the lives of protagonists in dramatic confrontations. The novel, and literature as craft, involves the self-conscious manipulation of words, symbols, styles, novelistic structures, points of view, suspensions and inversions of time sequences, inner and outer voices, and other novelistic devices. These can be viewed as methodologies and techniques which have an autonomy and dynamic of their own. Manipulation of these techniques, exhaustion of the possibilities in their self-consciously selected, limited assumptions results in the "need" for changes in assumption, techniques, methodologies and devices, and helps to produce a set of dynamics which results in a continuous meth-odological and technical innovation and self-consciousness.

But literature involves more than narrative, storytelling, and technologi-cal inventiveness. In portraying dramatic confrontations in the lives of his protagonists, the novelist presents, whether he likes it or not, his image of human life as it is, as it might be, or as he thinks his audience will under-stand it or would like to understand it [11]. Thus, it happens that the author cannot help importing into the generic form and the craft of literature all of the elements which influence his images of human life. In a relatively simple society with a dominant religious myth and poetic or political structure, literature cannot help but reflect these surrounding structures. In a society undergoing change, the novelist cannot help but comment upon these changes, cleavages, and conflicts. He may do so from the standpoint of one or another of the current positions, he may reflect without intending to comment upon those positions, or he may even attempt to reconcile or redefine those positions. He may even attempt to avoid the conflict by retreating to earlier positions, but in doing so he must take into account that the earlier positions are not accepted in the same way that they were in earlier times. The earlier myths may be intellectualized, simplified, or glorified from a position of intellectual sophistication imposed upon him by the later conflict. But as society evolves so that political ideologies, theological articulation, economic theories, psychological and sociological doctrines expand, novelists cannot help but become spokesmen for almost every intellectual tradition that emerges in the intellectual and historical development of man. Thus, we have the Freudian novel, the Marxist novel, naturalistic novels, realistic, romantic, surrealistic and symbolic novels, developing as each of these intellectual traditions develops in its own primary sphere or as an intellectual current that sweeps not only through the novel but through all other means of artistic, cultural, intellectual, and institutional development.

LITERATURE'S UNIQUE CONTRIBUTION

Literature does more than give shape and content to intellectual and philosophic currents that predominate at a given time. Because literature can dramatize, personify, and give specific meaning and content to what might in other media be abstract and dry, it can make "nonliterary" movements meaningful to audiences that would not understand these movements in their own abstract, general terms. It thus has the effect of intensifying and disseminating the effects of all other intellectual movements, and making them accessible to the consciousness of men in terms that reflect the immediacy of their own experience.

In fact, all of the arts, in their own way, can do the same. And conversely, when literature becomes an object of its own technological, methodological, and experimental self-consciousness, its focus upon its purely craft and technical aspects can empty it of its ability to provide images of life which go beyond craft; and at other times, among some audiences, it can suggest or reinforce the notion that life itself reflects only an experimental or craft-like attitude which has no other meaning. But pure craftsmanship too can become a meaning to life, and in this too, literature can be influential.

Like the development in each of the other spheres, the uneven rate of development within an artistic sphere results in the fact that "no voice is wholly lost." Thus, while the most advanced experimental novels are being produced, reflecting the most recent intellectual currents, other novelists, working in the most archaic forms, with philosophies and intellectual systems that by modern standards are "reactionary," continue to produce novels which from time to time may be highly successful in evoking exactly those kinds of responses that constitute a critique of the new, the advanced, the "in" of the moment. Every decade sees the pronouncement that the novel as a form is dead. This is a manifesto for the construction of new forms of the novel, or new forms of the anti-novel. Similar pronouncements are made with respect to the drama. The persistence and repetition of these

elegies is perhaps the greatest proof of the vitality of literature as an enterprise, of the novel, and of those forms of the novel, both written in the past
and written in the forms of the past [12]. But this vitality selectively includes
novels of the recent past whose forms at the moment of construction were
the novels or plays that would end the novels or plays of the past. A major
criterion that gives meaning to the novels of the past and present is their
capacity to illuminate the world and the life of the reader. This goes beyond
storytelling and craft. It is a fact of continuous amazement to us that novels
and novelists that are poor in craftsmanship, in construction and structure,
often poor in diction and language, continue to endure, despite their con-
demnation by critics who make as their central critical axis these standards
and emerging standards of craftsmanship. Eugene O'Neill has been buried
and reburied time and time again for obvious defects of craftsmanship, as
have Theodore Dreiser, C. P. Snow, Balzac, Dostoievsky, and Stendhal.
The same can be said for Shakespeare. As in all art, music, philosophy,
theology, or any world of creative endeavor, there is a kind of transcendence
of technique, craft, of the form itself, and it is this quality of the novel,
drama, or poem, of providing images of both the meaning and the possibilities of life, which constitute both their greatness and their indefinable
mystery [13].

NOTES

1. Such exceptions to the classic model which involve abstraction, formality,
and the segmentalization of experience, will be noted below.

2. In this respect the literary attitude is closely allied to and anticipates professional journalism (to be treated in Chapter 14). However, one must recognize that
much of what is literature is actually a form of journalism; that is, literature has been
used and continues to be used as a means of announcing and explaining events that
occur in the world.

3. E. M. Forster, *Aspects of the Novel* (New York, Random House, 1952).

4. Wayne Booth, *The Rhetoric of Fiction* (Chicago, University of Chicago
Press, 1961), offers a survey of methods and styles of narration. Equally valuable is
Rene Wellek and Austin Warren, *Theory of Literature*, 3rd ed. (New York, Har-
court, Brace and World, 1956).

5. For a recent study, see Vivian Mercier, *The New Novel, From Queneau to
Pinget* (New York, Farrar, Straus, and Giroux, 1971). Especially important is José
Ortega y Gasset, *The Dehumanization of Art and Other Writings on Art and
Culture*, translated by Willard Trask et al. (Garden City, N.Y., Doubleday 1956).
Also, Wylie Sypher, *Loss of the Self in Modern Literature and Art* (New York,
Random House, 1962). A useful collection of recent experimental fiction, written in
opposition to the classic unities, and clarity and objectivity is Philip Stevick (Ed.),
Anti-Story: An Anthology of Experimental Fiction (New York, Free Press, 1971).

6. Erich Auerbach, *Mimesis: The Representation of Reality in Western Literature*, translated by Willard R. Trask (Princeton, N.J., Princeton University Press,
1953).

7. Northrop Frye, *Anatomy of Criticism: Four Essays* (Princeton, N.J., Princeton University Press, 1957) (reprinted by Atheneum, 1970).

8. Kenneth Burke, *A Grammar of Motives* (Englewood Cliffs, N.J., Prentice-Hall, 1945) (reprinted by University of California Press, 1969).

9. See Owen Barfield, *Poetic Diction: A Study in Meaning*, 2nd ed. (New York, McGraw-Hill, 1964). Also, Barfield's *Speaker's Meaning* (Middletown Conn., Wesleyan University Press, 1967).

10. The ritualistic function of drama which may well have been basic in the origins of Greek drama, has been an important aspect of non-Western drama, as well as medieval religious and guild morality plays. Western drama since the sixteenth century has emphasized, along with most secular literature, the confrontation of the protagonist with opposing forces within himself or with others, even when those others personify fate or the gods. The rise of new ritualistic drama in the twentieth century in the form of the open theater and experimental theater often focuses on the ritual, the action itself, rather than on the actor. In doing so, it abandons much of the tradition of the Western theater, and addresses itself to problems of ancient and non-Western dramatic performances.

11. See Ian Watt, *The Rise of the Novel: Studies in Defoe, Richardson, and Fielding* (London, Chatto & Windus, 1957) (reprinted by University of California Press, 1971).

12. For a valuable discussion, see John Lukacs, *Historical Consciousness, Or the Remembered Past* (New York, Harper & Row, 1968), pp. 119ff. and p. 340n. Lukacs suggests that the crisis of the novel develops from several sides: first, the levelling of social classes makes increasingly meaningless "the principal topics of the classical novel, involving social relationships, social ambitions, social aspirations, because of the increasingly fluid characteristics of society . . . this growing meaninglessness of social bonds . . . forces the novelist of the twentieth century to contemplate increasingly the individual's relationship with himself. . . . Thus the collapse of the once inflated category of objectivity has affected the novelist as he has become aware of the artificiality inherent in the impartial, detached stance from which an invisible narrator related what third persons have done and thought and felt. Thereafter novelists . . . resorted to all kinds of devices. . . . There is, however, reason to believe that most of these experiments lead—not in the least because of their increasingly difficult readability—to a dead end." More important than these factors, suggests Lukacs, is the absorption of the novel by history. See Chapter 7, above, and Nicola Chiaromonte, *The Paradox of History: Stendhal, Tolstoy, Pasternak and Others* (London, Weidenfeld and Nicolson (n.d. 1971?).

13. In addition to the works mentioned above, see Lucien Goldmann, *The Hidden God: A Study of Tragic Vision in the Pensées of Pascal and the Tragedies of Racine*, translated by Philip Thody (London, Routledge & Kegan Paul, 1964); Leo Lowenthal, *Literature and the Image of Man* (Boston, Beacon, 1957), and Leo Lowenthal, *Literature, Popular Culture, and Society* (Englewood Cliffs, N.J., Prentice-Hall, 1961) (reprinted by Pacific Books, 1968).

Chapter 12

Legal Attitudes and Changes in the Law

INTRODUCTION

The meanings and historic functions of occupations change over time, but the residues of past meanings and usages are retained in the traditions and rituals of the craft; these impose themselves on current practitioners. The historic functions of an occupation, in the sense in which we use the term here, are simply the means used by its practitioners, sponsors (masters), and clients to achieve their respective ends.

The historic functions of the law will be briefly reviewed here to see how it has changed over time and how these changes have impinged upon the development of the law as a profession. Further, to ascertain that which is unique to the law-in-itself we must understand the interrelationship between law and society [1].

ORIGINS AND FUNCTIONS OF THE LAW

The law, no doubt one of the oldest professions, derived as a separate institution from two others: religion and the emerging state [2]. Law itself grew out of tribal customs and traditions, or mores (*die Sitten*), which have a degree of sacredness and are compulsory in character [3]. Law, in contrast to custom, historically develops separate, distinctive institutions when, first, it is written down and, second, when a separate body of officials emerges to interpret, apply, and enact it. The written aspect of the law originated within the realm of religion as ethical and other normative rules were codified in written or tablet form. Thus was created a body of proscriptions and prescriptions for behavior. Violations of codes of conduct could no longer be

183

excused on the basis of ignorance. These written codes, however, could not encompass the entirety of human experience.

The codes of behavior set the boundaries of permissible and inadmissible behavior. They were originally based on religious precepts, charismatic visions, heroic annunciations, and the sanctification of tradition. They had their origins outside the law itself. What is essential to the law *per se* is its objectification in written documents, its codification, and the attempt to apply its written commandments to living experience. Its substantive content is as varied as the religions from which it draws its content; its uniqueness lies in the formal attempt to state and apply precepts in a systematic way. Among the first practitioners of the law were the priesthood, who tried to codify religious myths and documents and subject them to rationally consistent theories, theologies, and theodicies, as well as to more concrete ethical codes. For centuries, canon law in the West and religious law elsewhere has competed with secular law in the regulation of common life. This competition was in principle resolved only with the separation of church and state in the eighteenth century in France and in the newly emergent United States; but these conflicts still haunt us at peripheral levels, as in such matters as abortion, school prayer, censorship of the mass media and art, and tax exemptions for tuition in religious schools.

The second major historical origin and function of the law emerged when primeval societies asserted the superiority of tribal and neighborhood councils over the extended patriarchical family. Public law and the state both emerged out of attempts to attain some degree of domestic peace and order by regulating and controlling blood feuds and vendettas. In a similar way, the origins of the state can be traced to efforts to regulate external defense and warfare between kinship groups and tribes.

In the process of adjudicating disputes between kinship groups, tribal heads and elders became "jurists." The judgments they rendered accumulated over time into a body of cases or precedents that influenced subsequent generations of judicial elders. These precedents were eventually codified and legal norms were extrapolated from them. Even *Kadi* law—the arbitrary announcing of decisions by religiously sanctioned judges based on the Koran—while formally requiring only the the validity of the sacred position of the judge, became subject to the bonds of tradition. When the *Kadi*, or priestly judge, exceeded in personal or religiously sanctioned arbitrariness the bounds of traditional propriety, he could with impunity be overthrown, assassinated, or driven out. This is to say that lay parties to juridical procedures began to develop a sense of the constraints that tradition places on the arbitrary action of judges, and to limit purely arbitrary charismatic appeals of traditional law [4]. Secular law was thus codified in ways similar to that of canon or other forms of religious law.

When states evolved in the ancient world, especially great states and empires, the position of judge, under a variety of names, became a separate occupation. Priests, lay officials, and military commanders became judges, serving as agents of the state and thereby assisting in the process of state building. In principle, all served the state, though at times their loyalties were divided between, their commitment as priests to a particular god and their service to a state that demanded too much be "rendered unto Caesar." In the same way, military leaders might be asked to violate family, clan, or caste loyalties, or found that civil procedures violated codes of honor or the ethos of direct action present in prebureaucratic armies [5].

LAW AND JUSTICE

Part of the historic function of the law, the judge, and later the lawyer was to serve the interests of their political masters in state building and/or preserve the interests of external status groups or elites. Even in the ancient world, the law expressed conflicts between state and polity, kings and people, classes, and status groups; and lawyers represented all sides of these conflicts [6]. When, in addition, newly emergent groups demanded rights or the equality of rights, liberation from bondage, and the privileges previously held by hereditary entrenched groups, the law became an instrument of justice; that is, it became a legal means of combatting the existence of legally defined privilege. As early as the fifth century B.C., the idea of justice was firmly embedded in Athenian law.

Conflicts of interest over the substantive definition of justice have led to the development of abstract ideas of justice and ideas of natural law and natural rights. These latter, at a rational philosophic level, are attempts at discovering the *a priori* or god-given basis for the objectivity of law that is superior to its application in specific cases.

The systematic codification of statutes and decisions, in contrast, may be based on the attempt to systematize cases and discover the logical patterns that underlie them. Codification may only be a mode of technical rationalization, that is, systematization, designed to make the law as a whole more predictable, efficient, and easily applicable. This implies a rational habit of mind willing to accept the impersonality of the law over the concreteness and irrationality of personal relations. It asserts the importance of objective, formal procedures over personal subjectivity and substantive results [7].

Substantive justice, in contrast to intellectual rationality or an emphasis on objective procedures, is concerned with principles that are intuitively or naturally right. Thus, the phrase "there's no justice" implies that there ought to be. That higher justice is based on the common sense or intuitive discernment by those who claim it.

The rational codification of the law, as in Roman law, or the Napoleonic Code, and later the French Civil Code, is the product of professional jurists working in and for large-scale empires. They were responsible for the standardization and administration of justice over wide territories with diverse cultures and legal traditions. It is thus related to military and political expansion and to the extension of political domain. But the attempt to standardize and unify the law has also been affected by the desire of jurists to produce an inner sense of systematic rationality in the law itself. The law as an intrinsic institution thus predisposes its bearers and upholders to rational argument, discussion, and systematic procedures [8].

Commitment to the use of the law as a technical means of adjudication of disputes, as well as of political administration, predisposes lawyers to a commitment to the machinery and institutions of the law, regardless of their external interest in the law, that is, regardless of the interests of their clients, sponsors, and employers.

This subjects them to conflicting pressures. One set comes from their clients, who expect them to be their agents and advocates. But lawyers are also officers of the courts before which they practice. If they suborn the law they are sworn to uphold, they challenge the very system that makes their work meaningful, that is, legitimate in the eyes of others and themselves. The way individual lawyers respond is partly a product of individual factors and character, but also a host of other factors.

The economic and political setting within which lawyers operate will influence their performance. In a totalitarian or otherwise lawless regime, the lawyer is necessarily responsive to the demands of the state administration or of a party. In laissez-faire societies lawyers are likely to be more responsive to the demands of clients; in a theocratic society, to those of religious institutions and structures; and in a society dominated by notables (*honoratiores*), to those of their own status group. Yet, in all these cases, there is a push to the objectification of legal principles and procedures by virtue of lawyers' insistence on legal rationality [9].

LAW AND SOCIETY

Our first theme, that the content of the law is largely determined by external factors, is perhaps best illustrated by a quick overview of Western history. We noted that the development of codified law in Rome came out of the need to administer a large-scale state and empire rationally. Medieval secular law emerged primarily in the law of inheritance and estates, reflecting the importance of feudal and patrimonial principles and of hereditary rights to succession of land, legitimacy, and power. The independence and coexistence of canon law with private courts and law based on hereditary entitlements came under attack by the heads of emerging secular states. Legal modernism in all its forms was accompanied and in part facilitated by postfeudal changes in the law. Thus a central principle in the development of the law was the creation of new rights, first of the sovereign and then of the state. This included the creation of national court systems and centralized administrative law controlled by the sovereign's court and privy councils. The right of the state was asserted over the rights of the estates, and a battle ensued between the kings and "the people." The seizure of rights was often assisted by a rising bourgeoisie who purchased rights from the nobility in order to escape the feudal law of higher estates. In England, in the Tudor period, this resulted in a battle between centralized chancery courts and the common law, the latter being exercised primarily by notables and gentry.

The victory of the bourgeoisie in France, as well as in England, ultimately resulted in the triumph of a legal system that was highly codified, *de jure*, as in the French Civil Code, or *de facto*, as in English common law. Secular lawyers increasingly became agents of the law. Yet, without the legal rationalists who transformed the law as an instrument of national policy and into political institutions, this could not have been accomplished. They constructed legal codes and theories to justify the new centralization, which became intrinsic to the emerging bourgeois national state.

With the development of the national state and bureaucracy, all aspects of society became subject to formal legal definitions and jurisdictions. The law first widened its scope from emphasis on estates and inheritance to broader conceptions of property and political rights. But as society became increasingly complex, the law grew to include every aspect of life. This was especially true much later, with the almost total bureaucratization of society and the rise of the welfare state.

Law as a profession became more specialized as it encompassed more areas of life. It divided and subdivided into narrower and narrower fields, such as patent, marine and naval, health and safety, environmental, corporate, social welfare and civil rights, family and child welfare, municipal borrowing, bankruptcy, tax shelters, air rights, nuclear, space, labor, and administrative law.

FORMAL PROCEDURE

All areas of the law concern themselves with procedure and form. The procedures and formal processes of executive agencies in administrative law are subject to fewer constraints than are the courts. The emphasis on procedure leads to cries of bureaucracy and red tape, among other things. It leads to protests that the law has become inaccessible to those who cannot afford legal counsel and the resources to understand and carry out what seem to be interminable processes.

Lawyers as professionals have developed a special affinity for administration and politics; attorneys have become administrators in many different areas of society, whether or not they practice law. At the same time, other professions and occupations have become quasi-legal even if the administrators are not certified legal professionals. For this reason, the education of professional and business managers is more and more concerned with paralegal issues. Modern physicians must also become acquainted with the laws governing malpractice, patients' rights, Medicare and Medicaid, and, of course, tax shelters. Those who do not develop this expertise must engage assistants, secretaries, or lawyers to inform them of both their rights and their legal responsibilities—including possible mis- and malfeasances and other legal and administrative procedures that govern their practice.

A large part of the work of social workers involves the application of federal, state, and local laws to the needs of populations whose rights and benefits are legislatively defined. Certainly, business administrators must be aware, either directly or through their corporate counsels, of the legal constraints on the conduct of business and of the opportunities for profit-making present in the gaps in the law and the legal system.

The application and interpretation of the law is plain, it is subject to a multiplicity of interests among a variety of individuals and organized groups. This is to say only that the law defines the rights and access to rights and privileges of everyone, whether or not they employ the law in their own interest.

Lawyers become the agents for all groups who seek to define or redefine their rights and privileges in the maelstrom of societal change. Lawyers serve all parties and on all sides of the plurality of issues.

The impulse to make the law into a final and complete codification is continuously upset by its very operation and by the efforts to redefine, express, and apply the law to new parties or situations not previously covered by it. In this sense the law is eternally incomplete, and its rational codification can never be final.

The law is inevitably tied to the realm of politics. It is changed by legislative interpretation and enactment, is subject to political interests and processes, to revolutions or other drastic changes in the power structure of society, and to minor changes in procedure [10]. Legislators often are lawyers because they tend to be more sensitive to legal issues that embrace all aspects of life, and because of their facility in translating substantive issues into legal and administrative terms. Many lawyers have also become legislators because, as free professionals, they are less subject to constraints of time, place, and special interests in the conduct of their business. And last, but not least, their exposure to many clients and issues broadens their experience and enables them to represent a plurality of legal or administrative interests [11].

CHANGING LAW AND CHANGING SOCIETY

If and when major changes in the law occur as a result of dramatic shifts in the centers of power in society, new definitions of rights and new procedures will follow. Not all lawyers, however, are always ready to represent new constituencies and interests. They may be still attached to the law and interests of the past. A new cadre of lawyers comes to the fore to represent these ascending groups. But often, after sharp discontinuities in the legal profession, new definitions of rights are expressed that reflect the changes brought about by the "revolution" [12]. A laissez-faire legality, a welfare state, or an authoritarian state may emerge, yet all are subject to formal rationalization [13].

In periods of transition, the law may seem to diminish in importance as military, economic, or religious "charismatics," heroic leaders, politicians, and power brokers rise in importance. The process of legal rationalization is a process of institutionalization and in the long run confirms whatever external system happens to predominate at a particular time.

The adversary process is central to the common law. This may be a residue of trial by combat; but it is, in its modern forms, intrinsic to law. As adversaries, lawyers will disagree about the very definition of rights and the facts that apply to a case. In doing so they seek to enlarge the rights of their clients while restricting the rights of their opponents.

As judges, lawyers are constrained to act upon previously established legal principles; yet they may adjudicate the extension of rights to situations not previously covered by precedent. Clarity in legal principles becomes elusive as established law is forever overburdened by new issues and cases. The law then, is always open-minded [14].

The bureaucratic state and interest group politics tend to overload legislative and judicial law with administrative procedures. The focus of the adversary process is removed from the courts, first to legislative corridors, and then to administrative hearing rooms. Pressure groups may help or hinder the definitions of legal decisions and their administrative articulation. Yet, the courts have to a large extent usurped the process of reviewing these adversary processes in legislative and executive bodies by asserting the primacy of the principle of court-defined constitutionalism.

The centrality of the courts in the determination of justice has led to a bifurcation in the practice of law. In England, the barrister became distinguished from the solicitor, and in France, the *avocat* from the *notaire* (or *avoue*) [15]. In the United States the distinction is not formalized and differences in title are not indicated, though lawyers may seek certification in order to practice before specific courts, such as the Supreme Court. To be effective, those who practice before courts have to develop special skills and talents, similar to those of the performing artist. A special sense of timing, quickness, personal presence, and poise are required as they are apt to be confronted with interruptions, interrogations, and surprise witnesses in the courtroom. In the case of jury trials (survivals of the historic claim for the right to be judged by one's peers) lawyers, to be successful, must be able to evoke emotion, sympathy, and a sense of substantive justice. They must also evoke pleas for fair play or equity and human rights rather than mere statutory rights or rights based on precedent or technical procedures. Barristers must have command of courtroom procedure, but they need not have as great command of legal knowledge as solicitors, who prepare cases.

In the United States, where the distinction between barrister and solicitor is not maintained, a relatively small percentage of lawyers practice primarily in the courts, despite their ubiquity in the mass media. The greatest proportion of the business of the law falls into the categories of contracts, conveyances, divorces, inheritances and estates, taxation, and interpretation of and compliance with administrative codes and regulations [16].

PHENOMENOLOGY OF THE LAW

In this hasty overview of the historical and institutional factors underlying the law, we have noted some of the factors that constitute the basis for the construction of a phenomenology of the law. We noted, first, that there has been a continuous quest for rationality and codification of the law. In its extreme form such codification might result in total logically integrated and self-enclosed sets of axioms and postulates from which all cases could be settled with, in Weber's terms, "nothing left over." The basis for the settlement of each legal issue would derive from axioms and principles inherent in a particular code. Roman law and the French Civil Code approached this ideal of the codification of a legal system. Similar attempts were made to codify the common law and legislative and "constitutional" codes. This legal rationality is never fully achieved because many new situations, practices, problems, and institutions, which must be addressed, forever spring up outside the parameters of existing codified and enacted law. The new realities and the extension of law to encompass them are rarely unilinear. They take a variety of contradictory forms, necessitating much pulling, twisting, and bending of established legal principles. The decisions establishing the legality of "separate but equal" facilities for African-Americans in the latter part of the nineteenth century is an example of such bending of constitutionally guaranteed human rights. The closer the law reflects empirical reality the less consistent it will appear to be. To add to this confusion, legislation and judicial interpretation may be so vague, ambivalent, and even contradictory as to create headaches, while at the same time creating new opportunities for clients, lawyers, and judges.

Legal rationality must be distinguished from other forms of rationality such as philosophic or scientific. In contradistinction to Hellenic rationality, which is abstract, legal rationality, like Talmudic or Confucian codes of conduct, is embodied in concrete cases. In fact, the final criterion for the law is its applicability to specific cases and life situations. *A priori* principles are likely to give way to the exigencies of everyday life. Nonetheless, in applying the law, judges attempt to maintain the logical consistency of its principles.

Even at a "philosophic" level, it is difficult to maintain the idea of a logically self-consistent legal system. Logical principles are not necessarily immanent to the law. The law is based on the values of diverse, continuously changing, successive or alternating philosophic and ideological systems such as those of Judaism, Christianity, Hinduism, and Islam, laissez-faire liberalism, ideas of divine rights of kings, bureaucratic rationalism, and communism. Recent developments in the Middle East and Eastern Europe attest to the instability and fragility of philosophic and religious principles as the bases for law. Yet, the tendency towards rationalization of the respective legal systems reemerges as a society returns to a degree of normality.

The intellectual rationality of the law is primarily formal in character. It makes explicit, in legal terms, the substantive content of the external systems and restores them in appropriate legal forms. In the process, its original spirit may be snuffed out or devalued. Nor does the law by itself always determine the spirit of a society, even when it is highly rationalized. A high degree of legal formalization may, however, evoke the "spirit" of a culture when it becomes pervasive [17]. Critics of the law may emerge who challenge the direction the law has taken while accepting its basic principles. "True" Christians, for example, may feel the spirit of Christianity has been irretrievably lost or deadened in modern society by the formalization of law that originally was based upon it.

The rationalization of the law involves more than the codification of legal procedures. It has to do with, as well, the implementation of court procedures, the creation and determination of legal jurisdictions and forms of appeal, the specification of its rules, admissibility of evidence, use of legal documents, and the proper use of the language embodied in all of these. The vast amount of knowledge needed to comprehend it in its totality eludes laymen and professionals alike. And the underlying ethic, to laymen particularly, often appears to have been lost or negated in the process.

Administrative rationality, as distinct from the rationalization of the contents of the law, develops in opposition to the sense of the law as a set of consistent ideas. In the quest for administrative rationality a pursuit of perfect legal form takes place. Content is created that overrides all other intellectual or judicial considerations. Administrative law and positive law have therefore been at odds since the latter was developed as a distinct legal theory and achieved a degree of acceptance in the nineteenth century. At the same time, in the quest for a rational law based on principles that are themselves outside the law, various "philosophies" have come to the fore that seek to remove it from its criterion of caseworthiness. Rational consistency has been achieved at the expense of empirical applicability, which means that it sometimes becomes necessary to torture the facts into procrustean beds. The complexity of legal reasoning and violations of common sense, or substantive justice, are other sources of disenchantment to laymen, who are after all the law's ultimate clientele and legitimators. Laymen are, in the long run, the supreme judges of the judges, the lawyers, and the law [18].

JUSTICE AND RATIONALITY

The law inevitably creates its own standards of justice out of the many separate sources of ideas of justice [19]. One set, as noted above, is normative in nature and derives from the various religious, philosophic, ethical, and moral notions that are implemented by and codified in the law. The other set derives from the enactment of and application of the law. Thus, if equality before the law becomes a principle of the law, inequalities are negatively judged. When the law affirms a legal postulate it becomes the criterion for the way it is applied by its agents.

Institutionalization of the law and the creation of legal establishments are possible only if support and acceptance are forthcoming from other established groups and institutions. Those who accept the principles upon which law is based expect that they will be implemented and that the original promises will be at least minimally fulfilled. The underlying principles thus form a tacit social contract. When a legal system changes so greatly as to be considered new, promises are made to the class or status group that has been most active in its advocacy. But in the long run it is not possible to isolate one set of parties to a legal promise; others take up the cry to be included in the "social contract" and to be extended the same rights. In this way, the middle classes "expropriated" the rights granted earlier to the nobility in the course of the English constitutional struggles of the eleventh to the sixteenth centuries; and later the working classes, peasants, and farmers everywhere sought to "expropriate" these same rights on their own behalf. Women in the United States demanded rights that were being extended to exslaves, and later they began to protest their exclusion under antidiscrimination laws aimed at racial and religious groups.

Laws that exclude segments of a population from the rights they promulgate are viewed as instruments of injustice. The groups who find that rights granted to others do not apply to themselves may either attack the legitimacy of the legal system and attempt to overthrow it, or seek to reform it in the pursuit of justice.

SUBSTANTIVE LAW

Demands for justice that continuously arise in the course of societal development may take the form of complaints about the unfairness of the mechanical operation of the law. They need not be supported by a legal theory or philosophy in order to be converted into a new legal system. The demand for substantive justice is often intuitive, naive, and based on common sense rather than on abstract principles. The law, from this point of view, is seen as simply unjust or unfair in its operation.

The advocates of a particular form of substantive justice must succeed economically and organize politically if they are to convert their claims into legal principles, and/or demand changes in procedures and precedents. Even if they were to succeed in effecting an upheaval in the system they might find the very changes they sought again embroidered with complex, rational, legal procedures. And they might find them again inaccessible to those who are not studied in the law or represented by counsel [20].

Thus, the quest for substantive justice understood as fair play, equity, or equality is eternal. Specific changes in the content of conceptions of justice will vary according to the problems attendant upon any historical moment. What is considered an injustice will also vary from one type of society to another, as in pastoral, patriarchal, feudal societies, or under laissez-faire capitalism, a welfare state, or bureaucratic communism. Or, it may simply have different saliency in each of these systems.

Lawyers usually come to the fore to represent new rising status groups and classes. In their demands for the extension of justice, lawyers become the vocal initiators and advocates of societal change. They were among the vanguard of the French and American revolutions. In England, they were the advocates of the primacy of the common law and among the opponents of the Tudor state and the law of royal chancery courts. In the United States, lawyers for the NAACP Legal Defense Fund were at the forefront of the mid-twentieth-century Civil Rights Movement.

Battles over the content and procedures of the law result in conflicts within the law and the legal profession. The decision of the American Bar Association at their 1990 annual meeting in Chicago to maintain their neutrality after their previous commitment to and endorsement of legal abortion is a recent example of this. The constraints placed upon lawyers serving emerging classes of clients may trigger demands for change in the form and content of the legal system. As full-time specialists, lawyers can make the concerns of their clients central to their activities. They have the freedom to tinker with the law and concentrate on representing clients whose interests they wish to serve. Taking it a step further, African-American lawyers in the Tawana Brawley case were accused of exploiting their client for the sake of dramatizing *de facto* discrimination in the courts.

Many lawyers are concerned with the legislative phases of the law. In democratic societies they have been for centuries the major political representatives of all groups, at all levels of the political spectrum.

LEGAL ETHICS AND CREATIVITY

Legal ethics are primarily designed to inculcate and enforce respect for the law and its machinery among those who are its agents. While protecting the client's interests, lawyers must be concerned for the law itself, its language, procedures, and governing principles. Without these it would be inoperative; and the lawyer would have no legitimate basis for practicing law.

These two dimensions—serving the client's interests and protecting the law—often pull in opposite directions. Some practicing lawyers are not content to be merely instrumental practitioners of a received set of principles and procedures. They are particularly sensitive to the law as a total system, and concentrate on those principles that are ambiguous, in conflict with, or out of phase with existential realities. They seek to test the boundaries or lack of boundaries of the received law. They may be motivated to clarify or introduce new ambiguities or to define new concepts of substantive justice. They may be concerned with the law as a total system, or may in their "vanity" seek to change the law by the extension and amplification of its older principles. Or they may simply wish to make the law more just. Legal giants prepare and argue cases so effectively they are able to institute change in the law. They may be more than great advocates or judges; they may be legal intellectuals. As they continue to work with cases, legislation, and/or judicial reviews, their "scientific attitude" is more empirical than that of the purely philosophic, intellectual, or academic attitude.

These types do not exhaust the possible forms of legal creativity. Lawyers representing clients interested in the redistribution of rights and resources may attempt to redefine existing principles purely in the interests of their clients. Thus, legal creativity may be conservative in scope, as well as liberal or radical. Prosperous clients may engage creative advocates when they believe they can benefit from changes in the law or redefinitions of rights. Similarly, at the legislative level, special-interest groups may seek lawyers to represent them in their efforts to redefine existing rights.

Creative advocates may need help in accomplishing "the impossible." They must convince judges, legislators and elected officials, and the legal profession, as a whole, that creative reinterpretation is a necessary correlate for making the law more rational and consistent and to close gaps within it.

Judges have the task of creating a higher rationality than do lawyers who practice before them. The overwhelming number of cases before them concern relatively fixed legal matters and do not lend themselves to creativity. Nor is the task of judicial creativity given to most judges, especially at the lower levels of the jural system. Creative interpretation is subject to judicial review, where the highest priority is likely to be given to the maintenance of the ongoing system, not change. What is more, at lower judicial levels, the decisions of a creative judge may be reversed. A judge with a poor track record is considered incompetent.

At each successive level of appeal, as the percentage of cases involving ambiguous or conflicting legal principles increases, there is a corresponding increase in creative interpretation. By the time cases reach the higher courts, the parties to the law have calculated their chances of success or failure in gaining a reversal or of sustaining a decision and weighed the costs incurred. Such calculations of judicial response inhibit recourse to judical action all along the process. Cases are more often settled out of court. Hence, the maxim: "The best law is the avoidance of litigation."

COURT–MADE LAW

At each successive level of judicial review, and especially in the Supreme Court of the United States, judges are the arbiters of judicial rationality and creative interpretation. Their judicial interpretations become equivalent to enacted law. A particularly creative judge of the U.S. Court of Appeals, such as Learned Hand, could write opinions that were accepted almost without question by the Supreme Court [21].

Historically, individual justices of the Supreme Court, in responding to briefs submitted by appellants and to the decisions of the lower courts, have succeeded in reinterpretating the law in ways that have resulted in virtual legal "revolutions."

The direction of judicial creativity in the United States is greatly affected by the appointment power of the president, adding to the political basis of interpretation. Presidents, however, are not always able to control the judicial performance of their appointees; sometimes justices appear to gain independence during the course of their tenure because of the position they occupy and the very "logic" of the law. They may respond to the cases before them in ways that are unpredictable in the light of their past record and public pronouncements. Felix Frankfurter, Hugo Black, and more recently William J. Brennan, Jr., are examples of those who in the course of their term on the bench of the Supreme Court of the United States disappointed their appointers even as they gained the respect and admiration of others. The law seems to have an autonomy, at times, that appears to rise above and beyond the constraints of the appointment process.

The higher courts have the responsibility for making the content of the law as a total corpus rational in its principles, as well as for supervising formal, procedural rationality. In the latter case, they rule on violations of due process and procedures, and redress any perceived illegalities in the administration of justice. But in their deliberations concerning due process, they are defining the law as an intellectual system, as well as defining the rights of individuals and groups in the toils of the law. Due process was the category under which civil rights and liberties were expanded and restricted throughout American history. As a result, formal rationality inevitably and inextricably has become a part of substantive justice.

The court system is one means by which the rationality of the law, intellectual or formal in nature, is codified; legislation is the other major way. In the United States, the ultimate legal means is the constitutional amendment; revolution is the ultimate illegal means. Success in revolution may be equated with the legalization of formerly illegal measures or rights. As noted previously, in the aftermath of a revolution, the process of legal articulation, amplification, and rationalization is renewed.

In the overall, ongoing process, legal philosophers and commentators, law school deans, professors of law, and sometimes law students and clerks—who may not all be practicing lawyers or judges—also review judicial interpretations and distill from them legal issues and principles. In doing so, they may enunciate new or modified legal principles, and train new cadres of professionals who may influence the course of the law.

At other levels, publishers of textbooks, computer codes, and handbooks of procedures and cases contribute greatly to the field by making available to interested parties the administrative rulings of quasi-judicial bodies and the courts.

The law is also greatly affected by philosophies of law and the distillation of principles and procedures even though they, too, derive from outside the inner workings of the law [22].

THE LAW AS INFORMATION

In the process of rationalization, the amount of specialized information increases at an accelerating pace. The appropriate content and form must be known to all those who wish to practice law successfully. This requires lengthy education and apprenticeship (usually in combination). The sheer amount of information one is required to assimilate, together with the complexity of institutional structures governed by law, makes it impossible for any one lawyer to claim total mastery of the field as a whole. And to the layman it appears totally inaccessible, alien, and opaque. Lawyers are accused of speaking indecipherable, convoluted mumbo jumbo, typified by the popular term "Philadelphia lawyer" [23].

The complexities of their trade have become so much a part of lawyers' everyday habits of mind that there is a tendency to resist demands for simple, common-sense solutions to their clients' problems. They may feel a greater kinship towards their adversaries in a case, because of common training and gestalt, than they do towards the clients whose interests they represent. They can engage in discussion with their peers based on inside knowledge that clients cannot share, in language incomprehensible to the layman.

One of the tasks of the lawyer is to impress the client with the limits or advantages to be gained by delay and legal maneuvering and the necessity of prescribed procedures. Such practices increase the fees lawyers command; the client, in the meantime, incurs even greater expenses because of the capital and interest lost as the issues remain unresolved. These costs must be computed against the values or risks of victory or defeat. Economic rationality, then, applies to clients as well as lawyers and is an intrinsic component of the many kinds of rationality that underlie or are immanent to the law.

Balzac and Dickens described cases that lasted for decades and even centuries, in which only the lawyers stood to gain. While these are fictional portrayals, there are well-documented cases of prolonged litigation entailing hundreds of millions of dollars in legal fees, which have lasted, it appears, an interminably long time. The antitrust cases involving IBM, the Xerox Corporation, and AT&T come to mind as examples of this type of seemingly endless adjudication. There are also well-known cases involving smaller companies or individuals, whose assets or potential assets were greatly diminished by prolonged litigation. They add to the stereotype of the avaricious lawyer displaying very little concern for the interests of his clients.

Lawyers will try to counter such allegations by acquainting their clients with the relevant aspects of the law while retaining the mystique of the complexities they must contend with. The mystique constitutes the basis for their specialization, high fees, claims of expertise, and indispensability. Given the *de facto* complexity of the law, the mystique may reflect reality. Many, however, believe lawyers have themselves created or enhanced this complexity beyond all necessity, thereby contributing to the public's disenchantment with the law [24].

In most cases, clients have little choice but to accept their lawyers' projected agenda. If they choose early settlement, they forgo the possibility of gain. They may choose to abandon the case and thus relinquish their rights, or seek other counsel, which may or may not hasten the process and lower their costs.

LANGUAGE AND LEGAL REASONING

It is easy for most competent lawyers to learn the language of the law, translate it for the client, and explain how the client is affected by it. More difficult is discerning which laws, precedents, and principles govern a particular case, and then translating and interpretating the language of the appropriate law or statute.

The translation and interpretation of legal documents entail, first, a process of legal search and research; and, second, *linguistic* research. In practice, these are intermingled in the search for precedents for a particular line of action or defense. But the interpretation of the law, legislative or judicial, also involves linguistic interpretation—discerning what the law, code, or decision is actually saying. Legal reasoning, at its best, refers to the ability to reinterpret the received language of a law to fit the facts that were unavailable to those who originally designed the legislation or rendered the decision. Legal reasoning and linguistic interpretation permit the extension of the law to heretofore unknown situations that might arise in the future and the creation of new legal principles. These may stand alongside or invalidate older principles while keeping to the language and reasoning of the principles from which they were derived [25].

All of this is done, of course, within a framework of adversary proceedings where interpretations may be countered and alternatives cited by presumably equally competent opponents. These may again be subject to review and to similar evaluations by the courts. And, it must be remembered, it does not necessarily stop here, as decisions of the lower courts in turn are subject to review within the framework of the appellate system, if the client so chooses. In the light of such possible conflict and review, success in reinterpreting statutes and precedents is both a test of resources and a feat of virtuosity, a real hallmark of superiority.

The same linguistic virtuosity may be present, at simpler levels, in the preparation of every type of legal document. Though the language and formulas are largely fixed, lawyers aim for clarity and precision with respect to the obligation of the other party, while they seek to limit their clients' obligations under the contract. It may aim for precision and clarity, but the law is often one-sided in that negotiation comes to mean that each party to a contract will emphasize the responsibility of the other. Which party is successful in achieving its goals depends greatly on the skill of the counsel and his ability to foresee the contingencies that might arise in the future. In this sense, linguistic skill is decisive, and skill in long-term prediction and planning is also a valuable asset in the writing of contracts. Important too, in most cases, is the participants' sense of goodwill in a common enterprise.

The same issues appear when historical documents are subject to reinterpretation. The intentions of the parties that, say, drafted the constitution, a law, or a particular opinion must be evaluated. These intentions are extended to circumstances in the future which they could not have foreseen at the time the documents were created. It is often argued, under positive law, that intent need not be a guide to interpretation; rather, it is the underlying principle that must be decisive. Even here, the task of the lawyer or judge is to distill the legal principles embedded in the language of a document. In applying these principles to new facts and cases, linguistic research and legal reasoning are employed and established principles of law are utilized.

Those who celebrate the glory of the law argue that, in this way, new developments in society can come under the scope of the law. The law, they argue, can adjust to changes in society on the whole, by small, steady changes in interpretation, making great legislative upheavals unnecessary.

The argument is reminiscent of the defense of laissez-faire economics; that is, that the law naturally accommodates to the needs of society without planned intervention or new legislation. This overlooks the existence of continuous, deep grievances by parties to the law itself, and the fact that the law accommodates to every type of system of dominion. This view also assumes that all people have equal access to the costly and time-consuming processes of the law [26].

LEGAL EVIDENCE

The legal and linguistic search for the law applicable in any given case is only one aspect of the law as a research enterprise. More direct and immediate research is necessary to ascertain the facts of the case, and this requires the discovery, gathering, and assessment of evidence.

The use of evidence has been subject to sharp and precise legal definitions and procedures, which—as in all legal activity—are always being redefined. Originally, evidence was confined to the assessment of guilt. Magical formulas or divine judgments could be presented as evidence, such as the results of trials by ordeal or combat. Survival was evidence enough of divine favor. It was presumed that the deity whose judgment was evoked was a party to the case. In trial by combat the legal presumption was that the combatants were equal in strength, skill, or training, or that they had advocates or champions who were equal before the current form of the law.

These forms of evaluation of guilt and innocence were eventually abandoned in favor of other forms and rules of evidence such as those governing the admissibility of evidence in juridical cases. Included were rights against self-inculpation, which were later extended to take in the spouse, priest, counsel, and physician. These exemptions have more recently been claimed by the press, tenure committees, psychologists, and college administrators.

Evidence secured under duress became inadmissible, and hearsay evidence was abandoned. Circumstantial evidence would have to be noted and presented as such. Legal fictions and presumptions are sometimes allowed to stand as substitutes for direct evidence as, for instance, in the doctrine of the uninvited guest. A visitor injured on the property of a defendant to a legal action does not have to prove he or she was an invited guest. The crucial questions here are: Was the possibility of injury so clear that a reasonable person would have attempted to prevent injury to the "guest," who without invitation, had reason to be on the "host's" property, or were all reasonable means used to prevent entry? The owner of a lumberyard, for example, where the possibility of injury is great, would be expected to make reasonable efforts to keep children from playing on the premises. The doctrine of the reasonable man avoided the necessity for detailed and exact proof of motivation and concern. In general, however, the standards of legal proof are sharp and demanding, as in the image of the smoking gun. Direct evidence is demanded for serious crimes, at least in principle.

Documentary evidence is usually favored over eyewitness evidence, though this is a matter of interpretation. Eyewitness evidence is believed to be more subject to misinterpretation or misperception, and to the discrediting of witnesses. Especially in civil cases, it is generally less acceptable than documentary evidence.

In dramatic criminal cases the law is equated with the assessment of truth. This implies a deep quest for the truth in unique events that are defined by the law as criminal. Here, the law approaches an ideographic search for evidence that is characteristic of classical historiography. Yet, such a conception of evidence reflects a relatively simple world where individual actions and purposes are clear and accessible. In mass societies collective action may express intent that is hidden because of its very complexity. Moreover, the definition of the action may be unclear. One overall action may be expressed in thousands of distributive, small bureaucratic decisions, none "meaningful" by itself. These divisions take on the character of a meaningful pattern only when their collective impact is assessed.

The courts and legislatures, in the light of this, have broadened conceptions of evidence to include the use of survey data, statistics, and other summations of actions and responses to them. In the case of *Brown v. Board of Education of Topeka, Kansas* (1954), the Supreme Court allowed the attorney general to present statistical evidence as to the distributive effect of the doctrine of "separate but equal" on African-American students. This was allowed despite a legal precedent that had some seventy years earlier confirmed the legality of the doctrine.

Once this principle was broached, new forms of evidence were allowed in determining other community standards, as in obscenity, pornography, and some class action cases. By now, survey researchers and statisticians are used as both expert witnesses and friends of the court.

NEW TECHNOLOGY AND THE LAW

The demand for new forms of evidence has also arisen in anti-trust, negligence, and production and manufacturing suits, and in scientific and technical enterprises. Computerized coding of large numbers of documents has been found necessary in order to be able to assess the actions and decisions of large corporations. The very complexity of this research requires the use of computer experts and technicians, and lawyers working in or with these companies also to become at least computer literate. Whether the law can, in fact, cope with such complexity is unsettled; for the burdens of costs and time—while presenting a bonanza to the lawyers and technicians—are great.

Judges and the principal counsels in such cases have been stymied by the difficult task of gathering a clear enough picture of the facts to provide a judicial settlement [27]. As a result, civil actions often result in pretrial settlements before "all the facts" are in. The costs of judicial action may be greater than the projected return. Governmental authorities may decide not to prosecute simply because the burden of gathering and evaluating evidence is too great. As the cases go on and on, the turnover in prosecuting attorneys and administrations may weaken further the will to prosecute. Immunity from prosecution may be secured by stretching out the legal procedures, that is, stonewalling, for decades if necessary. The awareness of the limits of evidence operates in favor of those who can use its complexity to delay, stall, stonewall, or otherwise obscure a case so that the weight of evidence is never brought to bear on it. Victory is claimed by those with the greatest reserves and will to wear out the patience of the opposition, judge, or jury.

The awareness of the deficiencies of standard adversary judicial procedures in the face of complex technological and scientific evidence has led to the emergence of administrative quasi-judicial tribunals. In these quasi-courts, exacting judicial rules of evidence have been modified to include informal procedures. The task of the chief officers of such administrative tribunals is to confirm or reject the decisions of the investigative officer. Presumably, only the legal aspects of the case are subject to judicial review. It is assumed that the informal procedures and depth of investigation will elicit the bases for the facts in question. Yet, in these times marked by scientific turbulence and innovation, relevant facts may still be unknown. The parties to the conflict have vested interests that predetermine their presentation, and their search for and interpretation of evidence. The chief investigator and administrative agency may not have access to the facts because they may not even exist. Yet, in principle, all issues must be resolved even if the "resolution" is the decision to delay decision. The principle of *stare decisus* is to allow the existing state of affairs to persist even when the uncovering of new facts casts a received judgment in doubt.

The gathering of evidence entails more than the accumulation of a mass of documents, statistics, and reports of actions. In contemporary society, the nonlegal meaning of facts may be beyond the ken of lawyers, judges, and jurors. Engineers, scientists, psychiatrists are all called upon to lend their expertise to assess the facts, subject to prevailing rules of evidence. Experts, however, may appear on both sides of an issue and offer contradictory data and opinions. Other problems to be faced are, first, Who is an expert? and, second, Is the evidence presented relevant to the law as it is written or interpreted? Can, or should, the law recognize as potential evidence facts that psychiatrists, say, are able to bring to a case? Judges and juries who are not experts must assess the testimony of so-called experts though no consensus or definitive scientific evaluation may be possible in the field in question.

The law demands that each issue be resolved by a decision; the failure of science to provide answers does not mean that the courts are thereby exempt from arriving at a judgment. In criminal cases, the standard principle is to decide in favor of the defendant if the evidence is insufficient to prove clearly a presumption of guilt.

Despite the problems outlined above as to what constitutes evidence, the law as an ongoing system must act as if it were logically and procedurally closed. That closure operates, in principle, at every level of the system, even when the adversary nature of the law suggests otherwise. Under appellate review, the previous forms of legal closure are subject to contention "up the line" until they are resolved, for the moment, by final review or by legislation.

SUBSTANTIVE JUSTICE AND THE JURY SYSTEM

The greatest area of openness in the legal system is in the jury system. In the common law, at least, the jury system emerged out of an interest in substantive justice; defendants were to be tried by juries of their peers to ensure equality in and before the law. The sources of judicial decisions were changed, and control of the law by crown and feudal superiors was mitigated. In principle, the extension of the franchise and the legal denial of inequality should make the jury system unnecessary. Equality, at least formally, is guaranteed by such legal enactments. The jury system does operate to ensure substantive equality when, for example, lower-strata juries award compensation to the victims of corporate negligence and medical malpractice. These awards have been so huge at times that some states have sought to limit the power of juries to decisions concerning responsibility and guilt and have signified that the courts determine the actual amount of financial redress. Physicians, liability insurance companies, and the Reagan administration joined in this drive to limit jury awards.

The jury system has additional features. Jurors are laymen who know little about legal matters. The court must inform them of the legal principles and constraints under which they operate. Their sole legal task is to evaluate evidence. However, they are empowered to make the final decision as to innocence or guilt. Within the confines of their sequestration they are not subject to review, nor are minutes of the proceedings maintained. They are therefore free to apply their own standards of substantive rationality. It is presumed that jurors are reasonable and will act as such. Again, this is a necessary legal fiction. Potential jurors may be challenged by either side of a case under empaneling procedures if they display irrational or prejudicial attitudes. Jury tampering is, of course, illegal; but some forms of pretrial interviewing are permitted, and have been judged to come close to being jury tampering. In some cases they have been judged as just that.

Once the jury meets in order to arrive at a decision, the values and attitudes of the members come to the fore. They may be reasonable men and women but they may exhibit different values and standards of reason; nor are all the facts made equally clear to each jury member. The process of sequestering and impatience with delay caused by interminable discussion may cause jurors to seek a common basis for decision. The decision is assumed to reflect a community of meaning though personal differences in values, dominance, prejudice, persuasiveness, and perception are always evident. Sometimes the achievement of a rational consensus is a relatively simple matter. Civil cases in which the facts are clear-cut are unlikely to go to trial. In criminal cases, trials may be necessary; but even here the defense may be *pro forma*. Where the facts are unclear, the prosecution may choose to offer a reduced charge in exchange for a guilty plea in order to keep paltry or ambiguous evidence from the jury.

The reasonableness of the jurors is tested in their discussions. They may have a personal sense of fairness or substantive justice that differs from that of the law. Some are predisposed to favor the little guy, others the establishment types, or they may identify with particular status groups in the society. Some are subject to appeals to their humanity, others to objectivity or to the brilliance of a legal argument. Because jurors cannot be prevented from introducing substantive rationality into their deliberations, their decisions may break through the formal and intellectual rationality of the law [28].

THE LAW AS A SYSTEM

If all of its aspects are taken together, including use of evidence of all kinds now permissible and the role of the lay juries, one can see the law and the work and habits of mind of lawyers as a multifaceted and multilayered "system" with a logic of its own, or perhaps a series of logics that are often in contradiction. No one lawyer need have intellectual access to the entire system, nor does the entire system have to be understood as a total logical system by the totality of its members. A specialist in a narrow segment of the law may be highly competent in drafting conveyances, contracts, or wills without having to know much more than the legal forms and procedures for such work. A legal intellectual may be aware of the major unresolved and abstract legal issues in constitutional law, yet display relatively little know-how concerning the nuts and bolts of the day-to-day business of law. In this respect, the law, like other human institutions, may be viewed as a system. A total system is always larger than the actions of any set of particular individuals: it consists of collective actions. A system consisting of collective actions that may or may not be coordinated and controlled exhibits features that seem to be independent of planned human intelligence. Hegel called this the "cunning" of history; Marx, the dominance of the system over men. Parsons refers to "the social system," Robert Merton to "serendipity." Classical economists referred to "the invisible hand of the market." Social philosophers have suggested, at least by analogy, that such often formless sets of agreements constitute the "social contract." Robert Burns summed it up when he said that "the best laid schemes o' mice an' men gang aft agley." Yet these internal features, including their contradictions, paradoxes, and serendipities, as a system account for only part of the dynamics of the law. One of the major constraints upon the law, as we have noted, is that it must reconcile its ongoing process of rationalization with the multidimensional changes taking place in society at large. It is subject to emerging interest group politics, ideologies, trends in philosophy, new technologies, and changing institutions. The law, like every social institution, is thus subject to internal conflict and the conflicts introduced into it by external demands.

THE LAW AND EXTERNAL EXPERIENCE

The law, then, is not a closed system removed from everyday life and experience. Moreover, its connection to external life is intrinsic to its very operation. In the course of everyday life experiences, clients are confronted with problems that turn into law cases. Governments, in the process of maintaining order in society, regulate the actions of citizens and subjects, and again turn to the law to do so. The law thus covers almost all actions performed in a society [29]. Lawyers seek to make specific actions legitimate so as to make them part of normal everyday life. The legal system, as a whole, then prescribes the range of permissible actions in a society. Yet the achievement of legitimacy *per se* is not its primary object. Rather, individuals and collectivities pursue their own goals for a variety of specific reasons—economic, political, social, and religious. Some of the resulting actions are illegitimate by previous standards. Others are not subject to the ongoing criterion of legitimacy and are therefore not illegitimate. Part of the process of legal change is thus the legitimation of what was previously nonlegitimate action. Legal action extends and broadens the law to provide a cover of legitimacy for new forms and content of actions as they emerge in society. The intention and motivation for these actions may not be acceptable by the standards of existing legal, economic, political, or other "systems," but the actions may ultimately become part of the ongoing system. The source of societal change is therefore outside the legal (or other) system. The process of transforming nonlegitimate into legitimate action is, however, not a random one. The new actions themselves result from changes that have taken place in the larger society. The law responds, not without delays and discontinuities, to these changes, thereby recognizing and legitimating new forms of action.

As a result of the continuous evolution of the law, some actions are considered, at any given moment, more "right" than others, while some are considered less right. The less legitimate actions may be, for a variety of reasons, the more frequently performed ones. The demand for legitimation may result in attempts to change the law or even to attack the system that denies legitimacy to those who claim it. They perceive the law as an obstacle to legitimating actions that they believe are a product of the normal operation of society.

Access to the law requires resources, patience, and technical knowledge, all of which are unequally distributed within a society. Thus, the famous maxim by Anatole France: "The law in its majestic equality forbids the rich as well as the poor to sleep under bridges, to beg in the streets and to steal bread." The law in other words, responds best to those who already have established their rights and is slow to respond to new claimants for rights.

The sense of grievance within a legal system is closely related to ideas of justice, which we have noted are external to the law. They are based on ideological, philosophic, and religious principles that often are incorporated in the law. Those who hold these grievances ideologize or intellectualize their social, economic, and political positions in the process of seeking legitimation and demanding change.

In addition, a legal system must by its very operation validate its legal principles. Otherwise, it discredits itself by failing to recognize the "social contract." It may even be seen as delegitimating itself, if and when the legal system is viewed as grievously in violation of, or contradictory to, the principles upon which it is based. Thus, every system is obligated to act according to its own stated principles.

A legal system may also invalidate itself when those favored in the system seek illegitimate benefits to an extent deemed intolerable to those not so favored. This may cause the less privileged to reject the legitimacy of the law. A legal system that favors those who are able to "best" or "work" the system will be self-invalidating if it does not develop self-correcting mechanisms. The establishment bias of legal systems applies to agents of the law as well. They may reflect the material interests of clients who themselves control the resources to employ these professionals. Lawyers and jurists may also be subject to criticism if and when their mastery of the intricacies and arcana of the system reaches such proportions that they alone are its beneficiaries.

Yet, the law is never totally the creature of the establishment. That is, in major part, true because the latter is itself always changing due to societal developments. Since lawyers represent almost all emerging groups demanding rights, even those with minimal resources, they may become the advocates of change. Some lawyers then become the spokesmen for new criteria for the law, for substantive justice, and for economic and political rights for the disadvantaged. All major revolutions, including the French and English ones, were to a large extent the product of lawyers, or were aided or abetted by them. In the United States, if the Civil Rights Movement was not sparked by lawyers, certainly its basic strategy was devised by lawyers.

In each of these cases, the emergence of new institutions or changes in the center of power become the basis for legal conflict within the law. In the long run, revolutions within societies are accompanied by revolutions in the law. If a particular political revolution is successful, new legal principles are legitimated by the successful revolutionary regime. Even if previously expressed demands and practices are not immediately legitimated, in the long run they may provide normality to the actions of those who are later subject to the postrevolutionary system.

Viewed from this external perspective, the law is not an autonomous system. Only the operation of society can be said to be autonomous. However, the definition and delimitation of the totality of institutions and actions that constitute society is a task unto itself. Therefore to consider society as an autonomous, self-enclosed system with clear-cut boundaries is to perform a feat of verbal magic.

Viewed from the standpoint of phenomenology, law and the actions of lawyers and jurists represent only some selected aspects of an infinitely extensible whole. Within that whole, the particular attitudes and dimensions that underlie and constitute law are formal in nature: they include the habits of mind, the attitudes, the procedures, by which society in part defines itself. The content of the larger principles and the issues that the law expresses in the process of definition are largely outside the scope of law.

From the same perspective, all crafts and intellectual and artistic pursuits may be seen as resulting from larger external processes. The process is internal when seen from one perspective but external when seen from another. If it were possible to see them all operating simultaneously together, we would have some notion of the "totality" of human existence and society. That may exist only in the mind of God. We therefore have only a methodological fiction of the unity of all action, culture, and society. This, at best, enables us to pose specific, if limited, problems and to ascertain, with some specificity—and modesty—the contributions of one set of institutions and habits of mind to others. The imputed totality is ultimately undefinable and inaccessible.

NOTES

1. The major outlines of our central argument are based upon Max Weber's sociology of law, derived from the following sources: *Max Weber on Law in Economy and Society*, edited and annotated by Max Rheinstein, translated by Edward Shils and Max Rheinstein (New York, Simon & Schuster, 1954). Max Weber, *Economy and Society*, edited by Guenther Roth and Claus Wittich (New York, Bedminster Press, 1968) volume 2, pp 641–838. *From Max Weber:* Essays in Sociology, translated, edited and with an Introduction by Hans Gerth and C. Wright Mills (New York, Oxford University Press, 1946) particularly, "Politics as a Vocation" pp 77–128. We, however, attempt to go beyond this with respect to the past sixty years. In addition, the implications of Weber's work for phenomenological analysis are, within our understanding of the tradition, largely based on the works of Alfred Schutz, who taught at the New School for Social Research Graduate Faculty in New York from 1939 to 1959.

2. *Max Weber On Law in Economy and Society*, edited, annotated and with an Introduction by Max Rheinstein, translated by E.A. Shils and M. Rheinstein. (New York, Simon & Schuster, 1954) p. 86: "Characteristics of the charismatic epoch of lawmaking and lawfinding have persisted to a considerable extent in many of the institutions of the period of rational enactment and application of the law. Remnants still survive even at the present day. As late a writer as Blackstone called the English judge a sort of living oracle; and as a matter of fact, the role played by decision as the indispensable and specific form in which the common law is embodied corresponds to the role of the oracle in ancient law. . . . The only distinction between the genuine oracle and the English precedent is that the oracle does not state rational grounds, but it shares this very feature with the verdict of the jury. . ." p. 87: "Originally, legal sages were men of some general magical qualifications who were called upon in individual cases because of their very charisma." See also p. 89: "The primitive method of deciding legal disputes by resorting to an oracle was frequent in civilizations of otherwise highly rationalized political and economic structures as for instance, Egypt (the oracle of Ammon) of Babylonia . . ."; *et passim*.
3. See *Ibid*, pp. 92–3, on the encouragement by the medieval church of princely interference in folk custom as it enacted the law.
4. *ibid*, p 213: Khadi—judge of the Mohammedan *sharia* court . . . Khadi justice—used by Weber as a term . . . to describe the administration of justice which is oriented not at fixed rules of a formally rational law but at the ethical, religious political, or otherwise expediential postulates of a substantively rational law." See also Gerth and Mills, *op cit.* pp 216–217, where "Kadi justice" is described as "informal judgments rendered in terms of concrete ethical or other practical valuations." Even today in England, . . a broad substratum of justice is actually Kadi-justice to an extent that is hardly conceivable on the continent."
5. *Ibid.*, pp 93–95
6. Reinhard Bendix, *Kings of People—Power and the Mandate to Rule* (Berkeley, University of California Press, 1978). Bendix traces the transformation from monarchy and aristocracy towards more democratic forms in five societies: England, France, Germany, Japan, and Russia. The relation of lawyers to all sides of these conflicts is depicted throughout. In one illustration out of many possible, describing the struggle between Parliament and the monarch, Bendix points out: "During the Long Parliament, the leaders of 'the country' engaged in a concerted drive against the monarchy's traditional authority. But these oppositionists were not 'progressives' in any modern sense of the word, nor were they prompted by social resentment. On the contrary they could claim to represent 'the country' in the old-fashioned sense that they were pillars of society who had always had the right and privilege to do so. All these oppositionists in parliament were landed aristocrats, justices, lawyers, and other members of England's high society. . . . Without the backing of these aristocratic leaders, divines and lawyers could not have sustained their claim of opposing the 'misguided' policies of church and crown in the name of the nation" (p. 307). Bendix's book richly documents the complex relation of the legal profession to changing forms of power and privilege; the resolutions of such struggles, whether short- or long-lived, always take the form of new legal decrees and forms.

In ancient Greece, a separate legal profession had not yet emerged; great men such as Solon and Cleistenes were "lawgivers" rather than law interpreters. Raphael Sealey's *A History of the Greek City-States ca. 700–338 B.C.* (Berkeley, University of California Press, 1976) documents the relations between these lawgivers and social classes in their struggles with tyrants and would-be tyrants.

"Aristotle's exposition of the economic crisis and of Solon's work . . . contains elements that appear genuine and others that may be due to speculation. He says that the poor, together with their children and wives, 'were slaves to' the rich. They were called 'serfs' and 'sixth-partners' *(hektemoroi),* since they worked the land of the rich 'at that rent.' All the land was owned by a few; and if the poor did not pay their rents, they and their children were subject to personal seizure. Until the time of Solon loans could only be contracted on the security of the borrower's person. Solon, according to Aristotle, freed the demos for the present and the future, by forbidding the practice of pledging the person as security for debt. Besides issuing laws, he cancelled debts, both private and public, and this cancellation was called *seisachtheia* or 'the throwing off of burdens.' " (pp. 108–109). As a result of Solon's work, Sealey writes, "the Athenian state thereafter did not have any class of citizens in dependent or semi-servile status" (pp. 111–112). Solon's legal code attempted to be as comprehensible as possible (p. 115). Sealy documents the complex groups and interests involved. See also pp. 150ff. for the reforms of Cleisthenes.

7. Weber (in Rheinstein, *op. cit.)* p. 228: "Formal justice guarantees the maximum freedom for the interested parties to represent their formal legal interests. But because of the unequal distribution of economic power, which the system of formal justice legalizes, this very freedom must time and again produce consequences which are contrary to the substantive postulators of religious ethics or of political expediency. Formal justice is thus repugnant to all authoritarian powers . . . because it diminishes the dependency of the individual upon the grace and power of the authorities. . . . To democracy, however, it has been repugnant because it decreases the dependency of the legal practice and therewith of the individuals upon the decisions of their fellow citizens."

Also pp. 230–231: "[T]he high cost of litigation and legal services amounted for those who could not afford to purchase them to a denial of justice, which was rather similar to that which existed, for other reasons, in the judicial system of the Roman Republic. . . . This denial of justice was in close conformity with the interests of the propertied, especially the capitalistic, classes . . . capitalistic interests will fare best under a rigorously formal system of adjudication, which applies in all cases and operates under the adversary system of procedure. In any case adjudication by honoratiores inclines, to be essentially empirical, and its procedure is complicated and expensive. It may thus well stand in the way of the interests of the bourgeois classes and it may indeed be said that England achieved capitalistic supremacy among the nations not because but rather in spite of its judicial system. For these very reasons the bourgeois strata have generally tended to be intensely interested in a rational procedural system and therefore in a systematized and unambiguously formal and purposefully constructed substantive law which eliminates both obsolete traditions and arbitrariness and in which rights can have their source exclusively in general objective norms. Such a systematically codified law was thus demanded by the English Puritans, . . . the Roman Plebians, . . . and the German bourgeoisie of the fifteenth century. . . . But in all these cases such a system was still a long way off."

8. Max Weber (in Rheinstein, *op. cit.)* pp. 268ff. "The Driving Forces behind Codification": "Systematic codification of the law can be the product of a conscious and universal reorientation of legal life, such as becomes necessary as a result of external political innovations, or of a compromise between status groups or classes aiming at the internal social unification of the political body." "The consequences of the purely logical construction often bear very irrational and even unforeseen relations to the expectations of the commercial interests. It is this very fact that has given rise to the frequently made charge that the purely logical law is 'remote from life' (lebensfremd)."

9. Weber (in Rheinstein, *op. cit.* p. 278: "This logical systematization of the law

has been the consequence of the intrinsic intellectual needs of the legal theorists and their disciples, the doctors, i.e., of a typical aristocracy of legal literati. In troublesome cases, opinions rendered by law school faculties were the ultimate authority on the continent. . . . The university judge and notary, together with the university trained advocate, were the typical legal honoratiores."

10.   Otto Kirchheimer, *Political Justice—The Use of Legal Procedure for Political Ends* (Princeton, N.J., Princeton University Press, 1961), especially Chap. VII, "Trial by Fiat of the Successor Regime, pp. 304–305": "While the logic of the Communist system leads to a revamping of the sum total of conditions under which the judiciary operates, more traditional political orders have reserved their special attention mostly to organizing jurisdiction in politically tinged trials. . . .

"When Charles I and Louis XVI met their fates, there was, as they and their counsels spoke of amply, little doubt as to the complete irregularity of both jurisdiction and procedure. Those who framed the indictment and those who judged the case were practically indistinct from each other. As their cases and their ultimate disposal were at the same time the constitutive acts of a new era, the decisions on the cases and principles applied formed identical manifestations of the same political will. But did the fifteenth, sixteenth, and seventeenth century sovereigns act much differently when their own political interests were at stake? The British king might not only order a command performance of his judges . . . but he might also dismiss them should their opinions give him sustained reason for displeasure. The French King . . . might entrust instruction and judgment of his enemy's cases or any other delicate matter to specifically appointed extraordinary commissions, in which learned friends of the king or cardinal and open enemies of the persons to be judged might find a strategic place."

11.   Weber (in Rheinstein, *op. cit.*), Chap. VI. "Forms of Creation of Rights," p. 98, surveys "the fusion of all those organizations which had respectively engendered their own bodies of law into the one comprehensive organization of the state," a process in which "the law serves the interests, especially the economic interests, of the parties concerned."

Also, p. 143, on the difficulties that arose in conflicts between persons subject to different bodies of law: "Law was not a *lex terrae*, as the English law of the King's court became soon after the Norman Conquest, but rather the privilege of the person as a member of a particular group."

12.   Kirchheimer, *op. cit.* p. 307, on the new German Constitutional Court, a structure found also in postwar Austria and Italy: "It functions mostly as a kind of arbiter between the highest organs of the state within the constitutional system . . . , as a guarantor of individual rights . . . , and as a general guarantor of the constitutionality of all legal and administrative enactments." See also note 6 above.

13.   See Kirchheimer, *op. cit.*, pp. 308–319, for a description of the legal changes of various successor regimes.

14.   Ronald Dworkin, *Taking Rights Seriously* (Cambridge, Mass., Harvard University Press, 1980), pp. 90–94: "Types of Rights," wherein the author distinguishes between "background rights, which are rights that provide a justification for political decisions by society in the abstract, and institutional rights, that provide a justification for a decision by some particular and specified political institution." Dworkin's entire work explores the relation of "emerging" rights to established rights.

15.   See Weber (in Rheinstein, *op. cit.*), pp. 209–210, on the relation between professional practitioners of the law and the specialists in commercial law and contracts; see also Rheinstein's note 39, p. 210: "the continental notary is also a specialist in legal drafting, especially of real estate conveyances, but also of important

commercial documents. He is thus not only a lawyer but a lawyer of special training and competence." See also note 17 below.

16.   Martin Mayer, *The Lawyers* (New York, Harper & Row, 1967) Chapter 9, "Pieces of Paper," p. 317, describes the routine work of the members of Wall Street law firms, including tax work, corporate charters, banking and financial matters: "Registration statements are today the classic 'boilerplate' of the large law office." Chapter 10, "Business in Washington," p. 346, quotes James McInnes Henderson, general counsel of the Federal Trade Commission: "If you'll read the Trade Commission Act or the Clayton Act or the Robinson-Patman Act, you'll know that you can't tell what the law is by reading the act." The growth of regulatory agencies has led not only to a jungle of unintelligible administrative legal decisions, but to a corresponding growth of legal specialists. Especially interesting is the proliferation of administrative codes to the point of obscuring the laws on which they were based. Thus Mayer, p. 371: "The case in which most of this came out was an appeal from an injunction to prohibit violations of 'fair competition' under the Petroleum Code. When the brief for the government came to be written, Professor Jaffe recalled a dozen years later, 'it occurred to the brief writer to examine the originals (which were found after some difficulty). He discovered the sickening fact that by reason of a mistaken use of terms—the Code had been amended out of existence.'

"What had happened, as Merlo Pusey put it, was that 'men had been arrested, indicted, and held in jail for violating a law that did not exist.' Justice Brandeis, after listening to this incredible story, asked from the bench, 'Well, is there any way by which one can find out what is in these executive orders when they are issued?' And the government counsel admitted, 'I think it would be rather difficult.' One does not have to be fanatical about the rule of law to be shocked by this sort of governing."

See also Chapter 11 on legal specializations (broadcast licenses, admiralty law, labor law, as well as lawyers specializing in certain industries such as restaurant, their specific licensing and real estate requirements, or copyright law, contracts in the performing arts, bankruptcy, taxes, and patents).

17.   Martin Mayer, *op. cit*, p. 462, "A professor at the Texas Law School recently wrote, at the conclusion of a research project: "How 'good' is the brand of justice administered by the Texas courts? Do the litigants and the public get a fair deal? . . . Must the answer be that there is no answer—that the system defies analysis? Unfortunately, this may be the necessary reply, unless an even more gloomy one is appropriate." Much the same can be said anywhere in the country. But meanwhile, let us look about us."

18.   The literature of disillusion with the law is very large and very old; much of it long ago passed into proverbs, such as that a peasant between two lawyers is like a fish between two cats, or that the law is a spider's web that traps the fly but lets the hawk go free. Charles Dickens's words, "If the law supposes that," said Mr. Bumble, 'the law is a ass, a idiot' " *(Oliver Twist),* like the dialogue in Shakespeare's *Henry VI,* have become proverbial:

Butcher.   The first thing we do, let's kill all the lawyers.
Cade.   Nay, that I mean to do. Is this not a lamentable thing, that of the skin of an innocent lamb should be made parchment? That parchment, being scribble o'er, should undo a man? Some say the bee stings, but I say 'tis the bee's wax; for I did but seal once to a thing, and I was never mine own man since.

For Americans the legal profession has for long been seen—until recently—as a support for democracy and people's rights, but here too a groundswell of complaint has arisen. A few recent examples:

1. *The New York Times,* June 1, 1983, offers an article by Stuart Taylor, Jr.: "Justice System Stifled by Its Cost and Its Complexity, Experts Warn."
2. *The Wall Street Journal,* June 7, 1984, offers an essay by Ernest Gellhorn (a dean and professor of law): "Too Much Law, Too Many Lawyers, Not Enough Justice."
3. *The New York Times,* December 6, 1983, in which Peter Megargee Brown (former president of the Federal Bar Council and a fellow of the American College of Trial Lawyers), in an essay entitled "Misguided Lawyers," points out the decline of the American legal profession by several measures.
4. *The Wall Street Journal,* November 2, 1984, offers an editorial, "Courting a Better Way," on the irrationalities arising from lawsuits by victims of asbestos-related diseases, resulting in years of complex negotiations even "before the plaintiff walks into court," and in the collection by attorneys of two-thirds of the damage awards. The resulting demand for private arbitration implies that "courts will learn they have no monopoly on dispensing justice." "The rest of us may see that the rule of law is sometimes better handled by individuals in private arbitration than by lawyers in public litigation."

19.   The Belgian philosopher of law, Chaim Perelman, has explored the problem of multiple sources and multiple ideas of justice. In *The Idea of Justice and the Problem of Argument,* translated by John Petrie (London, RKP, 1977,) pp. 17–26, he systematizes these various conceptions into six related but mutually irreducible propositions: (1) to each the same thing; (2) to each according to his merits; (3) to each according to his works; (4) to each according to his needs; (5) to each according to his rank; (6) to each according to his legal entitlement. His explorations lead to the conclusion that justice is an enescapably confused, yet indispensable, concept (p. 59). It cannot be reduced to clarity without distortion.

See also his *Justice, Law, and Argument* (Boston, Reidel/Kluwer, 1980).

20.   Weber (in Rheinstein, *op. cit.*), Chap. VI, "Forms of Creation of Rights," p. 147, describes the emergences of new rights and claims by many groups: "As long as the distinction between objective norm and subjective claim was but incompletely developed, as long, also, as law was a quality of a person determined by his membership in a certain group, one could speak of only two kinds of rules. The first were those which were valid in a group or organization because of the special status qualities of its members; the others were valid and binding because one had created them for himself by directly participating in a contract. All special law was indeed originally determined by status qualities."

21.   Arguments and decisions that at one time or another acquired "landmark" status are discussed in Mayer, *The Lawyers,* Chap. 15, "The Supreme Court: A Concluding Unscientific Postscript"; in Roscoe Pound, *An Introduction to the Philosophy of Law* (New Haven, Yale University Press, 1922); Edward H. Levi, *An Introduction to Legal Reasoning* (Chicago, University of Chicago Press, 1948); Raoul Berger: *Government by Judiciary: the Transformation of the Fourteenth Amendment* (Cambridge, Mass., Harvard University Press, 1977); and Guido Calabresi: *A Common Law for the Age of Statutes* (Cambridge, Mass., Harvard University Press, 1982).

22.   An example is suggested in a recent paper by David M. Trubek, *Where the Action Is: Critical legal Studies and Empiricism* (Madison, Wisc. Disputes Processing Research Program, University of Wisconsin—Law School, 1983). This paper notes the development of a "nondoctrinal" or "empirical" approach to legal studies,

in a complex relationship to another movement within the legal profession, which is labeled "critical legal studies." In Trubek's view, traditional legal scholarship ("doctrinal studies"), in its focus on what the law "is," disregards the wider social meaning and impact of the law. Social scientists have pioneered this wider field of study, and critical legal studies, practiced by lawyers themselves, is carrying this forward, with an avowedly leftist and partially Marxist aim in mind, that of transforming society by transforming consciousness, and especially consciousness of how legal institutions and ways of thought "legitimate" the present system: "the analysis of legal consciousness is part of a transformative politics" (p. 19); "if scholarship can change consciousness it is not merely a move toward an ultimate transformation; it is the real thing" (p. 22); "critical scholars see legal thought as *denial*. . . . Legal thought is a form of denial, that is, a way to deal with perceived contradictions which are too painful for us to hold in consciousness" (pp. 41–42); "the critical scholars share with others a concern to show how the law works and what impact it has; they, too, look at law from the outside, as it were, questioning its own self-understanding . . . critical legal studies is part of a broad movement in nondoctrinal thought on law that rests on the critique of legal order" (p. 52). The extent of this movement's influence is not yet clear. It is possible that criticism of the legal profession predates this movement.

Critical legal theory seems unclear on the extent to which the law is dominated by its own tendencies to the formalization of doctrine and to accommodate itself exclusively to external interests. If both processes occur at the same time, then it makes little sense to think of law purely in doctrinal terms or purely as a conflict of naked interests. Only in extreme situations do the conflicts between law and agencies of interests and between law and its own doctrinal unity become highlighted.

As critics of the law, critical legal theorists may attempt, quite self-consciously, to undermine established legal principles in the hope that, in so doing, they will create new principles upon which the law can then be codified. To the extent that they believe that one set of principles can be substituted for another, they betray great faith in the potentialities of the law as an instrument of reform or revolution.

23.   Philadelphia was for a long time the center of an American legal aristocracy; the term "Philadelphia lawyer" originally meant someone with exceptional skillfulness. "Some time after 1850 the term 'Philadelphia lawyer' became a national cliche. . . . 1950 was the Last Rally of the legal aristocracy of Philadelphia" (John Lukacs, *Philadelphia—Patricians and Philistines, 1900–1950* (New York, Farrar, Straus and Giroux, 1981), pp. 36–37, 314–318). At some point between those two dates, the term came to mean something less than scholarship and a concern for public service.

24.   See note 19 above. In more detail, as an article by Stuart Taylor, Jr., "Justice System Stifled by Its Costs and Its Complexity, Experts Warn," (*The New York Times*, June 1, 1983), "Complex cases in which opposing lawyers bury one another under thousands of documents and marshal legions of experts and other witnesses have become much more common. One index is the number of Federal trials consuming more than 20 days, which almost quadrupled to 164 in 1982 from 45 in 1960." Trials are only the top of a pyramid of legal activity: "Most lawyers rarely set foot in court, spending their time drafting memorandums, letters of opinion, interrogatories, motions and briefs, as well as counseling, lobbying, taking depositions and negotiating deals. The vast majority of all lawsuits are settled out of court." Quoting Derek Bok, the author says: "Too many of the nations most talented students are going to law school and then 'into legal pursuits that often add little to the growth of the economy or the pursuit of culture or the enhancement of the human spirit.' "

25.   Levi, *op. cit.*, pp. 58–59, discusses throughout the problem of ambiguity of legislative intent, and contortions of interpretation gone through by courts: "The

Constitution in its general provisions embodies the conflicting ideals of the community. Who is to say what these ideals mean in any definite way? Certainly not the framers, for they did their work when the words were put down. The words are ambiguous. Nor can it be the Court, for the Court cannot bind itself in this manner; an appeal can always be made back to the Constitution. . . . Added to the problem of ambiguity and the additional fact that the framers may have intended a growing instrument, there is the influence of constitution worship. This influence gives great freedom to a court. It can always abandon what has been said in order to go back to the written document itself." On shifts in interpretation, see also pp. 60ff.

26. A study of the costs of litigation is Lois G. Forer, *Money and Justice: Who Owns the Courts?* (New York, Norton, 1984). See also Richard A. Posner, *The Federal Courts* (Cambridge, Mass., Harvard University Press, 1984).

27. Ernest Gellhorn, dean and professor of law at the Case Western Reserve University School of Law *The Wall Street Journal*, June 7, 1984, "Too Much Law, Too Many Lawyers, Not Enough Justice": "the primary source of the lawyer explosion is the law explosion that began in the 1960s and reached its peak in the 1970s. New laws and government regulations were written in response to popular demands for protection from an unhealthy environment, for an assurance of safer products and wholesome workplaces, for an end to anachronistic discrimination because of race, religion or sex, and similar concerns. These rules were not limited to business regulation, and they have increasingly affected our daily lives.

"Thus, the major source of the law explosion is the legislature, acting not in ignorance or mendacity but rather in response to public pressure for yet more rules and laws. Nor can these pressures always be blamed on liberal activists. Recent propositions to allow prayer in public schools would probably require a government agency to rule on which prayers are permissible and which are not. The end result, of course, would be that we would chafe under yet another set of rules. And the public would complain that laws and lawyers are once again interfering and trying to rule our lives."

28. For a discussion of recent changes in the jury system, see Raoul Berger, *Government by Judiciary—The Transformation of the Fourteenth Amendment* (Cambridge, Mass., Harvard University Press, 1977), Chap. 22, "Trial by Jury: Six or Twelve Jurors."

29. The American Bar Association is the largest voluntary professional organization in the world." David Margolich, "Bar Group in Shift Adopts Neutral Policy on Abortion (*New York Times*, August 9, 1990, p. 20).

Chapter 13

Attitudes in Clinical and Scientific Medicine

MEDICINE AS SCIENCE

The prestige of the physician in modern societies is, at least in part, related to the fact that he embodies the application of science, not magic, to the solution of medical problems. Whether or not this is true is a central concern of this essay. A central question, in this context, is the meaning of science as it is related to medicine. Medicine as a craft existed for millenia before science as we know it was established as a mode of knowledge.

Medicine in its own domain is related to the problems of dysfunctions of the human organism, the easement of pain, and mortality. Science is only a particular set of means for achieving knowledge that are independent of these problems. Medicine as an intellectual discipline is also related to natural philosophy, the understanding of the human condition and existence apart from its pragmatic presuppositions [1]. As such, medicine as an intellectual discipline could follow all intellectual and philosophical currents present in the development and history of ideas, whether medicine as practice was *scientific* in the modern sense of the term.

Medicine as a science could only arise after the emergence of science and the beginning of the scientific era in the sixteenth century. Andreas Vesalius (1514–1564), an anatomist who based his work on the careful dissection of cadavers, was one of the chief exponents of actual observation in medicine. He was roundly denounced at the time for overturning the work of the second-century anatomist, Galen [2]. Medicine as a science progressed further in the eighteenth and nineteenth centuries with the great achievements of Harvey, Jenner, Lister, Pasteur, and Koch, though it is always possible to discover anticipations and prefigurations that stretch back even to the ancient world [3].

As a science, medicine rested primarily on strict observation of how the body operated, of anatomy, of the progress of diseases *in situ*, and of surgery on the battlefield. In the eighteenth century, the central problem of medicine was the discovery of physical systems in the body, such as the respiratory and pulmonary, gastrointestinal, cardiovascular, and nervous systems. Such observational investigations had to overcome taboos regarding vivisection and the invasion of the privacy of even dead bodies.

The plagues that had swept through Europe and other parts of the world helped the development of modern medicine. They were curtailed ultimately by techniques that did not require anatomical investigation or any refined theory of disease. The purification of water supplies, the burning of corpses, rat control, and the development of water and sewage systems were all used to contain death and illness long before medicine could in any theoretical or scientific way account for the diseases [4]. Nor did such solutions necessarily require the intervention of physicians.

The development of modern medicine, as we now know it, proceeded with the discovery of germs, bacteria, and viruses, following the invention of the microscope and the work of Pasteur, who applied and enlarged on some of these earlier findings. Louis Pasteur (1822–1895) was a chemist who in the course of his work on fermentation and bacteria developed the germ theory of infection in 1862. He then applied his findings to both human and animal diseases, but again, like Vesalius, not without meeting tremendous resistance from his colleagues [5]. Once Pasteur's approach to medicine was adopted in the late nineteenth century, experimental medicine—especially as defined by Claude Bernard (1813–1878) in his work *An Introduction to the Study of Experimental Medicine* (1865)—was on its way to becoming the science we now know it [6]. Bernard's experiments on the workings of the digestive system and the functions of the liver are especially noteworthy in the history of medicine.

THE GROWTH OF SPECIALIZATION

The investigation of specific body systems and subsystems continued and led to specialization within medicine; specific parts of the body also were studied—limbs, glands, tissues, nerves, sera, hormones, etc. Specialization has also accelerated with respect to diseases and to the chemicals that facilitate and inhibit the development of diseases. Moreover, each specialization, based on anatomy, body systems, or diseases of the organism, can be broken down further from the standpoint of biochemistry and the dysfunctions and physical operations of particular systems and subsystems.

A further form of specialization is based on the technologies of medical practice and research. Radiology, sonography, CAT scanning machines, dialysis, heart and other monitoring equipment, implantation of artificial organs and joints, transplants, and the use of computers at almost all levels of research, diagnosis, and monitoring are just some of the technologies used. They also include automatic diagnostic machinery in blood and other chemical tests, and elaborate surgical procedures using lasers, fiber optics, and scanners, to name just a few. Each form of equipment requires specialists not only in the disease or physical condition to which it is applied, but also in the design, operation, and interpretation of results. Many of the skills needed are nonmedical ones. Physicists, electronic engineers, computer scientists, biologists and biochemists, and an infinite number of other specialists all become necessary to the practice of medicine. Research, as part of the scientific apparatus of and practice of medicine, similarly requires a high degree of specialization. Again, the research in each field and its almost infinite subdivisions can often be conducted by specialists who are not physicians. Physicians may be necessary here in pointing to clinical problems and orienting nonphysician specialists to the clinical settings and applications of research problems. Some physicians do go on for Ph.D.s in biochemistry or engineering and other fields, and some people who initially held Ph.D.s or engineering degrees later go on for M.D.s in order better to bridge these technical and medical fields. Physicians who become superspecialists may have to expend a great deal of effort and give up much of their time keeping abreast of developments in these nonmedical fields [7].

Physicians do become indispensable in the reapplication of science to clinical practice. Such reapplication includes the determination of medications and the length and quality of treatments. Thus, the practice of medicine by superspecialists means having access to a group of patients all suffering from similar or related conditions [8]. This is most likely to happen in research-oriented teaching hospitals. Their clientele becomes a sample upon which they conduct applied experiments. In this case, the patient is but an instance of a disease that is relevant to the doctors only to the extent that the disease is amenable to their experimental practice. All other aspects of the patient's life, history, and diseases are likely to be of secondary relevance to the disease under research.

THE PRIMARY-CARE PHYSICIAN

If we view medicine from the perspective of nineteenth-century practitioners, the patient consists of a plurality of physical systems that in some ways are interrelated. The present superspecialization in medicine confronts a primary-care physician with a world of specialized knowledge of great complexity. This is not very different from the way laymen view the proliferation of science. Both primary-care physicians and laymen consider the abstractness, methodological density, and specialized theories, methods, and rhetorics of science as so many impediments for the making of informed decisions.

It is also beyond the ken of primary-care physicians, no matter how erudite, to master all the specialties that, in principle, they are required to know if they are themselves to treat their patients adequately [9]. They are required to keep up with research being carried out by specialists and need to be able to evaluate that research intelligently. If they are dedicated, primary-care physicians must turn to handbooks, journals, and texbooks written by medical journalists, who in turn try to keep up with scientific publications. They would probably also have to take refresher courses. In practice, they are forced to rely on specialists who may be medical researchers or physicians and who, on the basis of their specialties, are able to follow the literature more assiduously than they themselves can hope to do. Yet, even here, they are forced to make assessments on the capability of superspecialists when they lack the knowledge and criteria for making such judgments. They may, of course, abandon the attempt to make such judgments themselves. They may refer the patient to a university or research hospital, hoping to find physicians there who, on the basis of their institutional affiliation, should be more competent than they are to make the necessary judgments [10].

Increasingly, physicians practice in groups that cover broad areas of specialty, but this also may be insufficient in dealing with certain illnesses. These partners, too, may have to refer patients to a research institute or hospital dealing with the rare or complex disease in question.

In sum then, primary-care physicians, whether general practitioners, internists, or, more recently, family physicians (now a specialty unto itself), are often either forced to act as if they were the specialists or to become traffic managers among specialists and subspecialists. A seriously ill patient becomes the observational focus of a plurality of physicians, each viewing the patient from the perspective of the occupational blinders of his own specialty. Hence, the "zebra diagnosis" made only after hearing distant hoofbeats but without seeing their maker. This refers to the diagnosis of a rare and obscure disease (the "zebra") that just happens to be the focus of interest of a specialist [11]. Each specialist is likely to see the disease as a manifestation of a subspecialty or interest of his own. Thus, the patient becomes a corpus of potential interest for a variety of special interests, who then struggle to assert the primacy of their own interest. In a similar way, even general practitioners or family physicians may have some interest in a given branch of medicine, organ, or disease. They may follow up this interest in a particular branch of medicine, and be alert to nuances in symptomology and treatment practice in their favorite area. Yet, for other diseases and their treatment, they may have to rely on their recollections from medical school and textbook descriptions. The patient, on the basis of the particularities of his own condition and on its accidental relationship to the physician's interest and skill, may not be properly treated until the manifest pain or danger of the disease forces the physician to secure specialized assistance.

Primary-care physicians in such extreme situations become the mediators between specialists. Since they are less specialized than the consultants, they are not likely to be able to assert their interests in the patient as a totality. Nor are they able to defend the interests of the patient in the face of more knowledgeable and prestigious specialists.

This phenomenon within medicine is likely to result in what physicians call "Ping-Ponging" the patient. The patient is the Ping-Pong ball, and the players may be a group of specialists who bounce a patient from one to the other. They may hope that a satisfactory diagnosis will emerge that transcends the individual specialties of the collected assemblage of individuals and specialists [12]. The injunction of colleagueship may result in all other consultants allowing one to "test" his diagnosis before the others, who will have their turn in due course. In the meantime, the effect of continuous tests, diagnostic procedures, and examinations may be as painful and as life threatening as the disease itself. Such an image of medical practice may or may not be true, regardless of the interests of doctors in multiplying consulting fees or exchanging favors.

By the same token, the most forceful and aggressive specialists may be able to impose their diagnosis on the others. Their diagnosis is likely to persist until it fails; then another one is substituted, which is retained if the patient responds to treatment. The process continues until a workable diagnosis or treatment modality is found, the condition corrects itself, or the patient is no longer around as an object for diagnostic experimentation.

A word of caution that limits this black scenario must be entered here. The advance of pharmacological medicine, of broad-spectrum drugs, and of sulfa, penicillin, and other antibiotics has resulted at least in temporary victories over some diseases. (Bacteria may develop resistances to these drugs, after which new antibiotics must be developed.) In the meantime, the use of broad-spectrum antibiotics relieves physicians of the necessity of making detailed, specific diagnoses, and allows them to hope that the scientific researcher, the pharmacologist, and the chemist will have solved their problems for them. In a similar way, the great victories against contagious diseases such as yellow fever, bubonic plague, tuberculosis, scarlet fever, diphtheria, and polio allowed medicine to claim great victories as a science. The solution of these problems meant the profession could then turn to problems of the diseases of old age and others that are not easily prevented or cured by mass vaccination or innoculation [13]. But it should be noted that great increases in life expectancy took place before 1920; since that time, more people are living to a ripe old age, but life expectancy has only inched ahead, without any great leaps comparable to the period 1870 to 1920. Since the discovery of the polio vaccine, relatively rare diseases have received the greatest attention, and this may be one reason why life expectancy has not increased more sharply in recent decades. The advance of scientific research medicine has resulted in a concern with difficult cases that might not have been seriously approached by medicine as late as a quarter of a century ago.

If we return to the increase in specialization, when the patient is viewed as a totality, the problems are compounded. Even when a patient has one paramount disease or condition that, from the standpoint of pain or the imminence of death or deterioration, is critical, he is likely to suffer from more than one disease or condition. In addition, when he suffers from one paramount condition or disease, that disease may have secondary consequences throughout the physical system. Here the question is: Is the symptom related to the basic disease or condition? The plurality of specialists are all likely to be attracted to the symptom or condition that takes on a primacy because of their own specialty. And so multiple and often conflicting treatments are prescribed. The drugs used may also counteract one another, or produce negative synergistic effects [14].

In light of the above, medical schools have been faulted for not emphasizing pharmacology. In the absence of systematic training, graduate physicians are forced to rely on handbooks and textbooks, on pharmacists, and on the medical detailer of pharmaceutical manufacturers. Or they can read an almost unlimited variety of specialized journals. Yet, without adequate training, they are not likely to be able to evaluate both specialized and commercial presentations.

In principle, it is up to primary-care physicians to know the joint or combined effects of all the treatments, prescriptions, and dosages offered to the patient. In practice, this would mean that the primary-care physician should know more about the patient than the specialists and should be superior to them, even in their specialties and their collective impact on the patient. What is more, he would have to see the patient more often than does the specialist, and be the one to supervise treatment. Yet, in the absence of such integrated treatment, it is perhaps understandable that many people believe that patients may be as likely to die from the treatment as from the disease.

DILEMMAS AND CONTRADICTIONS IN MEDICAL PRACTICE

These contradictions and dilemmas in the practice of medicine are understandable in view of contemporary macroscopic institutional and technological development. Cleavages have developed because of the division between highly organized, highly specialized, "scientific" medicine, and medicine as a clinical art that deals with the individual patient in the uniqueness of the patient's ailments and personality. The attempt to resolve these cleavages has resulted in new specialties such as "primary medicine" or "family practice." This has been opposed to "general practice," which was often replaced if not by the two specialties, then by "internal medicine."

The ultimate result is that all physicians become "specialists." Yet, the creation of specialties is not merely a matter of labeling. It is a result of the complexity of knowledge and practice created by the necessary specialization of medicine as a science [15]. The research being done in each specialty is never productive of certainty, of definitive answers, diagnoses, or prescriptive treatment, or of transmittability to the physicians who practice on patients. Research focuses necessarily on areas of uncertainty. Thus, even if the scientific medical knowledge were accessible, it might not be entirely useful for general practitioners or primary-treatment physicians [16]. The publicity of dramatic research findings, however, raises the expectations of successful treatment among the population at large. New ills and obscure conditions are also thought to be amenable to treatment. This is because, at some levels, scientific medicine has been successful, though not usually or universally so successful as claimed by the current practitioners of "science."

The great successes in medicine have been at the preventive level, in what is by now regarded as elementary pharmacology, biochemistry, and preventive innoculations. Even here, the dialectic of diseases sometimes results in the creation of new strains of organisms, which may be resistant to previous syntheses of disease and cure. Again, the net effect has been to raise expectations of patients regarding treatment and adding to disenchantment when it is not forthcoming.

This dialectic of rising expectations and disenchantment is particularly significant because twentieth-century physicians have increasingly exploited their patients' desires for good health and fear of morbidity. Physicians have also claimed a unique status for their relationship to patients vis-à-vis trust and confidentiality, and immunity from the supervision of other institutions of social control. They have also claimed the right to exercise control over entry into all medically based practice, refusing to recognize the claims of midwives, podiatrists, chiropractors, psychologists, acupuncturists, and a host of others [17]. The revival and diffusion of new forms of folk medicine and the popularity of these excluded forms of treatment are perhaps another means by which patients express their disenchantment with expensive and not very understandable "scientific" medicine.

The legal profession has also been accused of adding to this disenchantment by holding out the possibility of lucrative malpractice suits and encouraging disdain for medical practitioners [18].

In part, physicians have believed their own claims; the vast knowledge they are required to master makes them feel superior to their patients and most other professionals and laymen. The sense of superiority gives them, like psychiatrists and psychologists (see Chapter 10), a godlike authority, especially since patients often consult them in a state of weakness bordering on desperation. If the physician accepts such an exalted self-image, he becomes the *deus abscondus,* not answerable to the patient or family, and keeping the patient in continuous fear or uncertainty in his refusal to communicate. This may be especially true in dealing with lower-class or lower-status racial or ethnic patients or those deemed to be otherwise socially and economically inferior to the physician, at least in terms of medical education.

These claims have been translated into demands: for high fees, for control over patient behavior in the name of health, and for deference, as expressed in waiting time, appointments, delays in treatment, and unquestioning acceptance of their medical decisions. If individual physicians incorporate into their professional and self-attitudes feelings of omnipotence and the claims these entail, they become the personification of the grandiose, arrogant side of medicine. And in light of the dialectic of rising expectations they become its victims as well. For general practitioners or primary-care physicians and specialists and superspecialists alike must become aware, even more than the layman, of the limits of specialized scientific knowledge as it applies to specific diseases and patients. Or they can evoke the glories of science, and face the prospect of explaining its failures in concrete cases after initial or successive diagnoses have been replaced, the operation has failed, or—for other reasons—the patient dies.

If they take the course of professional modesty, they help to undermine the previously established professional claims of the field. Yet, if they take this course, they are likely to increase the disenchantment caused by failure to meet the promises that they and their field have made. Moreover, if they know the risks and uncertainties of medicine, they are forced, by claiming medical omnipotence, to become actors, pretending to have knowledge that they know may not exist or is simply not available, not to them nor to the round of specialists at their beck and call.

As actors, they are subject to being found out by the clients—if not immediately, then over time. This intensifies patients' disenchantment. In either case, making excessive promises for science or exhibiting modesty against the background of these promises, doctors and patients will be bound in unhappy marriages in which grievances escalate. Yet, even bad marriages often prevail. Patients may shop around for another mate, one more competent or just more human; but ill patients cannot remain single for long. And doctors need patients not only to practice their profession as economic ventures, but also to acquire the body of data necessary to practice their science.

Certainly, in light of patients' complaints and the explicit and implied promises of the professions, legislative, institutional, and economic rearrangements are continuously being sought to bring medicine and its institutions under some form of control. But such attempts are limited by the fact that among those attempting to control medical institutions, the single most active group is that of organized physicians themselves.

OBJECTIVITY

Medicine in many ways recapitulates the history of science insofar as pure science distinguishes itself from the "merely pragmatic" or the utilitarian. Yet the distinction between pure science and clinical science is another version of the distinction between the scientific attitude and the attitude of everyday life. But, as it lies between the two, it is close to what we have labeled the planning attitude [19]. In medicine, the two basic attitudes are substantially different, yet they have a common element, that of "objectivity."

Objectivity has many meanings and causes. One meaning refers to the observer having an unbiased attitude in searching for and evaluating facts, or to the observer's ability to separate facts from opinion and values. Another meaning refers to the observer's unbiased image of events in the empirical world, one that is an accurate reflection of events taking place. A third refers to the emotional and evaluative distance between the observer and that which is being observed, so that he is able to view the world with some degree of detachment and analyze it without subjective bias. The first and third are close to essential ingredients in the scientific attitude.

If one probes into the causes of objectivity, additional dimensions emerge. Hegel and Marx explained the emergence of objectivity and a critical attitude toward the world of experience as resulting from alienation, or the inability of individuals immediately to impress their un-self-conscious intentions on the world. This enforced "distancing" causes the individual to perceive the world in terms of abstract categories, rather than intuitive, direct, emotional, and qualitative experience. Categorical thinking replaces the immediacy of direct experience.

George Simmel found yet other, or at least supplementary bases for objectivity. Like Marx, he found money and its quantification to be the means by which qualitative distinctions are reduced to a single quantitative one. Simmel added to this the idea that objectivity also arises as the number of people involved in a set of social relationships increases. Abstract categorical thinking replaces the intimate, subjective, and critical relationships of the dyad and small group [20]. People are forced to be objective in making judgments. The objectivity is based on reason and the categories they construct. And finally, social relationships in a metropolis cause the emergence of a blasé attitude, by which Simmel meant that people defend themselves from becoming emotionally involved with large numbers of strangers by becoming uncaring [21]. All of these dimensions—categorical thinking, (abstractness of thought), an emphasis on the cash nexus, and the blasé attitude—are related to medical attitudes in both research and clinical practice.

But the simplest form of the objective attitude in medicine, and perhaps in all other fields, is found in the very word "objective." Physicians deal with physical objects—organs, bones, veins, tissues, and so on—and the physical, chemical, and neural connections between all of these. Historically, physicians have had to rid themselves and the field of such prescientific concepts as spirits, humors, temperaments, animi, magic, and witchcraft [22]. They also had to learn to limit their desires to speculate, theorize, and imagine, in order to deal with the body as a biological organism, a physical object [23].

These have caused the medical profession as a whole and specific schools of medicine to concentrate on *objective* causes, effects, and processes almost to the exclusion of all other phenomena. This objectivity, based on the concreteness of the body, is similar to the "practical reason" of the lawyer, which abjures speculation and empty theorizing. This may have led to the way candidates to medicine are selected, and to the self-selection of those who are predisposed to thinking of objectivity as the physical manipulation of objects.

The same concern with objects as "facts" has characterized almost all medical education and has fostered the emphasis on memorization of body parts and of other aspects of medical knowledge. Students interested in principles, in theoretical sciences, and in humanitarian concerns find that overcoming the sheer burden of rote memorization is a task that demeans the intelligence and imagination. Certainly, if they have these qualities, they may be required to put them on reserve for at least the first few years of their medical education. The net result, in any case, will be the stagnation of those "antiobjective" factors—imagination, humanity, speculation, and a sensitivity to the subjective realities of both themselves and their patients.

Modern medical education also has fostered the institutional and self-exploitation of students, interns, and residents [24]. This is based on more than the exploitation by older doctors of the young. It is justified as hardening the doctor to the severities of professional life and helping to produce the distance from the patient that constitutes professional objectivity. Being able to cope with such untold deprivations may also produce an elevated sense of self-worth. And the physician who has gone through it all and survived feels peculiarly fit to prescribe or administer pain to others. This professional attitude may be the functional equivalent of Simmel's blasé attitude. The professional has to maintain distance from the client in order to maintain objectivity and not be drawn into the cycle of hope and despair that comprises the human condition.

RESEARCH MEDICINE

The objectivity of research medicine is quite different from that of clinical medicine. The research physician may not have to see the patient, only the test results. These specialists may see the patient only as related to a particular condition, and examine only a small part of the body. Thus they need not see the patient as a total human being. Objectivity here is based, in part, on the categorical generalization of the scientific attitude and, to a large degree, on the flattening out of time. The disease is but one in a sample of cases that constitutes the ideal type or theoretical model of the disease. Specialists may also be racing against time in competition with the progress of the disease. These means of maintaining distance limit the affectual or emotional and phenomenological sharing of communities of meaning with their patients.

THE SURGEON

Surgeons possess a different type of objectivity. Their objective world is a specific diseased or malfunctioning organ or physiological entity. It is revealed by tests or by previous diagnosis. Surgeons usually enter the treatment scene late, though they often ask for their own tests or X rays. They are not unlikely to recommend surgery, which entails objectivity in a radical sense, dealing with a specific part of the body.

But the objectivity of surgery entails still another form of objectification, that of procedure, as in the performing arts, sports (Chapter 3), and in legal and bureaucratic processes (Chapters 12 and 17). All steps can usually be standardized, and specified with precision as related to anatomical detail, instruments, sequence, order, and surgical method. Checklists, scenarios, or scores have been constructed and are available in textbooks, journals, and handbooks, and each step can be rehearsed, practiced, and prepared for. Repetition, either as a result of practice or specialization, sharpens and confirms the objectivity of technique.

The objectivity of technique of surgeons, however, is different from that in sports and the live performing arts. There, mistakes are most often visible to "informed citizens" who are fans. Surgeons' observers are confined to other operating theater attendants. Apart from these, the exercise of skill by procedural objectivity is hidden within the body, and mistakes or errors of judgment are covered up by suturing. Thus, the procedural objectivity of surgery is similar to that exercised by the performing artist in recording sessions. Only the artist's peers and attending technicians know of the takes, mistakes, and retakes necessary for finished performances. Botched jobs are of little importance and can be corrected relatively easily; usually it is only a matter of economic costs. In surgery, the finality of performance reaches its ultimate expression and the "trust" that is central to medicine is primarily among peers [25]. In musical performance, much less trust is necessary, and tales of fatuous mistakes abound and are diffused throughout the musical community. In medicine, public information of this nature usually emerges through the reporting of police actions and civil suits [26].

THE CLINICIAN

Clinicians are also objective, as indicated, but in more simple terms. Their objectivity is based on considering the patient as a physiological and biological entity. At the same time, their training has tended to reinforce these attitudes; but the rise of scientific medicine makes them susceptible to those aspects of objectivity that are peculiarly emphasized there. Thus the prestige of science is likely to cause them to act as if they were research scientists. To some degree this is true, for clinicians or general practitioners (or internists) become collectors of specimens for laboratory technicians and for higher level superspecialists, whether or not they are well versed in the language or in the referential meanings of their language. In presenting and defending these procedures, they are forced, often unwillingly, to "take over" the attitude of the scientist. They sometimes purchase expensive equipment that symbolizes "science" to the uninitiated layman. But that may not be appropriate to their degree of knowledge. It may also be uneconomical in terms of degree of usage. But the indiscriminate use of equipment ("overutilization") in order to reduce unit costs may be an even greater offense against the ideals of medical ethics, to be analyzed below.

THE OBJECTIVITY OF INDECISION

Many of the "scientific" forms of objectivity are based on tests that are ordered because of a failure to reach a diagnosis and result from and in the "objectivity of indecision." A scientific network team subjects the patient to a multiplicity of diagnostic tests without an agreed upon preliminary diagnosis, a hunch, or an idea. [With diagnostically related groups (see next section) they are forced to make a primary and secondary diagnosis. If they are unsure of or have not agreed upon a diagnosis, they make the broadest relevant one.] The tests are often given in no particular order and with little thought to the effect of one test on the others or on the patient.

Hannah Arendt might have seen this as mindless bureaucratic authoritarianism. Testing without an idea is reinforced by a complex system of bureaucratic rules and procedures, that is, medical payments. Compensation is based on the use of procedures, which then provide objective categories by which physicians and technicians can be paid. There is no objective category for thought per se, imagination, diagnosis, nor, as we have indicated, for ideas that emanate "between the tests." Diagnosticians do not fit into test-specialized treatment unless they are primary-contact clinicians known to possess a flair for diagnosis in addition to their test-based specialization. For the clinical, intuitive art of diagnosis most often falls between the cracks of objective specialized training and scientific practice, as well as through the interstices of the tests themselves.

CLINICAL DIAGNOSIS

Given all these forms of objectivity, general practitioners, whatever they are called, are likely to have the opportunity to encounter the patient as a whole person and to respond in terms other than that of research science. This is true, of course, only if the physician takes the time to get to know the patient. The physician must be willing to listen not only to the manifest language of the patient but also to his inarticulate gropings, and to have a sense of what is left unsaid. This requires time, repeated contact, a sympathetic response, and reflection over the meaning of poorly articulated symptoms in order to make that guess which is called diagnosis. Physicians, of course, combine these diagnoses with relatively simple tests to eliminate more extreme possibilities and confirm tentative hypotheses. This may involve the laying on of hands, and close repeated examinations. Later on, they may employ more elaborate testing and specialists to confirm or reject a hypothesis; but the initial formulations are based on skill in examination, interviewing, and listening, and creative imagination in synthesizing [27].

An opposite way of proceeding would be to rely on research science, feed all the results of tests into a computer, or hand them over to an ad hoc panel of specialists, and hope that with the collective wisdom of the specialists and the computer a diagnosis will be arrived at. This approach had been employed in many hospitals in the late 1970s, where all admissions were subject to a standard battery of tests regardless of the presenting problem [28]. The practice was in principle discontinued because Medicare and Medicaid refused to pay for tests and procedures that were not absolutely necessary.

In the 1980s, computers came to be used as well, in prescribing for
diagnostically related groups (DRGs) of diseases as a way of reducing medical
costs by enabling the patient to be removed from the hospital. Physicians
and hospitals are rewarded for cutting costs below the amount predicted in
the DRG handbook. The decision to terminate treatment is based on computer data. How successful this method is in treating patients while keeping
costs down is still, at this writing, in the balance. There is some indication
that a number of physicians are more inventive than the computer in
maximizing the diagnosis so that hospital stays are prolonged. Other research indicates that costs may be reduced by shortening hospital stays even
if the patient's condition is still poor. This use of the computer, like many
others described by Leyerle in her study of management-directed medicine,
is aimed more at cost reduction than at diagnostic or treatment effectiveness.
No doubt, computer programming of symptomology for facilitating diagnosis
is one of the frontiers of medicine. It may be particularly helpful in rural
areas where resources are limited. The question is, Can artificial intelligence
replace human intelligence? Many physicians believe diagnosis is a subtle,
intuitive art, often based on informed hunches. The computer might help
confirm or disconfirm a hunch. But can it replace it?

In drawing these two extremes of clinical and scientific medicine, we may
be constructing polar types, even stereotypes. But they empirically exist,
and each has its advantages and disadvantages. The pure clinician is unlikely
to have all the necessary information, and the physician who is a collector of
specimens and of specialists, or who is a computer operator *manqúe* is also
likely to produce endless delay and unlimited cost.

The professionalism of clinicians includes the ability to listen and sometimes to reject patients' descriptions of symptomology, especially when
based on hypochondria. This must be done with great tact, sometimes
utilizing placebos, for clinicians do have to be able to employ their time
efficiently in the service of genuinely ill patients.

In the case of hypochondria, the objectivity of the market and of money
may well be a form of objectivity present in medical practice. This form of
objectivity may also be present in the overutilization of medical facilities, in
"Ping-Ponging" the patient, in unnecessary surgery, and in overutilization
and overcharging in third-party payment plans.

The objectivity of medicine, as it is related to the operation of the
organism in all its parts, which underlies the history of clinical medicine, has
conflicted with the spiritual—here, psychological—theories and bases for
medicine. Thus, psychosomatic disorders may be the medical equivalent of
spirits, animi, humors, and temperaments; that is, they are intangible. It
was a long time before medicine recognized that physical symptoms could be
psychological in origin. Physicians had long recognized that the loss of the

will to live results in self-neglect. It has been harder for them to acknowledge that patients can postpone death through will and determination.

In all of these cases, concerning the boundaries of the purely physical, the medical profession has resisted the imposition of "nonobjective" aspects of medicine, especially psychiatry. Psychiatry had difficulty in becoming recognized as a specialty within medicine. Medicine has also had difficulty in accepting the idea of psychosomatic illness [29].

The resistance to the nonobjective aspects of medicine in psychiatry has led some psychiatrists to a total reliance on psychoactive drugs. If, so they argue, stability of temperament and emotional life are the products of bodily chemistry, then they come within reach of the objectivity of physical medicine. It is only a matter of prescribing and monitoring dosages. By doing so, inquiry into qualitative content, the emotional, the human, the psychic, is again banned from the practice of medicine or, if not banned, reduced to the objectivity of chemistry and numbers. Qualitative distinctions become reduced to quantitative variables along various chemical dimensions.

ETHICS

Medicine, like law and the priesthood, is a field that lays claim to special privileges and immunities that are based on the intrinsic qualities of its practice [30]. The very nature of clinical practice requires, it has been argued, unusual degrees of trust and deeply internalized ethical behavior on the part of the physician. Trust is necessary if the patient is to reveal private information about bodily functions. From the standpoint of the physician, trust means that he does not reveal such private or confidential information to any others, including the official establishment [31]. But trust is also required because patients—vulnerable because of disease, enfeeblement, and the possible imminence of death—surrender themselves into the hands of another who makes life-and-death decisions for them. The physician's recommendations must be followed in good faith. Patient's trust includes the belief that physicians will not exploit their weakness for their own financial gain [32].

The trust includes confidence in the physician's ability to render medical services and not be negligent, not cause unnecessary delays in treatment, and be dedicated to preserving the patient's health and life. All of these ideas have been embodied in the Hippocratic oath, and have been reaffirmed repeatedly and ritually, ever since that oath was accepted by the profession.

The oath has been the basis for the ideal that physicians serve not only patients but also the best interests of the community. They serve the community and the patient in a disinterested manner, that is, not from the standpoint of the physicians' own egoistic needs, profits, and opportunities.

However, over the course of centuries, physicians—with some exceptions—have been held in low repute. Yet, the claims based on the Hippocratic oath have been institutionalized—in the United States—initially by the Massachusetts State Medical Association (1899) and by the American Medical Association shortly thereafter, as the basis for establishing medicine as a profession [33]. The claims include the right of the organized medical profession to monopolize the practice of medicine and keep out those with less rigorous training, faith healers, and charlatans. The claim to professional monopoly, involved a post hoc attempt to improve the quality of medical practice by the creation and regulation of medical schools, postgraduate training, and internships. The Flexner Report was responsible for part of this program [34]. Implementation of the claims included setting strict standards for admission to medical schools and the profession, and regulating education and training. For professional practitioners, explicit ethical codes were formulated by the profession and the means of sanctioning unethical behavior were set down [35]. Such codes entail the objectification of unethical medical practice by defining explicitly and in behavioral terms ethically taboo practices. Review committees have been created to hear cases in which intolerable and substandard behavior is reviewed and censored by professional peers. In addition, at least in hospital practice, review committees are established to judge the competence and adequacy of treatment after the death of a patient. In many cases the medical profession has to share its power with the state, for licensing is a state function, and "disbarment" (revocation of the license to practice) requires state intervention [36].

Critics have charged that these ethical codes and procedures were designed for quite different motives. They claim they may have been designed (1) to limit medical practice to a relatively small number of professionals [37] and (2) to restrict the number of practitioners entering the field, thereby limiting competition in order to maintain high fee schedules. The restrictions concerning who may enter the profession also favor those who have the social, racial, sexual, and economic characteristics of those already in the field and have led to nepotistic practices [38].

Are these charges true? The question cannot easily be resolved empirically, given the distributive nature of the practice of medicine, that is, the sheer numbers who have been physicians or patients over the course of time. Violations of the code are surely not uncommon; but such violations reflect and validate the very existence of the norms. On the other hand, violations may go largely unreported. The distributive nature of medicine and its confinement to the relative intimacy of a personal but physiologically and psychologically complex relationship make the discovery of failures in treatment, whatever their cause, a difficult topic of research. It is difficult enough to compute objective rates of successful treatment, but the very privacy involved in the trust relationship (as well as the perishability and the "covering up" of diseases by the body) make such objectivity difficult to achieve. Certainly, quotas operated for women and African-Americans, effectively keeping all but a small number out of the profession and greatly restricting the hospitals with which they could affiliate even when they did go to medical school.

At one time, charges of fee-splitting abounded, but the charges are now less frequently heard. Fee-splitting may well have been replaced by reciprocity of referrals. A number of studies have noted that many surgical procedures are unnecessary, or unwarranted, including cesarian operations, hysterectomies, and bypass surgery. According to a study of the Columbia College of Surgeons in 1977, about one-third of all surgery was unnecessary [39]. With the advent of Medicare and Medicaid, other abuses have proliferated, such as kiting bills and billing third-party insurers for services never performed or for the performance of peripheral services. "Overutilization of services" has been charged among a substantial portion of those who practice medicine [40]. This has been accomplished in cooperation with hospital administrators, who may or may not be physicians themselves [41].

From time to time, physicians employed by industry have had as a major function the task of cutting down the claims and treatments of employees for industrially related accidents and illnesses. They have been the spokesmen for industry in the struggle against industrial culpability for diseases and disorders caused by environmental pollution and for negligence in hazardous occupations. Abuses of Medicare and Medicaid by physicians have also raised skepticism about the claims of the disinterestedness of the profession. There have been, in addition, struggles over jurisdictions over diseases by the various specialties, and over Medicare and Medicaid fees [42].

Another ground for skepticism and suspicion of the ethical claims of the medical profession is the overall failure of the machinery of medical ethics to sanction physicians who fail to comply with their ethical codes [43]. Very few physicians are sanctioned, at least publicly, and very few have their licenses revoked. The revocation of a license is usually due to publicity initiated by public prosecutors or following civil actions [44]. Such scandals have revealed kickbacks from suppliers of medical aids, especially pacemakers; mass prescriptions for narcotics, amphetamines, and other forms of "uppers"; padders of Medicare and Medicaid bills; and billing for services never rendered. Physicians and dentists have also been indicted for rape, molestation, murder (usually of wives), conspicuous flight from the scene of an accident, running illegal abortion clinics, and operating nursing homes in which residents, in addition to being overcharged, are neglected, abused, starved, and robbed. Malpractice suits, based upon surgery performed on the wrong organ or limb, or the discovery of sponges or other medical supplies in the bodies of patients after surgery, also contribute to a grim humor that undermines physicians' claims to special competence, concern, and a service ethic [45].

Validation of the claims for trust, ethics, and professionalism would be based on the response of patients to physicians. This refers to patients' reactions to excessive waiting, deferment of treatment, judgments as to competence, and perception of the overuse of specialists and superspecialists. The incompetence and neglect, accompanied by high fees, are attributed to greed. When a patient dies, the family or survivor may develop a lack of trust, in addition to the reasons cited, because they may sense that the death could have been avoided. They may also feel the course of treatment was too costly and unsparing of the patient and of them, economically and emotionally, and that critical information was withheld from them.

These types of grievances strip away the mystique of medicine and physicians, and with this follows an increase in malpractice suits and tremendous financial settlements for the adjudged victims of malpractice. Fees are then raised to cover the increase in malpractice insurance premiums of up to $100,000 per year. Physicians threaten to abandon or limit their practice and new recruits to the field may be discouraged from entering the profession, or at least those specialties that have had the highest rates, such as obstetrics and pediatrics. Ultimately, it is the consumer who pays the cost of malpractice. The objectivity of the need for medical services may be the initial and final objectivity governing the practice of medicine.

The medical profession seemed to have achieved its highest goals, in the United States at least, by the end of World War II, when it was rated as the most prestigious occupation of all, apart from that of Supreme Court Justice [46]. Since this rating was quantitative, it is not easy fully to ascertain its meaning. Certainly, part of the prestige of medicine within the framework of American values may have been its reputation as to income and the managerial practices of the profession, rather than the recognition of skill or ethical superiority. The profession had, for some thirty years, resisted heroically and virtually singlemindedly, all efforts at group practice and third-party payment schemes, governmental and cooperative, as "socialized medicine." It did so on the grounds of the sacredness of the physician-patient relationship. When it lost the battle it sought to keep control over the agencies managing these forms of practice and to set terms and fees. Characteristically it has succeeded. By now, however, group practice is pervasive, usually combined with third-party payment plans, private or governmental. The profession has also struggled to keep control and resist regulation by all third parties, be they insurance companies, industrial firms, hospitals, or governmental agencies. One could argue, as Eliot Friedson has done [47], that these resistances are in the cause of the autonomy of the physician, which defines professionalization. Yet such autonomy is not that of the individual in a private practice, but rather the collective autonomy of a group of partners in group or otherwise organized practice.

Autonomy is, of course, an ambiguous term. It may mean freedom from all external restraint to do one's own intrinsic thing. It may also mean freedom from all external constraints as a means of achieving motives other than those of doing one's intrinsic thing. Thus autonomy may mean freedom to charge what the traffic can bear, organizational and social power, freedom from criticism and prosecution, and freedom from the supervision of hospital administrators, third-party payers, government, and the skepticism of clients. The language used to defend both forms of autonomy is identical, that is, the language of positive, intrinsic autonomy. The underlying motivation and behavior springing from the respective forms of autonomy may be entirely different. Thus, one must go beyond rhetoric in ascribing the drive for autonomy as a central characteristic of modern medicine.

The achievement of the physician's high status in the 1940s and 1950s was short-lived in any case, judging by the number of malpractice and malfeasance suits, and the willingness of juries to grant huge sums in compensation. Insurance costs skyrocketed, and fees along with them, even exceeding the double-digit inflation of other goods and services. Since there is no alternative besides the objectivity of dying, patients, government, and third-party insurers pay the price, though all such payments constitute a tax on the patient as patient, consumer, and citizen.

The practice of defensive medicine as outlined above may be a device against prospective self-incrimination, which, however, also results in higher fees and costs. Thus medicine today is the single largest industry in the United States [48]. Yet the sense of powerlessness and resentment that individuals feel towards medicine as a whole results in endless proposals to restrict or limit the fees physicians charge and to discover new ways to test the competence of physicians.

The medical profession has lost the battle it waged to control entrance to medical school and hospitals by keeping women and minority group members out, or by restricting their entrance into the profession. Affirmative-action rules, it found, apply to the profession as well. It has also been accused of all manner of abuses by women associated with the feminist movement. These include insensitivity, sexual molestation, and aggressive, invasive procedures because shibboleths as to women's emotional and physiological makeup were perpetuated by the profession. Women were often left out of crucial research studies, so that almost no data exists concerning heart disease in women, though it is the number one killer of older women. African-Americans have accused doctors of refusing to treat them or of uncaring and discriminatory treatment. The high infant mortality rates among blacks, and the high mortality rates in their community bear out the veracity of their complaints. The suggestion that physicians are no better or worse collectively than anybody else is not a claim that physicians can make in light of their claims to prestige on the basis of their ethical superiority. In order to maintain their claims physicians are required either to behave ethically or to prevent instances of unethical behavior from becoming public knowledge. The incidence of muckraking against the medical profession is evidence of its failure to sustain the promises of its original organization [49].

The original ethical claims of the medical profession were claims for professionalism based on the physician as a free professional, an individual in private practice who saw patients in the confines of his office on a continuous basis extending over a substantial portion of the lives of both parties. The privacy, trust, confidentiality, concern, and mutual respect were ideally the product and the necessity of this long-term, relatively intimate relationship. Historically, these claims for privacy and trust may also have reflected a "Victorian" ethos in which the social dangers of public exposure, the shame and guilt, were so great that only in the employment of the physician, the priest, and the lawyer could one escape the oppression of a censorious public opinion. One could not reveal oneself and the less attractive aspects of one's moral, private, and physiological behavior and attributes to any others than these professionals. In return, they were obligated to maintain the trust, that is, privacy of the patient. Both these factors then—the continuity of interaction of doctors and patients and the necessity of self-revelation on the part of patients—contributed to the ethical claims of the profession.

In the meantime, however, the conditions governing medical practice have changed. The vast dissemination of medical science from the private to, by now, the group practitioner and the laboratory undermined many of the bases of these claims [50]. Thus, the specialist and superspecialist no longer directly share in the intimacy and confidentiality of the patient's self-reporting. To the extent that medical practice is based on objective tests, scans, and computerized reports, the intimacy upon which trust is based is not an intrinsic factor. At the same time, the knowledge of the results of the test, whom the reports are ultimately sent to—an insurance company, an employer, a government agency—certainly involve questions of ethics, which, however, are increasingly resolved at the level of law.

Third-party payers need such reports in order to calculate and check on medical costs. At the same time, knowledge of diagnoses and treatment in the hands of an outsider, especially an employer, may be used against the patient [51]. AIDS patients, or those who test positive for the virus, have been particularly concerned about confidentiality, fearing discrimination and loss of jobs if their disease becomes known to their employer. The CIA has for obvious reasons employed its own physicians and psychiatrists. Physicians have also been employed to protect the interests of industries and corporations.

THE STRUCTURE AND ETHICS OF SCIENTIFIC MEDICINE

We have indicated that scientific medicine operates on different principles, technology, structure, and social relations from that of clinical medicine. We have also indicated that being relatively new, as least in its dominance, the normative, philosophical, as well as ethical principles that govern scientific medicine are only beginning to emerge; and in the absence of such crystallizations, we can only speculate, based on observation and interviewing, what these principles might be.

Scientific medicine suffers from the same problems as all other highly specialized fields. The superspecialist will know a great deal about a given narrow subarea of the field, and not much else. Since patients and their maladies are not so specialized until after a diagnosis has been made, the treatment of almost all serious illness requires the use of many specialists; the number will depend on how readily the diagnosis is arrived at and a treatment plan is made available. The more intractable the disease, the larger the number of specialists called in. The limiting cases, of course, are the immediate reduction of symptoms or the death of the patient, after which only postmortem pathology may be required.

Specialists in the use of equipment and testing procedures, radiologists, anesthesiologists, and specialists in prosthetics and in postorthopedic rehabilitation become part of an overall structure of specialists, less on the basis of their knowledge of disease and the patient, and more on the basis of their knowledge of equipment and/or the interpretation of test results.

When a plurality of physicians is required to achieve diagnosis, the number and combination of specialists involved in a "case" are determined by the presenting symptoms and the tentative diagnosis. Physicians will have, among other things, a network of potential specialists whom they have worked with, know, or feel they can call upon. Each case results in the creation of specific case-related groups of specialists who are drawn from this pool or network.

Scientific medicine requires this because, unlike the case of clinical medicine, these physicians cannot rely on hunches. A large number and variety of tests are utilized to validate or reject an idea or hunch. And only when the test is positive does testing end; but even here subtesting may be indicated before treatment begins.

This results in the vast utilization (some have charged, overutilization) of equipment and personnel, and in the inflation of medical costs [52]. If the tests are negative, then further testing goes on until a positive result is found, the patient dies, or the problem disappears naturally.

Short of these extremes, scientific network medicine prevails. The assemblage of ad hoc networks around a given case must be understood in terms of the fact that the caseload of any given specialist may include hundreds of cases; thus a given specialist is likely to be involved with hundreds of other physicians, some of the same ones in more than one network and others distributed along different network continua. This causes a great strain on communications. Every time a new piece of information is gained or lost, the relevant physicians in the network must be informed. Physicians may be in hundreds of networks and are obligated to report, receive, remember, and file hundreds of communications coming in from and going out to hundreds of other physicians.

One of the virtues of the computer is that it provides automatic printouts of test results. Beyond this, specialists find it incumbent upon themselves to have a medical secretary whose job it is to receive messages and to take dictation or transcribe tapes on the results of a consultation. Among other things this is necessary so that test results are made available to the others in a given network. But given the total amount of information that the individual physician must send out, communicate, receive, and remember, it is not hard to imagine that much information is lost, forgotten, misfiled, or filed in systems for which there is no means of data retrieval.

The average superspecialist also spends many hours on the telephone, in addition to composing and receiving written reports. Phone calls from others in the network are a constant source of interruption and physicians must respond almost immediately in terms of their memory of the case, regardless of how systematic their record keeping. Of course, they may have to resort to their files, but they mostly rely on instant recall and must be able to shift attention to and from the case immediately before them. Minimally they must be able to take perfect notes, and at best be able to learn how to listen even with constant interruptions. It is not unheard of for surgeons to make phone calls to a nonsurgical specialist in order to find out what the initial symptoms were after the patient is on the operating table.

Again, the problem of information overload becomes one of attention overload. And the neglect of symptoms, information, and lack of consensus about what the case represents is almost a structural feature of scientific medicine.

There are also external factors operating. The panel of potential consultants and specialists can be drawn from among the various medical departments of a hospital, especially in a teaching hospital. Personal factors, such as antipathies and rivalries, also enter in. This means that some physicians and affiliates are barred from certain networks. Service technicians who are in private practice develop some personal and professional affiliations—client-patron relations—to either patients, physicians, or higher level specialists. Medical lectures, symposia, and seminars also become the scenes where physicians eat, meet, and treat, and establish contacts. Attendance at the same medical school or common residency may also qualify one; publications and speeches may prove important, giving in-house courses or teaching in medical schools or hospitals, and membership on review boards and panels or in country clubs, social clubs, or fraternities may serve the same purpose.

Those who aspire to elite status or wish to enter into particular networks must find some means of impressing older established members. Ideally younger aspirants become protégés of successful physicians until they reach that state in their career where they take on their own protégés. All of the above represents a major part of the background for the emerging ethics of scientific medicine.

Given the structural characteristics of scientific medicine as outlined above, the operative ethics are primarily concerned with physicians' relationships to each other, and not with physician-to-patient relationships. They appear to follow the following rules:

Rule 1: Physicians will not present differences of opinion about a case, a disease, or a diagnosis to the patient or the patient's surrogate. The patient may be referred back to the primary physician, to whom the report is sent. There should be only one voice for the disassembled network that constitutes the medical team. Other members of the team ought not be exposed to serious differences of opinion [53].

If differences exist, they must be presented with great tact and delicacy. The greatest violation of ethical standards is to tell a patient or surrogate that another physician is incompetent, negligent, or wrong. Thus ethics are designed to protect physicians as a team against the patient, surrogates, the public, and outside payment, regulating, and supervising bodies.

Rule 2: The team is constrained to develop a concept of group responsibility for the treatment of the patient despite the fact that at critical points there is no way to escape from having to make individual decisions.

Rule 3: Within the process of intragroup consultation, in principle, each physician must be treated as a valid expert specialist whose information, diagnosis, and opinion is to be listened to and taken into account. This is necessary despite the differences in specialization, which make it difficult or impossible for each physician to evaluate the opinions of others. This ethic of respect operates despite the existence of differentials in prestige, power (the ability to confer, by virtue of institutional position, benefits upon the other physicians), and perceived ability.

The problem of maintaining the integrity of specialization and at the same time abiding by the rules of structured interaction presents problems for those who would like to move up the ladder of network assignments.

Rule 4: Specialists on the way up to higher level network and professional status must exhibit a degree of deference to their network colleagues, while establishing themselves as sufficiently imaginative, original, brilliant, or solid. This involves tact, sociability, or solidity appropriate to the personae of the other team members. At the same time it may include withholding medical judgments if speaking out might interfere with their career. While appearing to be especially original, bright, and creative in diagnosis, they must make sure not to offend those who have already acquired a reputation and position. The judgment of when to be bright and when to allow others to be bright entails an ability to pick up often subliminal clues and cues. These become ethical problems, as well as career ones.

Rule 5:   The rules governing the purely research-oriented superspecialists are somewhat different. The patient is for them a case, a source of information, of tests, experimentation, and treatment. The pain and discomfort inflicted on patients, the negative consequences of overtesting or experimental treatment modalities, perhaps even the life of the patient, are not as important as the solution of scientific problems. And this takes on an ironical character when the patient or the government subsidizes the research-oriented tests and procedures.

Extreme examples of this are the research experiments conducted in the Third Reich; and the use of prisoners in research in the United States, as well as unsuspecting populations in Puerto Rico and the American South, who were used for testing contraceptive devices and in long-range studies on high blood pressure.

The purely scientific physician is ultimately concerned with truth and not with the patient. And a more humanistic physician is concerned with the patient even when the concern does not advance the quest for scientific knowledge.

In an earlier period, from 1900 to 1920, the dramatic issue presented to the public was: Should members of a control group be allowed to die in order to determine whether an experimental treatment is effective? Here the moral choice and the scientific choice ran in clearly opposite directions. Today the dominance of scientific medicine results in a set of scaled intervals between a purely moral medicine and an amoral scientific medicine in which there are no clear-cut cutting points, and compromises are made at each level of the scale.

The tentative rules stated above are not based on scientific tests of their influence and frequency, but are more in the nature of hypotheses. We do believe they are indicators of an emerging set of categories. They emerge because of the rise of science within a framework where its prestige is, in part, also governed by income and fees. The rules are adhered to by some of the best practitioners of modern medicine, and by some of the worst charlatans. However, it must be stressed that a relatively small percentage of physicians adhere to these rules in their purest forms.

Scientific medicine seems to be in the process of creating its own norms and principles, but these norms and principles govern *choices within networks of physicians* as opposed to the ethics between the physician and the patient as in clinical medicine. These changes in ethics thus reflect changes in the structure of medical practice.

CONCLUSION

Part of any set of ethics, medical or not, is designed to limit what is defined as unethical behavior by the practitioner. Thus one of the objectives of any set of ethics is to cause the practitioner to limit his behavior in support of values that have been internalized. The objectification of ethics, their embodiment in a code, is a negation of such internalized ethics in the sense that they are reduced to a set of external rules. The operative norm here is to practice in such ways that one stays within the letter of the code. This stretches into avoidance of prosecution. Depending on the effectiveness of policing, external ethics may limit violations of a code. When ethics are deeply internalized, stricter standards are maintained. They may be very difficult to adhere to, however, when prestige, power, and money accrue to those whose ethical standards are based on external codes.

Medical ethics has more recently taken a new turn. The awe and reverence given to the physician because he can postpone death is now subject to another dialectic. Scientific method has reached the stage where the patient can be kept physically alive although "brain dead." This possibility has caused a new debate as to how to define life and death. The debate parallels arguments over birth control and abortion, where the issue is again the definition of life or death. With reference to brain death, there are vast social and economic issues, not only about the definition of death, but over the consequences of maintaining bodily functions through artificial feeding and/ or breathing devices. The cost of such maintenance may not only impoverish the family of the patient, but also hospitals that are constrained to accept all cases regardless of ability to pay, and ultimately the state and society that must provide medical insurance. This will result in the necessity of putting a price on each definition of life. Some hospitals are employing "medical-ethicists," who are not physicians, but philosophers, to help with these problems on a case-by-case basis. This aspect of medical ethics and law is still unresolved [54].

In any event, we have reached the condition where progress in medicine, especially in the past two centuries, has increased the demands placed upon the medical profession, because that progress has undermined the resignation that makes death, illness, and pain acceptable. Illness may be an undesirable condition, but its particular definition and tolerance are subject to historical, cultural, and social evaluations. The level of acceptance and tolerance of these conditions is a function of the emphasis placed on other values such as work, mobility, and the active life. The evaluation of the inevitability and acceptance of these conditions is also a function of the progress medicine has made in increasing life expectancy and easing pain.

Organized medicine is thus a victim of its own successes; but, as we have noted, it is also a victim of the claims and demands it makes upon the public. These claims rest not only upon the successes of the past, but also on the explicit and implicit promises of continuing progress. To the extent that patients and the public accept these promises and claims, they expect medicine to continue to provide miraculous solutions to problems of health, life, and death.

Since the middle of the twentieth century, despite the successes and claims of medicine, the attitude of trust necessary to sustain and justify the claims for fees and monopolies, and the prestige of the profession, have been continuously eroded. The evidence of the erosion is in the willingness of patients to file suits against physicians, and the unwillingness of the press, novelists, journalists, and comedians to accept the claims of the profession.

Many of the assaults on the medical profession have been based on research reports, some from within medicine, such as the American College of Surgeons, others from prestigious research institutes and foundations, such as the Rockefeller Institute. Congressional investigating committees have added grist for the mill, as have reports of patients' malpractice suits.

The willingness of the public to accept these different negative images may, in part, reflect their own immediate experience.

Basic phenomenological attitudes derive from usages that continuously change with the passage of time and with technological, intellectual, scientific, economic, and administrative changes. Older attitudes persist long after the conditions under which they were first generated have changed.

New attitudes emerge along with rising new institutions and ideologies, including professional ones; but in the transition a number of competing attitudes often coexist. There may be gaps among these prevalent attitudes and images, or "cultural lags," between attitudes and the underlying realities they embrace.

Modern medicine is in such a state. The basic attitudes of clinical medicine have governed its practice, but they may not have attained its ideals. Their claims were bolstered and substantiated by contributions of scientific medicine during a period of exponential growth. Physicians are now forced to adjust to their inability under new conditions to produce mass miracles. The new medical miracles, by and large feats of virtuosity in surgery and medical engineering, including gene splicing and the use of lasers (nuclear magnetic resonance, or NMR, devices), while dramatic in individual cases, do not reach many people.

Physicians, for the most part, have not been able to adjust to the claims that their patients and third-party payers make upon them, though they themselves originally promulgated them. To surrender these claims would be disastrous to their professional prestige and economic practice. The absence of a comprehensive and integrated phenomenology of modern medicine is a phenomenological fact in itself.

NOTES

1. Max Weber, in H.H. Gerth, X. Mills, and C. Wright (Eds.), *From Max Weber—Essays in Sociology* (New York, Oxford University Press, 1946), "Science as a Vocation": p. 139: "The increasing rationalization and intellectualization do *not*, therefore, indicate an increased and general knowledge of the conditions under which one lives." See also pp. 143–145, on the relation of a discipline in practice to the presuppositions underlying its basis: "Consider modern medicine, a practical technology which is highly developed scientifically. The general 'presupposition' of the medical enterprise is stated trivially in the assertion that medical science has the task of maintaining life as such and of diminishing suffering as such to the greatest possible degree. Yet this is problematical. By this means the medical man preserves the life of the mortally ill man, even if the patient implores us to relieve him of life, even if his relatives, to whom his life is worthless and to whom the costs of maintaining his worthless life grow unbearable, grant his redemption from suffering. Perhaps a poor lunatic is involved, whose relatives, whether they admit it or not, wish and must wish for his death. Yet the presuppositions of medicine, and the penal code, prevent the physician from relinquishing his therapeutic efforts. Whether life is worth living and when—this question is not asked by medicine. Natural science gives us an answer to the question of what we must do if we wish to master life technically. It leaves quite aside, or assumes for its purposes, whether we should and do wish to master life technically and whether it ultimately makes sense to do so."

2. Andreas Vesalius, Flemish anatomist, explored the entire field of human anatomy through careful dissections; his work on anatomy, *De humani corporis fabrica*, of 1543 was greatly enriched by its illustrations, attributed to Jan von Calcar. See Charles D. O'Malley, *Andreas Vesalius of Brussels* (Berkeley, University of California Press, 1964); Jerome Tarshis, *Andreas Vesalius, Father of Modern Anatomy* (New York, Dial, 1969).

3. William Harvey (1578–1657), English physician, was the first to demonstrate the functioning of the heart and the circulation of the blood. William Jenner (1815–1898) did important work in the study of infectious diseases, especially diphtheria, typhoid, and typhus; he was the first to distinguish typhoid from typhus. Joseph Lister (1827–1912) pioneered many techniques and devices in surgery, especially the concept of antisepsis and the importance of antiseptic procedures in surgery, including heat sterilization. See Sir Geoffrey Langdon Keynes, *The Life of William Harvey* (Oxford, Oxford University Press, 1966); Rhode Truax, *Joseph Lister, Father of Modern Surgery* (New York, Bobbs Merrill, 1946). Louis Pasteur (1822–1895) did

important work in chemistry and in the development of vaccines against anthrax and rabies; the technique of pasteurization is, of course, named for him; his experiments with bacteria and his demonstration of the role of bacteria in the fermentation of beer and wine and in disease opened a new era in scientific medicine. Robert Koch (1843–1910) established the bacterial cause of many diseases such as anthrax, cholera, and tuberculosis. He pioneered many techniques and findings in bacteriology. See Paul de Kruif, *Microbe Hunters* (1926; reprint New York, Harcourt, Brace, 1954). See also William McNeill, *Plagues and Peoples* (Garden City, Anchor Books, 1976), Chap. VI, "The Ecological Impact of Medical Science and Organization Since 1700."

4.   In addition to McNeill and de Kruif, see also Geoffrey Marks and William K. Beatty, *Epidemics* (New York, Scribners, 1976), and Hans Zinsser, *Rats, Lice and History—The Biography of a Bacillus* (Boston, Little Brown, 1934; reprint 1963).

5.   Paul de Kruif, *Microbe Hunters*, Chap. 5, recounts the career and achievements of Pasteur, among others.

6.   Claude Bernard, French physiologist, did work of major importance to the development of experimental medicine. His studies of the digestive processes involving the liver and pancreas were especially important. His *An Introduction to the Study of Experimental Medicine*, published in France in 1865, appeared in an English translation in 1927, translated by Henry Copley Greene, (New York, MacMillan Co. 1927) See J.M.D. Olmsted and F.H. Olmsted, *Claude Bernard and the Experimental Method in Medicine* (New York, Schuman 1952). and *Claude Bernard and his Place in the History of Ideas* (Lincoln, Neb. University of Nebraska Press, 1960.)

7.   David Mechanic, *Future Issues in Health Care—Social Policy and the Rationing of Medical Services* (New York, Free Press, 1979), p. 168: "In the 1960s the growing imbalance of primary-care physicians and specialists became increasingly apparent. Although there was mounting concern about the inadequate number of generalists, departments of internal medicine in medical schools and, to a lesser extent, departments of pediatrics were intransigent about modifying their specialty-training orientations. Major emphasis was devoted to the training of subspecialists, with little focus on training for a more general role. Under the auspices of federal and state funding, encouragement was given for the establishment of a family-practice specialty. Although this development was not welcomed by more traditional departments in medical schools and often vigorously opposed (even sabotaged), the insistence of the public through their legislators led to the development of a vigorous family-practice program with a remarkable growth of family-practice residencies. While the early reactions of the traditional departments were disdainful, the threat of these programs contributed to their rethinking their own missions in response to the competition of family practice." Mechanic reports that significant changes of orientation were taking place. See also Starr, op. cit., p. 382 *et passim*, on specialization and overspecialization. Starr, p. 224, discusses the differing relations between specialists and referring physicians in Britain and the U.S.

8.   David Mechanic, *The Growth of Bureaucratic Medicine: An Inquiry into the Dynamics of Patient Behavior and the Organization of Medical Care* (New York, John Wiley, 1976).

9.   Charles E. Lewis, Rashi Fein, and David Mechanic, *A Right to Health: The Problem of Access to Primary Medical Care* (New York, John Wiley, 1976).

10.   *Op. cit.*, (Chap. 3) "The Consolidation of Professional Authority," pp. 355–356, reports on the drastic changes in students' plans while in medical school: "The proportion planning to be general practitioners dropped from 60 to 16 percent between the first and fourth years. Students planning to be specialists jumped from 35 to 74 percent, and those going into teaching and research increased from 5 to 10

percent." The primary reason was the growth of knowledge. The cited study was by Patricia M. Kendall and Hanan C. Selvin, "Tendencies toward Specialization in Medical Training," in Robert K. Merton, George C. Reader, and Patricia L. Kendall (Eds.), *The Student Physician* (Cambridge, Harvard University Press, 1958). See also a more recent book: Jack Haas and William Shaffir, *Becoming Doctors:* The Adoption of a Cloak of Competence (Greenwich, CT: JAI Press, 1987).

11.   Burton Roueche: *The Medical Detectives*, Volume II (New York, Dutton, 1984), pp. 345–358, "The Hoofbeats of the Zebra." (This records the problems involved in diagnosis of myasthenia gravis.) Gerald Astor: *The Disease Detectives— Deadly Medical Mysteries and the People Who Solved Them* (New York, New American Library, 1983), Chap. 5, "The Sound of Hoofbeats." Roueche's book reprints his many articles on medical problems that have appeared in *The New Yorker* magazine in recent years.

12.   *The New York Times*, February 24, 1983, in an article by Ronald Sullivan, "Physician Misconduct Said to be 'Rife,' " quotes Dr. David Axelrod, New York State commissioner of health, on the "overwhelming" problem of misconduct by physicians in New York. Among the abuses cited was "needlessly 'Ping-Ponging' patients from one specialist to another to generate fees." Many of these problems receive competent novelistic treatment in R.B. Dominic, *The Attending Physician* (New York, Harper & Row, 1980; reprinted by Pinnacle Books). A physician testifies before a congressional committee in exchange for a promise of immunity from prosecution (p. 139):

> "We call it ping-ponging," Costello told her chattily.
> "I've never heard that expression before. Could you tell me what it means?" Elsie asked.
> "You see, we all have offices in the same building. So when someone on Medicaid comes in to see me, I look him over and say he ought to see the internist across the hall. Then the internist sends him back to see the cardiologist, the cardiologist routes him to the neurologist and so on. By the time he gets to the end of the corridor, instead of just one billing, we've got eight or nine racked up. It really maximizes his visit."
> "So it would seem." Elsie was devoid of all human expression.

13.   William McNeill, *Plagues and Peoples*, Chap. VI. Also, John Lukacs, *The Passing of the Modern Age* (New York, Harper & Row, 1970), p. 74: "The standards and practices of medicine, surgery, and anesthesia current in 1920 bore no resemblance at all to the still largely barbaric standards of 1860. (In some places those standards of 1920 were also better than those of 1970.)" And pp. 140–141: "[In medicine] the greatest breakthrough occurred fifty to one hundred years ago, not after. In the most advanced nations of the Western world life expectancy rose by fifteen years during the fifty years after 1875: during the last fifty years it inched forward, adding another five or eight years at most. Infant mortality, on the average between 20 and 30 percent around 1865, dropped to about 6 percent by 1914 and to about 3 percent by 1965. . . . After 1945, however, it began to appear that the practice of medicine, too, was not exempt from the general degeneration of progress. The family doctor, especially in the United States, was disappearing; the personal contact between patients and physicians became, like hospital care, routine, mechanical, impersonal, often breaking down. Together with the advance of specialization the ethics of medical practitioners decayed. Against this were stacked up the claims of wonder drugs, and wondrous transplantations of entire noses, toes, and hearts. There rare achievements were comparable to the Men on the Moon: wondrous things, without much effect on the ordinary lives and tribulations of mankind."

14.   Among the ten leading causes of hospital admission in the United States is the adverse reaction to drugs or drug combinations prescribed by physicians: "one out of three hospitalizations today (1985) occurs as the direct result of the mismanagement of prescription and over-the-counter drugs." Alan S. Levin, M.D., in an address reprinted in *Dissent in Medicine—Nine Doctors Speak Out,* issued by the New Medical Foundation (Chicago, Contemporary Books, 1985), p. 80.

15.   Computerized information systems have been proposed as a means for mastering the great mass of knowledge that might prove relevant to a given medical problem. For a discussion of the problem of "information overload," see Anne J. D'Arcy, *Who Is Responsible When Computers Diagnose and Prescribe Medicine?* (Cincinnati, Pamphlet Publications, 1979). The problem of how a new scientific advance can be translated into clinical practice involving many variables is discussed in *Dissent in Medicine* by David Spodick, M.D., in an address on "Effectiveness of Treatment," pp. 124–126: "the computer . . . can do studies . . . considerably better than randomized studies can . . . one of the salvations for the medical profession will be the engineers."

16.   Spodick, in "Effectiveness of Treatment," *op. cit.,* pp. 111–132, discusses problems involved in following up on new modalities of treatment, and how they are introduced to physicians.

17.   Starr, *op. cit.,* pp. 229–230; *Dissent in Medicine, op. cit.,* p. 127.

18.   John P. Bunker, "When Doctors Disagree," *The New York Review of Books,* Vol. 32, No. 7 (April 25, 1985), p. 12: "But what of the widely advertised threat of malpractice suits that are brought when a physician allegedly fails to do everything that might help a sick patient? Such suits may be valid in life-threatening situations, when patients expect everything to be done to save them and are willing to accept the accompanying risks. For purely discretionary surgery, on the other hand, when the potential benefits are relatively small, patients are less apt to accept risks, even small ones. Indeed, it is exactly in these situations, especially if the physician allows the patient to harbor exaggerated expectations, that a disappointing result, or even a minor complication, is more likely to lead to a lawsuit. Thus, a patient undergoing surgery for cancer may suffer a wound infection requiring an extra week in the hospital but, glad to be alive, will not file suit. A thirty-nine year old woman undergoing elective hysterectomy for minor symptoms who suffers the same complication will probably be much less forgiving, and often will sue the responsible doctor. "There is, then, a clear need for basing medical decisions upon much more reliable evidence."

19.   See Chapter 1 and Chapter 17.

20.   *The Sociology of George Simmel,* translated, edited, and with an introduction by Kurt H. Wolff (New York, Free Press, 1950, reprint 1964), pp. 125–6 "The Characteristics of the Dyad."

21.   *Ibid,* pp. 413–415. The important essays by Karl Jaspers, "The Idea of the Physician" and "Doctor and Patient" in *Philosophy and the Modern World* (Chicago, Regnery, 1963) underlie much of our present essay.

22.   Henry M. Pachter, *Paracelsus, Magic into Science* (New York, Schuman, 1951), offers a study of this struggle.

23.   The distinction here is similar to one traditionally made within physics. Some physicists are given to specific, concrete, and matter-of-fact experimentation, and decry "global" theorization as unscientific. Others have been more abstract, "theoretical," speculative, and macroscopic, regarding scientific experiments as being merely building blocks of tests for grand theories.

24.   Fred Hechinger, *The New York Times* (May 29, 1984), records "New Attacks

Are Made on Medical Education" by, among others, Derek Bok, the president of Harvard, Dr. Lewis Thomas, Norman Cousins, and Drs. Richard Gorlin and Howard D. Zucker, staff members at the Mount Sinai School of Medicine.

William G. Blair, in *The New York Times* (October 21, 1982), cites a study by an eighteen-member panel of administrators and educators, ten of whom were M.D.s, headed by Dr. Steven Muller, president of Johns Hopkins University, initiated by the Association of American Medical Colleges: "Medical students are being over-whelmed by scientific detail at the expense of basic skills and a regard for human needs."

For a description of this exploitation by a physician, see the novel by Samuel Shem, M.D., *The House of God* (New York, Marek, 1978).

25.   Many surgeons have described their experiences, for example, Max Thorek, *A Surgeon's World* (Philadelphia, Lippincott, 1943); Robert T. Morris, *Fifty Years a Surgeon* (New York, Dutton, 1935); William A. Nolen, *A Surgeon's World* (New York, Random House, 1972); Richard Selzar, *Mortal Lessons: Notes on the Art of Surgery* (New York, Simon and Schuster, 1976). See also Chap. 3, on the performing artist, about the finality of performance in dance, music, drama, diplomacy, and surgery.

26.   See note 12 above; for a survey, see: Harvey Barry Jacobs, *The Spectre of Malpractice*, with foreword by Melvin M. Belli (New York, Nationwide Press, c. 1978).

27.   Roueche, *op. cit.*, recounts many of the problems and achievements involving difficult diagnoses. See also Jaspers, "Doctor and Patient," *op. cit.*

28.   Betty Leyerle, *Moving and Shaking American Medicine—The Structure of a Socioeconomic Transformation* (Westport, Conn., Greenwood Press, 1984), pp. 51–53, recounts attempts to limit the widespread application of a wide range of tests on admission, and quotes the American College of Physicians: "The injudicious use of diagnostic tests contributes greatly to the cost of medical care" (quoted on p. 52). Marcia Milkman, *The Unkindest Cut: Life in the Backrooms of Medicine* (New York, Morrow, 1977), also discusses this issue from a feminist perspective; women espe-cially appear to be targets for unnecessary surgery, particularly hysterectomies. But other studies suggest differently, pointing out that a high percentage of physicians' wives receive hysterectomies; physicians must believe in their necessity.

29.   Talcott Parsons, "Illness and the Role of the Physician: A Sociological Per-spective," *American Journal of Orthopsychiatry*, Vol. XXI, No. 3 (July 1951), pp. 452–460; reprinted in Clyde Kluckhohn, Henry A. Murray, and David M. Schneider (Eds.), *Personality in Nature, Society and Culture* (New York, Knopf, 1953). Parsons discusses briefly the reluctance of medicine to come to terms with the psychosomatic nature of many illnesses; he regards the continuity between medicine and psycho-therapy as being "deeply rooted in the nature of the physician's function generally" (p. 459).

30.   A.M. Carr-Saunders and P.A. Wilson, *The Professions* (London, 1933; Cass reprint of 1964), is a valuable history of professionalization up to its time. Page 104: "The doctor, aware that an essential requisite of successful treatment is to acquire and retain the confidence of his patient, and believing that the patient is incapable of appreciating the situation of the art of medicine, tends to a pompous assumption of knowledge and authority. He surrounds himself with an atmosphere of mystery and miracle. It is only too easy for the quack to imitate the doctor in these respects." But the same man may be both doctor and quack, depending upon the nature of the problem that confronts him, and the uneven depth of his knowledge, profound in some areas, thinner in others.

Harold J. Laski, *The American Democracy—A Commentary and an Interpretation* (New York, Viking, 1948). Chap. XII, "The Professions in America," offers a useful discussion of both law and medicine.

31.   See Laski, *op. cit.*, pp. 594ff., and Carr-Saunders and Wilson, *op. cit.*, pp. 102–106.

32.   Duane F. Stroman, *The Quick Knife—Unnecessary Surgery U.S.A.* (Port Washington, Kennikat Press, 1979), explores these problems throughout. See also William Nolen, *op. cit.*

33.   See Laski, *op. cit.*, pp. 566–571, 591–609.

34.   Starr, *op. cit.*, Chap. 3, "The consolidation of Professional Authority, 1850–1930," recounts the history of these developments.

35.   Stroman, *op. cit.*, pp. 125–131; Laski, pp. 595, 613.

36.   Starr, *op. cit.*, pp. 102–107 *et passim*, surveys the history of licensing efforts in American medicine.

37.   Laski, Carr-Saunders and Wilson, and Starr, *op. cit.*, all offer elaborations of these arguments.

38.   Jeffrey L. Berlant, *Profession and Monopoly—A Study of Medicine in the United States and Great Britain* (Berkeley, University of California Press, 1975), surveys the history of monopolization by the profession. See also Natalie Rogoff, "The Decision to Study Medicine" in Robert K. Merton, George G. Reader, and Patricia L. Kendall (Eds.), *The Student Physician* (Cambridge, Harvard University Press, 1957), pp. 109–129; John A. Denton, *Medical Sociology* (Boston, Houghton Mifflin, 1978), pp. 171–172.

39.   American College of Surgeons and American Surgical Association, *Surgery in the United States: A Summary Report of the Study of Surgical Services in the United States* (1975). (Chicago: The College, 1975)

40.   For a discussion of the shifting applications of the term "overutilization," see Leyerle, *op. cit.*, p. 21: "When overutilization of health care services first became a major social topic, critics of the system defined it simply as the unnecessary hospitalization of people who were not seriously ill; such services should be restricted to those whose conditions warranted them. Now we are told that overutilization means hospitalizing serious cases as well." See also pp. 39ff. "Overutilization" of course implies that someone knows what the "correct" level of utilization is. Leyerle shows that this is being defined in terms of categorical averages, rather than in the specifics of individual cases. This redefinition has operated as a major assault on the autonomy of the physician vis-à-vis the patient.

41.   Starr, *op. cit.*, Book II, Chap. 5, "The Coming of the Corporation," outlines this issue and related ones. More specifically, Leyerle, pp. 125–127, discusses the relations between hospital administrators and physicians.

42.   Starr, *op. cit.*, Book II, Chap. 4, "End of a Mandate," discusses much of this, especially pp. 381–387: "The reimbursement practices for hospitals and doctors were peculiarly designed to encourage higher costs" (p. 385); "Thus three powerful forces were now arraying themselves against the health care providers in a drive for greater state intervention—the insurance industry, the employers, and the government itself. In the seventies, these interests found themselves in alliance with long-time liberal critics of the health system and a variety of new social movements demanding reform" (p. 388).

43.   See note 12 above. In addition to the needless "Ping-Ponging" of patients, the article also quotes Commissioner Axelrod: "While most physicians take their responsibilities seriously, many hospitals and local medical societies are reluctant to report any suspected cases of physician misconduct or impairment to the appropriate authorities." The article adds: "hospitals and fellow physicians have traditionally

balked at reporting such cases to the medical conduct board. State health regulations stipulate that failure to do so constitutes misconduct itself."

44. A recent (1985) case was reported by the *Boston Globe*, August 28, 1985, in two articles. Richard A. Knox, "Sex Abuse by Doctors Called Hidden Problem": "A number of researchers and clinicians familiar with the problem concurred with Middlesex Superior Court Judge Robert A. Burton, who charged on Monday that professional societies and regulatory officials have failed to weed out doctors with histories of sexually abusing their patients." The judge's accusation followed the conviction of a Lowell physician on charges of sexual abuse, the doctor had successfully dodged "10 years worth of similar complaints in five states before finally being brought to account." The other article, "Judge's Attack Unfair, Says N.H. Medical Official," by Doris Sue Wong, quoted Peter J. Attwood, president of the New Hampshire Medical Society, as regarding the attack as unfair on the grounds that some hospitals are reluctant to take action against physicians accused of misconduct because of the threat of lawsuits; in addition, hospital administrators are often unaware of previous charges against physicians.

The *Boston Globe* article by Knox assembled data from a number of studies on abuses by doctors and on actions taken. It quotes one study by the Public Citizen Health Research Group indicating that in 1983, "state medical boards took action against 563 physicians out of an estimated 136,000 to 310,000 cases of medical malpractice—no more than one case of license revocation or suspension for every 250 cases of medical malpractice." The article continues: "Statistics on sexual abuse by physicians are sparse, but the available evidence suggests that . . . it is by no means uncommon." The article also refers to a survey by two Boston area psychiatrists indicating that "65% of a national sample of psychiatrists say they have treated patients who have been abused sexually by other health professionals. . . . Six percent of the psychiatrists surveyed acknowledged sexual contact with their own patients."

45. *Newsday, op. cit.*, cites cases from the files of Harvey F. Wachsman (a neurological surgeon who has become a malpractice lawyer) involving causal neglect of patients under anesthesia, doctors failing to follow up on significant symptoms, diagnosing symptoms accompanying a spinal fracture as "conversion hysteria," and the like. One case cited (p. 33) may be representative: "A child was followed over a three-year period of time for deteriorating vision and other symptoms. During that time four separate physicians (a pediatrician, a neurologist, and two ophthalmologists) saw the child. None of these physicians ever spoke to one another; none of these physicians ever obtained the others' records; and each of these physicians assumed that the other was taking care of the child's problems. The delay in diagnosing and treating the hydrocephalus by means of a shunt caused this child to be permanently and irrevocably blind." This instance, it appears, is far from "rare" or "exceptional," certainly not in the growing public perception.

46. National Opinion Research Center, "Jobs and Occupations: A Popular Evaluation," *Opinion News*, Vol. IX (Sept. 1, 1947), pp. 3–13; reprinted in Reinhard Bendix and Seymour Martin Lipsent (Eds.), *Class, Status and Power—A Reader in Social Stratification* (New York, Free Press, 1953), pp. 411–412: U.S. Supreme Court Justice ranked highest with a score of 96; physician and governor of a state tied for second with scores of 93.

47. Eliot Friedson, *Doctoring Together—A Study of Professional Social Control* (New York, Elsevier, 1975), Chap. 3, "Stances toward Demand and Supply"; also pp. 242ff., "The Collegium as a Delinquent Community."

48. Joseph A. Califano, Jr., "Putting A Lid on Hospital Costs," in *The New York Times* (Wednesday, October 20, 1982): "Since 1979, Medicare payments for hospital

services have jumped almost 20 percent per year. So far this year, hospital costs have increased three times faster than the general inflation rate in the economy. . . . The existing payment system in health care [has] turned traditional concepts of competition and free enterprise on their heads. . . . The average family spends more than 12 percent of its income on health care; about 15 cents of every Federal dollar go to the health-care industry."

Mechanic, *op. cit.*, "Future Issues in Health Care," pp. 10–11: "Medical-care spending in the United States consumed $163 Billion and almost 9% of the GNP . . . it is inevitable that greater energies will be given to controlling increased expenditures."

49.   See Friedson, *op. cit.*, and Nolen, *op. cit.*

50.   In addition to Friedson, see Louise Lander, *Defective Medicine: Risk, Anger and the Malpractice Crisis* (New York, Farrar, Straus and Giroux, 1978) Chap. 6, "The Ideology of Modern Medical Practice."

51.   The patients often have trouble seeing their records but many others have free access to them according to Jennifer Bingham Hull, "Patients are Often the Last to See Their Own Medical Records" (*Wall Street Journal*, September 30, 1985): "Only about half the states have enacted any laws about access to non-mental health medical records." Hull quotes a staff attorney for a Public Citizen Health Research Group, Allen Ginsberg: ". . . access is granted to a whole bunch of people, but patients don't have rights to their records, which is ludicrous." Although access laws grant patients the right to their medical information, "In practice, hospitals and doctors sometimes drag their feet for months, even years, before letting patients have their records." Yet third parties—insurance companies, employers, almost anyone with a plausible request—gain easy access to these files.

52.   See Friedson, *op. cit.*, on unnecessary referrals; see also notes 15, 25, and 32 above.

53.   Harold Garfinkel, *Studies in Ethnomethodology* (Englewood Cliffs, N.J., Prentice Hall, 1967), Chap. 6, "Good Organizational Reasons for 'Bad' Clinic Records," and Chap. 7, "Methodological Adequacy in the Quantitative Study of Selection Criteria and Selection Practices in psychiatric Outpatient Clinics," pp. 200–201: "When one examines any case folder for what it actually contains, a prominent and consistent feature is the occasional and elliptical character of its remarks and information . . . folder documents are very much like utterances in conversation with an unknown audience which is capable of reading hints . . . their sense cannot be decided by a reader without his necessarily knowing or assuming something about a typical biography and typical purposes of the user of such expressions."

54.   See Mechanic, *op. cit.*; see also Ruth Macklin, "Are We in the Lifeboat Yet? Allocation and Rationing of Medical Resources," in *Social Research*, Vol. 52, No. 3 (Autumn 1985); this issue, edited by Arthur L. Caplan, is titled "Bioethics."

The following articles also describe these "life or death decisions:

Andrew H. Malcolm, "For Doctors and Patients, Decisions on Death," *The New York Times* (December 23, 1984), "New Bioethics for a New Biology," *New York Times* editorial (June 27, 1983), and Macklin *op. cit.*, discuss some of these issues.

See also Katherine Bouton, "Painful Decisions, The Role of the Medical Ethicist," *The New York Times Magazine* (August 5, 1990) Section 6.

PART III

IDEOLOGICAL AND POLITICAL CONSEQUENCES

Chapter 14

The Journalist

The journalistic attitude is related to the reporting of events by media which have, as one of their central characteristics, periodicity in publication, whether it be a daily newspaper, a weekly or bimonthly journal, or a radio or television program. The act of reportage is limited. It conveys an image of the world defined within the framework of the reported event and of the periodicity of publication. Thus, time is a major dimension which determines a vast part of that reporting of events which defines and determines an image of the world. The time dimension in journalism is different from that in the natural, scientific, and ceremonial attitude described in Chapters 1 and 2.

The time feature is not the natural time of the natural man, but, because given the periodicity of publication, is an objective factor, subject to conditions and controls that are external to the psychological conditions of action though they may be incorporated into it. Nor, for the same reasons, does the journalistic attitude assume the objective constant, measured attitude that underlies the scientific attitude.

The externality of time is not the preordained rhythm of a ceremony or ritual, in which submission to the tyranny of time—rhythm—becomes a major aesthetic end. Time, for the journalist, is purely an arbitrary accident of the requirements of publication. It has no inherent rhythm other than the economics of publication and the expectations of readers that publication will occur at given periods. Thus, the journalist must consciously discipline himself to the tyranny of these objective forms of time. Having done so, he may enjoy the aesthetics of completing assignments within the framework of what might otherwise be purely arbitrary and capricious publication dates. Regardless of the completeness of his research and knowledge, he must present a complete story by his deadline. The appearance of completeness of a story, the who, when, where, and how of journalism, resembles the images of a total world as presented in a work of art, so that in this respect the journalist is an artist. The applied artist who works on schedule supplied by others and the performing artist quite often are subject to *the same* time requirements. The requirement, however, that the story appear complete forces the journalist to work for a closure which is not the closure that might have occurred had he not been subject to the time requirements.

The journalist, hemmed in by the periodicity of publication, and by the fact that he is selling some kind of media or publication, is forced to anticipate the response of his audience in terms of what the journalist calls newsworthy, or "human interest." He must anticipate what will excite, stimulate, and titillate an audience at the time of publication. This means that the flow of his attention must be consistent with the "natural" flow of attention of his audience. He must drop stories and his interest in events as the events themselves shift either in their dramatic impact on audiences, or in the journalist's estimate of the audience's rhythm of interest [1].

The cliché that there is nothing as old as yesterday's newspaper is no less true because it is a cliché. For this reason, journalism cannot or does not necessarily have the depth and the timeless quality of art, though in other respects it resembles the image-making of art.

In a third respect, however, journalism has much in common with science and art. One of the characteristics of outstanding journalism is that it results in a transvaluation, at least momentarily, of the natural world. Good journalism takes as its framework the world of everyday assumptions of routine, and the normal expectations of a natural audience, and discovers, through the significant story, the violation of the expectations of everyday life. So, the newsworthy, the dramatic, the "human interest" aspect of reporting looks either for the dramatic affirmation or the dramatic denial by events of the world of every day life.

In dramatizing the denial of everyday life by events, the journalist exposes the incongruities between image and reality, the fraud and chicanery behind many facades, and suggests the operation of more essential structures governing the world of appearances. At times, such activities result in a renovation of values which are frequently neglected because they are taken for granted. At other times, the effect of continuous exposures may cause the devaluation of values because they appear to be inoperative. But in both cases, the act of good reporting is something more than reporting; it is, like art, an act of creation and re-creation. Its effects, while they may be startling at a given time, are likely to be temporary, because the journalist is continuously forced to shift the focus of attention, as even the exposure in a given area becomes routinized, and as the response of his readership shifts.

While the result of such activities may from time to time cause public scandals, the arrest of malefactors, the redesigning of automobiles, the enactment of new legislation, or changes in the sensibilities of audiences, the journalist who lives at the point of the chasm between appearances and reality is likely at a personal level to feel that all appearances are fraudulent, managed, or engineered for reasons totally unrelated to the appearances. As a result, his personal attitude may be one of intellectual cynicism, which is not necessarily incongruous with intellectual honesty and the maintenance of high standards of personal ethics.

In presenting these characteristics of the journalistic attitude, we have tended to neglect the simple and more obvious characteristics of technical facility in the handling, arranging, and manipulation of words and symbols, so that taken together they produce for the moment total images of a reality as evoked by an event or story.

Viewed in terms of his technical virtuosity as a craftsman and artisan, the journalist is an information-disseminator. He is able to present images of the world in apparently clear, personalistic, simple, and dramatic forms that are not abstract, academic, or complicated. He is likely to look for the *specific* image, illustration, symbol, anecdote, or event that illustrates his point; and having found and presented that symbol, he is likely to allow the symbol or succession of symbols to convey his point without presenting the abstract argument. In his search for the specific, concrete image, he resembles the poet.

This latter aspect, the technical and aesthetic virtuosity of the journalist, not only constitutes his professional and artistic methodology, but constitutes his basis for evaluation and appreciation by others, including other journalists.

The qualities of the journalist as information specialist may be seen under two perspectives. First, that of the social functions of journalism, and the social consequences of journalism; second, the relation of this attitude to intellectual work of all types, including the scientific, the artistic, and the scholarly.

THE SOCIETAL SETTINGS AND SOCIAL FUNCTIONS OF JOURNALISM

Journalism as an activity becomes meaningful in various societal settings, which, if these settings were not extant, would not require a journalistic attitude. Thus, journalism is appropriate to only limited kinds of social worlds. In a small society in which all available knowledge is gathered through direct and personal experience, the journalistic attitude would not develop, or would be part of the normal cognitive and perceptual equipment of every individual in this society. This also applies to the extent of differentiation within a society. If all individuals in the society are equipped to understand from direct experience the total range of events and activities in that society, then the normal channels of personal communication would be effective in disseminating information within that society.

When the technical development of a society grows to the point where most of the basic issues and dynamics are too complex, abstract, or removed from the experience of the individuals in the society, there is need for the qualities of personification, dramatization, and the removal of abstraction and complexity from events and issues [2].

Thus, the journalist becomes necessary as the result of societal developments which coincide with the growth of large-scale civilizations, the increased differentiation within society, and the development of complex administrative, scientific, technical, and industrial processes which at an operative level can be understood only by highly trained, experienced professionals.

The journalist, by developing professional competence in one or more of the abstract technical areas in the society, and by combining them with his "communications skills," makes distant and complex areas of the world available to audiences who are presumed to lack either the experience or the equipment to understand those events and issues directly in their own terms. As a result, he is or seems indispensable to a mass society.

The second aspect of the information function of journalism is related to the uses of information in a large-scale society. Organized groups, business corporations, government agencies, universities, and other large-scale organizations are or become aware that information dissemination is related to their specialized public and private purposes. There is need to employ specialists at dramatization, personalization, simplification, in order to present most effectively the specialized claims of these groups to distant publics. It is no accident, then, that the beginnings of professional propaganda began with the beginnings of professional journalism. The information talents of the journalist develop in response to needs for substitute sources of information when genuine or direct sources of experience are not available. But this situation, in which the individual is not capable or is presumed to be not capable of evaluating issues and events in terms of direct experience, is precisely that situation which makes possible large-scale fraud, charlatanry, and deceit by misdirection. For the conscious manipulation of information becomes possible only when access to genuine information or direct sources of experience is obscured by the complexity of events, issues, technology, size, or differentiation in a society [3].

The development of a complex society provides the opportunity and the motivation, but the misapplication of journalism supplies the means.

PERSONIFICATION, CONCRETENESS, COMPREHENSIBILITY

The journalist, like the novelist, in avoiding abstraction and the cold dead-ness of difficult and abstract themes, seeks to find the image or the person-ality that embodies the idea, and deals with the image or personality in place 6of the idea. This enables him to communicate at levels that a large and nonprofessional audience is able to understand. Frequently, the characteris-tics of the journalistically treated personality begin to transcend that idea. Thus, the personal habits, the love stories, the leisure pursuits, the personal character or lack of it, all overpower that which would make the personality of journalistic interest original [4].

Thus the journalistic treatment of Albert Einstein would emphasize his eccentricities: his haircut, his hatred of shaving cream, his absentminded-ness, his proclivity for wearing old sweaters, all at the expense of any presentation of his contribution, which is defined as so abstract that allegedly only a dozen men could understand it [5].

The concreteness and "comprehensibility" embodied in this form of jour-nalistic treatment results in the "hero" or the "star," who symbolizes and personifies, in terms larger than life, a field of endeavor which would otherwise not be salient. Once the attempt is made to make the "star" salient, the person who is momentarily presented as a star has a fabricated image. The dramatic aspects have to be emphasized; traits are created either in the person himself, so that he is made to resemble his journalistic image, or so that the image is made independent of his genuine characteristics or qualities [6].

In this sense, journalism not only reports on the operation of appearances, and on realities underlying appearances, but also creates appearances or the appearance of realities.

JOURNALISM IN PUBLIC RELATIONS

The manipulator of public opinion, the propagandist, the public relations man, seeks from whatever source is available those individuals whose techni-cal skills, knowledge, and artistry will implement his purposes. The journal-ist possesses some of these skills, though in modern society he is not too different in these respects from the artist, the intellectual, the researcher, and the academician, who can become, if he desires, available for the same purposes.

Starting with the pure model of the journalist as developed above, a whole subsidiary set of occupations which can be called applied journalism can become available. These include the information functions, that is, the information specialist in large-scale organizations, and primarily as defined by the term in government. In this sense, the information specialist translates the often complex, scientific, abstract procedural documents of quasi-literate technicians into the dramatic, the personal, the concrete imagery characteristic of the essential journalistic model. As an employee of a specialized agency which has vested interests of its own, his job entails the repression of information which is not consistent with those specialized interests, the concealment of weaknesses, of original documents, and their restatement so that the positive interests of the agency are enhanced. In the private sphere, the same function is called public relations; it includes all of the same functions.

The essential devices of dramatization and personification enable both the public and the private agency to attain visibility or salience in a world where the overabundance of information tends to clog all avenues of information.

The journalist must work out dramatic devices. The public relations man, by means of hokum, teasers, and fraudulent stories gains access to media which allow the favorable story to become visible.

To the extent that journalism makes itself available for such uses, it destroys one of its original basic attributes: that of revealing conflicts between appearances and underlying structures. It reverses this relationship by contributing to the manufacture of appearances, and to a fraudulent public life. The journalist in these roles becomes a modern bureaucratic replacement for the primitive mythmaker. He also becomes, at the bureaucratic level, an ideologist. In his role as educator and purveyor of the thought, values, and screens to thought of others; he is neither a mythmaker nor an ideologist.

When "public relations" is conducted simultaneously for a vast number of institutions and organizations, the public life of a society becomes so congested with manufactured appearances that it is difficult to recognize any underlying realities.

As a result, individuals begin to distrust all public facades and retreat into apathy, cynicism, disaffiliation, distrust of media and publication institutions. They develop forms of psychological sabotage and rebellion. At this point the journalist unwittingly often exposes the workings of the public relations man or information specialist, if he operates within a genuine journalistic attitude.

Unfortunately, in a complex society where the sources of information are so varied and numerous, the journalist and his enterprises in their basic news reporting function are frequently forced to accept the press release or handout as a substitute for the genuine legwork that results in journalism as a peculiar art form [7].

In the above discussion, the journalistic attitude is primarily located in journalism as an occupation, and corruptions of the journalistic attitude are seen in the use of journalism by applied journalists for ends not related to the original ends of journalism. One must not forget that journalism in the original sense of our usage has been a "habit of mind," a way of viewing the world, and of creating articulate images of it. The point to be made here is that this journalistic habit of mind can become independent of a specific occupation, and can become applied to spheres other than that of journalism itself, or of bureaucratic information control and information manipulation. This is especially true since the social conditions which originally evoked the journalistic attitude are independent of journalism itself. The complexity, differentiation, abstractness, and social distances of modern society force everyone who wishes to communicate with others who do not directly experience the events communicated to do so in manners and styles that flow from the journalistic attitude.

These manners and styles, we have indicated, are the use of drama, personification, concreteness, simplification, imagery, etc. [8].

JOURNALISTIC TREATMENT

Journalism serves social functions in the articulation of images of the world of appearances and the appearances of reality. But it also has a set of techniques, which, with professionalization, specialization, and academic development, become fairly objective, and thus teachable. Then, the use of the objective techniques of journalism can become independent of professional journalism in its primary and original sense.

Once this occurs, it is followed by what we call journalistic treatment, in which the methods of journalism—personification, simplification, the quest for imagery along with easy treatment of almost incomprehensible information—are used in nonjournalistic enterprises. Whenever a new idea, institution, technological development, art work or form appears, in a society imbued with highly developed journalistic tradition, these new forms are almost immediately redeveloped, reported, and publicized, within the framework of journalistic treatment.

Modern art, or a new development in modern art, will become within a relatively short period of time, in journalistic form, invested with the glamour, the exoticism, and the chic inherent in a "hero" or "star" system. Given the appeal of the journalistic treatment to audiences whose interests have been aroused and jaded by past journalistic treatment, there is a high probability that the new development, if "taken up" either by journalists or public relations men, or even by sensation-seeking audiences, can have almost instantaneous currency, due both to the form of its treatment, and the media of mass dissemination for such material.

As a result, within the last hundred years, it can be argued that the time interval between the development of a style, a form, an innovation, and its acceptance at a popular level, has been shortened, so that by now, instant acceptance of innovation is often guaranteed, provided the availability of the innovation for journalistic treatment, even before the idea can be properly understood and developed by its protagonists. The individual as worker or innovator is pulled into the world of the stars and of public characters, before he has time to assess, criticize, and develop the innovation [9]. There is a probability that basically good ideas are exhausted or vulgarized before their immanent meaning emerges. In the absence of general ideas, effects may be forced by a willful experimentalism and sensationalism.

If this is true of innovators, it is even more true of audiences, who must be prepared, if they wish to be *au courant*, to leap from one journalistically created vogue to another, preferably before the high point of each succeeding vogue has been reached. The artist or innovator must risk the danger of becoming outmoded almost before he has done his work. And if he values his recently acquired stardom, he must learn to leave work which becomes passé as new styles replace it. The dangers of journalistically induced success are greater than the dangers of obscurity [10].

Other forms of journalistic treatment abound. The most frequent form occurs when journalistic treatment combines with academic treatment, in which the journalistic explicator must explain in journalistic terms how work that is independently valuable was really done, or how it can be understood in more simplified and "basic" terms. This results in the industry of commentaries. But it is not enough for the journalist (or nonjournalist who provides journalistic treatment) to amplify, and explain the original work. He must add elements to the original work and to previous commentaries, to justify his present commentary. This results in journalistic "improvements" of the original work by individuals who are not equipped to do the original work, but who know how to write about it.

As one example, in the field of music one of the largest critical industries is that of writing annotations—explanations of the systems of interpretation of such works as the Beethoven piano sonatas. Thus, for many original compositions, there are a host of editions, each annotated by an inferior musical mind, each introducing his own personal idiosyncrasies, preferences, and personality into his revision of Beethoven's works. In the process, the original annotations by Beethoven were lost or obscured, so that at a later date, a more advanced critical industry was forced to emerge, that of the discovery of the musical work in its original form. It is a tribute to recent musicological scholarship that it has discovered the necessity for removing the barnacles of past journalistic and critical growths.

Journalistic treatment results in a dialectic in which the creation of myths is but a phase. The removal of inaccuracies then becomes a necessary phase of another form of journalistic treatment, which may in turn result in the creation of new myths. In this sense, journalistic mythmaking becomes an autonomous process, almost independent of any reality towards which the myth may originally have been related. This autonomous process was most advanced, perhaps during the thirties and forties, in the treatment of Hollywood and the Hollywood stars.

THE JOURNALISTIC ATTITUDE OUTSIDE OF JOURNALISM

Given the growth of journalistic treatment as an activity apart from journalism per se it becomes necessary to consider the uses of the journalistic attitude by nonjournalists in nonjournalistic situations. Perhaps the simplest form of application of the journalistic attitude is the use of this device by a scholar or expert toward his peers who presumably have the experience, the background, and the technique at levels which do not require the simplifications of the journalistic attitude. Why this should occur so pervasively is not directly perceivable. Perhaps the habits of mind developed from dealing with outgroups become so pervasive that the trained professional presents his own materials to other trained professionals in ways that previously would have been considered inappropriate.

But other factors might be relevant as well. Among these is the technicalization of society to the extent that professional, technical, and occupational peers are so distant from each other that one treats them as strangers, as laymen, or as a general public. In addition, even within relatively narrow technical areas, the amount of information to be transmitted is so great that to gain the attention of one's peers requires the development of dramatic devices, which in specialized technical areas necessarily falsifies the data so presented. And, thirdly, the amount of specialization even within a narrow technical area is so great that the specialist does not feel confident that another specialist in a closely related field will be able to understand specialized information in its own terms.

Regardless of the cause, then, the specialist as receiver of information must guard himself against the forms of information which might mislead him, even though he himself, in his dissemination of information, might use the very same forms.

Related to these activities is the journalistic institution of the book review as a means of coping with the immense flow of information to be found in technical and specialized journals. This flow is so great that the academician is often forced to subscribe to reviewing journals, and to engage clipping services and graduate students to provide abstracts, digests, and quotations from unread books, monographs, and articles.

Beyond this, the specialist in any area must deal with audiences that do not and cannot have the technical equipment to comprehend his communication in the sense that he himself (hopefully) understands. He must thus become his own journalist.

The physician, for example, has a choice between developing or presenting descriptions of disease which are beyond the comprehension of the layman, or of vulgarizing the description. He may, in vulgarizing it, seek to maintain the essential accuracy of the description, or he may slant the information in order thereby to dramatize himself and the quality of his practice.

If, on the other hand, he presents the data in its original technical complexity, he can do so in order to be accurate but incommunicable, or he can do it in order to evoke the aura of science, complexity, and professional esotericism, and thus magnify and enhance his professional image. In this latter case, the use of the professional mysteries of science in its original complexity can become a public relations device in all the implications of the term. The example of the physician in dealing with the layman is the typical case, in which the complexity of a given field promises opportunity for material and psychological profit-making through either the simplification or the complexity of the specialized worlds of the expert.

Given the size of the various lay audiences for the products and by-products of specialization, the opportunities for such simplification or manipulation are boundless. Thus, the textbook industry, swollen in size by the number of subcollege and college students, provides vast opportunities for the specialist to simplify his materials so that they can be packaged and sold to neophytes in the field. A successful textbook can provide more material rewards than an entire career of undramatic but serious scholarly or technical work. The problem involved in such work is what level of simplification, dramatization, personification, and so on, is necessary to present the neophyte with a working knowledge of a field.

The journalistic attitude has a dual character. It has a specific attitude toward the material of scholarly work, and a specific attitude toward the audience [11]. The journalistic attitude treats the audience as a consumer: knowledge disseminated should excite, stimulate, titillate, entertain, surprise, and evoke temporary interest, but no effort, on the part of the consumer. A genuine educational attitude must treat the neophyte as a producer, must teach him to handle the complexity of the data of his field in its own terms. When the journalistic attitude becomes part of the process of education, then the would-be producer is treated as a consumer, and his perception of the field is distorted by the importation of dramatic elements into what might be serious, undramatic, persistent, long-term technical work. Disillusion must follow an orientation to work based on the expectation of the drama of work.

More important, the use of the dramatization inherent in the journalistic attitude delays the entry of the neophyte into the work itself, so that it is difficult for him to learn what work is. Again, to repeat a cliché, he learns *about* the work, instead of learning the work [12].

Ordinarily, genuine learning takes place during the process of working on real problems in real settings. Knowledge is acquired if and when it becomes useful to the worker in the solution of those problems. The salience of a technique or a method, or of information, is immediately perceptible in the light of the ongoing activity. It is never "theoretical," distant, or "abstract," because it is never removed from the problem.

However, the substitution of the consumer's point of view for the producer's point of view, through the journalistic presentation of nonjournalistic material, with its glamorizing and dramatizing of the activity, puts distance between the image of the work and the work itself, and creates a gap which cannot be closed until problems are confronted in the attempt to solve them.

JOURNALISM IN INTELLECTUAL WORK

Here we would distinguish between two ideal types of creation and dissemination of knowledge: "self-generated" material, and "externally generated" material. Externally generated material is developed simply to meet a deadline, to fill up space in a journal, or to fill time, as at a broadcast or popular lecture. Self-generated material includes all those books, art works, and scientific reports which are developed out of concern for immanent empirical or theoretical problems, out of perceptions or improvisations on the part of a writer or artist which are seen by him as promising and requiring further development or investigation, and which are not generated by immediate external pressures. Preoccupation with the material alone generates the work to be done.

A major component of journalistic activity and of the journalistic attitude is the pressure to have something written in time for a deadline, and of sufficient volume to fill the space or the time allotted to it. Thus, to paraphrase Karl Kraus, the journalist must write though he has nothing to say, and the journalist has something to say because he must write [13]. If, under this pressure, it happens that the journalist finds something to say, all is well; but if not, he must then have recourse to various devices.

One such device is to have recourse to that body of material which is, as described above, "self-generated," and to "popularize" it; that is, to explain it, "clarify" it, make it amusing or dramatic. One may go further, and in the process may "improve" the material by removing from it what one takes to be offensive to an audience, or merely boring, or threatening to one or another interest group. Here, the journalistic attitude actually acts as mediator between two groups. Towards the public, it decides what the public is fit or able to understand; towards the producers of work, it will dictate what may or may not be appropriate for an audience presumed to be rather lightly educated and having a somewhat limited capacity for attention. If this aspect of the journalistic attitude becomes internalized by a producer of self-generated material, he may become induced to shape this material in ways different from those he would have chosen had he not anticipated public responses. Thus, the extent to which the journalistic attitude becomes internalized may serve to distinguish various classes of intellectual work from one another, ranging from speculative philosophical works, works of high art, original theoretical treatises, on one hand, to works of popularization, "introductions," "how to" books, anthologies, readers, etc.

The distinction made here between "self-generated" and "externally generated" material actually describes the opposite poles of a continuum. At one end stands, in Schutzean terms, the expert, at the other end the journalist or the propagandist. Somewhere in between stands Schutz's model of the well-informed citizen [14], or Weber's concept of the cultivated layman.

JOURNALISM AND PROPAGANDA

Part of journalistic treatment is to present arguments for or against a given issue or idea in such a way that the arguments of the advocate can be understood and accepted without access to the complexities of the issue in its original form. Most points of contention in a complex society are dealt with in terms of legalistic, technical, administrative, procedural, and economic complexities. Their substantive merits are not immediately visible, especially as major substantive points will frequently turn on relatively innocuous but abstract legal or technical issues.

The argument at the level of abstraction of the original issue is often difficult to present, especially to a lay public, difficult to understand, difficult to evoke loyalties and passions, even though these arguments may involve the life and growth of major groups and institutions within a society. The journalistic treatment of these issues provides a solution to this problem. The techniques of personification, simplification, imagery, linguistic devices, and the truncated journalistic story can, at its highest point, provide a description of the issue, in which no argument is ever made. The selection of words and the emotional loading of words, the slanting of the treatment of events, the sympathetic or unsympathetic treatment of personalities all constitute the application of journalistic treatment to complex issues. The argument is contained in the form the treatment of the story, rather than in the argument itself. Argumentativeness, that is, the ideologized form of argument, is frowned upon from this point of view, for the ideological form or the polemic form of the argument alerts the individual to the idea that an argument is about to be presented. This signals him to adopt a critical stance in which the argument is to be subjected to logical or empirical criticism, or simply to emotional resistance. The argumentative form in its essential nature implies that the "other" should be prepared to resist the argument, and invites him to develop counterarguments. In using these forms of journalistic treatment, the individual is not alerted to the polemic situation, is not warned, alarmed, and invited to use his critical faculties. The argument is presented in such a way that the individual does not know that an argument has been made. If the presentation is successful, he accepts the argument as a series of facts, emotional tones, or as reality. He has been manipulated. This form of journalistic treatment finds its most concentrated expression in "mood advertising," in magazines like *Time*, and in indirect public relations campaigns. It is for this reason that ideology as a form of disputation has become unfashionable in a world where journalistic treatment replaces ideological or polemic treatment of controversial issues [15].

JOURNALISM AND PUBLIC RELATIONS

The public relations attitude requires a state of continuing innovation. One needs to have a story about something new and exciting occurring within an institution at relatively frequent intervals, so that press releases can be made. Since the routine operation of an efficient institution is not newsworthy, items that are newsworthy have to be manufactured. This means that new programs, new ideas, new personnel, the employment and application of new technology, machinery, and inventions all evoke the possibility of newsworthy public relations. When public prominence becomes a primary need for an institution, then the rate of innovation must be increased, even though on technical or intrinsic grounds there is no need for innovations. Thus, perfectly good ideas, programs, and techniques can be instituted even when unnecessary or misapplied. Their use is not intrinsic to the operation but only to the publicity. This is very important when related to considerations of the rate of innovation or change within a society. In a public relations world paralleling the development of innovation in the arts, the use of public relations techniques accentuates the rate of innovation and application beyond what one might expect from the need for such inventions or their usefulness.

Journalists who are insiders in large institutions and who are aware of both the public image and the internal image of the operations of institutions tend to be skeptical regarding the applicability of publicly valued technology to the institutions, such as high-powered computers, team teaching, teaching machines, operations research and linear programing, PERT systems, systems development, and many other similar ideas. This technology may be valuable, but its value becomes suspect because, at least in its early stages, it is highly amenable to public relations treatment.

Under this heading come such developments as the establishment of university chairs at very high salaries, for which an outstanding scholar is hired, primarily to enhance the "image" of the institution, the establishment of special curricula and educational programs and degrees, new construction of various types, and the establishment of various research institutions.

Applied journalism involves more than the selective presentation of favored facts and interpretations by means which make the desired story easy and attractive to accept. To convey an effective story from the standpoint of criteria that are independent of the story itself, it may be necessary to withhold information, to alter the facts, to be selective in the release of information, to color the story, and to provide the proper mood music and nuance. This has sometimes been called "information management." It may include the burning of documents, the shredding of papers, the firing of controversial figures, the deflection of issues from the embarrassing to the innovative, and outright falsification. In some cases, when the avoidance of a major scandal seems to be impossible, applied journalism will include the apparent exposure of a minor scandal in the hope that in so doing, the major scandal will be avoided. Furthermore, exposure of a specific contradiction between appearance and reality often has the effect of being an end in itself. The exposure is assumed to be self-remedying, and the action undertaken in light of the exposure may be limited. But since journalism operates most often at the level of the specific concrete case, the exposure of a concrete case, or even of an interlocking series of specific cases, quite frequently results in only the treatment, sometimes temporary, of those cases. The conditions which make the individual cases possible are often left untouched because the habit of mind upon which journalism rests, and which it reinforces, does not go beyond the specific case. The journalist, having operated successfully at the case level, will then go on to other cases, while the vested interest may well concede defeat in a specific case so long as the general condition favorable to their interests remains untouched. Journalism can thus reveal specific, extreme abuses and contradictions between official appearances and underlying realities; but, by itself, it cannot go beyond exposure. To be effective, the journalistic attitude must be transcended; but, of course, such transcendence need not be the task of the journalist: it may well be the task of the "well-informed citizen."

Thus the negative aspects of applied journalism include turning the journalistic attitude into its opposite: from the exposure of unseemly facts underlying appearances, it turns itself into the creation of new and intentionally false appearances. But it uses the methods of verisimilitude to do so.

THE JOURNALISTIC TREATMENT OF POLITICS

Political leaders can dramatically announce vast changes in policy, even if the change may be that of co-opting the language of the opposition without changing any behavior that might follow from the policy. The linguistic co-optation may be used to label a policy that has opposite intentions or consequences to that of the language employed. It may include the promotion and removal of officials who symbolize a policy that has become unpopular or controversial, with the change in personnel being used as a substitute for a change in policy. The journalistic personification may involve worldwide travels, publicly celebrated meetings and ceremonies under the eye of the television camera and the press. It produces drama, ceremony, personification and simplification, whether or not there is in fact a change in policy. The immediacy of personification introduced originally by radio with Franklin Delano Roosevelt's fireside chats, has been intensified by television, and includes the personification of issues in an aural and visual sense. It results in the attempt to select leaders who can personify policies whether they have policies in fact or not, and who can project images of warmth, sincerity, or masculinity. When these attributes are lacking, journalistic treatment involves the rehearsal, concealment, makeup, face-lifts and other anatomical alterations, and other forms of dramatic projection. As a result, part of the attitude of the performing artist is imported into the journalistic attitude to create newer forms of dramatic journalism.

The use of television, radio, and the film as means of simplification and personification in politics is only a technical advance over similar schemes of journalistic treatment based on different media. The most obvious of the earlier schemes was embodied in the slogan [16]. The slogan as a self-conscious method of political propaganda was developed to its highest point by Lenin during the Iskra period, from 1901 to 1905. The slogan was designed by the communists to embody in simple dramatic and emotional terms the aspirations of the downtrodden masses that were consistent with or could be used by the Communist Party in promoting the revolution [17]. There was an intense struggle among the various factions of the Communist Party as to what slogans (a) reflected the aspirations of the means, and (b) were correct from the standpoint of the revolutionary aspirations of the party. The use of the slogan by the Communist Party reflected an intense hundred-year study of the French Revolution, and the first dramatic political slogan, "Liberty, Equality, and Fraternity." The counterrevolution of the Congress of Vienna used an equally terse but not as emotionally powerful slogan, "Restoration, Legitimacy, and Compensation."

The intense study of the use of these slogans by the communists was first undertaken by Marx, who was himself, among other things, a journalist ("You have nothing to lose but your chains"). But after the development of this special field of applied politics, the use of the slogan became almost an intrinsic aspect of all politics. The slogan was based on the print media. The development of visual media in part collapses the slogan into the appearance of the man himself.

THE PRESENTATION

The journalistic attitude, as we have indicated, emerges out of a need for simplicity in a world that is increasingly complex. Part of this complexity is due to technology, or to the increased technology by which society operates, and part is due to the increasing knowledge of the way the world operates; the development of science and research provides an overabundance of information which tends to drown the cultivated layman (or, in Schutz's terminology, the well-informed citizen), such that even the information at his disposal becomes useless. The journalistic attitude responds by its own dialectic to the very problems it in part creates. For higher journalistic treatment includes the simplification of the presentation and the use of complex statistical devices to present simple dramatic facts and images of facts. These include the use of charts, simple indices, and animation, all aimed at presenting the most complex data in the world in forms that all but an expert in the collection of these materials can understand. This dialectic thus has further consequences: the deciphering of the meaning and basis for simple "facts" becomes the basis for some of the highest forms of expertise in our world, but so of course is the presentation of these facts.

JOURNALISM AND BOOK PUBLISHING

The "migration" of the journalistic attitude out of journalism and into various other fields has been discussed above. Its effects in the publishing of books may be briefly indicated. There are three principal loci of the journalistic attitude in book publishing. A firm may wish to fill out its catalogue in various subject-matter fields, for reasons of competition, and so may commission or generate books which would otherwise not have existed. Text-books are often generated for this reason. The second principal locus of the journalistic attitude in publishing is frequently located among editors. An editor who receives a manuscript from a subject-matter expert may find that its obscurity and disorganization of style require reordering clarification. In so acting, the editor is following the Schutzean model of the well-informed citizen. But a book editor may follow another model, as described above, namely that of anticipating audience responses to original, controversial, difficult, or otherwise disturbing material, and may in the process truncate, disfigure, or suppress a book entirely. This may be operative especially in the area of translating a major work into English, either from a foreign language or from technical jargon, in the process of which the editor fre-quently announces his deletion of considerable amounts of material which he has considered as not suitable for the English reading audience. Here, the editor has clearly adopted the journalistic attitude.

The third locus of the journalistic attitude in the field of book publishing lies in the area of reference books. The development of a complex technolog-ical world, and with it of journalism in all senses of the term, has led to a need for information about areas and fields which an individual cannot be expected to know at first hand. For the "well-informed citizen" reference books may serve a legitimate purpose, but they may serve journalistic purposes as well, enabling a popularizer, rewrite man, or commentator to assume the mantle of a depth of scholarship he does not possess. The influence of journalism may be shown not only in the proliferation of ency-clopedias, textbooks, and reference books, but in the regularity with which they are revised and updated, to the point where they begin to resemble periodicals, even though the developments reported on may be peripheral or of ephemeral interest in a subject-matter field.

At any given point in time in any field of study, the sum total of knowledge in that field is fragmentary and unorganized. A vast number of individuals are working on a series of frequently unrelated problems, others are working in terms of intellectual traditions which are often competing, antagonistic, or anomalous. An accurate summation of knowledge in any field, for those who expect a unified, organized, progressive march of science and knowledge, might prove discrediting to that field. When public relations purposes are first in mind, the presentation of the state of the art or science requires that the field by presented in an orderly, systematic, unified, and dramatic way such that all professionals have two orders of data about their own field: (1) inside knowledge which determines the operative data for the professional in his intramural work; (2) a pseudo-integration of his field, which is presented to laymen, neophytes, the general public, and to outside administrators whose work impinges on the field.

This may appear at times to be necessary. The attempt, however, to treat the pseudo-order as genuine often results in a falsification of the entire field. Furthermore, when a field is full of the conflicts and divergences of approach which is necessarily characteristic of a search for knowledge based upon free inquiry by independent minds, then the problem of orientation to the various approaches within a field is important not only to the public and to the neophyte, but also to the professional. Here, the scholar as intramural journalist operates by defining lines along which an individual can find avenues for the expression of loyalties and commitments. At the same time, the lines define the "enemies," and, with them, those schools of thought and approaches that are to be ignored, disdained, or accorded low prestige [18].

Journalism of this nature is necessary for the political organization of any intellectual field, and parallels the use of journalism as a device for controlling and manipulating information by the public relations man and by the information specialists of large bureaucracies.

Journalistic treatment combines with scholarship in other forms as well. The most frequent is that in which the journalistic explicator must explain in popular terms how work that is independently valuable was really done, or how it can be understood in more simplified and "basic" terms. This, as we have previously indicated, results in the industry of commentaries, in which each commentary on basic work encrusts itself on other commentaries, so that the original idea, which was sufficiently attractive to invite commentaries, gets lost in the total weight of commentaries. But it is not enough for the journalist (or for the non-journalist-scholar providing journalistic treatment) to simplify and explain the original work. He must add elements to the original work and to previous commentaries, to justify his present commentary, frequently "on the basis of more recent scholarship." This results in "improvements" on the original work by individuals who are not equipped to do the original work, but who know how to write about it.

The process of developing critical encrustations on original work by journalists or critics who have not done the original work results in further journalistic camouflage. The journalistic critic, in confronting both the original work and the audiences who know the original work or previous commentaries, must establish credentials to perform surgery upon these earlier stages. Therefore, scholarship, or the appearance of scholarship, becomes an indispensable tool for the journalist critic. In the light of this predicament, the journalist critic has greater need for such scholarship. Because of this situation, a secondary set of industries have been developed, to provide instant scholarship and instant credentials for validating the journalistic enterprise. These involve the use and creation of specialized encyclopedias, almanacs, dictionaries, and reference works, easily cross-referenced and indexed, which all allow the acquisition of the externals of expertise, at little cost of time and energy. To the expert who is not a journalist, knowledge of the same order of technical depth is based upon his total life history in the accumulation of such knowledge. The knowledge is an intrinsic part of him and manifests itself through his work at the moment of work, and not in the autonomous display of erudition. Only a genuine scholar can be simple in the manner of his presentation. There is a special type of scholarly paper whose format is by now fairly standardized, in which the scholar reveals in the course of the paper that he has read the original and every commentary thereon over the course of two thousand years. The amassing of citations, especially obscure ones, becomes the exclusive preoccupation of the paper as a work of scholarly erudition. The process reaches its culmination when the display of erudition is so concentrated that it leaves no room for a theme, a hypothesis, or a point.

One conceptual device which has become a major part of the critical industry, and which can be traced back to journalistic usages, is that of the establishment, within a subject-matter field, of a pantheon of the major historical figures of that field. Many a survey of a field for the beginner or for the layman, has the model of a guided tour of the pantheon, in which the leading figures are brought forth, their lives and works briefly sketched using the techniques of personification and simplification, and then their relative merits are established. Thus, one figure will be established in the main section, others in the lesser wings of the pantheon, according to their stature, as established by the critic describing the field. Thus, we will be given ratings of the figures in the field: the greatest and most important, the second after him, the next, and so on. This device of establishing, as though once and for all, the relative merits of the figures in a field, is journalistic in nature, borrowed primarily from the sports pages of the newspapers, in which individual athletes and teams are rated either according to their standings in the season's competition, or on the basis of long-term statistical measures, or according to public opinion polls.

In scholarly work, this results in the use of the biography or the anthology of biographical essays in which the life, glamour, travails and tragedies, the "agonies and ecstasies" of creative geniuses are presented as a substitute for the great work or thought itself.

The industry of commentaries also serves the political organization of an intellectual field in the problem of according recognition for original or valuable work which originates in an opposing or rival school of thought. If the concepts or findings developed are really indispensable, they can be gradually and anonymously appropriated, and sources for the appropriation can be eventually cited only among scholars of an allied, rather than an opposing, school of thought.

We have presented the development of a phenomenological model of an attitude as related to a specialized kind of treatment of information appropriate to given types of social and societal structures. The journalistic attitude is evoked by the needs for the periodistic presentation of images of the world to distant publics who are unable to comprehend parts of their world in terms of their direct experience. At its best, journalism performs an extremely important function in the creation, re-creation, and reemphasis of world images. It transvalues the world even in the process of trying to present it.

But the very development of the skills and techniques for manifesting such images demonstrates the possibility of use and abuse by those who would use the journalistic attitude for non-journalistic purposes. In a society in which the need for information is so great that, when fulfilled, the fulfillment cancels the need by drowning the public in information.

In addition to the overabundance of information presented to the society at large, one finds that public relations treatment has been imported into most other areas of life, even by those who are not professionally aware of using the journalistic attitude. Thus, when journalistic treatment begins to pervade a great part of the major institutions, and the thinking processes, of a society, the creation of images and appearances becomes an autonomous process in which the institutions, techniques, and methodologies of the society become the product of the attempt to manufacture images.

Thus, the image is no longer a by-product of the generic and necessary operation of an institution, but a major *raison d'être* of the institution. When this occurs, the activities and operations of the institutions are depleted of their intrinsic meanings, and extrinsic meanings become the only meanings available. If and when this occurs, self-consciousness concerning image-building, that is, the journalistic attitude and journalistic treatment, results in the devaluation of all intrinsic meanings. The articulation of meaning thus becomes a device by which meaning is depleted of its content.

NOTES

1. *The Sociology of Georg Simmel,* translated by Kurt Wolff (New York, Free Press, 1964), pp. 185–186: "The journalist give content and direction to the opinions of a mute multitude. But he is nevertheless forced to listen, combine, and guess what the tendencies of this multitude are, what it desires to hear and to have confirmed, and whether it wants to be led. While apparently it is only the public which is exposed to *his* suggestions, actually he is as much under the sway of the public's suggestion. Thus, a highly complex interaction (whose two, mutually spontaneous forces, to be sure, appear under very different forms) is hidden here beneath the semblance of the pure superiority of the one element and a purely passive being-led of the other."

2. Alfred Schutz, in his essay, *The Well-Informed Citizen: An Essay on the Social Distribution of Knowledge,* formulates this problem in a somewhat different

but related perspective, in which he constructs three ideal types: the expert, the man in the street, and the well-informed citizen as three separate forms of social knowledge (see the *Collected Works,* Vol. II, p. 129 *et passim*). The present essay on the journalistic attitude focuses upon certain aspects which Schutz developed only in passing. See also W. Lippmann, *The Phantom Public* (New York: Harcourt, Brace, 1925), p. 42: "Modern society is not visible to anybody, nor intelligible continuously and as a whole. One section is visible to another section, one series of acts is intelligible to this group and another to that."

3. Leo Gurko, *Heroes, Highbrows and the Popular Mind* (New York, Bobbs-Merrill, 1953), p. 236: "The enormous specialization that accompanied the spread of scientific and technical knowledge broke life up into smaller segments, and made the custodian of each segment increasingly important. In due course this custodian developed into the professional expert who, by virtue of his total knowledge of a single area (and often total ignorance of everything else), set up shop as middleman between his area and the public at large. His very concentration on a single sphere at the expense of every other kind of knowledge was a strong element in his functioning as an expert."

4. Leo Lowenthal, "Biographies in Popular Magazines," in William Petersen (Ed.), *American Social Patterns* (Garden City, N.Y., Doubleday, 1956), p. 71: "A biography seems to be the means by which an average person is able to reconcile his interest in the important trends of history and in the personal lives of other people." Also pp. 108–110: "The important role of familiarity in all phenomena of mass culture cannot be sufficiently emphasized. People derive a great deal of satisfaction from the continual repetition of familiar patterns . . . there has never been any rebellion against this fact . . . the biographies repeat what we have always known. . . . [The] distance between what an average individual may do and the forces and powers that determine his life and death has become too unbridgeable such that that identification with normalcy, even with Philistine boredom, becomes a readily grasped empire of refuge and escape. . . . By narrowing his focus of attention he can experience the gratification of being confirmed in his own pleasures and discomforts by participating in the pleasures and discomforts of the great. The large and confusing issues on the political and economic realm and the antagonisms and controversies in the social realm—all these are submerged in the experience of being at one with the lofty and great in the sphere of consumption. See also Lippman, *op. cit.,* pp. 13–14.

5. Orrin E. Klapp, *Symbolic Leaders: Public Dramas and Public Men* (Chicago, Aldine, 1964), Chap. 8, "Hero Stuff." See p. 127 for other props of famous characters: sweaters, spectacles, mustaches, stovepipe hats, etc.

6. Edgar Morin, *The Star: An Account of the Star System in Motion Pictures* (New York, Grove Press, 1960), p. 39: "The actor does not engulf his role. The role does not engulf the actor. Once the film is over, the actor becomes an actor again, the character remains a character, *but from their union is born a composite creature who participates in both, envelops them both: the star.* G. Gentilhomme gives an excellent primary definition of the star (in *Comment devenir vedette de cinema*): 'A star appears when the interpreter takes precedence over the character he is playing while profiting by that character's qualities on the mythic level.' Which we might complete: 'and when the character profits by the star's qualities on this same mythic level.' " p. 67: "Possessed by her own myth, the star imposes it on the film universe of which she is the product. Stars demand or refuse roles in the name of their own image. P. Richard Wilm wanted to make only films in which he would be victorious in love; Gabin, before 1939, demanded his death in every film he made." P. 66: "The star is in effect subjectively determined by her double on the screen. She is nothing since her image is everything. She is everything since she is this image too."

7.   Daniel J. Boorstin: *The Image, or What Happened to the American Dream* (New York, Atheneum, 1962), pp. 17–19: "[Our] whole system of public information produces always more 'packaged' news, more pseudo-events. . . . The common 'news releases' which every day issue by the ream from Congressmen's offices, from the President's press secretary, from the press relations offices of businesses, charitable organizations, and universities are a kind of *Congressional Record* covering all American life. To secure 'news coverage' for an event, . . . one must issue, in proper form a 'release.' . . . The release is news pre-cooked, and supposed to keep till needed. . . . The account is written in past tense but usually describes an event that has not yet happened when the release is given out. . . . The National Press Club in its Washington clubrooms has a large rack which is filled daily with the latest releases, so the reporter does not even have to visit the offices which give them out. In 1947 there were about twice as many government press agents engaged in preparing news releases as there were newsmen gathering them in."

8.   Israel Gerver and Joseph Bensman, "Towards a Sociology of Expertness," in *Social Forces*, Vol. 32, No. 3 (March 1954), pp. 227–229: ". . . symbolic experts may personify complexities not only for the distant public, but also for insiders under conditions which are sufficiently complex so that these complexities cannot be understood exclusively and immediately in terms of direct participant experience. . . . In many fields of endeavor the symbolic expert is not actually a substantive expert but appears to be one. The symbolic expert is not necessarily a particular living person but may be a complex of traditional evaluations and definitions which become personified . . . such as Rembrandt, Beethoven, Bach, Van Gogh . . . Copernicus and Galileo. . . ." "The interpretive expert who is attached to the organization publicizes the results and creates and maintains the symbolic expert. Both emphasize the magic of scientific technique to the public at large. Both are likely to pressure the substantive experts for publicly demonstrative results and both are more likely to announce these results before substantive experts would do so."

9.   Bernard Rosenberg and Norris Fliegel, *The Vanguard Artist: Portrait and Self-Portrait* (Chicago, Quadrangle Books, 1965), pp. 57–58: ". . . by becoming celebrities too soon, many of the young are deprived of experience. The quiet novitiate, an extended period of steady work without public celebration, toughens and inures a man to success. With adequate pre-conditioning and time to grow he can take it in stride. Young men in a hurry, overambitious to start with, who 'click' on the marketplace find it difficult to resist the ballyhoo which envelops them."

10.   *Ibid.*, pp. 194–195: "To get their work before a sizable audience, artists feel that they are forced into alien procedures; they must also accept the fact that much of their work will be acquired by aesthetically unappreciative buyers. They are elated when things go otherwise, but there is rarely any expectation that they will. Few can hold out for the 'perfect buyer.' The size of the purchasing audience often makes it difficult for the painter to know who his 'customer' is. The pervasive feeling is that the patron of yesteryear and the collector of yesterday have been replaced by a new and difficult-to-define breed of art consumers—a group whose motivations are at best suspect. Painters seem to accommodate themselves to these realities without excessive rancor. Understandably, they deplore the fact that the buying group . . . is often guided by extraneous considerations."

11.   See Chap. 1.

12.   William James, *The Principles of Psychology* (New York, Holt, 1896), pp. 221–222: "There are two kinds of knowledge broadly and practically distinguishable: we may call them respectively *knowledge of acquaintance* and knowledge-about. . . . In minds able to speak at all there is, it is true, some knowledge about

everything. Things can at least be classed, and the times of their appearance told. But in general, the less we analyze a thing, and the fewer of its relations we perceive, the less we know about it and the more our familiarity with it is of the acquaintance-type. The two kinds of knowledge are, therefore, as the human mind practically exerts them, relative terms. That is, the same thought of a thing may be called knowledge-about it in comparison with a simpler thought or acquaintance with it in comparison with a thought of it that is more articulate and explicit still." See also the development of this idea made by Robert Park in his essay, "News as a Form of Knowledge," in Everett C. Hughes, Charles S. Johnson, Jitsuichi Masouka, Robert Redfield, and Louis Wirth (Eds.), *The Collected Papers of Robert Ezra Park*, Vol. 3 (Glencoe, Ill., Free Press, 1955), p. 76: "What are here described as 'acquaintance with' and 'knowledge about' are assumed to be distinct forms of knowledge—forms having different functions in the lives of individuals and of society—rather than knowledge of the same kind but of different degrees of accuracy and validity. . . . 'Knowledge about' [is] . . . a body of tested and accredited fact and theory. . . . On the other hand, acquaintance with, as I have sought to characterize it, so far as it is based on the slow accumulation of experience and the gradual accommodation of the individual to his individual and personal world, becomes, as I have said, more and more completely identical with instinct and intuition." See also Chap. 10, "News and the Power of the Press." In journalism as in so many other areas, Park's work is as valuable as it is neglected.

13.   Karl Kraus, *Beim Wort Genommen* (Munich, Kösel-Verlag, 1955), p. 212. This and many other features of the journalistic attitude were first developed in the polemic and satirical writings of Kraus, e.g., "A historian is often just a journalist facing backwards" (p. 215).

14.   See Schutz, *op. cit.*, pp. 122–123 and 132–133.

15.   A by-product of this process is the development of a special journalistic language which conveys meaning by indirection, and by surrounding familiar words with new emotional connotations to convey meanings opposite to their traditional sense. In addition, new language, spelling, and coinages, elisions, and acronyms are invented. These debase the traditional usages of language, and introduce new forms of barbarisms. They do, however, facilitate the above-described journalistic treatment of events. See, for example, Dwight MacDonald, *Against the American Grain* (New York, Random House, 1962), pp. 12–13, and the essays, "The String Untuned," pp. 289ff, and "The Decline and Fall of English," pp. 317ff. See also Karl Kraus, *Untergang der Welt durch schwarze Magie* (Munich, Kösel-Verlag, 1960).

16.   See Joseph Bensman and Bernard Rosenberg, *Mass, Class, and Bureaucracy: The Evolution of Contemporary Society* (Englewood Cliffs, N.J., Prentice-Hall, 1963), pp. 351–354.

17.   Edmund Wilson, *To the Finland Station: A Study in the Writing and Acting of History* (Garden City, N.Y., Doubleday, 1940) (Anchor Books reprint 1953), pp. 383ff.

18.   Such practices of modern journalistic scholarship suggest the emergence of a new problem in the study of artistic and intellectual history: the fame of the ephemeral, and the obscuration of original or important work. What is visible on the surface of intellectual life and what is of lasting value are now sharply separated.

Chapter 15

The Attitude of the Intellectual

There is considerable difference of opinion among intellectuals concerning the precise definition of the term "intellectual"—who he is, what he does, and how he differs from such related types as the academician, member of the "intelligentsia," or of the "literati." In addition, there is considerable conflict concerning images of his stance toward society. To what extent is he or should he be detached or *engagé?* To what extent is he or should he be disaffiliated, alienated, or critical of society? To what extent is he necessarily a radical critic of society? Is it possible for an intellectual to be a "reactionary," a conservative, or a defender of the status quo?

These are some of the questions which are involved in the definition and discussion of the intellectual. The discussion was initiated by Karl Marx, who defined the intellectual as an alienated member of the upper classes, who because of his alienation was able to see the contradiction in his position, apply this insight to the society at large, transcend the limitations of his class origins, arrive at truth concerning society, and lead the proletariat forward by revolutionary leadership into a higher stage of societal evolution [1]. Marx's approach was elaborated, especially by Plekhanov, Trotsky, and Lenin, and the theory of intellectual as revolutionary leader became indispensable not only in justifying the revolution but in justifying the leadership of a proletarian revolution by middle class intellectuals [2].

In academic sociology, Karl Mannheim treated the intellectual in quasi-Marxist and Weberian terms as a product of societal evolution [3]. Mannheim argued that throughout world history individual intellectual bent and educational systems had produced a surplus of intellectuals, a group of highly educated, articulate, productive (of ideas) individuals who could not be rewarded by the on-going social system. The failure of the society to absorb, appreciate, reward or employ intellectuals resulted in the rejection by the intellectuals of the society that rejected them. The intellectuals became detached and disaffiliated from, and critical of, society, including

275

those classes from which they originated, and they identified themselves with classes and groups whom they perceived as equally exploited or under-rewarded by the society (and its exploiters) in which they lived. Thus the intellectual was able to free himself from the blindness of official ideology, to perceive true relationships, and to lead in the transformation of society on the basis of a newly revealed truth.

The above summation conveys three different dimensions of analysis: (1) the social and individual sources of the intellectual; (2) the social consequences of the intellectual enterprise; (3) the process of transcendence which allows the intellectual to create a particular world view, or in our terminology an intellectual attitude. Each of these dimensions, as we conceive them, can be separated analytically and treated as independent. Each dimension may be connected to the others in a variety of ways, and their combination may result in different constellations of intellectual attitudes than might be inferred from an invariant linkage of the three dimensions.

For the purposes of this essay, we will focus on the intellectual attitude, attempting to differentiate it from related attitudes and perspectives. We will then inquire into the possibility of exploring the history of the intellectual attitude as it affects and is affected by other aspects of society in terms of origins and consequences.

THE DEFINITION OF THE INTELLECTUAL ATTITUDE

First of all, we wish to differentiate the concept of the intellectual from that of the intelligentsia. The term intelligentsia, a Russian term, received world-wide currency, surrounding the discussion of alternative bases for revolution and/or reform, from the latter part of the nineteenth century up to the Russian Revolution. The term intelligentsia applies to an educated middle and upper class which concerns itself with things of the mind, social, political, and economic philosophy, and with the arts, literature, and politics. The intelligentsia is self-selected on the basis of these concerns. It regarded itself as a superior to the crass philistinism, materialism, backwardness, and provincialism of prerevolutionary Russian society. It hoped to share in all the advanced intellectual movements of European society, and was internationalist in scope, but its internationalism was Western in orientation. But the intelligentsia are primarily audiences for the intellectuals. They derive their unique stance to life by virtue of this propensity to value, absorb, and display the fruits of their intellectual consumption. To the extent that the intelligentsia were producers, they are also intellectuals. As consumers they are most interested in the intellectual product as a totality, as finished effect, in terms of how such products illuminate their lives, and produce benefits, material and ideal, for themselves and their society.

They were not primarily interested in the techniques, methods, and process of creation of intellectual products as these are applied in the act of intellectual work. These latter concerns are too narrow, technical, and disciplined for the intelligentsia as consumers. In short, the intelligentsia resembled Schutz's well-informed citizens or Weber's cultivated laymen, though classically the Russian intelligentsia were uniquely self-conscious and proud of their differences from the surrounding society, and felt that they had a mission to exemplify and disseminate the ideas of Western culture.

The intellectual may share in many (but rarely all) of the concerns of the intelligentsia. In his commitment to intellectual work, he is likely to be specialized in one or two areas of concern, and is likely to favor one or two intellectual or artistic media (the essay, the novel, journalism, politics, etc.) as the vehicles by which he articulates his thought. The intelligentsia, simply because they are primarily consumers, are free to engage equally or indiscriminately in all areas of high culture and intellectual life. They have no specialized commitment to production in any one area.

The distinction between the intellectual and the intelligentsia is ultimately based upon differences between producer and consumer within the same types of cultural activity. However, focus on production results in different levels of specialization, commitment, and, as we shall see, forms of thought about these activities.

THE LITERATI

Another distinction relevant to the definition of the intellectual is the distinction between the intellectuals and the literati. The distinction owes its currency to Max Weber's study of Confucianism in Chinese society [4]. The literati in this society are mandarins and bureaucrats concerned with mastery of the classical literary texts in order to pass examinations that qualify them for positions and promotions within bureaucracy that uses such mastery as criteria for promotion.

The literati are thus intellectual consumers of a more specialized sort than are the intelligentsia. First of all, the kinds of materials consumed are exclusively literary, though specialized codes of manners, ethics, dress, and speech all control the total behavior of the classical Chinese mandarin. Moreover, the literary materials to be mastered are prescribed and standardized by examiners into lists of classics. As a result, the work of the literati consists of the memorization of known, traditional literary classics. In this orientation, there was little room for an emphasis on modernism, innovation, or for being *au courant*, modish, or faddish. The intelligentsia value precisely these latter qualities, for social honor is bestowed when one has access to and demonstrates in prestigious intellectual circles the latest intellectual fashions shortly after they have been produced. For the intellectual engaged in the process of production, prestige derives from being able to do intellectual work, that is, to innovate within an intellectual pattern. Since innovation is valued, the traditional or classical is devalued. The literati achieved prestige, not by innovation or modernism in taste, but by mastering traditional texts and by acquiring greater ranges of knowledge.

The tradition of the mandarin presumes that the texts exist, that someone in the past has written them, that is, has done intellectual work. The intellectuals in a literati tradition may be priests or monks who are outside the bureaucratic system or literati who, becoming possessed by the intellectual aspects of their work (the meaning of the texts) lose interest in the examinations aspects of their tradition, and escape from it by doing productive, intellectual work. At some later date, the products of their work will enter into the examination system by being listed in the syllabi of prescribed texts.

The meaning of the literary orientation of the mandarin is governed by the examination system. The texts studied, while qualifying an individual for a position as tax collector, canals manager, or provincial governor, are totally unrelated to the techniques and activities needed for such positions. Presumably they qualify the official to be an educated gentleman. A government bureaucrat had to be, above all, a cultivated gentleman. But since passing the examination was a prerequisite for occupational success, mastery of the texts was required whether one was interested in their contents or not. An intrinsic interest in the text, to the extent that it caused excitement, "possession," or passion, would disqualify one from office, since these qualities are not the qualities of the gentleman. Moreover, preoccupation with the substance of a particular text beyond the necessities of the examination would result in the failure to study other texts equally necessary to passing the examination. The rhythm of examination, extending through the total aspiring life of the mandarin thus serves to devalue intellectual *work* as creative activity. Beyond this, intellectual activity is only a means to other ends which are independent of the activity itself. To consider the content of the text as intrinsically meaningful in such a system would be equivalent to treating the means as ends. The fact that texts did exist suggests that a considerable number of scholars did make the kind of error that made the system possible.

From the standpoint of the bureaucrat, however, intellectual activity did not consist of either the enjoyment of avant-garde ideas and culture or the aesthetics of the production of such ideas and culture. It was totally pragmatic within the narrow framework of a system of bureaucratic promotion and preferment. From the standpoint of "social functions," the examination system was important in limiting the power of landlords, warlords, and the emperor.

THE ACADEMIC VERSUS THE INTELLECTUAL ATTITUDES

The academic attitude is similar to the attitude of the literati in that it is professionalized. The academic attitude is a subvariant of the scientific attitude. Like the scientific attitude, it emphasizes the self-conscious, methodologically explicit formulation of rules of work and procedure within the framework of a narrowly defined academic field [5]. Several aspects of the academic attitude are of interest to us here. First of all, since the decline of humanism, the academic man increasingly narrows the area of his specializations by the division and subdivision of his field. This is especially true since the middle of the nineteenth century. He accomplishes this not only by the politics of jurisdictional division within the university, but by creating a "culture" of academic and occupational specialization.

This culture consists, among other things, of the development of specialized concepts and definitions which are so dense in texture, so abstract and removed from the ordinary use of language, that they are not understandable by the intelligent, educated layman, "the well-informed citizen" [6]. Advanced graduate training in these concepts, among other things, qualifies one in the use of these definitions and concepts. As a result, each field creates a vocabulary, a rhetoric, and too often a grammar, that is relevant only to that field. Some unkind critics have called such linguistic inventions "jargon," and have gone so far as too claim that they add nothing but a species of "brand differentiation" which gives the field unique claims to prestige, income, and jobs.

Whether this is true or not depends on whether the field adds anything to our knowledge or ability to do worthwhile things that otherwise could not be done. Whether or not the field is linguistically self-enclosed, to prove its usefulness, it must be translated into insights and knowledge that can be understood or demonstrated to intelligent laymen. If the field has meaning only to its practitioners, there is a high probability that it has no meaning. Thus, linguistic specialization and density do not by themselves prove that a field is useless.

In the same sense, a specialized academic field, like all specialized fields, will employ specialized techniques, equipment, habits of mind, and will do work that in its own terms may appear to be inaccessible to outsiders but that permits useful work to be done.

Correlative with the development of overspecialization is the development (often by the same men) of generalizers or idea-mongers who seek to offer syntheses and world views of a shallow superficiality. Their acceptance is often based on the reputations these men have made as specialists.

In the artistic and scientific attitudes, the effect of the work is to create images of the world in the process of pursuing the work. The critical attitude explains to the nonscientific or nonartistic consumer how the artistic or scientific worker created the works whose methodology is embodied in the work itself. The critical attitude and much of the academic attitude, we have asserted, attempt this explanation without adding any substantive elaboration of the world images that are the inputs to criticism. In short, criticism is a form of reduction from the work itself into a world of criticism and academicisms, which substitutes itself for the work from which it derives its subject matter and its reason for being [7].

At any rate, the academic attitude is narrow, technical, and geared to teaching students or laymen how work is done. In addition, the preoccupation with methodology and technique leads to an attitude of scientific neutrality or detachment from values other than the value of the science itself. In order to analyze scientifically and objectively the work under discussion, it is necessary to suspend consideration of the values of the creator, and to consider the work as logic, technique, or method. Even the values of the creator are accepted, for the moment, as given, in order to ascertain how these values are worked out in the work under discussion. This suspension of evaluation can later itself be suspended, but the judgment of the work as technique is, ideally, always independent of the judgment of the values contained in the work. Whether academicians, scientists, and critics are always able to maintain such objectivity is open to question. Whether they should is open to debate. Ideologically committed intellectuals within the academic community deplore the value-neutrality of scientists who, in their value-neutrality, do scientific and technical work for immoral business men and immoral governments because the value-neutral scientists do not enquire into the values of their sponsors. At the same time, the moral ideologies take the supremacy of their own values for granted, and the morally superior ideologue may in some circumstances employ ethically neutral or morally committed scientists to implement his values [8]. Thus, the Nazis and the Communists, with attitudes of moral superiority, were able to accomplish, on their own moral grounds, what ideologues decry as value-neutrality. Neither commitment to science nor commitment to higher values by itself guarantees moral superiority. It is rather the personal values of individual men in their own historical circumstances which allow for the achievement of a moral life. Moral ukases imposed upon others by the ideologically overcommitted are more likely to result in death and destruction than is the value-neutrality of the scientist.

Against this background it is possible to understand the intellectual attitude. First of all, the intellectual decries narrow specialization. He is, or aspires to be, a "renaissance man." Art, literature, politics, philosophy, the whole world of ideas and culture, are his oyster. Hans Speier, perhaps in despair of the academic man, has defined the intellectual as a man who reads books in fields other than his own. The intellectual may be an academician, but his audience is one consisting of the intelligentsia, other intellectuals, and the cultivated layman. He eschews the specialized jargon, the methodologies, and procedures of his academic specialty, and regards the well-written sentence, the apt image, and a general penetration of humanist knowledge in his work as a hallmark of intellectual authenticity. He is likely to look down his nose at the barbarisms in the language of his academic peers, their pedantry and ignorance of nonprofessional materials, and considers that their lack of culture condemns them to a lower order of existence. Conversely, the intellectual in an academic environment is likely to be regarded as technically deficient in the methodologies of his field, as an amateur and a charlatan because he writes intelligibly for laymen, and as an intellectual snob who uses his reputation among educated laymen to compensate for his lack of technical qualification.

The intellectual differs from the academician in his attitude to value-neutrality. Regardless of his particular set of values, he feels it essential to express his values in his work. Scientific detachment and objectivity, in the sense of value-neutrality, are alien to the intellectual attitude. The intellectual believes in the supremacy of the "things of the mind," though particular intellectuals will define those things differently. Some may devalue music or the plastic arts as being insufficiently logical, discursive, and literal, and therefore as an escape from direct, logical, literal analysis [9]. (Thus, Freud could not understand, and did not like music.) Others will view the arts as an escape from the analysis of reality. Others will discover literary values in the arts, and thus translate these art forms into literary forms. Finally, a few like Susan Sontag and Marshall McLuhan will use literary techniques to attack literary values in the defense of nonliterary media [10].

One cannot exalt a particular set of values without exalting implicitly the bearers of those values. Nor can one describe a set of optimal societal processes without affirming the society that contains these processes or the groups or classes rewarded by them, and the values affirmed by these groups or bearers. In this sense all "scientific" social science, as well as scientific socialism (or scientific conservatism) are permeated with values. Value-neutrality thus does not mean being free of values, but only means being able to separate the means from the ends, in order to analyze the relationship between them [11].

The intellectual thus often makes little pretense at being objective. In fact, indifference toward values would be a denial of his task. If we then analyze the relationship between the various aspects of the intellectual attitude, we can arrive at an image of its formal nature.

The intellectual creates, presents, and disseminates an image of the world that denies or affirms ultimate values. He does this in terms of media that, being nontechnical, are immediately perceptible to reasonably intelligent laymen, and include a wide variety of literary, cultural, and artistic forms. His skill at communications is thus a central aspect of his activity. He not only creates images of values, but disseminates them throughout society or to publics that may be crucial to society. As a result, intellectuals are important far beyond their number. They can be valued as propagandists, public relations experts, or ideologists for a particular class or group, or they can be denounced as traitors, class enemies, as destroyers of society, or as impediments to the realization of other values. But whatever they are, they cannot be taken for granted, for in the long run they alter or confirm the total shape, goals, and structure of society and of human life.

THE "ENGAGEMENT" OF THE INTELLECTUAL

In the light of the above, it can be seen that the intellectual, because of his commitment to value positions, is always *engagé*. Whether he likes it or not, or is conscious of it or not, he is engaged in the transvaluation of society, or in resisting such transvaluation. This fundamental stance is in the long run more important than whether he is writing political pamphlets, or whether he is actively distributing leaflets, haranguing the masses, or storming the barricades. Intellectual work itself is a form of engagement which operates whether or not the intellectual engages in other forms of activity. Political activists, organizers, and propagandists frequently decry the detachment of intellectuals from the organizational work of party politics. Their criticism of detached intellectualism may be more a case of professional self-justification than a criticism of lack of attachment. Critics of intellectual detachment see political activity exclusively in terms of party and organization politics. The intellectual, however, pursues politics by the definition of values, the articulation of ideals, goals, programs and the criticism of these programs when presented by intellectuals of opposing camps. These intellectual activities may be as "practical" or more so than organizational activities themselves.

But the words "detachment" and "engagement" each have more than one set of meanings [12]. We have written of them with regard to values, ideas, and ideologies. But the idea of detachment and engagement have relevance to the historical world, to "society" as it manifests itself in concrete empirical forms. Here, detachment and engagement refer to social distance. The intellectual as image-maker treats empirical reality, society, and culture, as an object for his analysis. He is engaged in describing real and mythical worlds, and in the process he describes either explicitly or implicitly the world he perceives, as a point of reference for comparison with the world he describes. In order to analyze that empirical reality, he is obliged to put distance between himself and that reality. He must conceive of "reality" as a thing apart from himself, or he has no vantage point, no platform, from which to describe and analyze it. If there is no distance between him and the world, the assumptions, values, and understandings that make up empirical reality become part of his unconscious habits of thought, his "attitude" of everyday life. He lives them, acts them out. But if he does only this, he is not an intellectual. The process of becoming self-conscious about values, and about the locus of values in a world, implies that the intellectual can conceive of values and of the world, as abstractions removed from himself. Being so, they are separate, distant from himself, and because he recognizes this, he is alienated from both values and the world, simply because he does not take them for granted. At a phenomenological level, his self-conscious commitment to ultimate values serves as a platform by which he separates himself from the world. For if the intellectual attaches himself to ultimate values, he inevitably realizes that finite, empirical reality at least provides an approximation of the best of all possible worlds, and at most a denial of those values. Thus, the intellectual may be separated from the world in two ways: (1) he is separated from it as an object of his consciousness, and (2) as a vehicle in which his values are achieved or not achieved.

But in both senses he is separated from the world and becomes aware of his separation. In one sense he is separated from the world because he disapproves of it; in the other sense, he is separated from it despite the fact that he approves of it. In both cases he is detached from it, despite the fact that he is attached to values and engaged in political, social, and ideological activity.

Should the engagement in political, social, and administrative activities become so total that the intellectual takes his values for granted (or loses his self-consciousness of them) or accepts the framework of political activities so completely that he becomes an object to his party or organization, and loses his consciousness of the world or party as a thing apart from himself, he ceases to be an intellectual. This is no crime. But the intellectual, to the extent that he values intellectual activity, preserves a part of himself from this involvement, and the activity itself as related to his commitment to activity and the values that evoked the commitment. If he fails in this regard he becomes a party hack, a bureaucrat, a journalist, a careerist, a narrow professional, a creation of his world, rather than an evaluator of the world. He loses his sense of detachment.

THE ORIGINS OF THE INTELLECTUAL ATTITUDE

The intellectual is defined as a creator or destroyer of world images who performs these functions on the basis of an intense commitment to values, but who is detached from society by the very nature of his attempt. He creates images, not in terms of narrow, technical, and objective professional ideologies, but rather on the basis of general, "amateurish," holistic, non-technical means, vocabularies, and styles. His audience consists of other intellectuals and educated laymen, and he attempts to be understood in their terms. He values generalized cultivated expression (but not as an end in itself—he is not an aesthete), rather than the narrow specialization of science or careerism.

But the definition of the intellectual attitude does not by itself tell us much about the origins of intellectuals or about the intellectual attitude, nor does it tell us much about its consequences. Moreover, it tells very little about the role of the intellectual in history. Here Marxism is important for having defined the issue although it has not resolved it. Marx, as well as Mannheim, defines the intellectual as deriving his world image from his relationship to the means of production. His consciousness is determined by his existence, and the conditions of his existence are determined by his class origins, in relation to income, wealth, the market, and his freedom to dispose of and withhold his labor from the labor market. His ideology reflects class interests as well as a class-bound social horizon. The free intellectual transcends his class position by developing self-consciousness concerning his relations to the means of production and all that is implied by it. Contradictions within his class position and between class position and ideology impose themselves upon his consciousness in such a way as to make it impossible for him to accept his class position as a basis for his ideology, and forces him to reconstruct one free from class bias. Thus, most free intellectuals are held to come from the upper, favored classes, or from lower class individuals who encounter ideological exposure and training at the hands of alienated upper- or middle-class intellectuals.

ALIENATION AND CREATIVITY

The argument is persuasive, but there are difficulties: Only a small proportion of the favored class are "class-alienated." Others who are alienated may be so in nonintellectualized ways. Such alienation may take the form of neurosis, psychosis, despair, alcoholism, or the pursuit of pleasure. To understand why intellectual alienation may occur is a separate problem from that of the discovery of alienation. Furthermore, we have argued that in the sense that the intellectual attitude involves the development of detachment from society and attachment to values, a conservative or reactionary ideologist may well be both intellectual and alienated. A theory of the intellectual must explain this phenomenon as well as that of radical intellectualism.

It is quite clear that alienation in its psychiatric sense, and in the sense that it involves the quality of separating oneself from one's immediate environment is not connected with class. The capacity for alienation lies within the framework of the very processes of the maturation and growth of the individual. For in the process of socialization, the individual at a very early age is forced to surrender some of his instinctual energy, demands, or drives in order to achieve the sustenance, warmth, and love which are offered as a condition for meeting parental demands [13]. If the demands are severe, and presented at a very early age, psychosis or the extreme repression of instinctual life is possible. If no demands are made, the individual is likely to become a psychopath or, in sociological terminology, a sociopath, that is, he internalizes no restraints. If, however, strong demands are made but accompanied with love, warmth, and affirmation, the individual will surrender some of his instinctual demands, but will resent or be ambivalent to those who force him to accept these demands. Moreover, he will resent the surrender of part of himself in order to gain a new, socially approved self. Out of his resentment, he will construct alternative worlds of play, of fantasy, of imagination, which exist as alternatives to the "real" world. If the demands of reality are too strong, the individual, as he matures, will repress all fantasy and imagination, and become an automaton. If these demands are overrepressive, and not accompanied by warmth, the individual may retreat into a fantasy world through psychosis. Alternatively, the individual, as he matures, may stylize his imagination by playing socially defined games or sports, drama, or humor. Because such activities are defined as being outside the realm of serious life, they are permitted, and serve to channelize the energy "left over" in the process of socialization. If the individual does not accept these forms of social stylization, his imagination seeks other channels of expression.

But these forms of stylization of the imagination are not determined by the fact of alienation itself. For some individuals the form may be wit, humor, and the free play of disguised hostility; for others it may be rebellion, expressed as negativism or as satire or poking fun at the overdemanding society and its representatives. For others, this form of rejection of the "real" world may take the form of creating alternative and perhaps more comfortable worlds. These newly created worlds may disguise the rejected world by the very act of creation.

The media for the construction of such alternative worlds may be words, pictures, sounds, or the fashioning of objects, or it may be a rearrangement of social structures in the forms of games and play. The particular forms depend upon the biological makeup of the individual, his talent and facility, trial and error, and on the social and cultural resources made available to him.

The social and cultural resources may be, from the standpoint of the individual, "accidental," or they may be determined by his social class or position. They are accidental in the sense that the individual meets adult others who affirm, discipline, and stylize the forms and media of imagination. A parent, a teacher or an older adult can, if available, recognize the creative aspect in fantasy and play, appreciate it as an affirmative phenomenon, demonstrate that the purely individual activity is linked to an established cultural style, artistic or intellectual medium, and may teach him the objective forms, styles, and techniques which organize and discipline the diffused and random subjective reactions which are the bases for these objective forms. Once the individual enters the social and cultural worlds of intellectual, artistic, scientific activity, he creates and re-creates the world in terms of these traditions. He may re-create the traditions by adding his unique, subjective insight to them, or he may fail because of difficulties in mastering the objective techniques. Or, the demands of "reality," that is, nonartistic or nonintellectual life, may be too strong.

Whether he succeeds or not, the possibility of intellectual and artistic creativity emerges from the linkage between subjective fantasy and objective, on-going intellectual and artistic traditions. This linkage is accidental in that the potentially creative individual may not happen to be exposed to the other who helps him to confirm and objectify his creative fantasy. It is also accidental in that the kinds of support given may be too weak to offset the demands of mere reality.

THE AUTONOMY OF INTELLECTUAL LIFE

An analysis of social class is a necessary but insufficient condition for explaining the rise of the intellectual. It is based on the assumption that prior circumstances and the process of socialization create the opportunity for a kind of alienation or separation that allows the intellectual to become detached from his immediate life circumstances as a merely natural, taken-for-granted framework of assumptions which govern his perception of the world. This process of detaching oneself is confirmed and strengthened by the acceptance of the literary and artistic and intellectual traditions which make up the medium, art, or style, which he seeks to master. To the extent that one is an intellectual, artist, or scientist, and is immersed in the techniques, theories, methodologies, culture, and social activities appropriate to his field of interest, one is less than what one might have been, were it not for the immersion. The new viewpoints, values, sensibilities, and interests may be alien from those one has abandoned, and this distance is, among other things, a distance from one's class of origin. But such distance does not mean necessarily that one becomes a self-conscious critic or antagonist to that former life, in the sense of being a radical. One may, as an intellectual, affirm the values of bourgeois or aristocratic life, or, in a communist society, of communist life, while being separated from the matter-of-factness of these respective lives due to the social distance of one's intellectual position.

Thus, De Maistre and De Bonald were intellectuals, yet reactionaries; Burke, Disraeli, De Tocqueville, and John Adams were intellectuals yet conservatives; Alfred Rosenberg, Goebbels, and Mussolini were intellectuals, yet fascists, and Max Lerner and Daniel Moynihan are intellectuals, and liberals. An intellectual orientation does not by itself predispose one to a particular political philosophy. Much more is necessary to explain such tendencies.

Given this mosaic of intellectual traditions, it is difficult to account in general for the sources of appeal of various intellectual traditions, or of their relationship to social origins. In fact, the relationship of the individual to a tradition is "accidental." It is determined by the visibility and accessibility of an intellectual sect to an individual. In part, the connection of individual to sect reflects personal taste, talent, and harmony between origins and intellectual tradition. But to a greater extent it reflects the relationship of intellectual traditions to the non-intellectual society and to audiences.

THE INTELLECTUAL AND SOCIAL STRUCTURE

Even though the origins of an intellectual attitude may be found in the peculiarities of the individual's response to his situation of socialization, to class origins, and to the qualities of intellectual preoccupations and traditions, the intellectual is never able to erase a living connection to his society at large, or to particular aspects that become relevant to him. Among other things, he needs a minimum economic connection to that society to be able to live. Moreover, the amenities of life are often attractive to intellectuals. This being the case, intellectuals must make some provisions to come to minimal terms with some segments of their society.

Those intellectuals who are independently wealthy may not feel the same economic pressures to get respectable jobs, to manage family businesses, or to participate in more valued activities and life styles. The blandishments of alternative opportunities quite frequently turn would-be intellectuals into dilettantes, though it is not unusual for a Marx and Engels, a Corliss Lamont, a Maurice Baring, a Lord Russell, to become full-time, serious intellectuals despite family pressures. In the same way, Hans von Bulow, Mendelssohn, Stravinsky, Berthe Morisot, and Cezanne, after a struggle, affirmed their art or music, despite family pressures.

For the less favored, other kinds of accommodation are necessary. These forms of accommodation are of two kinds. The first involves the aggregate demand for intellectual work by society, and the second involves the origins of that demand. As we have indicated, the supply of intellectuals at minimal levels is independent of demand; that is, the supply is determined by intrinsic interests, talents, and psychological predispositions toward intellectual work. The demand is determined by the felt need for intellectual work. The intellectual product which makes intellectual work marketable is the ability of the intellectual to manufacture symbols, create or disseminate ideologies, and to train or educate individuals in these qualities. The market for intellectual work is thus determined by the extent a society in question consumes symbols. In the past, the level of development of the society was so low that primary rather than intellectual production was rewarded in the marketplace. The level of literacy was low and the educated, cultivated minority was so small that there was only a small market for the output of intellectual activity. Intellectual work was poorly rewarded, on the basis either of prestige, income, or power. Intellectuals were thus aware of the fact that society rejected their values, their work, and their claims to the importance of their work.

In the same way, the peculiar talents of intellectuals have resulted in their employment by princes, emperors, and other political figures. They have been employed as scribes, administrators, and as lawyers, advisors, and as apologists, mythmakers, soothsayers, and prophets of good fortune. They have been instruments by which rulers can free themselves from depending on their feudal vassals, whose administrative talents were based on personal and military, rather than on educational qualities.

Intellectuals as state functionaries have always served as means to the centralization of dynastic or state power, and the weakening of local, decentralized feudal administration. As mythmakers, intellectuals have created ideologies for state and dynasty, while other, unattached intellectuals were creating counterideologies for antistate groups.

The third major traditional source of intellectual occupations has been education. Literacy and access to received knowledge have made education the major source of employment for intellectuals. The social consequences have not been unambiguous. Parents have most often wanted their children to acquire skills and knowledge to use in and grace adult life, but they have not wanted their children to take education too seriously. Nor have they wanted their children to be exposed to ideas that were hostile to their own values, way of life, and institutions. Educational administrators have often been forced to assure parents that education would not conflict with traditional values. Intellectuals in education, however, have not always agreed. Moreover, the fact that youth has frequently not been absorbed into adult institutions, reinforces and confirms the impulse of intellectuals in education to detach themselves from the values of professional educators of the society at large, and of the parents of their students.

Education, until it is totally de-intellectualized, contains within it the seeds for both detachment from and discontent with the society at large. Moreover, the intellectual as academician serves to exemplify and demonstrate the value of intellectual life to students, and to recruit neophyte intellectuals to their community. The solution to the problem of the conflict between intellectuals and traditional or academic education is to employ academicians rather than intellectuals as teachers.

The interpenetration of academic and intellectual "functions" causes difficulties. Intellectuals can respond either to the intellectual or to academic aspects of the teaching role. As our society has been more and more bureaucratized, formal academic training, qualification, and academic productivity have been stressed. Academicians have increasingly replaced intellectuals as teachers, and as intellectuals have been co-opted into the university, the quality of their thought has increasingly become academic. Intellectuals in academic positions, if they wish to remain intellectuals are increasingly forced to resist the academicism of their environments, usually by developing an intellectual life away from the campus.

As formal higher education has grown to mass dimensions, it has penetrated into areas of culture which previously had been occupied by intellectuals, the arts, and the sciences. Once drawn into the academic orbit, these areas have in turn been academicized. As a result, academic attitudes have grown, all too often at the expense of intellectual, or artistic, or scientific attitudes.

When the university, for public relations reasons, employs a conspicuously successful intellectual as artist-in-residence, the relationship is reversed. These are usually temporary relationships which often are celebrated by a literary or intellectual attack, in writing, on the sterility of academic life.

In considering the three classic forms of intellectual employment together, we can conclude that as intellectuals enter the institutional life of society, they begin to take over some of the attitudes that originate in the needs, interests, and class positions of these new statuses. Intellectuals who are not so co-opted retain some of the autonomous attitudes of intellectual life itself. Thus, the intellectual world fragments itself.

But even when co-opted, the intellectual rarely simply "reflects" the perspective of his position. In some instances, merely by articulating his position he raises to self-consciousness the implicit assumptions of his fixed position. He may weaken these positions by disenchanting them, or he may strengthen them by giving systematic, literate articulation, and energy to these assumptions. In the extreme case, he may develop the implicit assumptions of his position until the point is reached that causes a total revolution within the institution (as did Jesus, Luther, Calvin, Marx, Lenin, Trotsky). Another resolution is found in an uneasy tension between intellectual and occupational position, which can result in malaise, guilt, irony, exposes, on the one hand, or the surrender of intellectual pretensions to new occupational perspectives, on the other hand (with or without additional forms of self-devaluation or justification).

Given these various possibilities, even in a relatively simple society, the intellectual life of a community is likely to be fragmented, reflecting not only the plurality of intellectual positions, but all of the combinations of attitudes that reflect the adjustment of intellectuals to co-optation.

In a more advanced society, the fragmentation of the intellectual world is almost infinitely wider.

THE INTELLECTUAL AND THE BOURGEOISIE

Since the demand for intellectual products is a function of the level of development of a society, the slow but increasing rate of the development of life at the end of the feudal period began to alter both the supply and the demand for intellectuals. The rise of new classes, especially of the bourgeoisie and the associated rise in wealth for artistic, cultural, and intellectual consumption, stimulated by a rise in education among both the bourgeoisie, and the petty nobility, created new markets for intellectual work. The secular patron of arts and letters began to "compete" with the church, and the courts of sovereigns and petty princes became the scene of a rich competitive intellectual and artistic life [14]. Princes sought to be recognized as artists and intellectuals, they corresponded with and employed intellectuals, and intellectuals became the companions of kings.

The rise of the absolute state provided an increasing number of jobs for intellectuals in the state civil services, and a large number of intellectuals shifted their perspectives from that of the intellectual to that of the bureaucrat. As education became valued, intellectuals were increasingly employed as tutors of the young of both the secular aristocracy and the wealthy bourgeoisie. In these situations, they received the opportunity to "study" the life of the upper classes, and endured the slights and high-handedness of their social superiors. They responded, in part, by beginning to portray the life at court or in the home of their lords. Beaumarchais, for one, portrayed the decadence, immorality, and arrogance of his lordly superiors, and showed the superiority, resourcefulness, and the resentment of the picaresque servant. In fact, a whole genre of literary, artistic, and philosophical works in the period of the Enlightenment and the Baroque and Romantic eras was aimed at exposing, satirizing, or opposing, bourgeois and lordly patrons.

In the past, such opposition could be the product of an increased self-evaluation by self-conscious intellectuals and artists, who despite patronage were exposed to the condescension and arbitrariness of their patrons. In part, the very factors which increased the demand for intellectuals increased the supply. The growth of the bourgeoisie, and the increasing opportunities for both education and culture, made it possible for a larger and larger number of the bourgeoisie and the aristocracy to be available for seduction by the intellectual life. While the demand for intellectual work increased, the supply of intellectual workers increased at an even greater rate.

Through almost the whole of the modern era, with few exceptions, there was an oversupply of intellectuals. The system of secular patronage was unorganized. It was subject to the whims and vanities of patrons, full of the possibility of humiliation and dismissal. Even when not so, the system was inadequate to employ the host of intellectuals who because of their attachment to valued activities felt they deserved a better fate. The growth of opportunities for intellectuals created a "revolution of rising expectations" that was larger than the rise in opportunities. The intellectuals allied themselves predominantly with and became ideologists for the bourgeoisie. They aided in the bourgeois revolutions of the eighteenth and nineteenth centuries, becoming democratic ideologists. Other intellectuals were employed as servants of the *ancien régime* or as members of the aristocracies who served the régime on purely ideological bases. At a later date substantial numbers of intellectuals who arose from the bourgeoisie and the petty aristocracy turned against the bourgeoisie and became ideologists for socialism, communism, anarchism, and later, fascism.

The numbers of intellectuals increased continuously well into the nineteenth century, as did the numbers of intelligentsia who constituted their audiences. This increase made it possible for intellectuals to form social circles of their own, salons, residential sections and quarters, and cliques. In some cases, the bourgeoisie, or rather their wives, provided centers in which the intellectuals gathered and intermingled with their clients. In other cases they provided the funds for intellectuals to create journals, newspapers and reviews, and in still other cases they employed intellectuals as journalists on newspapers and periodicals, whose character was not predominantly intellectual.

The rise of the newspaper and the political pamphlet, as early as the eighteenth century, provided an opportunity for the co-optation of intellectuals as journalists and confirmed the literary character of the intellectual enterprise. The rise of mass political parties from the end of the eighteenth century to the nineteenth century provided opportunities for intellectuals as journalists, agitators, and organizers. Intellectual organizers created their own opportunities by organizing the parties which served to provide occasional and long-term employment for themselves and their followers. Intellectuals became attached to the expanding universities where, as staff members, many became co-opted into the academic world. Many others, especially the students, organized intellectual circles and revolutionary cells and clubs of all types.

Thus, throughout the nineteenth and well into the twentieth century, the worlds of the intellectuals flowered and expanded [15]. The varieties were enormous. Some were self-consciously intellectual, others served as leaders, energizing political groups and parties and still others served as technicians, journalists, and educators for established groups whose values were not primarily intellectual.

Intellectuals embraced all spheres of values in society, representing and articulating every point of view and confronting each other as ideological opponents. Moreover, since they had special skills, they did more than represent or reflect points of view; they created them. The intellectual trained in symbol manipulation was able to understand the logic, interest, and aspirations of his clients. He also attempted to understand the historical, political, and economic evolution of his society. He attempted to define these trends and pointed to their implications for the future of his clientele. He thus defined their interests, their enemies, and suggested the programs, the slogans, the strategy and tactics for their realization. In doing so, he helped (though he need not have intended it) to define a need and market for his continuous and increasingly valued services.

They advanced the internal development of purely intellectual theory, subjecting past theory to a critical scrutiny, discovering and attempting to correct contradictions in past intellectual output, and attempting to reconcile intellectual theories with on-going events. They revised, modified, and substituted theories, and created new ones in an endless process. The ferment of intellectual activity in the nineteenth and early twentieth centuries does not prove the correctness of such theories, but it indicates its increasing importance both internally and as related to leadership and to the definition of non-intellectual trends.

THE SELF-HATRED OF THE INTELLECTUAL

An interesting, but of necessity briefly treated aspect of the rise of intellectual self-consciousness in the nineteenth century, is the concomitant rise of intellectual self-hatred. In the seventeenth and eighteenth centuries, intellectual rationalists believed that the intervention of reason in human affairs could solve the problems of superstition, ignorance, tyranny, war, and the failure of men to control their social relations. With the triumph of reason as represented by the French Revolution and the reforms of 1832, 1848, and the 1870's, they found that wars, tyranny, nationalism, revolution, ignorance, and violence had not decreased. Moreover, intellectuals were pitted against intellectuals in acrimonious debates that were often as irrational as those they inveighed against. They found that reason was often sterile, empty, devoid of content, and that the values they were attached to had been reasoned out of existence. Some intellectuals began an intellectual attack on reason. They rediscovered God, they discovered myth, and attempted to create myths. They discovered the emotions, and intellectually attempted to induce deep emotionality. They discovered violence as a means to myth and emotion, as well as sexual adventurism, sadism, war, and revolution. They glorified at times the mystical unity achieved with others in God, in war, in revolutionary activity, in mythic communities of blood and honor, and in sex, heterosexual and homosexual, normal and perverse.

But most of all they discovered action. For in action they could suspend their doubts, their sense of alienation, and their frustration with reason. As a result, they added some permanent features of the modern intellectual attitude: anti-intellectualism, or intellectual self-hatred.

Anti-intellectualism has remained a permanent feature of the intellectual attitude, but it takes many forms, some of which are disguised. From the beginning of the nineteenth century onward, the intellectual tradition was permeated with continuously evolving styles of anti-intellectualism, which in part fed into a tradition in which intellectuals could easily jump the gap from advocacy to severest criticism of intellectual activities, whenever being an intellectual became difficult. The anti-intellectual, despite his position, remained an intellectual.

The one constant in all of this period is the relative oversupply of intellectuals, relative even to the increasing demand. This oversupply tended, despite all processes of co-options, to throw the preponderant direction of intellectual thought into the camp of the enemies of the "establishment." Intellectuals were predominantly both intellectual and social outsiders. As a result, they became identified with democratic, reformist, revolutionary, and even reactionary political activities, who, from a variety of positions reject the "norms" of established society.

This situation persisted up until the end of World War II in most of the world. Before that time, the Social Democratic Party and trade unions in Germany co-opted intellectuals into their bureaucracies, and, in part domesticated them. The Russian Revolution resulted in the co-optation of vast numbers of intellectuals, reducing them either to puppets or bureaucrats [16]. Those whom the Revolution could not control, it purged, imprisoned, or silenced. The success of the intellectuals as propagandists and as ideologists led to the death of intellectual activity itself, and to the murder of intellectuals, all too frequently by exintellectuals. The same phenomena were repeated in Nazi Germany and Fascist Italy, as later in Eastern Europe, and continue to occur in Communist China.

After World War II, a new phase in the history of the social framework for intellectual life began. Up until this period, the dominant fact determining the conditions for intellectual life was the oversupply of intellectuals. After World War II, in the United States and in many of the Western European countries, the dominant fact was the increased desire and the ability of established society to appreciate, use, and employ intellectuals in their own institutions [17].

Such changes on the part of established institutions, in the most general sense, are related to the cumulative effects of economic development of the respective societies. Society produces material well-being and the luxury which allows for the employment of intellectuals in secondary, tertiary, and higher forms of employment. The increased production of "services," as separate from concrete, physical objects and products is part of the trend. As a result, opportunities exist for intellectuals working alongside of trained professionals in the following areas:

1. *Mass Media*: Television, radio, advertising, mass journalism and the specialized journalism of smaller papers and magazines aimed at variegated specialized professional and cultural audiences. These include public relations work, both in public relations firms, and as employees and consultants to government and private organizations.

2. *Entertainment*: As managers, impresarios, performers, critics, and publicists.

3. *Management*: As civil servants, and managerial technocrats, either in private, public, or nonprofit bureaucracies, including trade unions and foundations.

4. *Research*: As researchers in all of the bureaucratic institutions and in philanthropic agencies.

5. *Advisors*: As advisors to all these institutions.

6. *Education*: As academicians and teachers.

Moreover, intellectual attitudes have entered into a wide variety of occupations which are not necessarily intellectual. Thus, psychiatrists, social workers, mathematicians, physicists, performing musicians, among others, are likely to be ex-intellectuals, or to be currently infected with the intellectual disease.

Because of these opportunities, intellectuals are often able to earn respectable incomes, they are appreciated and rewarded, and are promoted in the nonintellectual world. The results of this unique situation are manifold. As previously indicated, the intellectual world is fragmented into an uncountable number of subworlds. Moreover, many of these subworlds are characterized by ideologies, habits of thought, and interests of the new worlds into which intellectuals are co-opted. In the extreme case, intellectuals cease to be intellectual, and become creatures of the institutions to which they are attached. But when they do so, they bring into these new worlds the habits of mind, the self-consciousness, and the skills in analysis and image-making characteristic of them. As a result, they disturb, by their self-consciousness, their new worlds at the same time that they help their employers to make their particular bureaucracies more effective.

Intellectuals in such situations suffer guilt, become ironical, and develop defenses, some of which result in further disenchantment of the worlds they participate in. Others achieve an overaffirmation of the institutions to which they now belong. In part, these are problems of transition. But when they cease to be problems of transition, intellectuals will cease to be intellectuals, and become functionaries.

The overall result of co-optation has been to place intellectuals in an uneasy position with respect to their own past. For the traditional position of intellectuals, of being rejected by their society, has resulted in a traditional response of rejecting their society. The acceptance of the intellectuals by their society has undermined a major social support of the intellectual attitude. But many intellectuals have proved able to surmount these difficulties. After World War II, an increasing number of intellectuals have, in addition to being ideologists for specific institutions and groups, become ideologists for society at large. Unkind intellectuals called this group "celebrationists" "sell-outs" and apologists. Whether this is merely name-calling or not is perhaps irrelevant. But what is true is that individuals who in the past were radicals, revolutionaries, and leftist reformers, increasingly found this the best of all possible worlds. The United States in the sixties was proclaimed to be increasingly democratic, or as democratic as a mass society can be. All groups were claimed to be represented in the decision-making process, even when decision-making was controlled by bureaucratic elites. The competition of elites assured representation of all groups. Social mobility, under new definitions, was seen to be on the increase, and the intellectuals its chief beneficiaries [18]. Pluralism guaranteed the cultural autonomy of all groups, and voluntaristic activity enabled any interested, active, constructive, and energetic individual to reach leadership positions. The failure to do so was, by implication, a result of lack of ability or lack of effort, and was therefore justified. The mass society was so large, fragmented, and multidimensional that political action must occur under the domination of the mass media and large bureaucratic organizations, dominated by intellectual elite groups. But the mass media and mass bureaucracies were considered essentially democratic, because their survival depended upon acceptance by the masses. The cultural tone and level of modern society has been improving, as more and more individuals began to enter the middle-class, cultured worlds. Income in the Western world was becoming more evenly distributed. Urban life was better than in the past, despite the claims of alarmists. And finally, these ideologists an intellectuals announced the end of ideology. Pragmatism, the specific solution of specific problems by an interested public and by trained technicians, became the substitute for the scarcity-based ideologies of the past. The new ideology became the ideology for the managerial technocrats, the bureaucratic elites—whose ideology is that of having no ideology. The world belongs to those who manage it.

But this ideology of defining a future world, evaluating it positively, and then by implication suggesting the groups necessary to reward to make the system work, is precisely what all ideologies of the past have done. The new intellectuals were constructing their own ideologies, but they are doing so by both redefining themselves, and remaking themselves, into bureaucratic and technocratic leaders. If they were to succeed, however, they would do so by ceasing to project themselves as, or be considered as, intellectuals.

REACTIONS AGAINST BUREAUCRATIC CO-OPTATION

The bureaucratization of society has depended upon the co-optation of vast numbers of individuals who, in other times, might have become intellectuals. For the first time in the history of the world, in the United States at least, there was immediately after World War II no oversupply of intellectuals. Intellectuals became apologists for the system, technicians, ideologists, and publicists. In violation of all previous experience, this did not produce a dominant climate of intellectual acceptance of the system. A part of the second generation of post-World War II intellectuals rejected entirely the compromises and ideologies of their parents. Moreover, they appeared to reject intellectual activity altogether. In part, this revolution is based on the prosperity of the intellectual as parent, and the easy life of the would-be intellectual as child. The second generation of intellectuals were primarily the children of university-trained intellectuals, bureaucrats, experts, the new middle classes. They were raised in an atmosphere of affluence and in an atmosphere where the highest ideas were expressed but not necessarily lived. They saw, or thought they saw, the betrayal of values by intellectual sell-outs, and they could not appreciate the benefits from that "sell-out" because these benefits were the everyday affluence that became part of the taken-for-granted framework of their lives. Thus, they rejected as spurious both the fake and the genuine culture which they associated with this sell-out. In part, they rejected intellectual activity itself, to the extent that such activity implied disciplined organized, "linear" activities carried on over extended periods of time. They rejected, at least intellectually, the "establishments" which constituted the framework of their affluence and the parental "sell-out." Some of them, both parents and children, compromised to the extent of enduring nine-to-five jobs in these establishments and became, after hours, "swingers," whereby their nonwork lives could be an affirmation of the values they rejected during their ordinary work. New forms of art, culture, literature, became the media of this new intellectuality. At a political level, almost all forms of traditional activities were rejected, though the new intellectuals were unable to develop any stabilized forms of the expression of political activity. At the extreme, ad hoc bombings and the cult of violence were emphasized. At less extreme levels, politics was burlesqued by such groups as the Crazies and the Yippies. But the majority of the new radical intellectuals tended to "freak out" of politics [19]. All of these forms became part of an intellectual tradition that appears to be different from established modes of intellectuality; yet we would argue that such forms of "intellectual activity" have a consistent social base. The children of the upper and upper middle classes in many societies reach the stage where they can take for granted the benefits which their social position confers upon them. They are exposed in their education to the highest values of the Western humanitarian tradition, but they see, in the ongoing institutions of their society, little opportunity for the realization of those values. A vast percentage of this group is not given the opportunity to share in the wielding of power within their society. The numbers in the favored classes necessary to rule are usually less than the numbers available, and large numbers from the upper classes are left in affluent idleness or genteel poverty. In past eras warfare and colonization were the usual means by which members of the middle and upper classes were given opportunities to serve. In the absence of such activities, remittances were used to keep idle scions away from their families and away from activities where they could become dangerous to the establishment. Forms of personal debauchery were stylized to absorb their energies. Gambling, sports, gourmandizing, sexual liaisons were ways of using up energy and filling time. The fop, the dandy, the Beau Brummel, are names given to such persons. By and large such activities have been inadequate in absorbing the energies that are freed by relatively favored social positions and not absorbed by the work of the society in question. Political activity is one means by which this energy can be at least partially absorbed. The presence of high ideals allows the members of the favored classes to project their emptiness onto the deprived classes and permits the favored to act as if they were members of the lower classes, and to select themselves as leaders. In this sense they become alienated from their own class. In some cases these intellectuals have become actual leaders of the deprived classes (Lafayette, Lenin). In other cases, their revolutionary activities are autonomous. Thus they became "populists" (*narodniki*), anarchists, and revolutionary romantics. At other points they have become actual leaders of revolutionary movements, whose membership consists of the deprived classes. In the United States, this new upper and middle class intellectuality thus became a product of the bureaucratic middle-class revolution. In other countries, the social sources of almost all revolutions are similar, though in most other countries the lack of economic opportunity for intellectuals was a basic aspect of the recrudescent radicalism of the 1960s (Japan, Germany, France). Bureaucratic affluence seems to be a major feature of industrial technological society; and an intellectual bureaucratic class will continue to produce offspring with high ideals whose economic opportunities are limited to the narrow technical tasks that a bureaucratic society requires. As a result, the contradictions between high ideals and narrow technical means remain a major source of discontent among the newly emergent "intellectual" classes of industrial society [20].

RESISTANCE TO CO-OPTATION IN A PERMISSIVE SOCIETY

The problems of un-co-opted intellectuals are of a different order. At a relatively simple level, the production of a vast number of intellectuals has resulted in the fragmentation of the intellectual community. In addition, older intellectuals have had to deal with the results of previous eras of co-optation. They have seen the results of Stalinism as it operated both in the Soviet Union and in the Stalinist political parties in the West. They are somewhat chary of the escape from alienation into political movements whose organization and center lie outside their purview and control. At the same time, many reject the role of detached observer or academic analyst as being a violation of the ethical positions that constitute the bases of their self-definition.

Younger intellectuals, not having been burnt by a "proletarian" past, are less likely to have these scruples. They confront the problem of dealing with a permissive society, which not only co-opts the intellectuals, but enjoys their antics, adopts their styles, symbols, and vocabularies as fads and fashions, without visibly being affected by them. The temptation, under such situations, is to go to increasing lengths to offend and outrage one's audience, in order to reach some point at which one's intellectual position is one's own and not a toy of the philistine. In going to such extremes, the intellectual may adopt some forms of religiosity and cultism, in which the intellectual attitude is either a totally inward one, or is repressed, not expressed by easily co-optable programs, imitation, and not available to argument and discussion, and thus not negotiable by a permissive society. The inner attitude, the mystique, is rather a mode of sensibility, beyond interpretation, and ultimately totally subjective. It makes no explicit promises, no claims, and accepts no responsibilities for action taken under its aegis. The outcome of the action is only a successive series of identities which define themselves only in the course of action, but which in turn constitute no commitment. This type of "radical" ideology is also anti-ideological, and is based upon a presumed "end of ideology."

A major weakness of this position, in intellectual terms, is that it defines itself purely in opposition to its enemies, the "system," the older intellectual circles, parents, and bureaucrats. But since the "system" is permissive, such definition must be constantly changing. In short, there is basically no position except the transvaluating of established values, whatever they may be. As a result, the radical existential intellectual is dependent upon the bourgeois world for his values, and does not develop a stable basis for doing sustained, serious work. It degenerates into a series of gimmicks which exhaust themselves before they develop. Purposeless movement and equally purposeless quietism becomes the operative principle.

In the past, intellectuals were able to define themselves because the external world ignored or rejected them. The hostility and indifference of the world thus provided them with a stable basis for affirming their distinctive values, and for working out intellectual positions and ideologies which helped to transform the world. Opposition to intellectual activity by suppression, purges, censorship, and violence never succeeded in wholly destroying the urge for intellectual development, as witnessed by the emergence of intellectual production, in the Iron Curtain countries, during the "thaw." The immediacy of such response suggests that intellectuals go underground in a repressive society, and that young intellectuals continue to emerge and develop in the shade. The moment the shade is lifted, a full crop is available, partly crippled by the inability to communicate, to be criticized, and to learn from other intellectuals who are concerned with their own problems.

When there is a shortage of intellectuals, when they are co-opted, rewarded, tolerated, and appreciated, intellectuals have much greater problems. They are usually rewarded for activities that are only by-products of their intellectual role, their skill at symbol manipulating, at analysis, in communication. Their basic intellectual attitude is rarely understood, or if understood, regarded as an encumbrance. In accepting the rewards for incidental attributes and functions, they are in danger of redefining themselves in the terms that constitute the basis of their appreciation. By accepting the rewards they risk the dangers of ceasing to exist as intellectuals. They surrender their identity for a mess of pottage. If they resist co-optation, the act of resistance all too frequently becomes the basis of their identity, an identity that must continuously change in a permissive society. In a hostile world, the action of the world tends to confirm the identity of the intellectual; in a permissive world, the action of the world tends to alter or fragment his identity.

Thus, in a permissive world, if intellectuals are to remain intellectuals, and to do work that is based upon an intellectual attitude, they must define their own identity, that is, develop an autonomous self that requires neither opposition nor social approval for its sense of validity. Whether this is possible or not is open to question. Large numbers of intellectuals have succumbed to the negative sanctions of a hostile world; even greater numbers, to the blandishments of a comfortable life in a permissive world. Yet, despite the opposition to and deflection from intellectual work, the surprising thing is that large numbers of autonomous intellectuals continue to exist and do productive intellectual work. The urge towards intellectual autonomy is as deep in the human psyche as the forces which would restrict and contain it.

NOTES

1.   In the "Manifesto of the Communist Party" in Lewis Feuer (Ed.), *Marx and Engels: Basic Writings on Politics and Philosophy* (Garden City, N.Y., Doubleday, 1959): ". . . a portion of the bourgeoisie goes over to the proletariat, and in particular a portion of the bourgeois ideologists, who have raised themselves to the level of comprehending theoretically the historical movement as a whole." See also the title essay of George Lichtheim's *The Concept of Ideology and Other Essays* (New York, Random House, 1967), and Lewis Feuer's essay, "Marxism and the Hegemony of the Intellectual Class," in his *Marx and the Intellectuals: A Set of Post-Ideological Essays* (Garden City, N.Y., Doubleday, 1969).

2.   See George V. Plekhanov, *Art and Society*, translated by Paul S. Leitner, Alfred Goldstein, and C. H. Crout (New York, International Publishers, 1940); Plekhanov, *Fundamental Problems of Marxism*, translated by Julius Katzer (New York, International Publishers, 1969); V. I. Lenin, *What Is to Be Done?*, translated by Joe Fineberg and George Hanna (New York, International Publishers, 1969); Leon Trotsky, *Literature and Revolution*, translated by Rose Strunsky (Ann Arbor, Mich., Michigan University Press, 1960).

3.   Karl Mannheim, *Ideology and Utopia. The Sociological Problem of the "Intelligentsia"* (New York, Harvest Books, 1965), pp. 153–163.

4.   Max Weber, *The Religion of China: Confucianism and Taoism*, translated and edited by Hans H. Gerth (New York, Macmillan, 1964), Chap. V, "The Literati."

5.   See Chap. 1.

6.   Alfred Schutz, "The Well-Informed Citizen: An Essay on the Social Distribution of Knowledge," in *Collected Papers*, Vol. II (The Hague, Martinus Nijhoff, 1964).

7.   See Chap. 1, pp.

8.   The term *ideology* appears first to have been used during the French Revolution, by Antoine Destutt de Tracy, one of the intellectuals selected to manage the Institut de France. The *ideologues* were those revolutionary intellectuals associated with the Institut, who were to provide the justification for revolutionary practice. They helped Napoleon to power, but later turned against him. See George Lichtheim, *The Concept of Ideology and Other Essays* (New York, Random House, 1967).

9.   Jacques Barzun, *The House of Intellect*, Chap. 1, "The Three Enemies of Intellect" (New York, Harper Torchbooks, 1961).

10.   Susan Sontag, "On Culture and the New Sensibility," *Against Interpretation* (New York, Delta Books, 1966).

11.   Thus, Alvin Gouldner's popular essay, "Anti-Minotaur: The Myth of a Value-Free Sociology," in Maurice Stein and Arthur Vidich (Eds.), *Sociology on Trial*

(Prentice-Hall, Englewood Cliffs, N.J., 1963) reveals a basic misunderstanding of Weber's concept of value-neutrality.

12. Francois Bondy, "The Engaged and the Enraged," in *Dissent* (January–February 1969), pp. 49–58.

13. See Joseph Bensman and Bernard Rosenberg, "Human Potentialities and the Healthy Society," in Herbert A. Otto (Ed.), *Explorations in Human Potentialities* (Springfield, Ill., Charles C Thomas, 1966). Also, Bernard Rosenberg and Norris Fliegel, *The Vanguard Artist: Portrait and Self-Portrait* (Chicago, Quadrangle Books, 1965), Chaps. 3, 4, 5, and the Appendix. Also, Renato Poggioli, *The Theory of the Avant-Garde* (Cambridge, Mass., Belknap Press, 1968), Chap. 6, "The State of Alienation."

14. Lewis Coser, *Men of Ideas* (New York, Free Press, 1965), Chap. 2, "The French Rococo Salon."

15. *Ibid.* See also Levin L. Schucking, *The Sociology of Literary Taste* (London, Routledge and Kegan Paul, 1944); Albert Salomon, *The Tyranny of Progress* (New York, Farrar, Straus & Giroux, 1955); Frank Manuel, *The Prophets of Paris* (Cambridge, Mass., Harvard University Press, 1962); Cesar Graña, *Modernity and Its Discontents: Bohemian vs. Bourgeois* (New York, Harper & Row, 1967); Lewis Feuer, *The Scientific Intellectual* (New York, Basic Books, 1963).

16. A major program for the bureaucratization of the intellectual in a bureaucratic revolutionary and underground party is to be found in Lenin's *What Is to Be Done? op. cit.*

17. A. Alvarez (Ed.), *Under Pressure—The Writer in Society: Eastern Europe and the U.S.A.* (Baltimore, Penguin Books, 1965).

18. See Daniel Bell, *The End of Ideology* (New York, Free Press, 1961); also Chaim Waxman (Ed.), *The End of Ideology Debate* (New York, Simon & Schuster, 1969).

19. See Richard Lowenthal, "Unreason and Revolution," and Paul Goodman, "The New Reformation," in Irving Howe (Ed.), *Beyond the New Left: A Confrontation and Critique* (New York, McCall, 1970).

20. Joseph Schumpeter, "The Sociology of the Intellectuals," *Capitalism, Socialism and Democracy* (New York, Harper & Row, 1962), pp. 145ff. See also Harold Rosenberg, *The Tradition of the New* (New York, McGraw-Hill, 1965), Chap. 19, "The Orgamerican Fantasy," and John Lukacs, *The Passing of the Modern Age* (New York, Harper & Row, 1970), Chap. 10, "The Dissolution of Learning," and Chap. 11, "The Meaninglessness of Letters."

Chapter 16

Political Attitudes

Our discussion of the intellectual focused in large part upon the intellectual's attitude toward politics. It examined the differences in fundamental attitudes towards the world that are based on the degree to which one rejects or is rejected by the external world—external from the standpoint of the actor. The intellectual is of course interested in politics, and his interest is a basic one. Most often, in the past, his stance toward politics was determined by his being excluded from participation in political decision-making. In recent periods he has very often been included in the political process. His very technique of intellectual activity—the attachment to symbolic presentations of ideological and intellectual perspectives, his knowledge of historical, philosophic, humanistic, and artistic traditions—and his desire to present his thought in intellectually articulated wholes, have all contributed to his availability for co-optation.

The intellectual contributes to politics by defining political values, by constructing images of the world and ideologies which are the object of politics. He articulates positions, makes them appear reasonable, and attaches passion to them. In addition, intellectuals become involved in the political process as parliamentarians, researchers, writers, orators and propagandizers, administrators, advisers, and strategists [1].

But the intellectual is only one type of politician, if he can be considered a politician at all in the classic sense of the term. His attitude towards politics is meaningful only in contrast to other types and styles of politics [2]. These other styles often express elements of the attitude of everyday life more than do the intellectually rationalized styles of the intellectual. The major historical styles and attitudes, in politics, are those of (*a*) the patrician, (*b*) the businessman in politics, (*c*) the professional politician, (*d*) the intellectual in politics, (*e*) the bureaucrat, and (*f*) the philosopher-king.

THE BUSINESSMAN IN POLITICS

While historically the patrician in politics represents the oldest tradition of political attitude, the style of the businessman represents the immediate background to contemporary politics [3].

The businessman's attitude toward politics has been governed by a matter-of-fact practical interest in politics. Politics has been imposed upon him from outside, it has been a constraint upon him in the practice of business. He dislikes politics and politicians, but since he operates within the framework of a society where politicians and political matters make it impossible for him to function purely as businessman, he has been forced to engage in political activity in order to achieve ends that are not primarily political [4].

The feudal and mercantilistic systems were seen by businessmen as politically saturated economic systems that made it virtually impossible for businessmen to do what was essential to their practice, that is, to act as businessmen. To achieve this necessary freedom, businessmen were forced to engage in politics, to make alliances with absolute or would-be monarchs and with segments of the intellectual community, and to create a class of professional politicians who were not businessmen to advance the political interests of business. But, as Schumpeter has argued, the purpose of all this was to allow businessmen to act as businessmen. "The business of America is business" is a slogan that only a businessman could subscribe to. Business as an activity was seen as being so meaningful and so involving of the total energy of the businessman that concern with politics appeared as an undesirable but necessary deflection from the main task. In achieving or attempting to achieve their own goals, businessmen destroyed the existing forms of legitimacy and the political fabrics of their respective societies, but they were unwilling and unable to devote time, energy, and talent to any genuine reconstruction of that society. They left this task to others, to professional politicians and patricians, so the charge is made. Beyond this, it is clear that the approach of the businessman to politics is different from the approaches of all other groups [5].

The special approach of the businessman usually disqualifies him from the successful practice of politics. Business consists of a multitude of narrow, specific, limited contractual engagements, which involve the parties to the contract only to the extent that they are specified in the contract. Loyalties, depth of feelings, symbolic and poetic expression, are all precluded from the thought processes involved. Sentiment is excluded or is at most a private affair. The expression of sentiment, the evocation of loyalty, in nonmarket terms, is excluded from the pure marketing mentality. The marketing mentality of the businessman assumes that the firm has a single, relatively narrow goal, profitability. This includes, when short- and long-term considerations are involved, the preservation and expansion of the capital of the firm. All other goals of the firm, while relatively narrow in range, can be linked in a definite order of priority to the central goals. The emphasis on profitability, in addition, provides a central criterion and mechanism for the judgment of individual projects and plans; and, even more importantly, it provides a common framework of judgments within which consensus can be arrived at.

Political decision-making, on the other hand, is based upon the reconciliation of competing groups whose goals and values are often conflicting and competing and for which there is no given common criterion for measuring or judging the effect of any single action or project. Political bargaining often consists of constructing the criteria for decision-making in the process of arriving at a decision.

When businessmen, on marketing grounds, discover the commercial value of poetic loyalties and intangible sentiments, they will, on rational grounds, pay others to supply a measured amount of these intangibles, measured in terms of their market assessment of the return on such intangibles. But to the extent that they act on their own account, they are not likely to be able to express and evoke these intangibles on their own. Thus, businessmen, as spokesmen in politics, as mobilizers of consent, as creators of loyalties, have suffered historically from hoof-in-mouth diseases. Their discussions, presenting the matter-of-fact dollar pragmatism of business, evoke the distaste of all other groups in society. Thus, the statement that "what is good for General Motors is good for the country," may reflect the sincere belief of a Charles S. Wilson, but nonbusinessmen in such a situation, if they believed a similar idea, would have known enough to avoid stating it. Honesty by a businessman in expressing his true attitudes towards politics would disqualify him from politics. This is because politics as an activity is essentially different from business. Politics involves, at the public level, the evocation of loyalty, sentiment, unlimited, and long-term commitments to deeply felt values which provide expression to deeply felt social or communitarian needs. The ability to express and evoke these sentiments is essential to creating and maintaining a political community, whether the spokesman believes them or not. The businessman, in being true to his commercial philosophy, cannot but help express contempt for the hypocrisy of those politicians who express political values, but he uses them as a guide for his own more limited interests. In expressing his contempt, he ignores even those needs which make hypocrisy necessary. This is most apparent when the businessman employs the professional politician, and professional politicians as a group come into existence only to provide both the technical know-how and the full-time devotion to politics that businessmen are unwilling to acquire or are unwilling to devote themselves to. They see their agents as political hacks mired in the mud, they see the deceit and the intrigues of politics. They feel that on the basis of their commercial morality, they are above politics only because they employ such inferior types.

THE PROFESSIONAL POLITICIAN

The professional politician makes a different kind of commitment to politics, and as a result develops a different kind of attitude or style in politics. Since he is a professional, he is in politics for keeps [6]. He does not have the security of the businessman's income, or of the patrician's ownership of land or of aristocratic prerogatives, or of the academician's university post. He must literally live off politics. Living off politics may include the receipt of graft or other graft-like emoluments (which in some societies are not defined as graft), having jobs that are a result of patronage, fees, retainerships, and commissions that come to him as benefits of having "friends" in power. But since he is in politics for keeps, he knows that there are few final victories or final defeats. As a result, he is always forced to come to terms with the specific "realities" of any situation. He must come to terms with others in that situation, and must work out specific arrangements, deals, compromises, and formulas which avoid final or absolute "solutions" or confrontations. As a result, he works at the level of the mechanics of politics; he makes the system work in its day-to-day mechanical arrangements, and is forced to be responsible for his actions in terms of the operation of the system. Knowing that the evocation of sentiment and loyalty is necessary to politics, he develops competence in and respect for these loyalties, and attempts to articulate and evoke them. At the same time, his sense for the mechanical details of day-to-day politics causes him to operate at levels that are much less absolute or idealistic than is the rhetoric necessary for politics. In the best sense of the term, he is a hypocrite. For only by combining the symbolic and emotional aspects of politics with the needs of day-to-day operations can a political system work. At the same time, all individuals in a society who are removed from the political process and who have absolute approaches to values, have contempt for the lowly politician. They consider him a compromiser and a sell-out. The ideological, committed intellectual is likely to consider himself betrayed by the politician whenever the latter attempts to realize goals that the intellectual attributes to the politician and which the politician accepts in principle, but does not insist upon in practice.

The politician in the exercise of his function must deal with others who do not share these goals. Within the framework of these and other goals, and of groups committed to other goals, he must attempt to work out agreements which allow for either the assembling of majorities or the creation of blocs large enough to achieve some degree of political effectiveness. In doing so, he must blunt the exclusive demands of any one interest or ideological group, even though, in attempting to secure the support of that group, he accepts some of their goals to some degree. The very fact of working out a political majority or an effective political bloc requires the "betrayal" of the absolute interests or demands of any one group. Moreover, the compromises he achieves are often not "rational" or logical from the standpoint of any one set of premises. For in reconciling the interests of a plurality of groups, he accepts as a basis for the compromise, the varied and often contradictory premises of the various groups involved in the decision. The compromise is thus incapable of being "rational," having no major premises. The "logic" that the politician operates upon is minimization of conflict, rather than the construction of a logical scheme. The politician must thus always operate on the assumption that society is multidimensional, has more than one issue, and is based on a pool of many unrelated and often conflicting values. The ideologically committed intellectual, like the businessman, can operate on the basis of one issue, one value, and can be absolute in his adherence to issues and values. If he operates on such assumptions in a society that is complex, multidimensional, multi-issued, and pluralistic, he excludes himself from achieving power or even from influencing the political apparatus, except in those extreme cases when all issues are polarized into the one issue that is salient to the intellectual. In all other cases, if one desires to achieve some of one's demands, and to influence in his own direction the content and structure of politics, the intellectuals (and all other groups) must limit their demands, compromise, or defer the achievements of all of their demands at any one time. Such an approach is the *sine qua non* of the professional politician. It is for this reason that all other groups must go to the politician in order to achieve *some* of their demands. In doing so, they face the prospect that other of their demands will be deferred, limited, and compromised by the politician. The latter must necessarily bear the burden of scorn and charges of betrayal, and must accept the notion that he will be treated as a morally and socially inferior person. This is a consequence of his function, and he could not achieve success in his function without enduring the opprobrium attached to it.

The totally committed intellectuals can thus achieve, through the professional politician, some degree of attainment of their ends, not only at one moment, but at successive moments, because of the politician. They are permitted to enjoy the righteousness of their total commitment to values without having to compromise and endure the messy business of compromise. The professional politician allows the intellectuals to retain their sense of righteousness by doing the dirty work of politics for them [7].

Viewed from the standpoint of the operation of a total society, the politician, performing the functions cited above, makes it possible for the various interest and ideological groups to coexist without total confrontation and civil war. He adjusts and balances the ideological and interest demands upon him, upon his party, and upon the government, in terms of the relative strengths and pressures which these external groups make upon the political machinery of the state. He thus transforms economic, ideological, and other nonpolitical interests and ideologies into political, legal, and policy terms. In doing so, he rarely creates new societal issues and trends, but transmits, translates, and transforms these nonpolitical trends into the political machinery of the society. In doing so he makes it possible for that society to function. In that sense, no matter how unworthy and lowly the politician may appear, his function is indispensable to all societies that are sufficiently large such that political pressures cannot be transmitted to government by direct, personal action.

THE PATRICIAN IN POLITICS

The patrician in politics represents both an older tradition and a continuously self-renewing tradition. The patrician was, like the businessman, most often financially independent, had the time available to indulge in politics, as the businessman had not, and quite frequently could develop an ideology which made the pursuit of politics for him a meaningful and self-fulfilling task. The patrician could see that politics was the art of government, and, being drawn from ruling classes, felt that government was a necessary and desirable task, a task which naturally should fall upon him. This is especially true in classical Greece, in the late development of feudalism (in the Italian city-state, in eighteenth-century France and nineteenth-century England). In the early development of feudalism, politics was instrumental to the upper classes in terms of their immediate political and economic interests. When feudalism as an economic and political system had become stabilized, the patricians had developed a tradition for government, a skill, and the freedom to develop the aesthetics of politics, which at times was free from their own immediate economic interests. The upper classes provided scores of disinterested leaders, who in their concern for values that often transcended their immediate economic interest, paved the way for the destruction of feudalism and of the economic basis of their own power. The French Revolution was in part led by products of the *ancien regime*, such as Lafayette and Mirabeau, the Russian Revolution by such products of the upper-class intelligentsia as Lenin, the American Revolution by such patricians as Washington and Jefferson. The tradition is still a viable one: as American capitalism has advanced, it has produced, in the descendants of its "nonpolitical" business giants, a new corps of patrician leaders who act in much the same way as did the descendants of the feudal robber barons.

Thus, the Roosevelts, the Harrimans, the Stevensons, some of the Rockefellers, and the Percys represented not only high-minded but totally committed and technically capable politicians, men who in their immediate divorce from the economic interest of their class have often been liberal, humanitarian, and in the humanitarian sense of the term, disinterested. They have also been often viewed as "class traitors."

The English country squire took it for granted that he was politically able and qualified to administer the affairs of his shire in a gentlemanly, disinterested, but amateur way. Politics was part of his way of life, but it in no way separated him from the nonpolitical life of his county. In moving from one political jurisdiction to another, from one committee to another, not as a professional but as an amateur, he could control the politics of his jurisdiction. Since he dealt with others like himself, and with his total constituency in various political and non-political roles, he could express the interests of his community. He could often be above the petty and narrow class and economic interests, could be fair, humane, and always a gentleman. Thus, participation in politics as an amateur was his political role. In a larger sense it was also his class interest. At the same time, there was no separation between the mechanics of the day-to-day operation of politics and the higher loyalties, sentiments, commitments, and values in politics. All were part of the way of life of the gentleman. Until at least the first quarter of the nineteenth century, this style was part of the style of the American Founding Fathers. The development of popular democracy and the dominance of business interests threatened to destroy this style. The separation between values and politics, and the techniques of politics, were embodied in the dominance of businessmen and the instrumentalism of the professional politicians as reflected in the rise of urban political machines.

The rise of the professional politician, the boss, and the urban political machines of the nineteenth century produced a tone, morality, and an ethics in politics, which were reprehensible to the patrician. It caused some of them, like Henry Adams, to withdraw from the hurly-burly, the dirt, and the corruption of politics. In part, this was a question of political morality and political taste; in part, the patrician, because of an earlier historical development, had assumed that the right to participate in and control politics was a right reserved for the patrician, and that as a gentleman he did not have to lower himself by competing with others, especially the lowly, for the right to play the game. Now, with the competition from the professional machine politician, and, through the instrumentality of the politician, and of the businessman, he could not wait to be called, but had to scramble in an undignified way. Through the nineteenth and into the twentieth century, the patricians held themselves above what was then the new politics of the nineteenth century. At the same time, the patrician as plutocrat, as urban landowner especially, had economic interests of his own, and in these conflicts his morality was no different from the morality of his less worthy political competitors.

The production of new business fortunes and of new multimillionaires in the latter part of the nineteenth and early twentieth centuries, resulted in the stabilization of gigantic fortunes, and, with the passage to time, second and third generations of individuals with secure wealth. Their fortunes were in many cases so great and stabilized that they could be entrusted to professional managers and counselors. Freed from the limits and constraints of day-to-day economic involvement and management, the scions of these great fortunes became a new patriciate. The activities of this new "aristocracy" included philanthropy, polo-playing, patronship of the arts, intermarriage with the remains of European nobility, and international party-going. An additional gentlemanly activity became that of politics. For, not unlike other groups, the stable upper classes often find it necessary to construct a framework of meaningful life activities. Politics is one medium for so doing. There emerged a new generation of political patricians. In such a group one might include the Rockefellers, the Lehmans, William Scranton, Averill Harriman, G. Mennen Williams, and more recently, the Buckleys and the Kennedys. They joined the older group of patricians which include such family names as Lodge, Bundy, Percy, Saltonstall, Adams, Reid, and Taft.

As politicians, these patricians betray a dedication for politics that is greater than that of professional politicians. They live "for" politics, not "off" politics. At times, they betray a level of high-mindedness and disinterestedness which is not characteristic of the professional politician, though such high-mindedness is sometimes corrupted by personal, not "class" ambition, when the possibility of supreme victory, the presidency, is in the offing. In addition, unlike older patricians and political bosses, and like many intellectuals, they betray high concentrations of self-righteousness. Since they often do not "profit" from politics, they often feel that the purity of their motivation constitutes a claim for obedience to or acceptance of their programs and proposals, and that rejection of them constitutes a betrayal of an implicit agreement (to which they are the only party). In some cases, as in that of Henry Adams, they feel that rejection provides them with the opportunity to respond with a curse on both houses, or the right to withdraw with a sense of injury, or to retaliate out of injured pride. In such instances, they are neither true politicians nor true patricians [8].

But regardless of these apparent limitations in the political perspective of the new patricians, a new stratum of patrician has come into being, disproving Schumpeter's thesis that businessmen could not develop an indigenous leadership corps, and needed the older aristocracy as a governing elite, as a source of legitimacy, and as symbols for a business civilization. If there are difficulties and even crises in contemporary society, the lack of a patrician governing class is not the source of the difficulty, though their lack of orientation may be a difficulty.

THE INTELLECTUAL IN POLITICS

If the patrician symbolizes a political system that has a unified governing class, the development of the politics of business and the corresponding professionalization of politics emphasizes the separation of "intellect" from the ongoing process of politics. As we have indicated, the intellectual has at his disposal the means of expressing political perspectives in highly articulate and expressive forms [9].

He is a creator of ideologies, political myths, and Utopias, and he can articulate in highly reasoned and polemical forms the perspectives and interests of groups in politics in terms that raise issues of politics above the level of narrow interests and immediate concerns. At the highest level, he can provide a medium of discourse which allows issues to be argued and debated in terms of the issues themselves. At the lowest level, he can be accused of providing rationalizations and screens for interests which can only be understood as the narrow class interests of particular groups who employ the intellectual, or whom the intellectual selects as a potential clientele.

Through his ability at political journalism and propaganda, he can express the ultimate goals for societies and their political systems in ways that go far beyond those of the businessman, the professional politician, and the nonintellectual patrician, though it must be added that some patricians were also intellectuals.

The tendency for intellectuals to see the issues of politics in terms of logical wholes, in terms of ideological systems that have completeness, finality, and consistency, means that starting from any limited value base, the ideology they develop, whether from the right or the left, is always more extreme than the ideology of the politicians engaged in day-to-day politics on the mechanical, operative level. As indicated above, the professional politician and the patrician are necessarily compromisers. The intellectual, not operating in day-to-day operations of nonintellectual institutions and valuing logical consistency because it is intrinsic to his intellectual attitudes, tends to construct ideologies which are always more logically consistent than the patchwork compromises which an operating politician is forced to live with. As a result, the ideologies constructed by intellectuals, while being more consistent, by the nature of their consistency are often more extremist. Intellectuals as a group create ideologies for the status quo as well as both revolution and counterrevolution, depending on their initial assumptions, and patricians and professional politicians have tended to produce ideologies of compromise and consensus.

When the interests of other groups in the society corresponded with, or could be reinterpreted as corresponding with the ideologies of various brands of intellectuals, intellectuals have always been co-opted into the structure of those groups who were interested in revolution or counterrevolution, reform, or defense. Intellectuals became spokesmen for the bourgeoisie, the reactionary nobility after the French Revolution, the proletariat and the peasantry, and the military and technocratic elites, even though in their original ideological activity they operated purely as ideologists and not as exponents of interests. In earlier periods, the intellectual as scribe, bureaucrat, and myth-maker was co-opted by patrimonial rulers to legitimate their rule, to perform technical administrative functions, and to offset the claims to power and claims of indispensability of lesser feudal nobility.

The success of every revolution or counterrevolution reveals to the intellectual ideologists that there are other than purely ideological or intellectual elements and interests in the revolution or counterrevolution. He discovers that his ideological and intellectual talents, his articulateness, and his polemical and propagandist abilities have been used by persons who are not constrained by the values expressed in the slogans and propaganda that the intellectual constructs. To the extent that the intellectual is constrained by his own ideology and is not willing to see the betrayal of that ideology by a revolution, he may become one of the children eaten up by the revolution. To the extent that he is willing to go along, he can be viewed as betraying his own ideology and values. He ultimately discovers, and we would assert, universally, that ideology is not only a mask for interests, but for new forms of oppression and repression. He is forced to make a new series of choices. He can, in the case of a revolution, become a counterrevolutionary, and risk being liquidated himself. If he rejects this choice, he can become a functionary or public relations man for the new regime, defending new forms of oppression. This seems to have been the more frequent choice.

If the intellectual retains his original sense of values, he is likely to be a permanent revolutionary. Yet, all of this sad phenomenon is merely a recounting of the synthetic form of past history. We have indicated that a profound change in the structural position of the intellectual is occurring with the bureaucratization of society. Two aspects have been important. One is that intellectuals have been vastly more appreciated by the bureaucrats in contemporary industrial society, government, politics, business, and foundations than they ever were in the past. Secondly, the intellectuals have been increasingly absorbed into academic institutions which have provided them with relatively prosperous and stable bases from which to operate.

As a result, intellectuals have been less and less at tension with their dominant societies than they were in the past, and more and more available to co-optation by these nonintellectual elites in modern societies. Moreover, their relative affluence has made it difficult for some of them to conceive of ideologies as being outside of or opposed to the system. This process of institutional co-optation began in the United States with the New Deal, in England, with the Fabian movement. Since World War II, it is almost universal.

Ideologists have been available as technicians not only to bureaucratic elites but to all groups in society. The habit of mind of constructing articulate ideological wholes is independent of the social base of the ideologist. Thus, once the ideologist achieves occupational independence in the academy, ideologizing becomes pure technique. Ideologists either sell their ideologizing function to all interest groups or create ideologies for groups that are unaware of the need for ideological self-definition until the ideologist has proven the need by creating the ideology. In doing so, they contribute to an ideological ferment which exists even after "the end of ideology."

To validate their functions, ideologists have from time to time moved out of their relatively secure academic positions, seeking political allies who express their ideologies. They have become the speech writers, manipulators, articulators of all groups, left and right. They have particularly located themselves in the moderately liberal, moderate left, especially among the bureaucratic moderate left. They have moved in and out of politics, and have constructed a new political style; the style is politics with a Ph.D. The style is articulate, intelligent, bright. It relies on big words, and big words that translate themselves into popular consumption almost immediately. It tends to be cool and at the same time glib. It caters to the educated new middle class in societies where education is no longer a rarity. It is unabashed in its confidence that all societal problems can be resolved by the proper doses of intellectual rhetoric and formulae. It is, in the most genuine sense of the word, elitist, because the practitioners of intellectual politics are better educated, more articulate, and more self-confident than either the politicians or the masses. Politicians are often viewed as figureheads, or, more exactly, as media through which political messages are expressed. The masses are viewed as raw material who will be refined by the techniques, intelligence, education, and the know-how of the intellectuals. Unlike the professional politician or the patrician, and in many ways like the businessman, the new academic intellectual has his social base outside the political sphere. His base is the university. As a result, he can for the moment make absolute demands upon the political system, and can, like the patrician, withdraw in moral disdain whenever he finds that his demands are not met by the political system. When he enters the political arena, he knows that he is not committed to it in the same sense that a professional politician is. He is less likely to accept the restraints and even the personal sense of honor of a professional politician who knows that ordinary politics never results in final solutions. As a result, the intellectual politician does not know the restraints of politics. When he enters the dirty world of politics, he will accede to all the dirt of politics without its restraints, with all the extremism that is characteristic of total commitment to any ideological position, and finds, all too often, that he is dirtier than the dirtiest politician. When he is rebuffed, he is rebuffed because *politicians* are dirty; he is able then to retreat to his ideologically superior social base, to make, at a later point, another foray into the real world of politics. Thus, to the new intellectual, politics and ideology become a game which is not necessarily played for real; it is played for kicks, to prove that an intellectual is not an intellectual, that he is capable of living in the real world. But since he can withdraw from that world at will, he has few of the commitments that make the world real to him. He gets the best and the worst, at the same time, of all possible worlds.

The pattern of the intellectual's entrance into and retreat from the political sphere is not unlike the pattern of the businessman. The businessman retains his base within his firm. He uses politics to attain nonpolitical goals, he employs political tactics and political persons whom he sees as morally beneath him, and he feels disgust for those who exercise these tactics for him. At times, because of his distaste, he minimizes his engagement only to that which is necessary on economic grounds; at other times, out of outbursts of moral superiority, he sets out to introduce the clean, honest, idealistic politics of business. But when he becomes contaminated, he withdraws to lick his wounds and to feel morally superior.

The patrician and the professional politician, being committed to politics, are much more likely to remain in politics even when the political game goes against them. They are likely to be "more responsible," that is, they stay behind to "pick up the pieces."

While businessmen and intellectuals can afford to be irresponsible in their political engagements, the patrician and the politician, being based *in* politics, must accept responsibility for the results they achieve [10].

A relatively new pattern of "politics of the intellectual" emerged in the late Sixties. This pattern reflected the relatively large number of intellectually oriented college graduates who have increasingly become the technical, administrative, and symbolic technicians for a large-scale society. Such groups tend to live in relatively dense concentrations in selected enclaves within the urban society. In the past they focused either on the production and consumption of "culture," or in national, "serious" ideological politics. They were first called to local political work in their attraction to Adlai Stevenson, later to John F. Kennedy. In their youth they became activists in the civil-rights movement, which was not locally based, and in the peace movement, only partially based on locality, and in the youth movement oriented to university issues. Nationally, and at times locally, they became involved as supporters of Eugene McCarthy and/or George McGovern. With the decline of the national organization of these movements, many discovered local politics within their own residential areas as a basis for a new politics. In some cases this involved attempts to take over local political machines. In other cases, they tried to create local community groups which would be independent of established political groups. Such a focus on local politics may have been partly a response to or an emulation of the attempt of national and local governments to create local communities for blacks and other local poverty groups. In other cases, it may have been a response to the attempt of local government to create civic planning and advisory groups to assist them in the governmental planning processes.

In still other cases, such groups have emerged in opposition to the plans of governmental bureaucracies when such plans impinge upon or threaten the integrity of the local community.

In still other cases such groups have emerged in opposition to the plans of governmental bureaucracies because they impinge upon or threaten the integrity of the local community. Cases in point are the groups that have risen to defend residential living space from the incursion of crime and drugs; invasion from commercial and industrial construction; school busing schemes to promote or evade integration; the establishment of drug treatment centers, and other such plans.

The constants in the emergence of the new intellectual politics are an almost ceaseless activism plus an ideological style in politics. The effect of the ideological style is to cause a continuous splintering among such groups, in which each political sect achieves a higher level of purity at the expense of political effectiveness. In many areas, such intellectual activism has destroyed the power of established political machines manned by political professionals, but it has not replaced the older machines with any organization that can wield the power of a community, the power to withhold or deliver votes [11].

THE BUREAUCRAT IN POLITICS

The academic intellectual in politics overshadows a relatively new but historically prior type of politician, the bureaucratic politician. The perspective of the bureaucratic politician is limited and determined by the structural constraints of the bureaucracy he serves, and therefore is more limited than is that of the academic intellectual [12]. This new political perspective is the result of the development of bureaucracy as a major social force. Almost from the beginning of history, there have been groups in society, such as the priesthood, whose perspectives in many ways correspond with that of the modern bureaucrat [13].

The bureaucrat, as paid official, identifies with the mission of his particular bureaucracy, whether it be a military, business, public health, educational, or traffic-control bureaucracy. By the virtue of the nature of his employment, he becomes a member of a special-interest group. His special interests are twofold. First, the values of his institution become his political values, and his occupational success is related to his effectiveness in proving that his institution is functionally indispensable to the operation of his society. The institution must grow and its values be more and more disseminated in order for him to secure prestige, favorable budgets, and favorable legislation.

Second, he is interested in job protection, in civil-service regulations, tenure conditions, and other forms and conditions of employment that remove him from the vicissitudes of the market and of political control. Beyond this, within his institutions and his trade associations and professional associations, the bureaucratic politician creates and staffs public relations departments, "information dissemination" departments, that advance both interests. He also organizes political pressure and interest groups in support of his bureaucracy.

The politics of the bureaucratic class consists of securing from administrative and budgetary bodies favorable consideration for their specialized claims. But because the bureaucrats have information-gathering and information-disseminating staffs, their politics is highly professionalized, highly technical, and highly intellectual. Bureaucrats, or a considerable number of them, are part-time or exintellectuals, and a considerable number of them are technical experts.

Since this is true, and since they have access to information-gathering and information-disseminating functions, they are likely to be highly effective. The bureaucratic elites have not only their own corps of intellectuals, but, using the budgets of their institutions and of their technical associations, they are able to employ "unattached" intellectuals, by subcontracting, grants, consultancies, and research and developmental projects. They can co-opt unattached intellectuals into support of the bureaucracy. In addition, academic intellectuals in the same fields as the respective bureaucratic institutions become unpaid detached intellectuals for these bureaucrats.

The co-optation of the intellectual by bureaucracy is always a source of tension for the intellectual. He prides himself on not having narrow intellectual jurisdictions, on his ability to see the world in its totality and its history. As a bureaucrat, he is forced to confine himself, at least on the job, to the narrow technical and bureaucratic interests of his agencies and his masters. The focus of his interests, the problems he addresses himself to, the styles of expression, and the outcome of his thought, are more often than not prescribed for him. His success as bureaucrat in part depends on his fulfilling these prescriptions at a technical level. His self-image as an intellectual often forces him to reject the role of the technician in favor of the role of the free-ranging, self-determining, autonomous creator and definer of values and thought. Thus, the literature on and by the bureaucratic intellectual is full of guilt, self-hatred, recrimination, and of charges and countercharges of "selling out" to bureaucrats for narrow monetary gain or for political influence or prestige [14].

THE PHILOSOPHER-KING AND THE SCIENTIST

The conversion of the intellectual into the academic or the bureaucratic worlds, or both, has other, and, we think, more important consequences. Historically, the intellectual has always tended to consider himself above routine politics and the narrow vested class interests of his time and place. He has attempted to achieve this independence from narrow structural interests on the basis of his historical and philosophical knowledge. His broader literacy and intellectual interests, to the extent that his pursuit of knowledge operates as a constraint upon him, often alienate him from his class of origin. His alienation is further increased by the fact that his peculiar talents and abilities have usually not been employed and appreciated by others as they are employed or appreciated by himself. The broadness of his knowledge and interests and the high-mindedness of his endeavors often permit him to think that he is morally superior to the grubby servers of self-interest or narrow occupational, economic, or political interests. He thinks that he has a deeper and wider grasp of the truth and of the ultimate knowledge of reality. Given the two factors, superior morality and superior knowledge, the intellectual thinks that in the interests of mankind, he should be allowed to rule, or if not to rule, to determine the policies by which men are ruled. Regardless of terminology, the intellectual, at least since the time of Plato, has implicitly or explicitly been a policy scientist. Unfortunately, his claim has not often been recognized. When it is recognized and he is allowed to share in power, he has not proven more successful than any other group. Since the claim of the intellectual is in part tied to the development of knowledge, science, and the methods of the acquisition of knowledge and science, it is forever renewed despite past failures, always on the basis of the acquisition of new knowledge, methods, laws, and sciences. With the development of science, beginning with the Renaissance and the Enlightenment, the development of natural and social sciences has produced new versions of ultimate truth which justify new claims to power for the intellectual. Saint-Simon presented the beginning of ideologies based on science and art. Comte restated the claim of Saint-Simon, based on the discovery of social structure and on comparative methods. Adam Smith and David Ricardo based similar claims on the discovery of an ultimate knowledge of the operation of the market on society. Marx based his claim on his discovery of the laws of capitalism and on history, and Engels based his on the discovery of the dialectics of nature. Sorel based a different claim on the discovery of the function of myth, poetry, and violence for society, a claim that was repeated by Benito Mussolini and Alfred Rosenberg. Le Play wanted to reconstitute earlier forms of the *ancien régime,* based on his scientific discovery of the laws resulting in the constitution and destruction of moral order in society. De Bonald and De Maistre contributed similar claims, based on less scientific pretensions than those of Le Play.

The twentieth century has seen the rise of science in far more sophisticated forms than in the past, and this has resulted in new claims based on new methods and new technologies. Since World War II, the rise of the computer, and a theory of knowledge based on the computer, systems theory, has become the basis of a new claim [15]. Under such a theory, the world or some aspect of it is seen as being amenable to treatment as a closed, logical system in which all the factors are hypothetically able to be posited (or, if not able to be posited, the results of the failure to posit them can be measured by the failure of the system to predict). All the parameters in such a system can be discovered. If some are not measurable, their value can be asserted, and that assertion can be validated by the efficiency of the system in predicting. All of the variables in the system are subject to measurement, or, if not measured, they are subjected to an estimate that leads to a "best fit." Finally, all of the values or the hierarchy of values to be gained by the achievement or nonachievement of a social policy can be quantified. Given the development of such a model or system, all that remains is to gather the necessary data and program it; the output is the inevitable and ultimately desirable social policy.

Such an approach can be understood either as science or as ideology. As science, if the system were to work, it would require the ability to conceive of the empirical world to which the system is applied as being as logically closed as the system is. But since the empirical world is as subject to as many systems as there are theories, the empirical world is never a closed system. Only the logical models of scientists are closed. Therefore, the scientist can never deal with the empirical world as a totality, and he cannot draw conclusions from his model about the empirical world as a totality. He can only draw conclusions that correspond to those assumed by his questions, hypotheses, or theories. His knowledge is necessarily fragmentary—it is not applicable to those aspects of the world which are excluded from his original model. While it may be possible to determine by inference the weight of any one parameter when the other parameters are known, it is not possible to estimate the weight of a number of parameters, and a number of variables, when the weights and quantities of other variables and parameters are not known. Thus, the possibility of mutual cancellation of errors may produce results which, while totally logical, are empirically inaccurate. The attempt to substitute logical consistency for empirical accuracy as a criterion in science is medieval in its scholasticism. The notion that one can establish numerical weights for values or for hierarchies of values, when presented in its own terms, suggests images of absolute bureaucratization, dehumanization, horror. What quantitative weights does one attach to life itself, to love, health, friendship, spontaneity, or creativity? It can be argued that each human being does in fact render all his values into some kind of hierarchy in order to make a choice. It could be said that the systems model does no more than individuals do in a much less "informed" way in their everyday actions. This may be true, but individuals ordinarily have the right, within limits, to make their own choices and to face the consequences of their choices, no matter how ill-informed they are. They also have the right to be inconsistent. The use of the systems model, based on inputs of information from, hypothetically, thousands or millions of people, results in (*a*) the centralization of all information, (*b*) the centralization of choices, and (*c*) the centralization and concentration of both accuracies and errors. It is not centralized organizations, however, but individuals, who must face the consequences of such choices.

As ideology, the new science of systems would result in the centralization of decision-making in those who have (*a*) the knowledge and the wisdom to design the appropriate system, (*b*) the technology for data-gathering, and (*c*) the technology for processing data into a computer. In addition, it means that those who design the system will by some means have to define the value of values, and the hierarchy of values, upon which policies are to be based.

A claim for power is implicit in systems models for determining social policy at several levels. The first such claim is that if at a purely technological level the men performing these indispensable functions are to provide the basis for the formulation of policy, they need the power to do so. The very notion of doing so provides a claim for the indispensability of their function, and at least implicitly, for the prestige, power, and economic rewards accruing to those who perform so necessary a function.

Secondly, it would mean that all groups who are obstacles to the operation of these unique functions would have to be devalued. For the system to work, they would have to be removed as obstacles. Thirdly, this systematic centralization of values, it would seem to us, regardless of how done, represents the assumption of total power over a society. It also represents, from the standpoint of the original thought that prescribes the use of science to solve issues of policy for a society, a fundamental confusion of thought. We would argue that scientists, including social scientists, because of conditions of specialization, training, and expertise, may be qualified in the gathering and collating of data; but we are sure that training in the collection and processing of data does not in any way qualify the specialist in these areas, any more than any other layman, in the matter of what the proper values for an individual or a society may be. When it comes to the prescription of values, each individual, assuming only sanity, is equally qualified to prescribe his own. This does not mean that we do not believe that some values are superior to others, but it does mean that the belief in the superiority of our values is only a matter of belief. We believe we have the right to assert our belief, but that others with different beliefs have the right to assert theirs, and that the development of scientific technology and methodology cannot abrogate that right. To believe otherwise would be to assert a scientific totalitarianism, as described by Huxley or Orwell. The implication of systems theory is not only of that of an ideology for a scientific elite in the classic sense that all ideologies end up as assertions of superiority for an elite, but that it is a peculiarly totalitarian elite, and for a world in which the beliefs of the scientist are treated as facts, and then imposed upon all others.

As we have indicated elsewhere, such a program is not inappropriate, not necessarily in conflict with the ideologies of higher management, foundations, and patricians new and old at the top levels of governments. Conflicts would occur at the level of who is to control the articulation and manipulation of the system, the system as model, as science, and as instrument of control. These other elites, in a complex world, have vast needs for information, means of processing information, means of stating the probability of success, and knowledge of the costs of success or failure in order to make informed decisions. The right to make those decisions are their own, since they are subject to their own structurally imposed values, and to their own righteousness. They can thus join with the scientific intellectual at all levels of the operation of the system, avoiding for the moment the problem of the struggle for ultimate control. These other elites have additional resources in money and central positions from which the systems approach can be applied.

At least temporarily, the scientific intellectual must subordinate his demands for power until he achieves the financial and positional resources which would enable him to operate independently. He is forced to ally himself with establishments that have the resources and the willingness to accept his technical program, and he must subordinate himself to their ultimate goals. This applies whether those establishments are "left," "right," or bureaucratically "liberal." We would think that such an alliance would work in regimes that are capitalistic, socialistic, or communistic. The ability of the scientific intellectual to realize his claims depends in part on how well he can at a technical level serve his masters. We have reason to believe that the greatest possibility of society's not being subject to the horrors we suggest above (though not all would agree that they are horrors) is the inability of the new scientific intellectuals to realize such goals at a purely technical level—the systems do not work. In a sense, the vast errors of the Pentagon and other agencies using such systems models to design the F-111, the Dewline, the SST, and to predict the consequences of their own actions in Vietnam, was as yet the best omen for our society that we can imagine. In the absence of such errors, the second line of defense is that various systems theorists, aligned with competing institutions, will demolish each others' predictions, arguments, and policy recommendations. But if that is the case, the survival of a free society depends on the absence of a supersystem, a condition for this line of defense [16].

At any rate, we are now for the first time in the history of the world close to the realization of the ideal of the philosopher (or scientist) king, where wisdom will be forced upon us whether we like it or not. If we dislike it, for the sake of the higher system, we will be either superseded or forced into the system, unless we ourselves are scientific intellectuals.

NOTES

1.   Karl Mannheim, *Man and Society in an Age of Reconstruction*, translated by Edward Shils (New York, Harcourt, Brace, 1940), Part II, "The Sociology of the Intelligentsia."
2.   A formal definition of politics both as an attitude and as an activity is that of Bertrand de Jouvenel, *Sovereignty: An Inquiry into the Political Good*, translated by F. J. Huntington (Chicago, University of Chicago Press, 1947) (reprinted 1963), p. 18: "We thus arrive at a first conception, very narrow, but very precise of the art of politics: it is a technique for increasing the human energies at our disposal by rallying other men's wills to our cause." Central to our discussion is Max Weber's "Politics as a Vocation," in Gerth and Mills, *From Max Weber*, (New York, Oxford Univ. Press, 1946) especially where he distinguished between those who live for politics and those who live off politics.
3.   For some studies of the relation of businessmen to politics, see Miriam Beard, *A History of the Business Man* (New York, Macmillan, 1938); Henry Demarest Lloyd, *Lords of Industry* (New York, Putnam, 1910) and his articles and essays collected in *Wealth against Commonwealth* (Englewood Cliffs, N.J., Prentice-Hall, 1963); Gustavus Myers, *History of the Great American Fortunes* (New York, Random House, 1936) (originally published 1907); C. Wright Mills, *The Power Elite* (New York, Oxford University Press, 1959); Robert Engler, *The Politics of Oil* (Chicago, University of Chicago Press, 1961); Arnold Rose, *The Power Structure* (New York, Oxford University Press, 1967).
4.   C. Wright Mills, *The Power Elite*, p. 86, cites the instance of Owen D. Young, President of General Electric, considered too valuable a man to be president of the United States.
5.   Joseph Schumpeter, *Capitalism, Socialism, and Democracy* (New York, Harper, 1962) Chaps. VII and VIII.
6.   Max Weber, "Politics as a Vocation," in Gerth & Mills (Eds.), *op. cit.*, pp. 84ff. "There are two ways of making politics one's vocation: Either one lives 'for' politics or one lives 'off' politics. By no means is this contrast an exclusive one. The rule is, rather, that man does both, at least in thought, and certainly he also does both in practice. He who lives 'for' politics makes politics his life, in an internal sense. Either he enjoys the naked possession of the power he exerts, or he nourishes his

inner balance and self-feeling by the consciousness that his life has *meaning* in the service of a 'cause.' In this internal sense, every sincere man who lives for a cause also lives off this cause. The distinction hence refers to a much more substantial aspect of the matter, namely, to the economic. He who strives to make politics a permanent *source of income* lives 'off' politics as a vocation, whereas he who does not do this lives 'for' politics. Under the dominance of the private property order, some—if you wish—very trivial preconditions must exist in order for a person to be able to live 'for' politics in this economic sense. Under normal conditions, the politician must be economically independent of the income politics can bring him. This means, quite simply, that the politician must be wealthy or must have a personal position in life which yields a sufficient income. . . . The leadership of a state or of a party by men who (in the economic sense of the word) live exclusively for politics and not off politics means necessarily a 'plutocratic' recruitment of the leading political strata . . . there has never been . . . a stratum that has not somehow lived 'off' politics . . . the professional politician need not seek remuneration directly for his political work, whereas every politician without means must absolutely claim this."

7.   For valuable material on the rise of urban machine politics, see M. Ostrogorski, *Democracy and the Organization of Political Parties*, translated by Frederick Clarke (New York, Macmillan, 1908), Vol. II, pp. 161ff., on Bosses and Rings, and Chap. VI, "Genesis of the Politician." See also John Thomas Salter, *Boss Rule: Portraits in City Politics* (New York, McGraw-Hill, 1935), and his *The American Politician* (Chapel Hill, University of North Carolina Press, 1938); Lincoln Steffens *The Shame of the Cities* (New York, Hill & Wang, 1957), contains material on the relation of businessmen to political machines. Important as a defense of the machine politician (though not necessarily written for that purpose) is William L. Riordon, *Plunkitt of Tammany Hall* (New York, Dutton, 1963). A valuable discussion of the financial and personal costs incurred by nonwealthy persons entering political life is to be found in Stimson Bullitt, *To Be a Politician*, with introduction by David Riesman (Garden City, N.Y., Doubleday, 1959).

8.   Traits of the patrician in politics are described in E. Digby Baltzell, *The Protestant Establishment* (New York, Random House, 1964), and in his *The Philadelphia Gentlemen* (New York, Free Press, 1958); James Bryce, *Studies in Contemporary Biography* (New York, Macmillan, 1903), especially the chapters on Disraeli, Lowe, Viscount Sherbrooke, and Gladstone; John Maynard Keynes, *Essays in Biography* (New York, Horizon, 1951) (reprinted by Norton, 1963); George F. Kennan, *Memoirs (1925–1950)* (Boston, Little, Brown, 1967) (Bantam reprint 1969); Max Weber, "National Character and the Junkers," in Gerth and Mills (Eds.), *op. cit;* Max Weber, *Economy and Society*, edited by Guenther Roth and Claus Wittich (New York, Bedminster Press, 1968); Alexis de Tocqueville, *Recollections*, translated by George Lawrence, edited by J. P. Mayer (Garden City, N.Y., Doubleday, 1970); Albert Salomon's "Tocqueville (1959)," in *Social Research*, Vol. 26, No. 4 (Winter 1959), reprinted in Salomon's *In Praise of Enlightenment* (New York, Meridian, 1963); Joseph Epstein, "Adlai Stevenson in Retrospect," in *Commentary*, Vol. 46, No. 6 (December 1968); Roger Starr, "The Aristocrat in Local Politics," in *Commentary*, Vol. 51, No. 1 (January 1971).

9.   Sources on the intellectuals have been listed in Chap. 15 above. See also Dennis H. Wrong, "The Case of the New York Review," *Commentary*, Vol. 50, No. 5 (November 1970); Irving Howe, "The New York Intellectuals: A Chronicle and a Critique," *Commentary*, Vol. 46, No. 4 (October 1968); Henry Fairlie, "Johnson and the Intellectuals," *Commentary*, Vol. 40, No. 4 (October 1965); George Lichtheim, "Rosa Luxembourg," *Encounter* (June 1966), reprinted in his *The Concept of Ideolo-*

gy and Other Essays (New York, Random House, 1967); George Orwell, "England Your England," in George Orwell, *A Collection of Essays* (New York, Harcourt, Brace & World, 1953); James Joll, *Three Intellectuals in Politics* (New York, Pantheon, 1960).

10.   Hans Morgenthau has described and deplored a confusion, prevalent in American thinking about electoral politics and foreign affairs, which confusion he designates as operating to the detriment of American politics: the equation of the good man with the effective politician or with the great statesman. Those traits which define the individual as good or admirable in private life are frequently irrelevant or disastrous in the politician. See his essays, "The Decline of Democratic Government," and "The Problem of National Interest," in *Politics in the Twentieth Century* (Chicago, Ill., University of Chicago Press, 1971). Important here is Weber's classic discussion, in "Politics as a Vocation," of the contrast between an absolutist ethic and an ethic of responsibility, Gerth and Mills, Eds., *From Max Weber* (New York, Oxford, 1946).

11.   See Aaron Wildavsky, *Leadership in a Small Town* (Totowa, N.J., Bedminster Press, 1964); David T. Bazelon, *Power in America; the Politics of the New Class* (New York, New American Library, 1967).

12.   See Chap. 17.

13.   See Piet Thoenes, *The Elite in the Welfare State*, translated by J. E. Brigham, J. A. Banks (Ed.) (London, Faber and Faber, 1966); Fritz Morstein Marx, *The Administrative State* (Chicago, University of Chicago Press, 1957); Karl Mannheim, *Freedom, Power and Democratic Planning* (New York, Oxford University Press, 1950); Robert Merton, *Social Theory and Social Structure*, Chap. VII: "Role of the Intellectual in Public Bureaucracy." Important also are the writings of Richard M. Titmuss, *Essays on "The Welfare State"* (London, George Allen and Unwin, 1963), and his *Commitment to Welfare* (New York, Pantheon, 1968). For fuller documentation, see Chapter 17.

14.   In addition to Merton's *Social Theory and Social Structure*, see also Joseph Bensman, "Who Writes What in the Bureaucratic University," *Dissent* (July–August 1968).

15.   There is a large variety of movements of thought which fit loosely under the heading of "systems theory," some originating in biology and physics, others in the theory and practice of automation (cybernetics); others in psychology, communications theory, games theory, and computer science. Some representative documents include Ludwig von Bertalanffy, *General Systems Theory* (New York, Braziller, 1968); Walter Buckley (Ed.), *Modern Systems Research for the Behavioral Scientist* (Chicago, Aldine, 1968); an excellent short anthology is F. E. Emery (Ed.), *Systems Thinking* (Baltimore, Penguin, 1969); two popularizing introductions are C. West Churchman, *The Systems Approach* (New York, Dell, 1968); Ervin Laszlo, *The Systems View of the World* (New York, Braziller, 1972); for systems theory as a means of governance of the world by computer, see Grace J. Kelleher (Ed.), *The Challenge to Systems Analysis: Public Policy and Social Change* (New York, Wiley, 1970), Vol. 20 of *Publications in Operations Research*, edited by David B. Hertz for the Operations Research Society of America. See also Jay Forrester, *World Dynamics* (Cambridge, Mass., Wright-Allen, 1971); *Urban Dynamics* (Cambridge, Mass., M.I.T. Press, 1969); Jay Forrester, *Principles of Systems* (Cambridge, Mass., Wright-Allen, 1969). Strikingly enough, the social claims and philosophies among these quite diverse disciplines are almost identical.

16.   Two important sources are: Dean Schooler, Jr., *Science, Scientists, and Public Policy*, (New York, the Free Press, 1971), especially valuable for its bibliogra-

phy; also, H. L. Nieburg—*In the Name of Science*, revised edition, (Chicago Quadrangle Books, 1970); see also Aaron Wildavsky, "The Political Economy of Efficiency: Cost-Benefit Analysis, Systems Analysis, and Program Budgeting" in *Political Science and Public Policy*, edited by Austin Ranney, Chicago, (Markham Publishing Company, 1968); Wallace S. Sayre, "Scientists and American Science Policy," *Science* CXXXIII, March 24, 1967; for the pretentions of scientists in other areas, see Anthony Oettinger and Sema Marks, *Run, Computer, Run*, (Cambridge, Harvard University Press, 1969); also, Robert J. Art, *The TFX Decision: McNamara and the Military*, (Boston, Little Brown 1968); Daniel S. Greenberg, *The Politics of Pure Science*, (New York, New American Library, 1967); Irving Louis Horowitz, editor, *The Rise and Fall of Project Camelot: Studies in the Relationship Between Social Science and Practical Politics*, (University of Chicago Press, 1946), reprinted 1965. See also Paul Dickson, *Think Tanks*, (New York, Atheneum, 1971).

Chapter 17

Bureaucratic and Planning Attitudes

IMAGES OF THE BUREAUCRATIC ATTITUDE

By now, it is almost a cliché to speak of the bureaucratic attitude. Weber, Merton, Mills, Mannheim, Michels, Blau, and Selznick have presented us with images and models of emerging structures which dominate much of the modern world, and which, because of their pervasiveness, dominate many of the styles of thought [1]. In this chapter we will attempt to see if it is possible to go beyond these traditions of modern political and social theory.

Conventionally, the bureaucrat is defined as a paid official employed in a large-scale organization whose work is delimited by relatively narrow, written, legal spheres of competence or jurisdictions arranged in strict hierarchies. The official enters the job as a career and derives his major income from his office. By virtue of training on the job, and preparatory education, he becomes a narrow, "technical" expert. He advances through the hierarchy on the basis of examination and merit ratings which are presumably objective and impersonal. He exercises his function on the basis of standardized, legal, objective procedures which are written down and specified in detail.

In doing so he is subordinate to bureaucratic law, and to the rights, duties, and privileges of offices that are prescribed by the legally constituted codes and tables of organization of his organization.

He is enjoined in principle to separate personal considerations, money, and influence from the objective forms and procedures of his organization. He does not provide his own capital, tools, books, office space, or resources, but depends on the organization for them.

He is a cog in a gigantic machine which has an objective character to which he must submit himself. All of this breeds a specific type of social character, or, in our terms, a set of attitudes. These include the habits of mind of disciplined obedience to impersonal causes, organizations, and institutions. It includes matter-of-factness or impersonality in dealing with others, the denial of sentiment, personal loyalties and attachments, warmth, and anger. It implies the disenchantment of all that is poetic, myth-oriented, chivalrous or humane, when such humanity conflicts with the objectivity and impersonality of bureaucratically specified procedures. It implies an emphasis on rationality in action, but more so of procedures. In large-scale organizations the total flow of rationality of action is broken down into thousands of formal procedural acts, each or only a series of which fall within the jurisdiction of any one bureaucrat. No one official may know, or needs to know, the substantive rationality which governs the action of the total enterprise. Formal or functional rationality may be devoid of content as far as any one official is concerned, though that official may have faith in the rationality of the entire enterprise. That faith can be called *morale*, a submission to objective "reasons of state," organizational purposes or mission. Such morale conditions the employee to accept his total dependence on the bureaucracy as a whole and to act as a willing cog in the machine. In addition, this morale is sustained by the fact that one's career will advance with one's willingness to serve and to accept the rationality of the entire enterprise.

Other aspects of the bureaucratic attitude have been criticized. Among other reasons, as his narrow expertness increases, the bureaucrat becomes less and less able to see the overall intentions that govern his actions and the consequences of his action; more and more he becomes an expert over less and less. As a result he becomes a "trained incompetent," or exhibits forms of "occupational psychosis." Such a criticism of bureaucracy per se or of the bureaucrat would be unfair from the standpoint of the functional theory of bureaucracy, unless the bureaucracy was so imperfectly organized that the official in his trained incapacity could not exercise the functions that lead to the substantive rationality, the policy purposes of the organization, whether the bureaucrat, in fact, was or was not aware of the intentions that governed that substantive rationality. This criticism might be valid on aesthetic or social-psychological grounds since it portrays man without substance, soul, or heart, devoid of feeling, interest, passion, wisdom, or humanity. Such an image of the bureaucrat as a human being may not be appropriate unless it can be established that the bureaucrat takes over the habits of mind from his work into his nonwork life. The separation of office from domicile, at least in principle, allows the bureaucrat to exist in other, perhaps more human terms, when not on the job. But certainly the image of the soulless bureaucrat has become so prevalent, we believe, that it constitutes a major source for the rebellion of youth against possible careers as "clerks" in modern bureaucracies. Beyond this, there is sufficient evidence by now that, despite or perhaps because of the very formal nature of bureaucracies, individual

bureaucrats at all levels conspire (perhaps unwittingly) against the bureaucratic system to violate its formal nature. Thus, bureaucratic environments
are interlaced with cliques, friendship groups, informal organizations and
procedures, which tend to make the environment (at times) more human,
personal, warm, and frequently, for these very reasons, less efficient. It is
perhaps because of the violation of the formal nature of bureaucracy that
complaints on the grounds of inefficiency equal complaints against bureaucracy on the grounds of inhumanity [2].

At another level, bureaucracy is complained about because, despite its
rules, bureaucrats exceed their authority. The very powerlessness of the
bureaucrats, a powerlessness caused by strict delimitation of jurisdiction and
by standardized procedures, causes some bureaucrats to attempt to enhance
what minor powers they have in dealing with less powerful officials, and with
their bureaucratic clientele. Thus, petty sadism, obstruction, and delay are
standard complaints made against bureaucrats by clients who must deal with
them even when the latter are bureaucrats who are not acting in their role as
bureaucrats themselves [3]. In a society that is highly bureaucratized the
proportion of people who are not bureaucrats must necessarily be low. But of
course the opposite complaint is also made, that bureaucrats, in their subservience to bureaucratic and class superiors are often subservient to the point
where they confirm the sense of omnipotence of their superiors, and deny
superiors access to necessary but often unwelcome information. But in both
cases—bureaucratic subservience and bureaucratic authoritarianism—the
bureaucrat, in overcompensating for powerlessness, or in expressing it
through subservience, responds primarily to the dimension of power, and
subordinates other aspects of his social relationships to power relationships.

At still another level, the bureaucrat is charged with being a legalist, a
pettifogger, fully aware of all of the procedures and limits on jurisdiction
which make it impossible for him to act in any positive way. He thus
becomes an expert in inaction, buck-passing, and in bureaucratic obstruction. At the same time he is able to insist on his own officially defined rights,
privileges, precedents, rank, and exemptions from obligations, agreements
or work demands. Such charges alternate with charges of exceeding one's
bureaucratic authority, abusing one's position, power-grabbing, and expanding one's prerogatives. Both charges may be true with variations in major
orientation according to bureaucratic level. Bureaucratic expansiveness is
more likely at the higher levels, and bureaucratic intransigence or immo-
bility more prevalent at lower levels. Length in grade and mobility aspirations may be another significant variable, with the least aspiring being most
given to bureaucratic intransigence.

Dependence on procedure in bureaucracies has led to the charge that
bureaucracy results in the development of ritualism; that forms, procedures,

and methods of bureaucracy result primarily in the multiplication of paperwork that has no other function. Bureaucratic inefficiency is a byproduct of
such ritualism.

The very conflicts between bureaucracy as a formal means of carrying out
action, its dependence on rules, procedures, paperwork, and the necessity
for fast, immediate, efficient action at times lead to a contradiction between
the appearances of bureaucracy and its reality. Regardless of whether the
action undertaken by bureaucrats is legal or illegal, personal or impersonal,
oriented to substantive action or purely ritualistic, the action so undertaken
is always presented publicly in legalistic, formalistic, "ritualistic" procedures, language, and form. This is true whether the action of the bureaucrat is generous, personal, malevolent, or illegal. The bureaucrat must
follow the bureaucratic form at the expense of his personal generosity or
malevolence in order to escape charges that he violates bureaucratic law,
jurisdictions, and procedure. The bureaucratic milieu always conveys an
aura of hypocrisy. It is always more legalistic than the actions it undertakes,
more proper than honest, more impersonal in form than in content, and
more righteous than right. The atmosphere of hypocrisy offends laymen who
enter the ambience of bureaucracy. But because bureaucracy is "hypocriti-
cal" in its form, it is not as legalistic, impersonal, and inhuman as the form
suggests.

Other charges against bureaucracy are more serious. At a societal level,
bureaucracies are charged with an inevitable tendency toward expansion.
The very *esprit de corps,* the reasons of state, and the ideologies necessary to
create the sense of disciplined morale within a bureaucracy result in the
tendency for each bureaucracy to see its mission or function as indispensable. An alleged absence of funds, personnel, and jurisdictional limits are
seen as impediments to the complete fulfillment of the original mission or of
carrying out that mission in related fields or jurisdictions. Almost all bureaucracies tend to find reasons for expanding and to find objective bases for such
expansion. Expansion creates new jobs, new opportunities for advancement,
and validates the original service ideal. Such expansionist tendencies are
further promoted by the fact that the specialization and expertise assembled
in a bureaucracy as a whole provides the bureaucracy with access to information which justifies its case. Moreover, the withholding of information by the
same bureaucracies may weaken the power of the political overseers of the
bureaucracy, or in political bureaucracies, the electorate, so that the only
sources of information operate in favor of the bureau. Such withholding of
information protects the bureaucracy from evidence of its own incompetence, and allows bureaucrats to escape responsibility for actions which are
illegal or incompetent. But even more important, the central position of the
bureaucracy results in the assumption of policy powers by bureaucrats,
resulting in the conversion of elected officials to figureheads. Bureaucracy

tends to result in a centralization of power, and the usurpation of power over policy by those who legally do not have such powers. Bureaucracy, it is argued, is fundamentally authoritarian, not only in its internal structure but with respect to its external relations.

THE FUNCTIONAL INDISPENSABILITY OF BUREAUCRACY

The original Weberian discussion of bureaucracy was based on a number of premises. The first of these was that bureaucracy as a means of administration replaced such other forms of administration as feudalism, patrician rule, and boss rule in urban political machines. In comparison with these other forms of administration, there is no doubt that bureaucracy is faster, cheaper, and more efficient. All the inefficiencies of bureaucracy must be understood in comparison with the still greater inefficiencies intrinsic to the other systems of administration. On this basis, there is no doubt that bureaucracy with all its imperfections still remains that most efficient means of administration. Moreover, all large-scale organizations, and all pressures within society that are based on increasing the scale and efficiency of organizational operation result in further extensions of bureaucracy. Most attempts to reform bureaucracy focus on humanizing it, making it more acceptable and tolerable. Few of these attempts alter its fundamental structure.

Some recent attempts at decentralization and community control are aimed at making administration more responsible by breaking up large-scale bureaucracies into smaller units and subjecting these smaller units to local political control. It is not clear at this time whether such attempts will result in the reinstitution of local boss rule, or whether the subdivided units are in fact so large as to result in merely smaller bureaucracies [4]. Certainly the much celebrated decentralization of General Motors in the early forties resulted in the creation of five gigantic bureaucracies subject only to the financial controls of a central board of directors in place of the one gigantic bureaucracy that was being "controlled."

From a technical point of view the growth of bureaucracies has largely been a product of the expansion of those functions which are most efficiently administered by bureaucratic organizations. Some inefficiencies of coordination, control, and integration become central when bureaucracies grow so large that the constituent units and officials lose awareness or knowledge of who their colleagues are and of the functions which they jointly manage. At this point, hosts of problems emerge. Problems of communication, record-keeping, filing, coordination, processing of paperwork, transmitting of orders become so large, that mechanical errors in the carrying out of routine functions, as well as bureaucratic sabotage caused by poor "morale," and inadequate training, can cause large-scale error and inefficiency simply because the bureaucracy as a whole is so complex and delicately balanced. At the same time, the very complexity of bureaucracy depends on the willingness of lower-ranking officials to be punctilious in processing the flow of paperwork, in filing, and in observing detailed bureaucratic codes. Some social scientists have suggested that segments of this officialdom, penetrated by a new consciousness, by rising expectations, and by disdain for the petty clerical work that constitutes the lifeblood of bureaucracy, engage in positive acts of sabotage, or develop unreflective attitudes of indifference, carelessness, or repugnance; and in doing so weaken the very basis of bureaucracy at the level of mechanical efficiency. To the extent that these are simply problems of scale, of the scope and complexity of functions involved, decentralization of the bureaucracy may not be a solution, since it may not be possible to divide complex interrelated functions among a number of separate organizations. Thus, it may be difficult to subdivide the functions of a telephone company in any one metropolitan area even though at times it appears that the telephone system as a whole is decreasing in efficiency. If the problem of efficiency is to be solved, it would appear that it would have to be solved in terms of more perfect coordination, more effective personnel policy and administration, greater knowledge of the internal communications of the system, better planning, and provision for the balanced growth and coordination of functions. More carefully planned bureaucratic extension may be the solution to such problems, not the elimination of bureaucracy itself.

SUPRABUREAUCRATIC POLICY FORMATION

A second major aspect of the growth of bureaucracy is that regardless of technical function, bureaucracy is a power instrument. The development of state bureaucracies grew as a means of controlling and limiting the power of local feudal lords; military bureaucracies were an answer to a decentralized mercenary or feudal army, and industrial bureaucracy was a means of centralizing economic power. Yet in all these cases, beyond the bureaucracy were political and economic overlords. While bureaucracy is primarily a means of administration, it is not necessarily the goal of administration. The tendency to confuse the internal authoritarianism of bureaucracy with its external ends is far too easy a solution to the theoretical problem of bureaucracy.

Bureaucracies have existed within totalitarian states and within democratic states. Totalitarian states have rejected the theory of bureaucracy, as in Nazi Germany, in which the Fuehrer principle was used as an alternative to stable bureaucracies, and Italian fascism was notably weak in its adminis-trative effectiveness.

Bureaucracy as a technical instrument of administration thus is subject to political, economic, and social pressures emerging from sources other than the particular bureaucracies. As modern societies become increasingly bu-reaucratized, individual bureaucracies provide part of the political pressures that constitute the framework for policy-making that govern bureaucracies other than the one in question. Thus, the totalitarian aspirations of any one bureaucracy are limited by the plurality of pressures created by all the bureaucracies that govern the actions carried out by any one. But individuals and pressure groups in a society can be organized by political parties and by other groups that are not organized primarily as bureaucracies, or if so, that cut across the jurisdictions of a particular bureaucracy in such ways that the pressures and interests represented by a pressure group cannot be con-ceived of as being bureaucratic in nature. Though oil companies, for exam-ple, are organized internally on bureaucratic lines, the political interest of these companies is not particularly bureaucratic but rather reflects their interest in oil, markets, taxes, privileges, government regulations, pipelines, etc. In such cases, the struggle of interest groups to dominate or control the formulation of social policy in a given area go on almost as if bureaucracy were not a factor in the given area. To be sure, the central bureaucracy carrying out the policy in that area will have bureaucratic interests of its own, but these will be limited by the activities of numerous other interest groups, which, while themselves bureaucratically organized, will not make, in the given area of interest, its bureaucratic interests the central focus of concern.

SUBSTANTIVE, FORMAL, AND FUNCTIONAL RATIONALITY

But all of this has consequences for our very image of bureaucracy. For the theorists of bureaucracy, notably Weber and Mannheim, have all empha-sized the rationality of bureaucracy; bureaucracy can be conceived of as having substantive, formal, and functional rationality [5].

Substantive rationality is defined as the relationship between means and ends. Formal and functional rationality refer to the procedures by which the means lead to an end. By formal rationality is meant the use of systematic, legal procedures in an objective and impersonal way. Functional rationality refers to the integration of jurisdictions and procedures so that they interlock in a consistent and organized way, despite the fact that not all bureaucrats need be conscious of the relationship of their function to the ultimate end of action. The notion of substantive rationality, however, implies that there is a clear-cut set of goals that are consciously articulated in a consistent and rational manner, and that these goals can be implemented to produce a desired effect. The notion of rational planning, consistency and harmony of goals, all imply a higher rationality than merely the formal or functional rationality of bureaucratic procedures, means, or internal operations.

We would not argue with notions of formal or functional rationality, but our previous discussion of the pluralism of bureaucracies, interest groups, and pressures that operate on the formulation of social policy for a particular bureaucracy opens the question of whether substantive rationality in fact governs bureaucratic or other forms of the modern planning of social policy. The discussion of bureaucracy in its traditional forms assumed that bureaucracy is capable of developing centralized planning within its jurisdictional area. It viewed bureaucracy as an institution within a nonbureaucratic world. It did not envisage either the competition between bureaucracies in a bureaucratized world, nor did it fully envisage the state machinery above the level of a single bureaucracy, the legislative or policy-making organizations, as being fully subject to pluralistic pressures. In short, planning functions were seen as artifacts of a single set of hierarchical values which were assumed to be logically interrelated. In fact, one of the major ideologies for modern planning has been that planning introduces order. Implicit in the assumption that planning is rational may be the notion that the planners operate within the framework of a coherent set of values at the political level, perhaps symbolized by the state or the nation, in which national goals are assumed to be clear and unified. Taking place within the framework of such clarified goals, planning becomes a technical means to realize goals that are outside the planning process. Yet if one were to conceive of the state, the nation, as a collectivity of individuals and groups, classes, organizations, political parties, each of which may have goals, interests, ideologies, and structures of relevance which are sometimes unrelated to each other, and often in conflict, then the goals within which planning takes place are not to be regarded as given, and are often defined and articulated only within the process of planning itself.

THE PLANNING ATTITUDE

Planning may involve more than an ideology of order. It may emerge from the desire to extend the jurisdiction of an existing bureaucracy over a wider and wider sphere of operations, and in doing so subject them to the order given by that bureaucracy. It may arise out of the expansion of the sense of felt needs, new functions, services, and goals which arise out of a sense of ideological changes, political pressures, and the emergence of new groups and interest in society, whose needs can only be met by the development of planning and the expansion of bureaucracy. The failure of existing institutions, bureaucratic and nonbureaucratic, to meet needs that were already present, or newly emerging needs, may call for the extension of bureaucracy and planning, or the reconstitution of existing bureaucracy and planning.

But wherever planning occurs, it is the end product of usually a long period of ideological, institutional, and interest-group pressure, propaganda, bargaining, and policy determination. The need for planning in this sense is never self-evident except to ideologists and interest groups of particular forms of planning and policy. The specific content of the plan is never self-evident to those involved in the development and articulation of planning. That specific content only emerges during the process of planning.

The above discussion allows us to state systematically the elements and ingredients necessary to conceptualize bureaucratic planning. Some of the elements, to summarize, are as follows.

Most of the manifest classical features of bureaucracy, as described above, refer to its internal operation below the level of policy-making and planning. Bureaucratic planners must take into account the existence of other bureaucracies, their interests, ideologies, jurisdictions, resources, potential rivalries and competitions, and their capacity to deflect, inhibit, or advance policy in a given area. In doing so, the bureaucratic planners must treat these other groups, though bureaucracies, in virtually the same way that they treat nonbureaucratic interest and ideological groups. These other groups may include political associations and parties, journalistic specialists, formal and informal voluntary associations, and other powerful leaders in the area for which planning is contemplated. The process of constructing a plan or a new or changed policy must envisage in advance or anticipate the interests and ideologies of all groups relevant to the policy or planning area. This is necessarily so, since the adoption and implementation of the plan rests upon the ability to anticipate the resistance of these other groups to the contemplated plan or policy. Successful planning also depends upon the ability of the planners to secure support for the adoption of the plan, and, if adopted, support in the implementation of the plan. Technical planners are frequently forced to call into consultation all groups who have an ideological or interest relationship to the area of planning or policy under consideration. Consultation may be direct, immediate and informal. When informal, the groups consulted are usually considered to be an "establishment." An establishment is the self-selected, relevant, and powerful representatives of the dominant institutions in a given area. At other times, the planning process involves the more formal assemblage of commissions or committees. Committees are usually selected to represent all the relevant and powerful agencies and organizations involved in the planning area. Even when such formal processes are not adopted, planners who sense that the contemplated plan must be adopted and implemented, must take into account the existence of relevant establishments by anticipating their response, their possible support, their resistances, and the bases of such support and resistance. If they do not take these groups, interests, and ideologies into account, they can expect that their plan will generate its own opposition [6]. As a result of these processes, planning as a social process involves the following.

1. The process is highly formalized.
2. Major groups who would respond to the plan are brought into the planning process before the plan is actually formulated.
3. Their perspectives, interests, ideologies, are taken into account in the planning process regardless of whether their perspectives, interests, and ideologies are consistent with the intention of the plan. In this latter case, the ignoring of these other perspectives is only possible when:

    a. The area being planned is too unimportant to be worthy of notice by otherwise potentially impeding groups, or
    b. The planning group has sufficient power and authority to be able to ignore the resistance of the potentially impeding groups.
    c. All other bases for ignoring relevant publics and interest groups must be classified as oversight, ignorance, and incompetence.

PLANNING FUNCTIONS

In taking into account the ideologies, interests, and perspectives of the potentially supporting and impeding groups, the planners incorporate them into the planning process. In doing so, the planning function becomes less the formulation of a substantive plan, and more the organization of interests, ideologies, consent, and support, for a plan that will emerge only after the outside groups in question have been organized. The planning function, at least at the highest political and professional levels, consists of organizing the interest groups in question, rather than manifestly constructing a plan. It includes discerning what are the relevant interest groups in question. This is no mean task since the relevance of a potential responding group to a planning operation is in part a function of the plan, which at early stages is unknown. Yet there is sufficient experience in all planning operations for planners to realize that the neglect or oversight of a particular relevant group may destroy the plan when the relevant group finds either that it has not been consulted, or that the plan does not take into account, because of neglect and oversight, its interests and ideologies. Unless sensitivity to the possible effects of a plan or policy on a potentially powerful responding group is continually maintained, major political faux pas, resistances, and opposition can emerge. This is especially true in the later stages of a planning operation when the planners are considering what appears to be the purely technical implementation of the plan. At this stage, their attention is likely to be deflected from the political consequences of what appears to be purely technical considerations. The re-emergence of unforeseen political dimensions of planning in the technical stages of planning disrupts the planning process.

After the relevant "publics" to the plan are discerned, the planning process shifts to the solicitation of points of view, consultation, the mediation and conciliation of different interests, ideologies, and points of view to be incorporated into the plan. It includes the creation of agendas for such consideration, the organization of conferences, committee meetings, and joint consultations. In these stages the technical planners are concerned with mediation, negotiation, bargaining, and the facilitation of compromises between divergent points of view.

To a large extent planning becomes purely technical facilitation, administration, mediation, and bargaining between interest groups whose ideologies and interests represent the substance out of which the actual plan emerges. The professional planner exercises purely technical functions. Major functions, technical in nature, may have substantive consequences. The planner, first of all, usually assembles the technical information relevant to the area of planning, and may have access to information that may not be available to any of the direct interest groups (though the reverse is also likely to be true.) In carrying out the mediating and negotiating functions outlined above, the planner may by now have more access to the interests, ideologies, points of resistance and compromise among the various groups engaged in the planning process than any of these groups may have with respect to each other. Therefore the planner can arrange compromises, or focus the plan in a given area more easily than any one of the parties. By being outside the major ideological and interest areas, the technical planner may have some degree of "objectivity" and distance from such issues and may be able to suggest alternatives that the ideologists and interest groups cannot.

The discussion above indicates that within any area of planning, a broad range of interests, perspectives, and ideologies are operative among a plurality of persons, groups, and agencies, all of which have different amounts of power, influence, and resources to aid or implement the plan. The primary task of the planner is to reconcile these varied interests and ideologies in such a way as to organize a consensus that will enable a plan to be drafted, and to organize sufficient support for the plan, once drafted, to gain adoption and implementation [7].

Since the various groups and agencies that focus upon any area under consideration for planning or policy formation have often competing or unrelated policy perspectives and interests, the construction of a plan involves a series of compromises, the adoption of often unrelated and at times contradictory or mutually antagonistic goals and purposes. Some statements of goals may be incorporated only as a sop to neutralize the opposition of a relevant interest group to a plan. Some may be only verbal formulas whose implementation is not intended. Other incorporations may be designed to gratify the vanity of an individual consultant. Still others may be intended to placate the constituency of a co-opted representative of an interest group who would like to go along with the plan because of a sense of community, good fellowship, and morale that the planning process creates in its very operation. Beyond this, the prestige offered to a representative of a low-prestige interest group in a high-prestige planning operation may often, at least temporarily, force him to suspend his "better"—or at least narrower—judgment. The plan will embody a vast number of conflicting goals, values, interests, and means. Since separate means are related to individual goals, but since means are often treated or considered separately from ends in any plan, the means to one goal quite frequently contradict or conflict with the means to another goal. Those who understand the political nature of a plan are often aware of the relationship of particular means to particular ends. Those who at later times are given the task of implementing the plan are not privy to such hidden understandings, and thus see the plan as a "mess" or as self-contradictory and self-neutralizing guides to action. Yet, all of the above is necessary to organize a consensus and to secure the adoption and implementation of the plan [8].

THE RATIONALITY OF PLANNING

But since the planning process emphasizes the rationality implicit in the planning process, the process of drawing up the final draft of a plan requires that the plan be stated as a logical, rational, systematic, orderly scheme for action. Regardless of the inconsistencies, contradictions, congeries, and lack of clarity between means and ends, the form and style of the plan as a document always suggests the kind of substantive rationality that is present in theories of planning, bureaucracy, and social policy.

So far as we know, there are very few plans that do not involve these elements of planned irrationalities in their hidden scenarios. When they do not contain these irrationalities, they are the plans of a single, monolithic agency dealing with at most very narrow technical problems which do not have an impact on a wide number of audiences and publics.

Once a plan is formulated with respect to its overall goals and means, the problem of technical implementation emerges. At this point formal or substantive rationality is salient, for the planners must work out the administrative machinery and the jurisdictions by which a plan must be carried out. However, even at these levels the process of functional rationalization involves political considerations, if and when implementation involves the loss of jurisdiction or the realignment of jurisdictions with respect to the bureaucracy entrusted with the implementation of the plan, and other organizations upon which that bureaucracy impinges. Such conflicts may emerge in the technical implementation of the plan, or they may emerge after the execution of the plan has been undertaken, when hidden and unanticipated implications of the plan become apparent. At this stage, reconsideration of the political dimensions of the plan may take place, or, as is more often the case, a new plan is proposed. Such reconsideration may occur only after years have passed.

In addition, technical implementation of the plan involves pricing out the cost of the operation of the plan, the creation of tables of organization involving the use of personnel, and costing out the salaries of such personnel. When this is done, quite frequently the costs may far exceed anything anticipated in a planning operation. If this does happen, means must be devised to cut back the scale and focus of the plan. Theoretically, this could involve reconsideration of the overall goals and purposes of the plan; but since such reconsideration would also involve the reconstitution of the complicated and unwieldy machinery of organizing consent, the tendency is not to tamper with the overall agreements which became the basis for the plan. The tendency is to thin out the resources needed to implement relatively ambitious plans so that few goals are attainable. The process of "thinning out" the implementation of the plan may take the form of cutting back the means of achieving each of the plurality of ends so that the means are below the threshold of effectiveness. The alternative of concentrating all or a major part of the means to a restricted number of ends might result in greater effectiveness in achieving these ends, but such a strategy might involve violation of the agreements which made the planning possible. In working out a strategy of covering all bases, the plan that emerges is often an empty shell. In addition, the implementation of a plan often requires estimates of the technical efficiency of the scientific or technological apparatus on which the plan depends. In areas of innovation, such estimates are only "guesstimates." As a result, the success of the plan as a whole and its technical implementation can only be determined after the fact, even allowing for test operations and contingency plans. When such technological innovations do not produce the estimated effects, then costs may rise at unanticipated rates and the planners, bureaucracy, or policy-makers become subject to criticism. When technological results are better than anticipated, a budgetary surplus may be possible. At this point, the task before the bureaucrats is to use up the funds in such a way as to make it not appear that they made a mistake in planning or estimating.

When technological innovation is not a factor and when the basic costs and administrative implementation rest upon incidence of use of services and facilities, imperfect estimating may result in the same kinds of binds and squeezes that are produced by technological change. Cost estimates must take into account the rate of inflation in the society as a whole as well as the increasing costs of the goods and services to be required over the length of a plan. Mistakes in estimating costs are a major source of failure and an excuse for the failure of long-range planning. At another level, the competence and efficiency of those entrusted with the execution of the plan must be evaluated. Planners, we suspect, are loath to build into their planning estimates factors such as incompetence, laziness, inefficiency, bungling, and red tape [9]. If such factors are anticipated, they are usually concealed in other budgetary and personnel categories. All too often, people engaged in planning are socially and organizationally far above the personnel engaged in actual execution of the plan. They tend to take execution for granted. Failures in such estimates are usually compensated for in time periods occurring after the initial implementation of the plan, and are subsumed under the category of "experience" [10].

BUREAUCRATIC NARROWNESS

An interesting problem in planning that runs contrary to the image of planners and bureaucrats as power-hungry, often occurs. At times the ideological and interest groups pressing for a plan propose planning and bureaucratic operations that appear to be technically unrealizable. Public pressure and ideological interests suggest that certain planning tasks are highly desirable, and that not planning to meet felt needs is politically indefensible. Yet the resistance of an area to planning or the lack of resources likely to be allocated for a highly desirable goal will cause bureaucrats to try to avoid responsibility for the planning operation or its implementation. This is especially true when established bureaucracies have already developed a clear-cut, narrow, and stereotyped image of their own operation, based on techniques which do not "fit" the contemplated planning. In such situations, bureaucrats are likely to resist attempts by others to saddle them with new functions and duties, despite the fact that the functions would entail larger budgets, promotions, and expanded jurisdictions. Even when such missions are handed to established bureaucracies under the above circumstances, some are tempted to shrink the mission to performing what already has been done, or performing the new assignment by using familiar techniques. In such cases, the problem is not bureaucratic "imperialism" but bureaucratic "narrowness."

SOCIAL AND ADVOCACY PLANNING

Planners and others concerned with urban problems have begun to recognize that planning which is conceived in purely physical terms can be disastrous. Lewis Mumford, Jane Jacobs, and Herbert Gans are among those who have maintained that attention to purely physical planning without concern for social relationships, could produce plans whose effects were inhuman and which intensified urban problems [11]. Gans described the demolition of Boston's West End as crude, heavy-handed, and as resulting in a net loss for the city. Mumford and Jacobs, though in disagreement over what is to be done next, agree on the pernicious results of project housing plans [12].

As a result, there has been a turn to planning for social policy in terms of a mix of factors other than the purely physical, and in some instances such planning is directed entirely towards such goals as the elimination of poverty, with little or no discussion of physical or urban planning; these plans include programs aimed at increasing earning power, job development, encouraging community action, the invitation of industry into poverty areas, planning for the life-cycles of the poor, encouraging local community leaders to participate in the planning of neighborhood services, and so forth. New York City's Model Cities Program is one outgrowth of such planning [13].

These developments are too recent to permit conclusions to be drawn, but Richard Titmuss' studies of the effect of welfare-state programs in Great Britain suggests distortive and unforeseen results which may prove as disheartening to social policy planners as previous results have proven for the planners of urban renewal. The provision of "welfare services" to the urban poor may result, Titmuss argues, in a failure to make changes in their real income, inasmuch as the provision of such programs may be regarded as an adequate substitute [14].

Bureaucratic professionals may promote and encourage the development of new planning jurisdictions and organizations in areas that manifestly compete with their own. This is likely to occur when bureaucrats are asked to take responsibility for problems that are regarded as being unsolvable, or whose techniques of solution lie outside of the traditional competence or imagination of the bureaucrats. In creating a new agency to handle extremely difficult problems, established agencies can divest themselves of responsibility for solving problems whose lack of solution might otherwise embarrass them.

Policy-making and planning are not as rational a process as is assumed by such terms as "substantive rationality," or by the very word "planning." Much of what is usually thought to be planning is the rational articulation of the forms of planning. In substance, planning is a highly political operation based on the reconciliation of conflicting interests and ideologies in order to gain consent for policies and programs, and to overcome opposition to such policies. These political processes must be thought of as the primary planning processes [15]. The articulation of planning in rational form is at best a secondary process. But planning as an ideology emphasizes its rational components and tends to deemphasize the political components which are neither rational nor are they subject to the control of the planner as technician or planning ideologist. Because this is true, it would seem to us that one of the persistent and compelling problems facing planners as professionals is how to deal with the violations of the ideology of planning, wherever planning is undertaken.

One of the continuous problems is that the planner who believes in the ideology of planning as the basis for the creation of an orderly or humane society continuously discovers that he is being used as a tool by vested interests whose interest in planning is only a means to secure what to the planner are narrow, selfish, personal, and jurisdictional ends. The recurrent disillusionment results, at times in cynicism, at times in the abandonment of planning ideals, and in the joining of nonplanning "interest establishments." At other times it results in a professional mobility in which the planner moves from planning field to planning field, hoping to find an area where both his technical talent and ideological commitment can be simultaneously gratified.

NOTES

1.   Major documents on bureaucracy include Max Weber, "Bureaucracy," in Gerth & Mills, *From Max Weber*, (N.Y.: Oxford Univ. Press, 1946). Robert Merton, *Social Theory and Social Structure*, rev.ed. (New York, Free Press, 1957), Chaps. VI and VII; C. Wright Mills, *White Collar*, (New York, Oxford University Press, 1959); Karl Mannheim, *Man and Society in an Age of Reconstruction* (New York, Harcourt, Brace, 1940); Robert Michels, *Political Parties* (New York, Macmillan, 1962); Peter Blau, *The Dynamics of Bureaucracy* (Chicago, University of Chicago Press, 1955); Philip Selznick, *TVA and the Grass Roots*, (Berkeley, University of California Press, 1949) (Harper reprint 1966). Important studies include F. J. Roethlisberger and J. Dickson, *Management and the Worker* (Cambridge, Mass., Harvard University Press, 1939); F. J. Roethlisberger, *Management and Morale* (Cambridge, Mass., Harvard University Press, 1947); Elton Mayo, *The Human Problems of an Industrial*

Civilization (New York, Macmillan, 1933); William F. Whyte, *Human Relations in the Restaurant Industry* (New York, McGraw-Hill, 1948). Useful readings are to be found in Robert K. Merton, Ailsa P. Gray, Barbara Hockey, and Hanan C. Selvin (Eds.), *Reader in Bureaucracy* (New York, Free Press, 1952); Amitai Etzioni (Ed.), *Complex Organizations: A Sociological Reader* (New York, Holt, Rinehart & Winston, 1961); valuable also is Melville Dalton, *Men Who Manage* (New York, Wiley, 1959). One such study is David Rogers, *110 Livingston Street: Politics and Bureaucracy in the New York City School System* (New York, Random House, 1968), especially Chap. VIII. See also Joseph Bensman and Bernard Rosenberg, *Mass, Class & Bureaucracy* (Englewood Cliffs, N.J., Prentice-Hall, 1963) Chaps. 9 and 10. Our discussion of bureaucracy draws upon and summarizes the materials above.

2.   Mayo, Roethlisberger and Dickson, Blau, Dalton, and Whyte, among others, have all emphasized the informal as part of bureaucracy, and by now they are part of the dominant tradition in the field. For other aspects of the bureaucratic character, see Arthur K. Davis, "Bureaucratic Patterns in the Navy Officer Corps," *Social Forces*, Vol. XXVII (1948), pp. 143–153, reprinted in Merton et al., *op. cit.*, pp. 380–395.

3.   See the discussion by Philip Selznick in his "An Approach to a Theory of Bureaucracy," *American Sociological Review*, Vol. VIII, 1943, no. 1, pp. 47-54, reprinted in Lewis A. Coser and Bernard Rosenberg, editors: *Sociological Theory: a Book of Readings*, 2nd edition, New York, Macmillan, 1964.

4.   An illustration of a failed attempt of two decades ago is the decentralization of New York City's public schools. The *New York Times* of May 8, 1971, carried a story by Emanuel Perlmutter: "Decentralization of Schools Fails, Kenneth Clark Says." Dr. Clark is quoted as seeing those involved in decentralization as having forgotten its original purpose, and as having become involved primarily in struggles for power and control.

5.   See Weber's "Bureaucracy" in Gerth and Mills, *op. cit.*, p. 220. In Mannheim's *Man and Society in an Age of Reconstruction*, see Part I, sections V and VI. (Translated by E. Shils, N.Y. Harcourt, Brace, 1940.)

6.   Martin Meyerson and Edward C. Banfield, in *Politics, Planning, and the Public Interest* (New York, Free Press, 1955), record this process in their chronicle of public housing plans for Chicago; similar processes and problems for such areas as Minneapolis and St. Paul are recorded in Alan Altschuler, *The City Planning Process* (Ithaca, Cornell University Press, 1965).

7.   The difficulties these conditions make for planners who must reconcile their actual functions with the professional ideologies are discussed cogently in Altschuler, *op. cit.*, pp. 323, 354, 359. See also Robert C. Hoover, "A View of Ethics and Planning," in the *Journal of the American Institute of Planners*, Vol. XXVII, No. 4 (November 1961), pp. 293–304. For other views, see Norman Beckman, "The Planner as Bureaucrat," *Journal of the American Institute of Planners*, Vol. XXX, No. 4 (November 1964), pp. 323–327; Herbert Gamberg, "The Professional and Policy Choices in Middle-Sized Cities," *Journal of the American Institute of Planners*, Vol. XXXVII, No. 3 (May 1966), pp. 174–178. Gamberg argues that planners must learn to play local administrative politics in order to achieve their goals. Beckman suggests a more resigned attitude on the part of planners, who should accept the limitations inherent in their positions Beckman says (p. 323): "Not everyone is built for the bureaucratic life, and for those planners whose 'idealism' and 'professionalism' make life difficult, [planning] cannot be recommended."

That planners themselves carry a potentially authoritarian, "higher" morality is inherent in their ideologies and in their roles, at least earlier along in the history of planning. Contact with local politics may serve in part as a sobering experience.

These points and much of the illustration of these points are documented in detail by Maynard Robison, in *The Ideological Development of American Planning in the 1960's,* unpublished Master's Essay, (City College of the City University of New York, 1971).

8.   Readers may wish to follow, by way of illustration, an issue which, at the time of our first edition was in relatively early stages: the New York City Master Plan, which dates back to 1938. The *New York Times* of May 29, 1972, carried a story by Ralph Blumenthal, "Critics Forcing Changes in Master Plan."

"A deluge of community criticism of the city's proposed Master Plan will bring major changes in some neighborhood projects, according to Donald H. Elliott, chairman of the City Planning Commission. However, he said, critics who have denounced the plan . . . have misunderstood its function as a guideline. The concept of the massive document itself will not be changed, he added. 'We have been pushed—and I like to think we have pulled a little,' said Mr. Elliott, the city's top planner, who was good-humored but tired after what he called the 'physically punishing' series of night-time hearings that ended last week. . . . In addition, Mr. Elliott said, the hearings have helped to foster some changes already. . . . Mr. Elliott's publicly stated eagerness to seek changes in the plan was in contrast to his comment in an interview in February. Asked then whether the hearings . . . have forced a change of view, he replied . . . 'No.' "

Students of planning as a bureaucratic process will follow its history with interest.

9.   The need of the planner to reconcile contradictory goals, and to count on waste in his plans, is discussed in F. Stuart Chapin, *Urban Land Use Planning* (Urbana, University of Illinois Press, 1965), pp. 62ff. A certain "resigned opportunism" on the part of planners is also suggested by Robert T. Daland and John A. Parker, "Roles of the Planner in Urban Dynamics," in F. Stuart Chapin and Shirley F. Weiss, (Eds.), *Urban Growth Dynamics* (New York, Wiley, 1962), pp. 188–225. It is possible that regional planning in underdeveloped countries may serve as outlets for the idealism (and latent authoritarianism) which some planners try to retain. See Lloyd Rodwin (Ed.), *Planning Urban Growth and Regional Development* (Cambridge, MIT Press, 1969), and also his *Nations and Cities: A Comparison of Strategies of Urban Growth* (Boston, Houghton Mifflin, 1970). The hazards described above, however, are no less present, albeit in different form.

10.   None of the above necessarily "proves" that plans are not adopted, that "plans do not work," or are stillborn, but we believe it does prove that virtually all implementations of planning result in something other than that intended by the planners at the time of the inception of the planning. As a matter of fact, at the time that plans are adopted, it is most often necessary to forget or conceal the aspirations and intentions which governed the plan. If the planning is reasonably acceptable to its audience at the time of its realization, the audience will tend to forget a major part of the extremely complex steps, adjustments, and readjustments which took place between conception and delivery. If the plan is conspicuously so successful that it surprises the parties involved, then awareness of the planning process will be salient and celebrated, though all the confusion, conflict, misunderstandings and inefficiencies will be "repressed." If the plan, when implemented, is a sudden, conspicuous, and important failure, then awareness of the planning process becomes an object for historical research. The intentions here are usually to distribute and redistribute the blame and to create the confidence that such disasters will not reoccur. When this is done it is possible to undertake new planning ventures. See, for elaboration, Arthur J. Vidich and Joseph Bensman, *Small Town in Mass Society,* rev. ed. (Princeton, N.J., Princeton University Press, 1968), Part IV "The Reconciliation of Symbolic

Appearances and Institutional Realities," and Part V, "The Findings, Methods, Theory and Implications of a Community Study." See also Joseph Bensman and Israel Gerver, "Crime and Punishment in the Factory, a Functional Analysis," in Alvin W. and Helen P. Gouldner (Eds.), *Modern Sociology* (New York, Harcourt, Brace & Jovanovich, 1963) (reprinted in Edward Quinn, Robert Lilienfeld, and Rodman Hill (Eds.), *Interdiscipline: A Reader in Psychology, Sociology and Literature,* (New York, Free Press, 1972). Planning can be reasonably successful when the planning agency rests upon grants of authority from outside groups or agencies or opinions that are relatively strong, focused, and clear. The necessity of compromising mutually exclusive and contradictory ends and means is not overwhelming. In this sense, planning is most likely to be effective when the planners are subject to authoritarian constraints.

11.　Lewis Mumford, "Home Remedies for Urban Cancer," in *The Urban Prospect* (New York, Harcourt, Brace & World, 1968); Jane Jacobs, *The Death and Life of Great American Cities* (New York, Random House, 1961); Herbert Gans, *The Urban Villagers* (New York, Free Press, 1962). On the fate of plans, see also Gans' *The Levittowners* (New York, Pantheon, 1967), Chap. 14, "Politics and Planning."

12.　The history of St. Louis' Pruitt-Igoe housing project is a case in point.

13.　Edward M. Kaitz and Herbert H. Hyman, *Urban Planning for Social Welfare* (New York, Praeger, 1970); Leonard Duhl, *The Urban Condition* (New York, Basic Books, 1963); Harvey S. Perloff, "New Directions in Social Planning," *Journal of the American Institute of Planners,* Vol. XXXI, No. 4 (November 1965), pp. 297–303; Lyle C. Fitch, "Social Planning in the Urban Cosmos," in Leo Schnore and Henry Fagin Eds.), *Urban Research and Policy Planning* (Beverly Hills, Cal., Sage Publishing, 1967), pp. 329–358. See also Peter H. Rossi and Robert A. Dentler, *The Politics of Urban Renewal* (New York, Free Press, 1961), and Martin Anderson, *The Federal Bulldozer* (New York, McGraw-Hill, 1967). Also valuable here is Charles E. Silberman, *Crisis in Black and White* (New York, Random House, 1964), especially Chap. X, "The Revolt Against Welfare Colonialism."

14.　Richard Titmuss, *Commitment to Welfare* (New York, Pantheon Books, 1968), Part III, "Issues of Redistribution in Social Policy:" also Richard Titmuss, *Essays on "The Welfare State,"* 2nd ed. (London, George Allen & Unwin, 1963), Chap. 2, "The Social Division of Welfare: Some Reflections on the Search for Equity."

15.　The decision to escalate and de-escalate the war in Vietnam was in part a very carefully planned operation, and in part it represented a conflict of a variety of different governmental pressure groups, in part the normal operations of both optimism and inefficiency, and the unwillingness of subalterns to question the political authority of their superiors; all these factors contributed to the planned chaos that ensued. In a similar sense, John F. Kennedy's decision to invade Cuba, and later Lyndon Johnson's decision to invade the Dominican Republic, were all highly planned operations, in the sense that we have described above.

Chapter 18

Class Attitudes

CONTRADICTIONS BETWEEN PHENOMENOLOGICAL
AND CLASS ANALYSIS

To discuss the phenomenology of social or economic class is a contradiction in terms. One of the major precepts of phenomenological analysis is that of treating the object of intellectual, ideological, or human thought only in terms of itself. The phenomenological method permits no reduction but the reduction to the meaning of the things described [1]. By definition, even the term social and economic class suggests that "class" perspectives, thoughts, ideas, and ideologies can be reduced to economic or social realities other than conceptual or ideational materials. The economic reduction devalues ideas and subjects them to criteria of thought which are outside the framework of analysis, and whose determinations are frequently unexamined.

It is possible that an examination of the perspectives that lead to social class analysis can show that they are themselves determined by the social, economic, occupational, personal, or philosophical biases of the analysts, and are therefore not themselves free from the biases from which the sociological or economic analyst assumed himself to be free when he purports to describe other people's biases [2].

Phenomenologists, however, face the same problem, for in making the phenomenological reduction, they tend to define phenomena in terms of categories of consciousness which may well be the product of the consciousness they are attempting to define. This is the problem raised by Hume, and it has continued to plague epistemologists and philosophers ever since. The act of constructing and defining experience implies prior concepts and

345

consciousness which must first be defined. In attempting to define such prior concepts and consciousness, the phenomenologist undertakes a continuous regression into more basic states of mind, until he reaches one last concept of pure consciousness.

Pure conciousness is consciousness without any content. If pure consciousness is to have content, one would have to go backward in one's analysis to discover the basis of the definition of such content [3]. A pure consciousness without content, however, even if it is possible to imagine, does not help us analyze specific ideational materials. The leap forward from pure consciousness to analytical concepts is, by definition, a leap across an unbridgeable gap.

At this level, it would seem to us, it is possible to destroy any system upon which one could base a theory of knowledge, whether such a system were based on reductions from external phenomena or on the phenomenon being considered in its own terms. For the sake of our present analysis, we think that all that can be done is to suspend the epistemological reduction, that is, to assume that knowledge is possible, and, having assumed this, to ask, What are the forms that knowledge takes [4]?

This means we can postulate that corresponding to social and economic classes are distinguishable forms of knowledge, experience, ideology, interests, commitments, and concepts, and that different social and economic classes will exhibit differences in these ideational forms. The analyst is forced to claim the right to stand outside the system he analyzes and to act as if his thought is not itself determined, even though he may believe that this assumption is not true. He allows the uncertainty of his assumption to come into play only after he has performed his work; the uncertainty is expressed by the criticism, debate, and discussion which is focused on his work by other men who also claim the philosopher's privilege. The value derived from making the assumption that knowledge is possible and that the question is of determining its forms and content, is derived from the consequences of making the assumption. We are being pragmatic about the use of concepts in what we understand as the technical sense of the term "pragmatic." We do not believe that this contradicts the original impulse to phenomenological work.

The argument resolves itself into a debate about what is known rather than one of how we know. If there is any resolution, it is on the basis of a consensus as to what is known, even though all parties to the consensus may be men whose thought is itself determined. On these grounds, we simply assume the fact that we can describe the nature of class-determined thought without waiting for the analysis of thought to determine whether one can use the concept of class at all.

CLASS AND OCCUPATIONAL ATTITUDES: BASIC DIMENSIONS

In much of our preceding work, we have indicated that the occupational methodology, the habits of mind and "attitudes" of men in various fields of endeavor, determine the way they view the world, and that occupation is an important ingredient in determining their consciousness.

Here we are thinking primarily of the methodology, the habit of mind, developed from an occupation, rather than the structural position and perspective which an occupation may produce, or the vested interests that become associated with an occupation, as it relates to market, income, or capital structures. These other dimensions of an occupation will be treated subsequently. By and large, they have been the focus of most Marxian occupational and class analyses. The occupational methodology has been less important in Marxian analysis, though one can find it even in *Das Kapital*. To our way of thinking Veblen, in applying John Dewey's concept of habit of mind, emphasized the importance of occupational methodology on ways of viewing the world (or on the development and articulating of images of the world).

An occupation, however, is not a class, though it may well be that occupations, or a number of them, may be similar enough in their occupational methodologies or craft to produce a "class" perspective. Moreover, we have indicated that individuals in various occupational positions perceive restricted segments of the total horizon of experience available to a society because of the selective and restrictive nature of their social position.

It is quite obvious that the world of experience presented to an assembly-line worker by virtue of his job is quite different from the world presented to an investment banker. Both respond to very narrow and restrictive aspects of the world, and are prevented by their respective restrictions from seeing, in concrete specific terms, the world that the other sees [5].

Conversely, there is a richness of descriptive texture that each occupational group is able to draw from its experience, based upon the very specialization and preoccupation with limited areas of experience. It is now a cliché to note that the nomadic Arab has some forty words to describe sand, and the Eskimo some thirty words to describe snow. Such richness in capacity for description reflects the respective specialization and the respective necessity for the articulation of experience, since the restricted area constitutes so much of their totality of experience [6].

Still another dimension of class corresponds to the conception of economic, occupational, and political self-interest which reflects the particular claims of an economic group upon other groups in the society. These interests can be expressed in the distributive feeling of being under-rewarded, or can be communalized or socialized through political, social, or occupational and trade groups. Once the latter occurs, the articulation of a class or occupational interest takes an idealogical or intellectual form. [7].

A fourth dimension of class can be conceived as involving a sense of identification with or commitment to the established forms of society. The identification or commitment can range from total acceptance to total rejection of the dominant social arrangements of a society. Total acceptance and rejection may be expressed in forms which go beyond the explicit embracing of ideologies. An individual who totally accepts a society may do so by simply embracing the forms and procedures of a society without knowing that he does so. His acceptance manifests itself in his behavior, temperament, character, but not necessarily in an ideological articulation of his position. In a sense, total acceptance of a social system means that the system is not external to the individual, it has become part of his unconscious perceptive apparatus. Since the system totally governs his thought, he is unaware of the system [8].

The problem of discovering the phenomenological aspects of a received identity and commitment to a total social order or part of one is a difficult problem, since by the very nature of the commitment and identification, the individual is unable to articulate it. Simply because it is true, it *appears* to be not true. The phenomenological model would be constructed by developing an ideal type of the kind of motivation that appears to explain the actions, commitments, and identities of the person. The truth or falsity of such a model depends on its ability to predict.

In positing these motivations, and attributing them to the actors, despite the fact that the actors do not attribute them to themselves, we are to some extent violating the rules of phenomenological method. We are constructing models of the "as-if" character of motivations.

An individual who totally rejects "the system" may reject it by retreating from all thoughts or activities that force him to come to grips with the system in explicit intellectual or ideological terms. His rejection is manifest in his behavior. It becomes readily apparent from the observation of his behavior. In both cases, the unconscious acceptance or rejection of the system can be reduced to phenomenological terms by imputing a world of conscious thought to the individual that reduces the variance of his behavior from the model to zero. Thus, the behavior becomes phenomenologically accessible even though the individual is unable or not called upon to express his intellectual attitude [9].

The dimension of commitment to a form of society is broader than the commitment to an established, ongoing order of society. Commitments can be held to a past order of society after it has been superseded. Commitments can also be made to an order of society which never has existed, that is, to an order of society that is a romanticized and idealized image of a previous world. The commitment can also be made to orders of society which are conceived as being emergent but whose "emergence" is as much a product of the commitment as it is of a preordained future, that is, the self-fulfilling prophecy. Marxists may well have this type of commitment. Finally, commitments may be made to a Utopia, an order of society which is believed in or hoped for. Whether such a Utopia can emerge is more a question of faith than prognosis. The validity of the Utopia can only be established after all the efforts to make it emerge are undertaken.

CLASS AND IDEOLOGY

Acceptance and rejection of a system can develop in intellectual and ideological terms, usually as the product of long and systematic intellectual and ideological development. Such a process involves the development of the awareness of class, economic, occupational, and political consciousness. It means that the consciousness becomes socialized or communalized. This involves the development of explicit ideologies which are often the product of specialized intellectual and ideological articulation by specialized ideologists or intellectuals. The development of such ideologies involves the creation of systems of thought with internal logic, consistency, assumptions, and emotional overtones that can be treated as structural wholes. It doesn't matter what the basis of their origins are in the social and economic position of those who create them or are their intended audience.

An ideology, being an intellectually constructed structural whole may be different from the attitudes of the members of an economic or social class. Certainly there is no requirement that members of an economic group internalize what may be at times the infinite variety of ideologies and subideologies that are attributed or presented to them. Nor need they be aware of the structural unity and logic that can be inferred from a formal ideology. Nor do we assume that ideologies or class attitudes need to be "true" or appropriate for a given class or "class system." The truth or falsity of an ideology at most is revealed after the historical fact, and, as we know, history does not often reveal unambiguous verdicts.

All one can say at this point is that ideologies do exist and that to some extent they may or may not be internalized by particular populations to which they are presented. They may be internalized by populations for whom they were not intended. But once they come into existence, both ideologies and class attitudes can be made subject to analysis in order to discern their structure and content, and to infer their manifest or latent purpose.

A systematic ideology that affirms a social system is usually the product or the "descendant" of an earlier ideology which attacked a previous system but has grown affirmative with the success of the class of its bearers. At the "high point" of its success, however, the ideology may not exist in a systematic intellectualized form, but becomes internalized as part of the perceptual apparatus of its bearers.

The ideology may reappear in its manifest ideational form when it is attacked by a newer or older ideology which has now grown in strength. Explicit ideologies may become defensive, and the defensiveness forces groups to make their ideology explicit in order to use it as a weapon. In short, ideologies are not always weapons. Ideologies, as intellectual systems, are alternative to attitudes "taken for granted." The conditions which make an ideology a formal system rather than an implicit system are always of interest, but it is always necessary to distinguish between "latent" and "manifest" ideologies.

Whether such attitudes are distributive, communalized, or socialized is a question of the difference between class-in-itself and class-for-itself. The difference between distributive and communalized forms of class consciousness and class interest are substantial, and are based on major processes of intellectual, cultural, and social developments within societies. Such "external frameworks" to the development of class consciousness and awareness of class interest are in part independent of the development of class itself in any of its forms, and constitute a pre-condition for the historical determination of the forms that class takes.

IDEOLOGIES AND CLASS CLAIMS AND INTERESTS

Most ideologies do not completely affirm or reject a total system. Ideologies usually specify the definition of an ideal social system, the necessary conditions for the operation of that system, and the groups and skills necessary to operate the system to achieve the idealized goals of the system. They usually suggest or imply that a given group, class, or occupation are indispensable to the system, and either deserve the rewards that they get or are under-rewarded, depending on the economic, social, and political situation of the class or interest group.

Thus, some groups will demand modification or change within the framework of the ongoing social system, alteration of the prestige and reward systems, and perhaps modification of laws or structural elements in that system.

All of these ideological arguments will favor a claiming group and disfavor a competitive group. But since in the majority of cases the demands are usually for less than total destruction and reconstruction of "the system," the level of commitment to or rejection of the system is usually less than total. Partial acceptance and rejection of the dominant system need not be made on explicit ideological grounds. Individuals may feel that they are adequately rewarded, and may affirm or accept the system without developing any ideological attachment to it. They may announce that the system is rotten and corrupt, but that it favors them; therefore they can accept it, even as they "cry all the way to the bank." Other groups may be highly critical of the system, but express their criticism by individual deviancy, murmuring and complaining, but will not systematically ideologize, organize, or politicize their complaints or sense of injustice; these are the true conservatives. It is well known that many individuals and groups who ideologize, politicize, and organize their complaints, do not feel that such ideological activity should interfere with their enjoyment of the benefits of the system or with their favored position in the system. Some kinds of disaffection from the system take the form of apathy, retreatism, and the avoidance of all political consciousness, and thus of all ideology other than the implicit ideology of having none.

All of this is relevant to social class because the experience of commitment to a social system, or of disenchantment with it, is frequently made on the grounds of common class situation. Arguments for reform and revolution are made in the name of, and directed to, working-class groups, peasant groups, the old bourgeoisie, the new bourgeoisie, the new working classes, the silent or neglected majority, and, of course, in the name of aristocracies, nobilities, and ruling classes. The members of these classes will respond to such ideologies in terms of the consistency of the ideology ("elective affinity"), its plausibility in the light of their experience, including their experience of the consciousness of being members of a class. In responding to the ideology, they accept such definition and membership, though not all individuals in a given class situation need accept an ideology that is beamed to them, or accept it on the same grounds or to the same degree [10].

We would reject the notion that there is a "true" class interest or class consciousness which is necessary to any stage of economic or historical development and which can be inferred deductively from the class position itself, or from immanent "laws" of classes or of the evolution of classes. We would argue that if given stages of class interest or consciousness emerge at given stages in the economic or historic process, they can be derived only from the empirical materials, and they are valid only insofar as they explain and interpret the empirical materials. The notion that some deductive process can explain what class consciousness ought and should be is subject to the same charges of reification which Marx made against his enemies.

Occupational Perspectives

We have indicated that an individual's occupation in large part determines his view of the world. It does so in two ways. First, in that the methodology, technique, or technology of an occupation creates and selects certain habits of mind which, while being specific to the occupational methodology, become generalized. To a substantial degree they govern the total way one perceives the world. Secondly, the world that is presented to a person in a given occupation will be different from the world presented to members of another occupation. Therefore, there is a different "reality" to which different occupations respond with different ways of perceiving that reality. But all of these multiple realities and multiple perspectives are related to occupation, not to class. The problem in the analysis of class is to discover if there are any typicalities of classes of occupation, a problem of great complexity because of the vast number and variety of occupations in a complex society.

The standard literature on the subject by now indicates a cultural dimension in the classification of occupations. This is based on the object of occupational activity. Individuals are classified as "object-pushers," "pencil-pushers," and "people-pushers." Object-pushers are viewed as members of the lower classes, pencil-pushers of the middle classes, and people-pushers of the upper middle and upper classes [11].

It seems to us that such a classification, though containing many useful implications, is not totally accurate. Certainly, a sculptor, a dental technician, even a surgeon, are to a great extent object-pushers, though they are not conventionally considered to be members of the lower classes. We shall demonstrate that people-pushing is an attribute of all classes. Moreover, within the categories, the range of possible attitudes is extremely wide. It is by now almost a truism that peasants and primitives generally tend to personify nature and objects in nature, so that while they are object-pushers, they respond to objects as if the objects were people [12].

Thorstein Veblen, in speaking of the industrial habit of mind, identified industrial workers as presenting a "matter-of-fact" attitude, a consciousness of cause and effect, and he identified this with the scientific attitude. Almost all subsequent research has indicated that industrial workers tend to concretize phenomena, to depict the specific object and not the generalized class of object or the generalized principle upon which objects are classed [13].

Scientific workers are concerned with the generalized attributes of objects and the generalized processes which transpire between objects, so that they rely on the specific appearance and nonappearance of objects as a test of the abstract relationship between the generalized attributes which are contained in objects.

Object-Pushing

The notion that industrial workers are scientific in habit of mind, as indicated by Veblen and some of his followers, appears to have been based upon the rejection of upper-class ideologies that are "magical" in character by the working class. Veblen argued that the upper class shares with the peasant a kind of personalization of natural forces, a love of myth and ritual, especially where such a love is associated with war, the manly arts, and the struggle for domination. The upper class conceives of this as a game in which victory and its display are the ultimate goal of upper-class activity. There may be merit in this position.

He also argued, however, that the scientist rejects this psychology of zero-sum gaming, and instead he is concerned with absolute output, a goal the scientist strives to achieve by disenchanting and depersonalizing nature. Again, it is doubtful that scientists (apart from viewing science as an abstract function) are capable of separating themselves from their occupational roles in the purity of their functions. It would appear to us that scientists are perfectly capable of exhibiting at the same time the highest degree of impersonal rationality in some areas of their being while maintaining perfectly irrational humanity in other areas of their existence.

Yet all of the above does not invalidate the major point. Factory workers tend to see the reality of the physical movement and metamorphosis of objects in the industrial process, and see that it is their direct actions that result in these physical changes. The more abstract managerial, financial, legal, and even scientific basis for their actions are doubly abstract. The principles accounting for the specialization of their tasks are not fully understood in their original character. Beyond this, the scientific basis for their work is not physically demonstrated in their immediate environment. These principles appear to be secondary in importance to their physical work. As a result, the special perception of work by the blue-collar worker results in a transformation in dimension of thought. Thus, the salience of their work is transformed into the importance of their work, which in turn is translated into the possibility of magnifying their ideological claims and interests in the final share for rewards of their work. Thus there is a direct linkage between perceptual density and restrictiveness of social environment, and the possibility of ideological claims emerging from that perceptual density and restrictiveness.

Pencil-Pushing

The concept of "pencil-pushing," as related primarily to middle-class occupations, was historically more valid at earlier times than it is at present.

In prebureaucratic societies, and societies in which literacy was available to a very limited sector of the population, the separation between object-pushers, people-pushers, and pencil-pushers was more cearly apparent. Certainly the occupations of scribe, priest, scholar, and notary, were the primary occupations of pencil-pushers. And these were, within the framework of these societies, more middle class than were the peasant or the feudal lord. With the development of large-scale bureaucratic industrial society, pencil-pushing became a minimally essential quality necessary to all occupations. The maintenance of control by "ruling classes" requires their personal evaluation of reports, balance-sheets, and operational summaries of all kinds which, no matter how simply they were prepared, require a mentality which can digest symbolic presentations. It is true that the upper-class comptroller must be able to translate symbolic presentations into possibilities for direct action (people-pushing), but he can never wholly succeed in avoiding dealing with a symbolic world. At the same time, the requirements for mastery of symbolic presentation are so great that members of the middle class who are superior in abstracting, summarizing, and presenting symbolic material become co-opted into the upper classes by virtue of these talents. Thus, the scientific consultant, computer expert, and technician cum millionaire enter the upper classes of all advanced societies.

At the other end of the class continuum, a minimum mastery of symbolic materials becomes indispensable for participation in the labor force. This means that the ability to fill out forms, to read signs, gauges, dials, to follow printed instructions, is the most general and necessary talent for even relatively primitive industrial work.

The groups and individuals who have not acquired these skills become the *lumpenproletariat*, excluded from the process by which minimal opportunity is presented to individuals in an industrial society. At this point, basic education becomes an indispensable quality for participation even in lower-class life.

People-Pushing

People-pushing has generally been associated with upper-class styles, again the primary reference being preindustrial society. People-pushing means the manipulation of others, the use of symbols that evoke loyalties to causes that are frequently the manipulator's, not the causes of those manipulated. It involves the invocation of obedience, discipline, and subservience. It involves skills of leadership, "management," and above all negotiation, compromise, and collaboration. The skills are necessary to the operation of a social system and the exercises of power within a social system.

The various emotional colorations of the terms used above imply either a positive or negative evaluation of a function. Whether or not the terms are positive or negative, however, the same function is the object of the terms. People-pushing is related to command functions. But again, while the over-all principle may be accurate, the world has become so complicated that the exceptions almost inundate the rule. Certainly the rise of the new white-collar classes has provided vast new opportunities for people-pushing.

The major forms of people-pushing include self-manipulation in order to ingratiate oneself with others. The white-collar worker in a bureaucratic setting finds that in order to succeed he has to win friends. He wins friends by first manipulating himself to be pleasing to customers as a salesperson, or to be pleasing to higher-level officials as an employee or bureaucrat. To the extent that he succeeds, he manipulates others. But this self-manipulation is in terms of criteria that are perceived to be the criteria of others. Therefore, it is not at all clear who is being manipulated and who is doing the manipulating. Since, in a complex sales or bureaucratic situation, the customers or the supervisor are not independent of the system within which they work, they must manipulate themselves. Even in relationship to the sales person or the subordinate, the practice of manipulation may be a mutual one. Thus, the round of self-manipulation may be continuous, with no set of goals outside of mutual survival within a system that requires the manipulation of oneself and others [14].

Freedom from being manipulated requires that one be outside the "system," or have the freedom to enter or leave the system. But as the system becomes all-embracing, few can resist being simultaneously both the subject and object of manipulation. It is undoubtedly true, however, that one's susceptibility to self-manipulation as described above is related to an absence of power and a desire for the fruits of power. Thus, individuals who little desire the fruits of the system are less amenable to manipulation by themselves and others. Individuals with relatively high degrees of authority may manipulate themselves and others more than may these less-favored groups, simply because they are striving for even greater authority or for the rewards of authority. Thus, favored position by itself does not guarantee freedom from manipulation, a fact that every courtier knew long before the modern bureaucratic revolution.

Lower-Class People-Pushing

While manipulation of oneself and others is generally considered to be an upper-class or middle-class phenomenon, lower-class manipulation of others is frequently overlooked. Lower-class manipulation of others is usually different in intention from either upper- or middle-class manipulation. By and large, such lower-class manipulation entails resistance to the manipulation practiced upon them by the middle and upper classes. Yet it involves social and cultural styles that are objective in character, in the sense that they are learned and transmitted among lower classes. The content and style of such counter-manipulation is historically and culturally varied, elaborate, and includes many subtypes. Perhaps the simplest and best-known can be called Schweikism, and it involves two types of behavior. One type involves acting the role of a lower-class idiot, which is attributed to him in such situations where being a lower-class idiot frustrates the manipulation by a superior. This involves the feigning of stupidity, the employment of destructive incompetence, and the incapacity to understand orders or suggestions. It may involve requiring of the superior an explanation that is more difficult and time-consuming than doing the task himself. Sometimes it involves carrying out orders literally and ritualistically when such execution defeats the purpose of the orders. It also involves playing on the guilt, the gullibility, and the innocence of the superior when such innocence involves favorable advantage to the lower-class individual. It may involve stealing, when the lower class is regarded as being morally incapable [15].

Incompetence, laziness, and malfeasance are all presented in simple innocence, since innocence is the expected attribute. It may involve embarrassing the upper-class person with friendliness, affection, or intimacy when the upper-class individual would prefer to maintain his position of superiority by maintaining social distance.

There is much speculation whether such lower-class incompetence becomes so ingrained that it becomes a fixed response, in which the chief victim of the incompetence becomes the actor himself. What started as a form of behavior oriented to a higher, more powerful class becomes the only possible form of behavior. At the other extreme is the psychology of the "put-on," "jiving," the "snow job," or the act of "conning." In each case, the very term implies a consciousness of technique and style which can be donned or discarded depending on the class situation, the ideology, or the degree of personal intimacy of the parties involved. Black Nationalists of the 1960s rejected the notion that there ever was something like a Sambo or an Uncle Tom. The Sambo or Uncle Tom was a put-on reflecting the powerlessness of the Negro in a system dominated by slavery and caste. The argument that the Sambo and Uncle Tom are put-ons allowed the Black Nationalist ideologically to reject the notion of impairment in slavery that colors contemporary race relations. At the same time the Black Nationalist accused other Blacks who held differing views, of being Sambos, Uncle or Doctor Thomases, without at all times making it clear that these forms of behavior were put-ons.

The objectivity of these techniques is seen in the fact that they become culturally standardized, that a great many individuals in the same class will adopt identical forms of defensive manipulation of class and racial superiors. Studies of folklore such as The Brer Rabbit stories, and a vast number of novels by Blacks on race relations and social science studies on race etiquette, emphasize the social character of such responses. Moreover, an elaborate put-on may involve the collective participation of two or more members of the same class or race, with extreme finesse and ability to respond to minimal class or cultural cues in spontaneously created performances that will evoke the desired effect in the upper-class viewer. A key dimension of such put-ons is that the extent to which they are a put-on must remain ambiguous, for the put-on is an act of retaliation for being cast into an inferior position. If the put-on is too obvious, it will evoke a direct reaction of the individual with power. If it is done too subtly, it will confirm the latter's sense of superiority. If it is ambiguous, the viewer will feel uncomfortable but unable to retaliate. At this point, he is helpless. Such put-ons, of course, assume the fact that the viewer can respond with guilt to the degraded and inferior position of the lower-class individuals. Thus, the liberal, sympathetic person will become more the object of the put-on than will the upper-class individual who is too obtuse, thick, insensitive, or reactionary to be affected by it. The subtlety, style, or sense of appropriateness as to what is an effective put-on suggests that at some level consciousness of the process is involved, though such consciousness does not require that the individual be able to spell it out in phenomenological terms. Of course, members of a lower class, having learned what manipulation and exploitation by an upper class means from bitter experience, will at times practice what has been practiced on them, when they can find an individual or a group that is even more vulnerable than they are. People-pushing thus becomes a compensatory device, even where there is little direct profit or gain from such people-pushing.

Such reactions to powerlessness are part of the phenomenological makeup of all powerless groups extending far beyond class. There is evidence to suggest that the psychology of women in the eras where males were dominant was governed by such indirectness and manipulative behavior, as was the psychology of youth. But since an essential ingredient of class is relative powerlessness, such attitudes can be expected in the phenomenology of classes. It involves people-pushing though such people-pushing is necessarily indirect. At times it is a defense against the more direct people-pushing by more powerful groups, and at other times is a form of retaliation against the more direct people-pushing of the superordinate group.

But lower-class people-pushing frequently does involve the highly skilled use of personal and social manipulation. In this perspective, then, the upper classes do not specialize in people-pushing, but only in some forms of it. Middle classes, as indicated, have different styles of people-pushing, as do the lower classes.

While object-pushing, pencil-pushing, and people-pushing are all related to class, it is not so much that different classes select one or more of these basic orientations toward action, but rather that they give different cultural content to all these forms of action. The reconstruction of the phenomenology of class, then, depends on the discovery of the appropriate substance or content to those orientations toward action.

Class Attitudes Toward Time

A considerable body of literature has developed to indicate that various class groups develop different attitudes toward time, and that the consciousness of past, present, and future is related to the experience of favorable and unfavorable eras in the development of a class. The literature in this area is so extensive that we will only outline the arguments.

Attitude toward time is not simply related to class, but to the sense of movement, accomplishment, and ascendancy in a society. It is related to optimism and pessimism. In a purely determinist perspective, it is related to differential accumulations of capital. This is to say that those groups that are expanding their accumulation of capital are likely to be optimistic about the future, and the groups who, having achieved some measure of social and economic success, but are no longer expanding relative to other groups in society are likely to be pessimistic and oriented to the past. At a societal level, those societies that are expansive are likely to be geared to the future and the present, and those that are contracting or stationary are likely to be more geared to the past.

Expressing this phenomenon in class terms, there is much literature to suggest that upper classes, especially aristocratic classes, having achieved dominance in a society that continues to develop, especially among and for new and ascendant classes, are likely to worship the past, their ancestors, and the pedigrees and social qualities of their ancestors. They tend to justify themselves in terms of bloodlines, character, and life styles that are tasteful and morally superior. Thus, ancestor-worship, heirlooms, public service, moral leadership, philanthropy, emphasis on stylized good taste, are characteristic of upper classes [16].

The same forms of response are possible among middle- and lower-class groups who, after having achieved some mobility which is now arrested, develop comparable forms of adherence to the past, and morally and socially superior characteristics associated with their own past. Thus, lace-curtain Irish have triumphed over Shanty Irish, and petty bourgeois enjoy the same symbolic victories over the blue-collar workers or the *lumpenproletariat*.

When the rate of descent of a previously favored class is extreme, rapid, and highly visible to that class, their worship of the past is accompanied by extreme status defensiveness, anxiety, and resentment. At times it becomes radicalized and politicized so that the desire to return to the past is revolutionary in character even though ideologically based on the images of conservatism and the past. The response of the lower middle class to inflation in

Germany in these terms contributed to the rise of a radical national socialism. In France, the desire to restore the *ancien régime* after the defeat of Napoleon contributed to hundreds of right-wing reactionary but revolutionary movements in that society by scions of the older nobility.

In the same way, older WASP groups in American society, both in the North and in the South have contributed to racist, radical, and revolutionary movements throughout American history. Almost every ethnic group that "makes it" in American society tends to develop an ethnic pride and attitude of superiority toward groups who follow their attempt. This process continues to the present [17].

Arrested ascendance makes the past more meaningful than the present or future, and mobility or ascendance makes the present and the future more attractive. This attractiveness is linked to attitudes of optimism, aggressiveness, and opportunity.

Ascendant groups are not likely to have favorable images of the past since the past does not convey a favorable image of themselves. They are likely to consider themselves as ancestors rather than as descendants, and only after they have achieved substantial success are they willing to make jokes about their youthful poverty, their horse-thief ancestors, and the nostalgic days when they or their parents lived in the ghettoes. Until such success is achieved, the ascendant groups are likely to be defensive about their pasts, and to develop personal and social styles which are emulative of the styles of older ascendant groups. They are likely to develop resentments against the very groups they emulate because such groups stand in the way of their full achievement in the directions in which they are moving. The extent of these resentments and the political implications of these resentments are a product of the extent to which their mobility is blocked by ascendant groups. The very fact of mobility and success permits groups that were previously quiescent to express outright hostility and resentment toward groups that "lorded it over them" in the past. At times this aggressiveness, hostility, and blockage will result in politically revolutionary movements. But such movements are usually oriented to an imaginary future world that is in the making rather than to an idealized present. While they are ascendant, they are likely to justify their ascendancy in terms of economic function. They construct ideologies which define their new function. Such ideologies define the rewards they hope to achieve by making these contributions. The ideological development for ascendant classes reflects both their optimism, their expectations and orientations, and resentments which suggest that their self-image is not accepted or appreciated by others, especially the others whose own favorable self-image precludes the recognition of others.

Groups that are not favored and never have been, who are "out of it" in terms of societally accepted canons of self-legitimacy, develop two distinct attitudes toward time. The first is an attitude of embracing the present in the hedonistic and self-indulgent senses of the term "present." Since the future offers nothing and the past offers no standards, restraints, or traditions, one might as well "make merry." The pursuit of pleasure then becomes the relevant time-locus for their action, and such pursuit does not allow for considerations of the future or the future consequences of their present action. Alcoholism, sex, narcotics, immediate excitements and gratifications become the psychological equivalents of an ideology. The *lumpenproletariat*, the shack people, the outcasts of respectable society at almost all times and places become bearers of this world now—the damned and the doomed.

Another group which finds no living space in the immediate present, the past, or in the short-range future attempts to rescue itself from negative self-imagery by focusing on a far-distant future, so far in the future, that direct comparison between the present and the near future does not embrace it. Thus, chiliastic groups look to Utopia, the millennium, and perhaps to the Revolution. With such a futuristic orientation, the present can be enjoyed because it is preparation for that distant day. Enthusiasm, optimism, and joy can be expressed because they are related to ultimate victory and the transcendance of the present, no matter how negative it seems. Underneath all of this, however, is a rejection of ordinary life, of the established scheme of values, institutions, and rewards within a society [18].

The sense of deprivation or lack of deprivation of a class need not be an objective fact. Some lower or working classes, after achieving moderate success relative to their own past, may feel that they have "arrived" even though in objective terms they are not particularly "haves." They may defend their relative success with greater passion than those who are objectively more successful.

On the other hand, groups that have been highly successful in the past, and by objective standards are still so, but less than in the past, may develop ideologies and attitudes of *ressentiment*, rejection, subjective deprivation, rejection of commitments to the ongoing system, and may develop reactionary or radical antiestablishment attitudes. Such groups may become incipient fascists, defensive totalitarians, and defenders of systems, real or imaginary, of the past.

CLASS ATTITUDES IN THEIR HISTORICAL CONTEXT

The same class will change its basic attitudes over time. A class may be unorganized, disorganized, apathetic, or incapable of expressing itself as a class at a given time in its historic experience. At other times, the same class may become rebellious, revolutionary, reformist, or conservative. A middle class at some phases of its historic experience may be optimistic, expansive, aggressive, and independent of established upper classes. At other times it will accept and submit to the social and political leadership of the upper classes. They may assert goals and objectives of their own, and may pull down the structure of the society that "oppresses" them. They may do this with a sense of optimism and progress. At other times they may be just as revolutionary, but their revolutionary impulses may be governed by a sense of defensive anxiety and the attempt to avoid social and economic defeat.

Newer middle classes may be located as isolated or nearly isolated and defensive individuals and groups among the older middle classes. The newer middle classes may discover life styles, interests, and forms of social and cultural behavior that are distinctly their own, and develop some sense of pride, self-satisfaction and vindication in the feeling that their life styles appear to reflect their authentic social basis and life experiences, education, and culture. At other times, the challenge to their occupational or status position may make them defensive.

It is possible to argue that the social, psychological, phenomenological, political, and economic characters of a class are always subject to change, and that a generalized timeless abstract model must, in the light of these historic changes, become "incorrect" or inapplicable. The more generalized models can serve, at most, as indicators for the asking of relevant questions, as heuristic devices when one wishes to confront the empirical worlds in which classes dwell.

PREDICTING THE FUTURE OF CLASS SYSTEMS

The attempt to transcend historical limitations of data on class frequently results in the attempt to construct total and general theories of the historical evolution of societies which in their operation define and redefine the classes and the class orders in their respective societies. Such theories attempt to account for and project the evolution into the future of the economic, political, and social bases of classes. Abstract laws of history and society are evoked which predict the ultimate nature of the classes, their situation, their interest, and the directions which classes must take in order to take into account the "new" laws of society.

It is apparent wherever such theories are constructed that the classes in question often fail to recognize their own class interests, as postulated by the intellectual theorist, that they fail to recognize their class situation, and often fail to take the actions that would be appropriate to such recognition. When they fail to do so, this is often called, especially by Marxists, "false consciousness." The sources of false consciousness are often attributed to ignorance, to lack of theoretical ability, to short-sighted sell-outs by class leaders, to brainwashing and propaganda by the ideologists and institutions of other classes. Implicit in such a conception of false consciousness is a conception of true consciousness. The theorist who constructs the laws of history which embody the true consciousness of history thinks that he knows the laws of history and can predict the future evolution of society, its institutions and its classes. But it must always be remembered that those who attempt to predict the future and therefore the future intentions and desired action of classes, do so on the basis of their own assertion of general historical laws. The true consciousness they assert may not be the "spirit" or the "laws of history," but rather their own perception or assertion of the spirit and the laws. They are therefore subject to the charge that the true consciousness of history is only their own, and it may be as false as the false consciousness they find in others. If we take as given the descriptions of the laws of history as provided by virtually all who have claimed to know them, we would find as much evidence of error, failure in prediction, and therefore "false consciousness" as they charged their ideological enemies with. Marx's prediction of increasing misery within capitalist society, of the growing polarization between capitalist and proletariat, of recurring crises and his failure to see the tremendous importance of the new middle classes and of the bureaucratization of society are not minor failures. His failure to see the emergence of a class system within communist societies which is not essentially different from the class system of advanced capitalist society is as great an error [19]; his willingness to see the end of the dialectic in the achievement of communism is as great but more a philosophic error.

The proponents of the concept of false consciousness see themselves as being the exponents of true consciousness, true laws of history, because they are exempt from the particularities, the ideologies, the bases of social and economic position.

Their opponents are limited by these particularities. If their predictions are wrong, then we have no right to accept their claim of freedom from historical particularization. They appear to be subject to the limitations of time, place and history, though the times, place, and exposure to history may be different from those of their ideological opponents. No social position by itself guarantees access to the truth, especially if truth is defined in such terms as to be below or above the level of testing.

True consciousness and false consciousness are continuous emergents, continuously being revised by actual historical and institutional developments. Classes emerge and change out of a dynamic which, in the long run, is often unpredictable, that is, it must be assumed to be unpredictable until such prediction is validated by subsequent experience. Thus, the asserter of the laws of history, of class development, and of definitions of class interest and ideology is in the same position as anybody else who makes statements of the same order whether he claims true consciousness or not. The prediction is only a hypothesis, and in the world of class definitions the existence of multiple and contradictory predictions must be accepted as given. In a free society, all prophets have an equal right to make predictions and claims; but so far as we know there is no objective social machinery which exempts any group on any ground from the process of history and from the necessity of proving its claims in the open competition of ideas. The suspension of the sense of one's removal from history, and from the limitations placed on oneself by one's own time, place, and class position must itself be suspended. One becomes necessarily and appropriately subject to the charge that one's own class-free and value-free images of history or philosophy are only new attempts at ideological construction. One is forced, ultimately, to defend oneself, and this defense cannot be based on a "philosopher's privilege." It can be made only on the ability of the "philosopher" to assemble the evidence necessary to defend the plausibility of his position.

The evolution of class and class groupings appears to be a continuous process which in the long run has a set of dynamics, development, and continuity of its own. We can make short-term assessments of future prospects, and we can, with perhaps greater accuracy, describe the present and the past. But such descriptions are subject to the criticisms and the alternative descriptions of others. While at times the analyst makes the assumption that he can directly describe a social reality, free from the biases which would determine his own analytic position, yet he must always entertain the possibility that his approach is limited and particular. As of the present, we know of no way that the social analyst can exempt himself from history and can claim, as a result, a special right to prophesy, or a monopoly on the truth, no matter what the grounds are for such a claim.

NOTES

1.   Edmund Husserl, *The Idea of Phenomenology*, translated by William P. Alston and George Nakhnikian (The Hague, Martinus Nijhoff, 1964), p. 7: The phenomenological reduction "is inquiry within the sphere of pure evidence, inquiry into essences. . . ." also, "it means the exclusion of. . . everything that is not evident givenness in its true sense, that is not absolutely given to pure 'seeing' . . ."

2.   For an exhaustive survey of the literature on the sociology of knowledge, see Robert Merton, *Social Theory and Social Structure*, rev. ed., 1957 (New York, Free Press, 1957) Chap. XII, "The Sociology of Knowledge," and Chap. XII, "Karl Mannheim and the Sociology of Knowledge." Other works to be consulted are: Nigel Harris, *Beliefs in Society: The Problem of Ideology* (London, Watts, 1968); Lucien Goldmann, *The Human Sciences and Philosophy*, translated by Hayden V. White and Robert Anchor (London, Jonathan Cape, 1969); also his *The Hidden God*, translated by Philip Thody (London, Routledge and Kegan Paul, 1964), Chap. V, "World Visions and Social Classes."

3.   Karl Marx and Friedrich Engels, *The German Ideology*, edited with an introduction by R. Pascal (New York, International Publishers, 1947), Parts I and II; see especially the section on Feuerbach. Central to this discussion is Karl Mannheim's *Ideology and Utopia*, especially the Preface by Louis Wirth, pp. xxiff. Also useful is the title essay in George Lichtheim's *The Concept of Ideology and Other Essays* (New York, Random House, 1967).

4.   See Chap. 6 above on epistemology. Important is Hans Speier's essay, "The Social Determination of Ideas," *Social Order and the Risks of War: Papers in Political Sociology* (Cambridge, Mass., M.I.T. Press, 1969), p. 95: "Relativists who point out the futility of any philosophy which concerns itself with human nature in general, since this nature is time- and space-bound, are sometimes unaware of the fact that their own relativism, whether it be social-historical, racial, psychological or any other brand, presupposes a 'philosophical anthropology': it happens to be no less general than the generalizations it would discredit. All theories of the relation between ideas and the world we call social have philosophical implications. They imply general propositions concerning the nature of social reality, history, man and reason." In discussing the Marxian view of consciousness, Speier notes (p. 100): "Man seeks to satisfy economic needs, produces means of satisfaction, creates new needs, and reproduces himself—and in these four activities he cooperates with other men. Only after we have recognized these four aspects of the original historical relations, Marx declares, do we find that man also has consciousness. 'Contemplation' was subsequently presented as a socially necessary illusion of man living in capitalistic society; the so-called fetish-character of that society serves to account for the contemplative attitude of philosophers who, failing to appreciate the dynamic and dialectical nature of the social structure, have no material interest in changing it. . . . In any case, it is worth noting that popular interpretations of contemplation as something old and useless do not take cognizance of the idea which has to be refuted if contemplation is really to be devalued. This idea is that 'practical' thinking is not that which is incident to the success of an action but that which is undertaken for the sake of truth and leads to it."

5.   For a summary and survey of Marx and Engels, see Vernon Venable, *Human Nature, The Marxian View* (New York, Knopf, 1945) (reprinted by Meridian, 1966), on the social division of labor as engenderer of "craft idiocy."

6.   For a general discussion of this problem in relation to language, see B. Bernstein, "Social Class, Language, and Socialization," in Pier Paolo Giglioli (Ed.), *Language and Social Context* (Baltimore, Penguin, 1972).

7.   See Max Weber, "Class, Status, Party," in Gerth and Mills, *From Max Weber*, pp. 181ff. Also in Reinhard Bendix and Seymour Martin Lipset (Eds.), *Class, Status, and Power*, 2nd ed. (New York, Free Press, 1966), their essay, "Karl Marx's Theory of Social Classes." In the same collection, see Stanislaw Ossowski, "Different Conceptions of Social Class," pp. 86–96. Also George Lichtheim, "Society and Hierarchy," *The Concept of Ideology* (New York, Random House, 1967).

8.   Max Weber, "The Social Psychology of the World Religions," in Gerth and Mills, *op. cit.*, pp. 271ff., for descriptions of how world views may be totally embedded in individual consciousnesses.

9.   Arthur Vidich and Joseph Bensman, *Small Town in Mass Society*, rev. ed. (Princeton, Princeton University Press, 1968) Chap. 11, "Personality and the Minimization of Personal Conflicts."

10. Selig Perlman, *A Theory of the Labor Movement* (New York, Macmillan, 1928) (Reprinted by Augustus M. Kelley, 1970). The entire work is valuable; especially relevant is Part II, Chap. VIII, "The Intellectuals' Programs for Labor"; also his

A *History of Trade Unionism in the United States* (New York, Macmillan, 1922) (Kelley reprint 1950), Part III.

11.   Joseph Bensman and Bernard Rosenberg, *Mass, Class, and Bureaucracy* (Englewood Cliffs, N.J., Prentice-Hall, 1963), pp. 229ff.

12.   While a host of anthropologists, sociologists, and social scientists have made this distinction, Oscar Handlin has described this mentality fully in *The Newcomers* (Cambridge, Mass., Harvard University Press, 1953) (Anchor reprint, 1962), and Basil Bernstein has made it a basic part of his linguistic research.

13.   See Veblen's *Theory of the Leisure Class*, and *The Instinct of Workmanship* (New York, Macmillan, 1914: reprinted by Norton, 1964), Chap. VI.

14.   F. W. Howton, and Bernard Rosenberg, "The Salesman: Occupation and Ideology in a Prototypical Occupation," *Social Research*, Vol. 32, No. 3 (Autumn 1965), pp. 277–298. See also Karl Mannheim on self-rationalization (the systematic control of one's impulses), in *Man and Society in an Age of Reconstruction* (New York, Harcourt Brace, 1947), pp. 55–56.

15.   Precursors of this line of thought are Mannheim on self-rationalization, C. Wright Mills in White Collar, and William H. Whyte, Jr., *The Organization Man* (New York, Simon & Schuster, 1956) (Anchor reprint, 1957). Whyte summarizes a whole line of analysis which became popular in the late Fifties and early Sixties as related to the problem of conformity in modern bureaucratic society. Allen Wheelis also develops this theme in *The Quest for Identity* (New York, Norton, 1958). Literary portrayals of powerlessness, in addition to Hasek's *The Good Soldier Schweik* translated by Paul Selver, (New York, New American Library, 1963), include the janitor, Spiridon, in Alexander Solzhenitsyn's The *First Circle* translated by Thomas P. Whitney (New York, Bantam Books, 1969). See also a recent reprint edited by G. Osofsky: *Puttin' On Ol' Massa: The Slave Narratives of Henry Bibb, William Wells Brown, and Solomon Northup* (New York, Harper & Row, 1969).

16.   See Karl Mannheim, "Conservative Thought," in Paul Kecskemeti (Ed.), *Essays in Sociology and Social Psychology* (London, Routledge and Kegan Paul, 1953); Hans Gerth and C. Wright Mills, *Character and Social Structure* (New York, Harcourt, Brace, 1953), Chap. XI, "Stratification and Institutional Orders." Also, Joseph Bensman and Arthur Vidich, *The New American Society* (Chicago, Quadrangle, 1951), Chap. 3, "Business, Bureaucracy, and Personality," and Chap. 4, "Economic Class and Personality."

17.   See Joseph Bensman, "Foreword" to Nicholas Alex, *Black in Blue: A Study of the Negro Policeman* (New York, Appleton-Century-Crofts, 1969).

18.   V. Lanternari, *The Religions of the Oppressed* (New York, New American Liberty, 1963); Norman Cohn, *The Pursuit of the Millennium*, rev. ed. (New York, Oxford University Press, 1970).

19.   Milovan Djilas, *The New Class* (New York, Praeger, 1957); *The Unperfect Society: Beyond the New Class*, translated by Dorian Cooke, (New York, Harcourt, Brace & World, 1969).

Conclusion

THE OCCUPATIONAL ATTITUDE

We have attempted to show how "world images" or basic attitudes toward life and the world have emerged from the occupational technique and methodology of the practitioners of a limited number of occupations and professions. We have argued that every occupation or profession develops and takes specific stands to the world as a result of its craft. This approach to knowledge, to attitudes, and even to character formation coexists with other aspects of occupations. The craft attitude is located, together with and inseparable from occupational interests, in the sense that such interests are claims for prestige, income, and power in the Marxian sense of the term. Occupational attitudes are also separate from, but coexist with, world views that derive from the selected social experience that the practice of any occupation necessarily entails. While one can argue, with Marx, that one's social experience determines one's consciousness, a major component of that social experience is the specific things one does in one's occupational and professional practice. This includes the peculiar quality of the social relations involved in the practice of a profession, illustrated in the social roles of the psychoanalyst, the doctor or lawyer, artist, and the intellectual as outsider or as adviser.

It also includes the nature of the materials with which an occupation works. Dealing with words, sounds, symbols, computers, and people all contribute to the technique which becomes generalized as a basis for an occupational attitude. The specialization in the handling of different materials and symbols creates habits of mind, attitudes, and loyalties which give each occupation its specific character, and which then go beyond that character.

The craft attitudes are also interlocked with interests and attitudes which are based on the historical success of the occupation in developing its professional acceptance and claims in the society at large. The occupational attitudes are linked to the success of the occupation, in establishing an occupational legitimacy for its members. This means that, depending on relative success, the development of an occupation results in attitudes of affirmation, denial, or defensiveness with respect to the society at large.

The sociology of knowledge is replete with studies and theories concerning the development of all the external aspects of occupational structures. We have chosen to concentrate on the effect of the craft itself in determining world images and occupational attitudes. We have selected those occupations and professions which are peculiarly related to the development of world images and attitudes that historically have and can be disseminated to the society at large. We have focused on such "occupations" as religions, philosophy, the arts, intellectual articulation, the university, literature and such central professions as law and medicine.

This focus may be due, in part, to the subjective biases on the part of the authors. It may be due, in part, to the fact that the attitudes and images developed in the selected occupations have consequences far greater than the numbers of persons involved, since these occupations are specialized in the articulation and dissemination of attitudes to wider publics, and therefore provide the raw materials out of which more generalized class, societal, and cultural images and ideologies emerge.

We are also aware that the attitudes and interests of members of other occupations who are less specialized in articulating and disseminating attitudes and images function as selective devices in the acceptance and rejection of images and attitudes created by the articulating occupations. We could have expanded our catalogue of occupations and professions to provide for an extended survey of occupational and professional image- and attitude-making activities.

There is no doubt in our minds that such occupations as medicine, architecture, teaching law, steamfitting, cobbling, taxicab driving, and rag-picking produce unique and peculiar combinations of attitudes appropriate to the craft as well as to the societal and social position, ideological and material interests, and commitment to the society at large. Every occupation, every skill at every substantive level produces such attitudes.

The task of articulating the effect of occupations on attitudes and images is as large as the number of occupations with all their subdivisions. In other work, we have attempted to describe some of these attitudes and the conditions out of which they emerge.

OCCUPATION AND "CLASS"

The peculiar unit of our analysis has been the occupation itself. Karl Marx and his disciples have attempted to broaden the conception of occupational attitudes and interests by focusing upon class, a concept initially based upon similarity of occupations with respect to ownership of capital and access to markets.

Such a procedure is possible when the occupational structure of a society is relatively simple, in which different occupations are highly delineated and demarcated, and in which the ownership of the means of production and the distribution of rewards and benefits of the occupational system is simple and highly visible. Even when such conditions exist, the development of classes cannot be based on occupation alone. The conversion of occupational attitudes to class attitudes requires, under Marxian analysis, concerted activity by the ruling or favored classes to create, through the conditions of exploitation, a consciousness of a common fate by members of classes who, because of their conditions of exploitation within an economic system, only then become aware of their common destiny. But even these conditions are insufficient. The creation of class consciousness requires, as postulated by Marx, the development of communication among members of an occupation and among members of similar occupations. It is usually the role of members of totally alien occupational classes, the intellectuals, who construct ideologies which remind the members of occupations of their common fate, interest, and ideology.

Occupation by itself does not create class consciousness or class identities. In our chapter on class, we have shown that members of similar occupations can have different "class perspectives" based on the differential fate of their occupation as it is related to its acceptance in the society at large. Occupation as craft creates, for any particular occupation, an attitude which is unique. One could further argue that even the occupational career of a particular practitioner will give him a different class perspective from that of his fellow practitioners. Class is something different from occupation if and when class emerges at all, and operates upon separate and often conflicting dynamics from that of occupation.

THE AUTONOMY OF OCCUPATIONAL ATTITUDES

Occupational dynamics can be totally different from that of class. We hope we have demonstrated that once an occupation emerges, its technique, methodology, and craft develop a dynamic of their own. The practitioners of the craft become self-conscious in their methods, and attempt to develop these methods as an autonomous set of skills and basis for their identity. The rationalization of occupational methods becomes the major means by which crafts and craft attitudes emerge. Prestige and esteem and commitment to craftsmanship itself become the bases for attempts to develop new methods, new approaches, new technology, and new skills in the craft. These become separated from the function or contribution of the occupation to others or to society. Occupations, for instance, develop jargons which are incomprehensible to all but the insiders. At times such linguistic devices are "functional" in the sense that they help protect the occupation from a scrutiny that might otherwise render the occupation suspect on the grounds that it does nothing but talk to itself. But if this is the case, then the disease and the cure are in the long run the same thing.

The very obscurity of occupations, however, provides the basis for new occupations which serve to explain, clarify, and often propagandize for occupations which would otherwise be meaningless. Thus, the journalist, the public relations man, and the intellectual all at times have functions of this nature.

THE DYNAMICS OF CRAFT ATTITUDES

The focus on craft methodology serves to provide a dynamic for an occupation because every technique, craft, and starting assumption which becomes the basis for a method is necessarily limited. The concentration on technique results in an elaboration and development of these various limited sets of assumptions which may cause such a proliferation of methods, vocabulary, and products on such a narrow base that the work done tends to collapse under the weight of overrefinement, complexity, repetition, and sterility. It may also collapse under the weight of its incomprehensibility and uselessness, for any craft or occupation can easily go beyond the point of diminishing returns in the pursuit of elaborate techniques with limited goals. When a set of technical, aesthetic, or other limited assumptions are exhausted through overdevelopment, then it may be necessary for innovators to alter the initial assumptions, methodologies, and techniques, so that these new assumptions can provide the basis for new or different methods, contributions, and content of an occupation. But even here there are dangers. The development of new assumptions, methods, and techniques may become an aesthetic and a dynamic of a profession which has no other impulse to its development than change per se. The emphasis on such change produces a kind of meaninglessness which can be called pure occupational virtuosity. Solutions to such problems of meaninglessness can be found by either the return to earlier methodological and aesthetic assumptions, or through the borrowing of such assumptions from related fields. The method of returning to simpler and earlier assumptions means that the history of the occupation becomes the source for new methods and new assumptions. Thus, in every occupation there are periods of archaic revivalism. In music one can return to an interest in the Baroque, Medieval, or Renaissance styles, or to "primitive" or ancient musical forms. Similar trends may be found in painting. In religion, the return not only to the primitive origins of one's own religion is a recurring phenomenon, but also the incorporation of the ideas and practices of alien religions is possible. In academic and intellectual spheres, the return to the classics is always a theme, and the discovery or rediscovery of neglected classics always adds to our knowledge of what the classics were. As a result, experimentalism in world images and attitudes includes experiment with what has been previously tried and at least temporarily rejected.

CHANGES IN CRAFT ATTITUDES

Our work on the phenomenology of law and medicine adds several new but not necessarily unanticipated conclusions to our work. The essay on law suggests that craft attitudes are subject to continuous change. The rationalization of the law entails a continuous formalization of the law in the creation of new procedures, new forms and quests of evidences, and new kinds of research, language, and codification. This formal rationalization results in new subspecializations within the law and in new "content." The new specializations and content of law not only reflect its internal rationalization, but new demands made upon it by new or changing classes, status groups, and new technological and administrative institutions. Law and, more importantly, phenomenological attitudes inevitably reflect the operation of this history. To this extent, phenomenological attitudes cannot be understood *sui generis*.

Our study of medicine makes this latter point even stronger. Since a craft is based on technology and the social administrative arrangements that surround its technologies, technological, organizational, and administrative changes may have great impact on craft attitudes.

Clinical medicine based on the individual practitioner dealing directly with the patient produces an attitude and ethic that reflects these basic social relations in medicine. Scientific medicine and technology has largely superseded clinical medicine and its associated attitudes and ethics; but it has not as yet created integrated systems of attitudes and ethics of its own. As a result we have a world of medicine replete with archaic survivals of clinical medicine and fragments of what may soon emerge as a new system of attitudes and ethics but is not as yet complete or accepted. In short, we have anomie and a system full of distrust, but one that is still necessary.

It thus might be possible in such a situation to project a hypothetically complete set of professional or occupational attitudes; but such a set of attitudes would have little resemblance to anything that empirically exists or would even come into existence.

THE BORROWING OF AESTHETIC ASSUMPTIONS

The borrowing of occupational attitudes and images consists of using the occupational attitudes of related fields and occupations as the basis for the development of new attitudes and assumptions within one's own field. There is a unity within the world of the arts, letters, sciences, which goes beyond occupational specialization and boundaries. Every innovation in aesthetic or methodological assumptions, whether appropriate or not, ultimately becomes applied to other fields if only as a means of escaping from the limits and overdevelopment of assumptions within any particular field. Thus, the Classic, Romantic, Gothic, and Baroque have meanings in literature, arts, letters, philosophy, and even the sciences. These meanings vary with the medium since the materials out of which they are constructed in a particular field are so different.

Such borrowings take place at uneven rates, so that the borrowings in one medium may occur at a time when the style is virtually exhausted or has taken different shapes in another medium or locale. Impressionism in music, for instance, began to be heard long after Impressionism was exhausted as a creative force in painting and poetry.

There may occur borrowings not only from the techniques and styles of another field but a leaning upon general intellectual currents which cut across all fields. We would venture that philosophy is extremely important as a channel of borrowing, while in the past both philosophy and literary criticism have been extremely important as major sources for borrowing across fields. At earlier stages religion may have been more important, while today it appears to have been eclipsed by science.

But even with these time lags and delays, the predisposition to borrow results in a ragged, straggling movement of ideas, assumptions, symbols, and forms of consciousness which move through a whole culture and society over relatively long periods of time, and which make it possible to characterize an age or a period.

These characteristics in the development of knowledge and cultural styles are products of the attempt to work out the methodological, aesthetic, and artistic assumptions of an occupation at a given time in its history and development. The borrowings from its own past and from other occupations are all products of the internal dynamics of an occupation. Because they have these aesthetic and methodological dynamics, they achieve some degree of autonomy from the marketplace, from the economic system, and from a "class system" which in occupational terms often does not exist. It is possible to argue that at least in the area of intellectual and artistic creativity, in the area of the creation of world images, the development of ideas does not directly reflect the material interests of either classes or occupations. Ideas, aesthetic, artistic, and intellectual productions have, in this sphere, an autonomy of their own.

OCCUPATIONAL ATTITUDES AND THE SPIRIT OF THE TIMES

The concern with method, technique, form, and style as central to the development of an occupation often leads to the criticism of the major fields of creativity that they are becoming technologically obscure, devoid of substance or content other than technique itself. Some critics argue that such preoccupation is either a reflection of the bureaucratic spirit of the times, or a spirit that is broader but includes the bureaucratic spirit of the times. Thus, formalism is seen as related to the development of late capitalism and of the "value-neutrality" and the technocratic determinism associated with late capitalism. While such an argument may seem attractive, and combines with the emphasis on instrumental rationality associated with the market rationality of early capitalism, the bureaucratic mentality of late capitalism, and the technical, stylistic, and aesthetic rationality in cultural and aesthetic spheres, yet we would conclude that it is easy to establish the separateness and independence of these various phenomena. Preoccupation with intellectual, aesthetic, and artistic methodologies has occurred in all periods prior to the development of capitalism. Focus on substance and content has occurred long after the development of capitalism. Medieval theology and philosophy had all of the characteristics of a method-centered system of thought, at least by the time of St. Augustine. Poetry has gone through innumerable cycles of preoccupation with the formal aspects of style and the rebellion against its own formalism. Late medieval music prior to the appearance of Dunstable was characterized by the exhausting of a limited style. Late Renaissance music achieved extremely high levels of sterility and was replaced by simpler music which in turn developed its own forms of complexity, replaced in turn by other styles. In painting, mannerist styles have risen to dominance almost as a signal of the decline of the dominant style. The concentration on technique was a symptom of the fact that painters in the dominant style had relatively little to say, except to extend, amplify, and caricature the style itself. Within painting, the rise and decline of mannerisms has been a recurrent phenomenon, each new style of mannerism being different from earlier ones.

We have indicated that the focus on method becomes part of a critical attitude in which the objectivity of method and style becomes the most teachable part of the art. The discussion of style becomes most communicable by the medium of the printed, and later, with radio and television, of the spoken word, rather than the medium in which the work is originally done.

Thus, criticism, and associated with it, the preoccupation with methods, is associated first with the rise of the large university, and secondly with journalism, and of course with literacy. Added to this is the abstracting and mathematizing approach of modern physics, with its implied devaluation of everyday appearances, and the need for a critical philosophy of knowledge. As a result, preoccupation with methods becomes an increasingly important phenomenon in the late nineteenth and twentieth centuries, while the growth of criticism and the preoccupation with the dissection of method and style begins much earlier.

OCCUPATIONAL ELITES

The concentration on method, technique, and style is a product and a cause of a methodological self-consciousness of the practitioners of a craft. Such self-consciousness goes far beyond craft or technique. The artist, the intellectual, the philosopher, or the scientist begins to define himself as a species apart from the normal run of mankind. He regards himself as the bearer of special values upon which he bases his craft. He becomes a spokesman for Art, Literature, Reason, Knowledge, Science, Philosophy, Religion, and so forth. The domain which he occupies takes on special value, and becomes the basis for claims for priority of that value. The "civilian" world becomes of secondary importance. As he defines his world of value as being of primary importance, he constructs a social world which intensifies the social, cultural, ideological, and aesthetic ambience of that world. He associates more and more with other practitioners of that world and of other worlds that are immediately relevant to each other in their joint hostility to outside worlds. Thus the world of the "civilian," the layman, the "feather merchant," becomes more and more removed, and is by and large conceived as a hostile world. The worlds of the arts, literature, etc., become more and more dense, not only in their aesthetic, symbolic, and technological systems, but also in their subgroups, cliques, schools, friends and enemies. These worlds can become the sum total of the worlds of experience for the practitioners.

At the same time, if the central world of the artistic or intellectual practitioner is to gain ascendancy appropriate to its primary importance (its primacy attributed to it by its practitioners), then the practitioners must engage in continuous ideological, cultural, and intellectual propaganda. As a result, the "civilian" world, the lay world, is always the receiver of "messages" and propaganda from these "higher" worlds. The very practice of the craft, the art, music, literature, is a message. To the extent that the art portrays an image of life or a form of sensitivity that is meaningful or superior, these messages serve as propaganda for their creators. Since intellectual and artistic craftsmen possess skills in communication, their success has been far greater than one would expect, based either on their numbers or on the resources available to them. But such communication is not by itself adequate to achieve predominance, given the conviction that preoccupation with a single value entails. While intellectuals, artists, philosophers, etc., are specialists at communication, they do not usually control the media by which their messages are disseminated. If the craftsman desires to exert the influence appropriate to his self-esteem, and to achieve the benefits therefrom, he must find means of gratifying the expectations of others, of coming to terms with their demands. This entails the discovery of the symbols, aspirations, "psychology" of an audience, whether that discovery is the product of the direct knowledge of the craftsman, or is mediated by publishers, impresarios, managers, researchers, or media specialists. To the extent that the intellectual or artistic craftsman accepts such definitions and tailors his work to them, he sacrifices the autonomy of his art. Though he may, within the framework of communicating at an expected level, develop high levels of virtuosity and technique, such virtuosity and technique are aimed at expressing the commonplaces already known to exist in the attitudes of his audience. A true genius in any field may create his own audience simply by defining his message and technique in his own terms, but in doing so he creates in the audience a response that did not exist before the existence of the message.

OCCUPATIONAL ATTITUDES AND THE ATTITUDE OF EVERYDAY LIFE

Intellectuals may thus define images of experiences and worlds of experience for lay audiences, but they also incorporate into their work the "attitudes of everyday life." The process is not a simple exchange in attitudes. There is a tendency among some academicians and intellectuals concerned with the sociology of knowledge to see "Culture," knowledge, and attitudes as direct reflections of attitudes of everyday life, which in turn are reflections of the direct, primary interaction of individuals and communities. Knowledge is seen as a higher synthesis of attitudes of everyday life. So far as we know historical societies, we can say that, to the contrary, the attitudes of everyday life are a simplified, vulgarized, de-intellectualized reflection of highly articulated systems of thought originally developed by intellectuals, and disseminated through the communication machinery of a society. In the process of dissemination and diffusion, the attitudes become simplified, and incorporated into the common sense of a populace that need not know of the origins and intellectual articulations on which the attitudes are based. The individual, in internalizing such attitudes, adopts them as a rhetoric and a medium for the expression of his actions and his presocial impulses. The attitude of everyday life does not emerge out of everyday experience in the sense that that everyday experience precludes direct and indirect contact with "higher" intellectual production. To think of the dichotomy between the attitude of everyday life and these more elaborate intellectual attitudes is to think in terms of a Robinson Crusoe isolated from his society and recreating a social and intellectual world *de novo*. But even Robinson Crusoe created his world with attitudes derived from the England from which he departed. He could not erase from his consciousness the memories of the ideas and practices which had emerged in his past. The isolated individual, creating a world out of his own experience and his own social interaction, enters such social interaction and each new experience with attitudes that are a product of his previous social interactions and the interactions of all those with whom he has had interaction. Thus, the notion of an isolated individual is, to all intents and purposes, an impossibility. Theories based on the conception of the microscopic and formal processes of interaction of undifferentiated individuals, by their very preconceptions, make it impossible to determine the degree to which these situations are permeated with culture and attitudes which are predetermined by other attitudes developed at more complex levels. It is far easier to make assumptions concerning the autonomous creation of attitudes and cultures in primitive societies, since they do not have a written history. The absence of a written history makes it difficult to assess the role of intellectuals and other institutionalized cultural creators of attitudes of everyday life. It is easy to assume that primitive culture is simply a by-product of the undifferentiated actions of individuals in a community. Paul Radin has demonstrated, to our minds quite conclusively, that primitive intellectuals, prophets, and priests have performed the same functions of creating new attitudes of everyday life which become the products of social interaction.

In the area of folk music and folk art, there is considerable literature which suggests that much of what is regarded as the naive, simple, direct creation of indigenous folk culture is actually the borrowed culture of other civilizations, hymns, popular music, and in some cases highly sophisticated symphonic music.

If attitudes of everyday life are reflections of highly articulated systems of thought, then the creators and communicators of new systems of thought must present their production to lay audiences who have internalized and incorporated, often in "non-systematic" ways, older products of the elaborate intellectual and communications machinery of the surrounding society. The process of internalization of such cultural and intellectual production is selective. Individuals incorporate such culture on the basis of their differential exposure to that culture, the affinity of old and new ideas, their position in a social structure, and the interests that emerge as a result of these various factors. Thus, the concept of the attitude of everyday life refers to a very complex phenomenon, a phenomenon that is not referable exclusively to the isolated social interaction of an individual or of an undifferentiated community.

The analysis of attitudes of everyday life must include not only these primary group relations but the whole complex of institutional machineries, social, and class structures, and the problems related to individuals and groups of individuals in highly developed cultures and societies. The original creators of the sociology of knowledge, Marx, Weber, Mannheim, and Veblen, were fully aware of such complexities. The more recent developments in the sociology of knowledge which reflect relatively simple models of "symbolic interaction," interpersonal relations, ethnomethodology, and role theory are all primitive in comparison. Their selection of data does violence to the realities under consideration—they define that reality as that which is necessary to their methodological preconceptions, rather than what must be studied in order to make a satisfactory solution to the problems under consideration.

RESPONSES TO SUCCESS

When responding to the taste of an existing audience, the craftsman may vulgarize his art. In responding only in terms of the technique and his artistic community, he may fail to communicate his message to any audience. When he creates his own audience, he may succeed in instilling the attitudes of his art in an audience of laymen. Artists and intellectuals create, define and redefine nonartistic and nonintellectual worlds. But audiences, in accepting the world so created, frequently misunderstand it, though their misunderstanding may be accompanied by "appreciation" and plaudits. The artist or intellectual, in responding to his own success, may accept and internalize the misunderstanding that was the basis of the success.

In doing so, the artist becomes the victim of his own myth and his own success. He also becomes the victim of the audience he created. The acceptance of the craftsman by the public or the bureaucracies which transmit his message tends to transform it. At the same time, the acceptance of the craft by outside groups, institutions, or markets causes a growth in self-esteem by the practitioners of the craft. This causes the craftsman to raise his own demands and expectations with respect to the capabilities of the audience. In such cases, the artist-intellectual-scientist, now a member of an elite, develops images of society whose dimensions are defined by his craft, and in which the structuring of society will be done by himself and his elite.

Thus, acceptance of an elite by the society increases the demands of the elite on society.

The artist-intellectual-scientist then begins to construct images of a society which, if it is to reach the true potential given by the elite's values, must be reconstituted. Its reconstitution must inevitably place the particular elite at the head of the entire society. The philosopher becomes the philosopher-king. The scientist provides the laws and methods for the governing of society. The politically superior intellectual becomes one of the ruling class of a postulated new society. Psychologists imagine an order in which they produce a mentally healthy society. Managerial scientists run society at levels of managerial efficiency that are heretofore unimaginable. The claims of specialized elites upon the total society have at specific times been unlimited. Their success, even when the opportunities have been given them, has been less than optimal. As a matter of act, they have everywhere failed in terms of their own claims, and most often have produced forms of barbarism and totalarianism that have violated every form of idealism and self-righteousness that was the basis of their claims.

Such failures are perhaps inevitable. The very condition of acceptance of the newly ascendant elite by the society is that the craft of the artistic or intellectual or scientific elite be subordinated to the needs of older dominant groups in the society. Thus the more the demand for change, the less substance there is to the change. And the more "radical" the demand, the less substance there is to the radicalism.

THE RADICAL INTELLECTUAL

The same analysis applies to revolutionary intellectuals. Rejected by or alienated from a society, they construct ideologies, images of a more perfect society, and negative images of existing societies, as a means of expressing their alienation or rejection. Such images may remain at the symbolic level, and have little or no organizational consequences. When intellectuals enter active organizational struggles, the party and the sect become the medium that restructures the original message that may have been the basis for the revolutionary movement. The intellectual as party member must then disci-pline himself to the demands of the party, to its strategy and tactics, and thus limit that vision may have been the intellectual basis of the movement. If he can enter an organization, he may succeed in rising to the top of a revolution-ary movement. If he retains his original habits of mind and emphasis on craft or vision, he is likely to be purged. If he does limit himself, his "art" becomes subordinated to the stereotypes of an official ideology, and he in effect commits intellectual, artistic, or scientific suicide. The problems for the left or right intellectual, the prophet and the priest, are essentially the same. The lust for power and influence in establishments that exist or that hopefully may exist by replacing present establishments operates to destroy what is intrinsic to the basic attitudes of the creative "crafts."

THE NARROWING AND EXTENSION OF CRAFT HORIZONS

In periods when social crises are less than revolutionary in intensity, the development of artistic and intellectual autonomy and imperialism has opposite effects. Each craft develops its own focus on values, and each subgroup and clique develops subfoci. The world of intellectual production becomes a cacophony of voices. A society at large is presented with an infinity of worlds of values, each presented as an ultimate value, each capable of sustaining the life of its audiences. Audiences are presented with conflicting voices, without a hierarchy of values or guides to choice. Each individual is left to choose on the basis of criteria that may be personal, arbitrary, or random. In one respect this represents a maximum amount of freedom, in another respect it represents chaos.

One of the limitations of occupational attitudes as a means of viewing the world and as a means of governing the world is based on the narrowness of the vantage point from which the nonoccupational world is seen. The artist may see only those aspects of the world that are relevant to art, and ignore all other aspects. The psychologist will see the world of habits, of mechanisms for the distribution of affect, of perceptual processes, etc., as the only relevant reality. Sociologists, as we have indicated, are likely to see the social content and processes as being dominant, and to ignore, or treat only as constraints, such factors as economic or technological processes and institutions. Even when they recognize such phenomena, they do so only as part of a stage on which they can perceive sociological dramas. Economists are "guilty" of similar procedures. In part such procedures are absolutely necessary. The total world of experience is so broad and subject to an almost infinite variety of perspectives, that to analyze it requires a limitation of the perspectives used in the analysis. Thus some forms of "reduction" are necessary and appropriate. But such reductions are merely methodological devices, self-imposed restrictions, which enable one to deal with the world in an orderly way. They enable the observer and analyst to concentrate his vision so that he can see more in a given direction than he would otherwise.

It is unfortunate that individuals who start their work with self-consciously created points of reference lose, in the process of doing the work, their awareness that they are viewing only a limited aspect of the world. When they do this, they are making a reduction of sorts—all phenomena are reduced to something that can be seen only from a very limited perspective. It is correct to criticize the materialist reduction, the psychological reduction, sociologism, logical, linguistic, and epistemological reductions, even reductions to the "thing itself." In the latter case the reduction consists of refusing to entertain alternative possibilities. This stricture does not apply to Edmund Husserl, for whom an unlimited horizon of further determinations was an essential aspect of any object of experience. The reproach is more applicable to studies which call themselves phenomenological, but which appear to be subjectivistic. No reduction is in itself "incorrect" so long as the observer or analyst is aware that, in using a restricted perspective or method, he is describing a limited aspect of experience. If the observer or analyst maintains such awareness he is likely to ask: How much of the phenomenon that I wish to explain is explained by the use of the methods that I have employed? How much remains unexplained? What other perspectives, or "reductions," need I employ in order to do justice to the phenomenon? If he asks such questions, he is more likely to employ a wide variety of perspectives or reductions. In fact he is likely to rotate perspectives as his mode of analysis, asking always how much is left unexplained by his use of various reductions. Since the world of experience is infinite, subject to an unlimited number of perspectives, there is little likelihood that one will be able to ascertain a true image or absolute knowledge of any one thing, but rather by the use of such methods, it would seem to us that the probability of error is diminished. Moreover, it might, by such efforts, be possible to achieve a truly humanistic image of the world, and to escape the blunders that often appear to be the hazards of occupational attitudes.

AUTHOR INDEX

SUBJECT INDEX